Also by Kyle Keiderling:

PRAISE FOR: *THE PERFECT GAME: Villanova vs. Georgetown For The National Championship*

"If you appreciate perfection, then this is your book! Kyle Keiderling has written a 'perfect' retrospective of the 'perfect' game." —*Alby Oxenreiter, Sports Director, WPXI-TV, Pittsburgh*

"Rollie and the 'Cats shook up the basketball world with their triumph in Lexington, KY. The flawless game plan and the disciplined performance by the Villanova players proved that 'miracles' can happen on the hardwood." —*Bill Raftery, CBS and ESPN commentator*

"It was the closest thing to a perfect game I've ever seen." —P.J. Carlesimo, former coach, Seton Hall University, Portland Trailblazers, Seattle Supersonics

PRAISE FOR: *HEART OF A LION: The Life, Death And Legacy Of Hank Gathers*

"Hank Gathers was an extraordinary player. He was a young man who dared to dream in a place where dreams go to die. Hank's dream ended tragically but his teammates carried on in his honor. Together they provided one of the greatest stories in NCAA tournament history. Hank has been gone 20 years but, the dream is alive."
                                                              —Jim Nantz, CBS Sports

"An inspiring story." —Wendell Maxey, USA TODAY

"Keiderling has written an elegant and stirring account of the life of a young man most recall best for his passing. This masterful, thoroughly researched account of Hank Gathers' short life is a long overdue tribute to an extraordinary individual. You may think you know the ending- but you don't. A great read." —David Diles, former ABC Sports broadcaster

"This is the real Philadelphia story about a young man who used the game to help his family while setting an extraordinary example for all to witness. Hank's life was a model for student athletes to emulate; he eschewed drugs, honored his family and university and earned his diploma. Hank made every player around him better and he enriched the lives of all those he touched." —Bill Raftery, ESPN college basketball

"A terrific book. . ." —Stan Hochman, Philadelphia Daily News

PRAISE FOR: *SHOOTING STAR: The Bevo Francis Story, The Incredible Tale of College Basketball's Greatest Scorer*

"One of the greatest stories in sports." —George Steinbrenner

"I was lucky in my youth because I got to see the amazing Bevo Francis shoot the basketball. I saw him score 48 points against Butler Univ. He is not forgotten by those who saw him play and this book does a good job bringing back those memories." —Norm Jones, author of Growing Up in Indiana: The Culture & Hoosier Hysteria Revisited

"Times may change, but some things stay the same – sports have a strong grip on the public. I had never heard of Bevo Francis before, and reading this story makes me wonder why. Truly a remarkable tale of a "superstar" who, along with talented teammates, took the country by storm. His story was covered nationwide, and record crowds gathered to see him." —R. J. McCabe, Seattle

". . . I was hoping that someday somebody would write the definitive history of Rio Grande's two legendary seasons. Kyle Keiderling has done it, and it is an excellent book." —R. Patterson, Indianapolis, IN

"I loved the book . . . I think that anyone interested in college basketball would find this book highly entertaining and informative!" —William J. Rush, Warren, Ohio

TROPHIES AND TEARS

Again, for Ky and everyone who believes that miracles still happen now and then.

TROPHIES AND TEARS

The story of Evansville and the Aces

KYLE KEIDERLING

Foreword by Marty Simmons

MORNING STAR BOOKS
MORNING STAR COMMUNICATIONS • NEW YORK

Published in the United States of America by
Morning Star Books, New York, New York.

Requests to the publisher for permission to reproduce selections from
this book should be addressed to the Permissions Department,
Morning Star Communications, LLC, 68 West 120th Street, New York,
NY 10027, (646) 709-7341, fax (212) 208-4570, or online at HYPERLINK
http://www.morningstar-communications.com and www.ljlagency@aol.com.

Trophies And Tears is available via **www.kylekeiderlingbooks.com,
www.trophiesandtears.com, www.morningstar-communications.com**, at your local
bookstore, Amazon.com, and via barnesandnoble.com.

Cover design: Kyle Keiderling, Jr.
Front Cover Photograph: Courtesy University of Evansville Athletic Department
Interior design and Jacket design by Oh Snap! Design
Production coordinator: Oh Snap! Design

Photograph of plane crash site courtesy Associated Press, all other photographs
courtesy the University of Evansville Athletic Department

ISBN: 978-0-977-8996-4-7
ISBN: 978-0-977-8996-5-4 (EBOOK)

Library of Congress Cataloging-in-Publication Data:
Keiderling, Kyle.
Trophies and Tears: The Story of Evansville and the Aces
p. cm.
Includes bibliographical references.
1. University of Evansville, Indiana. 2. NCAA College Basketball players—United
States—Biography.
I. Title.

Printed in the United States of America

CONTENTS

FOREWORD

In 2007, I felt that I was returning home when I returned to the University of Evansville as the Head Basketball Coach. I first came to the University of Evansville in 1986 to play basketball for Head Coach Jim Crews. Little did I know at that time what an impact this university would have on my future and my life. At that time, I didn't know about the history and tradition of Evansville basketball. Coach Crews taught it - the history and tradition – on a daily basis. He talked to us about the five national championships, the undefeated season and fourteen conference titles of legendary Arad McCutchan. He talked daily about the great players and coaches that came before us. We learned life lessons, leadership, discipline, humbleness, dedication, commitment and hard work! We learned from them and we respect what they did for Evansville Basketball.

We often refer to our "Basketball Family" because that is what we are. We are family who support each other in good times and bad – through life challenges. December 13, 1977 was surely the lowest point for Evansville Basketball – the night Bobby Watson and his first year Division 1 basketball team perished in a plane crash. Tremendous community support helped bring back UE's basketball program the following year. The people and the Aces tradition of excellence is one made possible by individuals who have contributed in countless ways to our success.

At Evansville, it has always been about the people. As a former player, my fondest memories are playing in front of the great fans that support Evansville Basketball. There is just no greater feeling than having those fans cheer you on and support you!

The enthusiasm, dedication and loyalty for Evansville Basketball in this community is what separates the Purple Aces from other Division 1 programs. The uniqueness of being able to compete as one of the smallest schools at this level is awesome! People make the difference! It is a lifetime commitment to become a Purple Ace. The University of Evansville is a very special place.

Marty Simmons
Head Basketball Coach
University of Evansville

INTRODUCTION

TROPHIES AND TEARS is the story of a city and a team. A city in search of itself and the team that gave it what it sought.

The city is Evansville, Indiana, population 125,000 in America's heartland in a state where basketball is as much a religion as a sport. One historian said "Evansville is an anomaly." Another described it as a "northern town with a southern flavor."

They were both right. It is a unique place with a unique character and in many ways, if you follow its history and development; it represents a microcosm of America itself.

In the early 1950's it was a city still yearning for attention, characterized by pride and prejudice, divisiveness, dissension and a place where social evolution came slowly but surely.

Evansville was a major manufacturing and industrial center surrounded by rural landscape for miles in any direction. A city that was part of Indiana, but remained apart from it. Yes, Evansville was an "anomaly" but it was also a city that mirrored most of the social and cultural changes that transformed America and left it a better place.

In the team they embraced, the city at last, found an identity that united them.

The team is the University of Evansville Purple Aces.

Outside of the Indiana tri-state area their story remains little known except for its grimmest chapter. The Aces were the UCLA of small college basketball. *Time Magazine* and *Sports Illustrated* covered the team. The Aces captured 5 National titles with the University of Evansville never having an enrollment of more than 2,500 students.

The attendance figures that the Aces posted in the late 1950's and through the 1960's were the envy of major colleges everywhere. The numbers were so impressive they remained in the record books for nearly half a century.

The team was the embodiment of the American dream. They believed anything was possible. They played anyone who would play them and upset major college powers, routinely. They were the quintessential American success story. The little guys of the world triumphing over the odds stacked against them time and time again. One of America's best sports writers called them "the best small college team in the nation."

Some years they may have been *the best* college team in America. Their coach, Arad McCutchan, was the first small college coach ever elected to the Naismith Memorial Basketball Hall Of Fame.

The Aces and Evansville were symbiotically joined and together they shared triumph and tragedy and managed, somehow, to move forward together after their collective hearts were broken and their souls shattered on a dark and dismal December evening in 1977.

In the story of Evansville and the Aces you will find, no doubt, familiar names. You will also find names that are not so familiar but are, nonetheless, important, not just for for Evansville, but for what they achieved, and surmounted, to attain their improbable lofty success in the only truly American game.

They wrote history and made history in a place and at a time when the country's landscape socially, culturally and politically was being transformed, in violent and turbulent times. Though they had no idea that they were doing so is of little import. That they did so, quietly and permanently, is.

TROPHIES AND TEARS is the story about a town and a team that are both, in their own way, unique.

Evansville isn't a social mecca. It isn't a tourist attraction or known as an educational and cultural center for the region. No one will ever mistake it for a renaissance city. It is however something that no other city can lay claim to -- it is the home of the Aces.

The Aces are now a major college team playing in a mid-major conference. They have a sparkling new downtown arena and have managed to achieve respectability at the major college level while remaining one of the smallest schools competing there.

The days of championships are a distant memory now. But each November the hopes and dreams are renewed for a return to the glory days. And dreams are what this country was built on.

TROPHIES AND TEARS is more than a basketball story.

It is an American story set in the heart of a land where hope beats eternally and where dreams sometimes come true; and where horrible things sometimes happen to good people for reasons none of us can understand.

In the end you will learn that there is a little bit of Evansville in all of us. And there is a little bit of all of us in Evansville. Evansville and the Aces. A town and a team. Trophies and tears. This is their story. An American story.

A Perfect Team (1964–1965)

It didn't start then, it had been building for a while: but 1964-1965 is a season Evansville basketball fans will never forget.

The Purple Aces of Evansville College and their popular coach, Arad McCutchan, had given their loyal fans much to cheer about in capturing the College Division (now Division II) national title -- their third overall the year before. The glow of that national championship season was still warm when a cause for alarm sounded. Jerry Sloan, a man whose tendency toward vacillation had brought him to Evansville in the first place, was once again mulling a decision that could have serious consequences for the Aces.

Sloan, who had garnered All-America honors again after the 1963–64 season, was considering leaving Evansville for the NBA. He would be eligible for the NBA draft because his high school class of 1960 would have completed four years of college in June. Although he remained eligible to play college basketball for another year, he was also available to the NBA under the rules in place at that time. And he was tempted.

He had told reporters that he might indeed make the jump to the pros "if someone made me a good enough offer." One of those who felt that Sloan was ready to move to the professional ranks was "Hot Rod" Hundley of the Los Angeles Lakers, who had seen Sloan play in the NCAA Tournament. Hot Rod's opinion was unequivocal. He called Sloan "the best all-around player I've seen this year."[1]

Hot Rod wasn't the only NBA observer at the finals. Scouts from the St. Louis Hawks, Baltimore Bullets, Boston Celtics, and Detroit Pistons had all been in Roberts Stadium and were similarly impressed. Hawks general manager Marty Blake said, "I don't think there's any question that Jerry will be drafted. Where he will be drafted and by whom will be dictated by the needs of the various clubs."

But for now Sloan was back in action at Roberts as part of the College Division team at the Olympic Trials in the end of March. He was on the team that had knocked off John Wooden's UCLA national champions, 76–59. Sloan went 6-for-8 from the floor, nabbed 5 rebounds, and limited All-American guard Walt Hazzard to just 7 points. Sloan did not survive the subsequent round of Olympic tryouts at St. John's University in New York, but that didn't dissuade the Baltimore Bullets organization. "Our coach [Bob Leonard, who was from Terre Haute] had been talking about him even before the season started," Baltimore president David Trager said. "He told us, 'Here's a boy to watch.' Then there were several other people we had confidence in who looked him over, and they all liked him."

Sloan was not unaware of the attention he was getting. "It's like a dream come true," he said. "Basketball has been my life since I was in the second grade." He also told reporters that he had been "real impressed" with the Baltimore organization. He'd been real impressed with Illinois at one time as well and that hadn't lasted long. But now he was mulling the reported $14,000 offer from Baltimore while Aces fans watched nervously.

Mac was not one to stand in the way of a person seeking to better his circumstances, even though it would mean a key loss to his team. "I've always emphasized to him that he shouldn't stay here out of a sense of duty to me or to the college. I've tried to make clear to him that he should consider what is best for him. If he does that, I hope he will be back next year," Mac said.

Sloan and his wife, Bobbye, pondered for several weeks. Then he made the Bullets a brash counteroffer. Jerry said they had added up all the expenses they would incur in moving to Baltimore, then asked the Bullets to pay him $15,000 plus a signing bonus of $7,000. Baltimore, understandably, refused to do so.

On May 26, after the team holding his draft rights rejected his counterproposal, Sloan made a public announcement: he had decided to stay in Evansville (not that he had any alternatives if he wanted to play basketball). He described the decision as ". . . even harder than deciding where to go to school in the first place."

A much-relieved Arad McCutchan joined thousands of Aces fans in letting out a long sigh of relief. "Now we'll be expected to beat everybody," he said after the announcement.

While Jerry and Bobbye had been pondering their next move, a bevy of highly regarded prospects were spotted on campus. Many had attended the tournament finals and, though the majority would end up signing somewhere else, the mere fact that they would consider a visit to a small College Division school was testament to Evansville's growing national reputation. Those who decided to go elsewhere ended up at West Virginia, Dayton, New Mexico, Kansas, and even UCLA. The Aces were keeping heady company in the race to sign talented youngsters.

One who choose Evansville was a local product, a graduate of Rex Mundi High School. Jerry Mattingly had chosen Evansville after being offered scholarships by Michigan, Florida State, and Purdue. Mattingly was a baseball and football player as well as a basketball standout. His younger brother Don would become a star for the Yankees. "I think I did the right thing," Jerry said after deciding to join Mac's Aces. "There's the Stadium and a championship team. I'm like anybody else. I like to win."

Another recruit Mac had landed was Howard Pratt, who had played for former Aces star Marv Pruett at Shoals High School in Shoals, Indiana. A 6-6 center who had averaged 22 points per game as a senior while leading Shoals to a 22–2 record in 1963–64, Pratt had received offers from 35 schools. Like many players Mac had secured through the years, Pratt had been influenced by one of Mac's disciples who had gone on to coach after college. Pratt also was on the long list of players who chose Evansville simply because they wanted to stay close to home.

Mac also landed Clarence Hupfer of Indianapolis; Roger Miller, a 6-5 center from Madison; and Dave Riggs, a Bosse High grad who had received the Kiwanis Award as the Bulldogs's best player.

Mac's recruiting forays were barely behind him when Sloan again began making noises about leaving. The Baltimore Bullets had been unable to sign their top draft pick, Gary Bradds of Ohio State, and were once more trying to entice Sloan to leave school for the pro ranks. Typically, Jerry was conflicted. "I don't know where I stand, and I don't know where they stand," he said in August. "Money helps anyone get by. But that's not everything. I want to get an education. I've been in school, or I will have been in school, five years after next season. A guy wonders if he's ever going to get out. I want to get out with that degree."

True to form, Sloan scheduled a trip to Chicago to meet with Bullets officials, while the team was playing there, then canceled at the last minute. When classes resumed in September, he was on campus.

Mac had five returnees from his championship team, and he told reporters, "I'd be kidding myself if I didn't think I had a couple of sophomores who could move into the starting lineup." One of them, the 6-3 Herb Williams, would be named to replace Ed Zausch in the pivot. Russ Grieger, a senior, would fill the other open spot opposite Sam Watkins at guard, while Sloan moved to forward alongside Larry Humes.

The 1964–65 Aces would be facing another trying schedule put together by Mac and Bob Hudson, with games at Roberts against Iowa, Northwestern, and Notre Dame. All three major powers would be visiting the spacious stadium in December. Fans would soon know how the current edition of their team compared with the championship edition.

Mac may have gleaned something early on, because he told reporters, "I won't say this is a better team. But, they seem to be a little further along in their development than the squad was at this time a year ago. They seem to work well together."

The euphoria from the championship season, coupled with the attractive marquee names on the schedule, generated record advance season ticket sales. Bob Hudson's office resembled a war room as he juggled requests for seats. The Aces had sold 134,622 tickets the previous season, making them sixth in the nation in attendance. They trailed only Ohio State, Illinois, Kentucky, New York University, and Wichita State. The Aces had sold all those tickets to a fan base comprised of only 2,500 undergraduates and a population of little more than 100,000.

Evansville wasn't New York or Lexington or Columbus—it wasn't even Wichita—yet the loyalty and enthusiasm of the city for Aces basketball had placed the team in the elite ranks of college basketball attractions. And basketball, always was big in Evansville, was about to get even bigger.

A harried but happy Bob Hudson, the Aces' multi-tasking promoter, publicist, ticket agent, sports information director and promoter proudly announced that the 4,000 fans who had purchased advance tickets for the season, a package of 14 home contests at $18 apiece, had set a new record. In anticipation of the burgeoning crowds, new bleacher seats had been installed, increasing the stadium's capacity by 4,835, for a total seating capacity of 12,309.

Now all the Aces had to do was to keep winning.

While Evansville was preoccupied with what Sloan would decide, much of the rest of the country dreaded learning the answer to what had happened to James Chaney, Andrew Goodman, and Michael Schwerner, the three young "Freedom Summer" volunteers who had disappeared in June while working in Mississippi.

The summer of '64 would be a momentous one for the United States. On July 2, President Lyndon B. Johnson signed the Civil Rights Act, which banned segregation in all public facilities and gave the Justice Department the power to intervene in any instances of segregation. It also prohibited election boards from using different standards to qualify blacks and whites as voters, required employers to provide workers with equal opportunities, and banned discrimination based on race, color, ethnicity, or gender in any federally funded enterprise.

But it was also a summer of racial unrest, the first of several. The fatal shooting of an African American teenager led to allegations of police brutality and sparked a riot by 8,000 Harlem residents on July 18; it lasted six days. One person was killed, 100 were injured, and 450 were arrested.

Less than a week later, on July 24, police in Rochester, New York, arrested a 19- year-old black man for public drunkenness at a block party. Rumors of police brutality spread quickly—that a police dog had attacked a child, that an officer had slapped a pregnant woman—leading to a riot that resulted in the arrest of a thousand people and $1 million in damages. The National Guard, mobilized by Governor Nelson Rockefeller, restored order to the city three days later.[2]

In August riots broke out in more cities: Jersey City, Paterson, and Elizabeth, New Jersey; Chicago; and Philadelphia. In December 1965 the McCone Commission traced the origins of the Watts riot to the unrest in eastern cities sixteen months earlier and identified the causes: few job opportunities, especially for blacks with no training; schools inadequate to meet the needs of "the disadvantaged Negro child, whose environment from infancy onward places him under a serious handicap"; and "resentment, even hatred, of the police, as the symbol of authority."

The riots, the Commission declared, "were each a symptom of a sickness in the center of our cities. In almost every major city, Negroes pressing ever more densely into the central city and occupying areas from which Caucasians have moved in their flight to the suburbs have developed an isolated existence with a feeling of separation from the community as a whole. . . . The conditions of life itself are often marginal; idleness leads to despair and, finally, mass violence supplies a momentary relief from the malaise."[3]

On August 4 Americans learned that the bodies of Chaney, Goodman, and Schwerner had been found in an earthen dam outside Philadelphia, Mississippi. (No one was convicted for their murders until 2005.)

It was also the summer of the Gulf of Tonkin incident, which led Congress to grant President Lyndon Johnson the power to take any action necessary to counter the Viet Cong.

Certainly the events of that traumatic summer heralded change. Evansville, like most places, watched what was happening with growing unease, perhaps even alarm, but apparently without violence, according to those who were there at the time. In Evansville, the one-time Indiana headquarters of the Ku Klux Klan, change came quietly, and it is no stretch to say that the city's affection for the Aces helped promote the acceptance of integration that other places had resisted with dogs and fire hoses.

Herb Williams remembers that catalytic summer, but his memories are mostly the recollections of any college student: "Larry [Humes], Sam [Watkins], and I and my roommate, John O'Neil, all hung out together. We lived in a dormitory, Hughes Hall, and my room was 101 and Larry's was 201, right upstairs. The stairwell was outside our door, and we were always running up and down to visit. We all had a lot in common besides our color. We'd all experienced segregated schools and racism to some extent. We had shared life experiences, and it was just natural for us to be together all the time.

"A big treat for us was when we'd all pile in one car and go to Una Pizza. They had a large plain pizza that we would get for four dollars. It was enough for all of us. We never experienced any of the problems in Evansville that the other African Americans in town had."

Although other blacks who tried to exercise their right to eat in downtown restaurants found that their presence caused the establishments to empty quickly, Herb said, "When we went to a local restaurant to eat, nobody got up to leave, and we were treated like everyone else. There were a number of white families that took us under their wings. Mac was one, Wayne Boultinghouse's mom was another, and there were others that would invite us to dinner and picnics. As members of the Aces, we were pretty much welcomed everywhere in the city.

"When we were in Kentucky, though, it was different. We stopped once at a popular barbeque restaurant in Henderson, and when we entered, we were told we could eat, but we'd have to do so in the back—in the kitchen. It was just across the river but it was a far different reality over there.

"In many ways I guess we were spoiled by the treatment we got in Evansville because we were basketball players. Our biggest problem was the lack of any black girls on campus to date. There was only one that I can remember. So, eventually, we all went over to the Administration building to see Mr. Patberg [the former Ace who had returned to campus as director of admissions]. We asked him if he would try to recruit more black females to the school. He said he'd try, and we were satisfied with that."[4]

Sam Watkins remembers their effort to diversify the student body: "Mr. Patberg was a good man, and we told him that he really needed to try to get some more black girls there." He recalls telling Patberg, "You are recruiting black athletes, but they have no one to socialize with here except themselves."

White students' memories of that period are, well, *white*. "Evansville at that time was much like the town depicted in the movie *American Graffiti*," said Russ Grieger. "It had a drive-in where we'd all go. We cruised the main drags. Life was really very good and relaxed; despite all the momentous changes that were taking place elsewhere, we never experienced any of that in Evansville."

That's not to say that those, like Russ, who grew up there were oblivious to racial tension.

"Once, when I was in high school, we were coming home from a basketball pick-up game. We were walking down Bellemeade Avenue on the fringe of the predominantly black neighborhood towards Central Turners, where they had a restaurant, a gym, and a pool," Grieger said. "There were three of us, and a group of five or six black kids surrounded us. It was pretty menacing, but just then two black kids that we had played baseball with in Little League…came along and rescued us. That's the only racial incident I can recall. You just knew that you don't go down in that area at night. Basically, we all got along and coexisted peacefully during that time."[5]

That three of the Aces' starters for 1964–65 were black undoubtedly helped Evansville come to terms with the need to comply with the Civil Rights Act and hastened the peaceful and quiet dismantling of the last of the barriers that had long existed there. "We were on television with our games and in the paper all the time. There was some tension in the city at that time but not very much," Herb Williams said. "We were part of the Aces, and we became one of their own."[6]

If you loved them on the court, how could you hate them in a restaurant?

As summer turned into fall and fall turned into basketball season, the attention of Evansville turned to its favorite question: Just how good were the Purple Aces going to be?

The season began like many others, with a visit from the Hawkeyes of Iowa, now coached by Ralph Miller, a graduate of Kansas who had been a protege of the legendary Phog Allen. One of Miller's classroom instructors had been a guest lecturer, James Naismith, inventor of the game of basketball.

Miller learned his lessons well. He had been named coach at Wichita University (now Wichita State) in 1951 and had taken the team to the National Invitation Tournament three times and the NCAA Tournament in 1964. In 13 seasons at Wichita he had won 220 games before moving on to Iowa.[7]

Iowa was 1–1 coming into the game against the Aces, having beaten South Dakota, then losing by six to Kentucky. Mac expected a hectic battle: "We know Iowa will press us, and probably all over the floor. We've been working against the press all week in practice."

Practice, as they say, pays off.

A crowd of 12,464, well beyond the expanded seating capacity, greeted the Aces warmly for the opening contest. The team managed to stand up well against Iowa's relentless pressure and took a 40–38 lead to their locker room.

Sam Watkins and Sloan had foul troubles, but midway through the second half Sam intercepted an errant Iowa pass and dribbled the length of the floor for an easy layup to put the Aces up by seven. The crowd stood and roared its approval. The Aces never were challenged again and went on to win, 90–83.

Mac had used only seven players in the win, and Ralph Miller, for one, was impressed by what he'd seen. "I believe Evansville has better balance and a better rebounding club than Kentucky," Miller told reporters, placing the Aces on a lofty pedestal in the rarified air of one of college basketball's greatest programs.

"I learned some things tonight," Herb Williams said after his varsity debut. Herb had battled the taller George Peeples, Iowa's 6-8 center and future pro, and managed to wrest nine rebounds. Sloan, with foul trouble, sat for 10 minutes in the first half and finished with only 10 points. His presence was barely missed because Larry Humes picked up where he had left off at the end of the previous season. Humes poured in 16 of 21 attempts from the floor and finished with 39 points to lead all scorers.

Larry's 39 points, his career-best mark, was just eight shy of Ed Smallwood's school record, and Larry still had two years to go. "If you get to close to him, he just ducks his head and goes. You have to play him all the way. We didn't . . . or couldn't," Miller said.

Ralph Miller would be only the first in a long line of coaches who would learn that stopping Larry Humes from scoring was like trying to stop a fast-moving freight train with a finger. It wasn't going to happen, and the results were not going to be pleasant.

Despite the recognition Sloan had achieved in the press, Humes was the fuel that propelled the Aces' engine. "When I was playing there it was always, 'Humes and Sloan,'" Humes said years later. "Then, when Jerry went to play in the pros and began coaching, it got reversed somehow," he laughed.[8] Maybe that's logical in view of Sloan's subsequent career, but in 1964 make no mistake: the correct order was Humes and Sloan. In fact, Sam Watkins, not Sloan, would prove to be the other most dangerous offensive component in the Aces' attack. Sloan was a valuable assist and rebound leader, but it would be Humes and Watkins who put the ball in the bucket most often. And they would prove to be a powerful duo.

Northwestern, another Big Ten school, was the next to succumb to the lure of hard cash and paid a visit to Evansville. "We can't hope to match them in size and strength," Mac told reporters. "so we're going to have to do something different or get beat. We have to go after them."

Going after someone was something the superbly conditioned and talented Aces were ideally suited to do. "I've never seen a team so high as those guys were when they went out there," student assistant coach Dave Fulkerson said. "You'd have thought they were going after the championship of the world."

They may have been a little too high. The Aces' offense sputtered in the opening half. They were so overeager they made just 3 of their first 24 shots from the field. Only Larry Humes's 15 points kept them within 9 points of the Wildcats at the half.

The intermission gave the Aces time to collect themselves, and the second half was a different story. When Sam Watkins nailed a 15 -foot jumper with 6:31 to play, the Aces took the lead. The game was still in doubt when Northwestern's Jim Burns stole a Watkins pass and was fouled from behind. Just under a minute and a half remained to play as Burns stepped to the line with Evansville holding a one-point lead. Burns, who was 6-for-8 from the free-throw line, put up the first—and missed.

Humes got the rebound and was fouled. Six seconds after Burns stood there, Humes was at the line with a one-and-one opportunity. "I was praying just like everybody else when I shot the first one," he recalled—not least because he'd missed four straight to that point. "I had been shooting them just a little too hard all night, and they were hitting the back of the rim and coming out."[9]

Not this time.

Larry coolly put the first one in. Then the second dove home, and the Aces led by three. A Grieger free throw and a Humes tip-in, followed by a Humes jumper, sealed the win.

Sam Watkins was celebrating—both the win and his twenty-first birthday. "It's about time I did something. I sure waited long enough," said the sophomore, who made seven of ten attempts in the second half. Humes and Watkins each had 26 points. Northwestern's coach, Larry Glass, had high praise for Sam: "We knew he could shoot, but not quite that good."

Sam himself was exuberant but already focused on the Aces' next task: "That's the thing about basketball. You only get to be happy for about five minutes after you win one. Then you've got to start worrying about the next one."

And the next one was Notre Dame. Mac had been eyeing the November date with the Irish since the first day of practice. "Of our first three opponents," he'd said, "Notre Dame might be the toughest." Indeed, Johnny Dee's Fighting Irish had humbled the Aces 91–75 the previous season, and they had since added 6-6 Ron Reed to the starting lineup, where he joined the 6-10 Walt Sahm.[10]

Notre Dame was 4–0 for the year when the Irish arrived at Roberts Stadium, where an SRO crowd of 12,807 was gathered.

Though the Irish were bigger and beefier, the Aces started the game strong. Because the 6-3 Herb Williams was facing off against Sahm, Mac abandoned his normal opening-tip play. "We usually used a play where I tipped it forward to the forwards," Herb recalled. "But Mac told me to tip it back to the guards. I told the referee, 'I might look little, but throw the ball high so I can get it.'"[11]

No one can recall Herb's ever losing a jump ball, and when he got that one too, the Aces scored easily. They built a 12-point lead with a little more than nine minutes to play in the opening half.

Then the shots stopped dropping. The Aces missed their next thirteen shots, and the Irish made their move to climb within two. When Reed made a layup at the buzzer, the Irish took a 43–39 half-time edge to the locker room.

Midway through the second half Dee switched the Irish to a zone defense. The strategy backfired. Grieger hit from the corner, Watkins made a layup, and a Humes jumper from the foul line put the Aces ahead. The Aces never trailed again and went on to claim an 89–82 victory.

The fans were ecstatic. So was Mac. "This has to rank as one of my greatest thrills in coaching," he told the press. "I'm speaking of this win right behind the wins over Iowa and Northwestern. That was quite a package. We just might quit right now."

The three wins by a College Division team over major college foes may be unprecedented. It was certainly an eye opener.

Watkins had spearheaded the second-half charge with 14 points after the intermission. Larry Humes hit on 13-for-24 to finish with 37. "If Larry Humes isn't an All-American, then there aren't many in the country," said Tom O'Brien, the Evansville assistant coach who was Mac's principal recruiter. Walt Sahm added, "As far as Larry Humes is concerned, I don't believe we'll see anyone much better all season."

Sam Watkins complimented the vanquished Irish: "That team isn't going to lose many games. But we may not lose many either."[12]

Having met and turned back three major college foes, the Aces turned to face some more in the upcoming Holiday Tournament. Among them was George Washington University, which had for years lured players from the Evansville area to its campus. The Colonials were joined by Louisiana State and Denver. Of the three, only the last boasted a winning mark coming in to the tournament.

Mark Clark was the latest in a long line of players from Evansville who had chosen GWU. "I'd love to play basketball for Evansville College," the former Reitz High School star told reporters, "but I have a much better opportunity to study medicine at George Washington and that's what I want to do after my playing days."

His return to Evansville wasn't a particularly pleasant one. More like bitter medicine. The Aces trounced the Colonials 105–80 before 6,253 fans. Mac used all 15 players and 11 of them scored. The regulars took seats on the bench after playing only four minutes in the second half. Larry Denton, who had been plagued by foul trouble in the earlier games, had five field goals in seven attempts. He attributed the improvement to Ed Smallwood's coaching. "He talked to me at half time and told me to 'Play it cool. When you shoot it you know it's in,' he told me. When I hit the first one in the second half I looked over at him, and Ed had a grin that split his ears."

Evansville was 4–0, which made everyone happy.

LSU would be the Aces' first Southeastern Conference foe since they had faced off against Tennessee in 1962–63. The Baton Rouge squad had nipped Denver by six in the opening round.

The Aces picked up where they had left off against George Washington. A stifling press upset the Tigers' offense, and the Aces led 48–32 at the half, with Larry Humes accounting for 21 of those points.

The lead widened to 63–41 in the second half as Larry poured in 12 straight points. He had 39 points with more than 10 minutes to play.

At the seven-minute mark, when Evansville held a commanding lead, Mac pulled Humes and the other starters. Larry had scored 45 points, only 3 points shy of the school record held by Ed Smallwood, who was sitting beside Larry on the bench. The 7,818 fans began to chant in protest: "We want Humes! We want Humes!"

Mac wasn't buying it. When he sent in a third-stringer instead of Larry, the popular coach heard boos for one of the few times in his career. Mac offered no apology. "In the past we've broken records only when we've needed the points, and I don't think we needed to change now," he said. LSU was down by 32 when the crowd had begun to urge Mac to put Larry back in.

"There's no doubt in my mind that Larry will eventually break every Evansville record in the book," the prescient coach said. Mac's refusing to have his star gain a record at the expense of a badly overmatched non-ICC opponent spoke to the coach's character. "I agreed with him," Humes said. "He was the boss and I respected him."[13]

Larry would observe years later: "There's no way of knowing how many I could have scored if there had been more close games and I was playing all forty minutes. We usually got far ahead, and then we came out, so I can't even begin to guess what I might have had. And, remember, there was no three-point shot then, either."[14]

Humes's torrid scoring pace had fans lining up early for the next contest. Against major college competition, Larry was averaging 34.4 points per game when the University of Massachusetts came to town.

Bob Hudson, whose latest promotional gimmick was playing-card size images of the players with a schedule on the reverse, had expected about 10,000, but 12,203 passed through the turnstiles.

Massachusetts was coached by Johnny Orr, who told reporters, "It's going to be quite an experience for these kids to play at Evansville. Most of them have never been out of New England. They don't know what Midwestern basketball enthusiasm is like."[15] And in the Midwest Evansville had the most enthusiastic fans of all, many of them dressed in red to watch Humes continue his torrid scoring pace.

Orr, whose Redmen were 5–1 when they got to town, elected to double-team Larry to try to stop the Aces' biggest gun. The Aces' guards, in turn, were left alone and responded with a barrage of their own. Evansville held a 58–41 edge at the half. When Orr abandoned his collapsing zone in the second half, Larry added five quick baskets. When Mac removed him and the other starters with six minutes to play, Larry had tallied 29. Sloan had profited from the UMass attention to Humes and scored 17 while grabbing 16 rebounds. Johnny Orr left Roberts with an embarrassing 113–82 experience for his kids. He tarried just long enough to offer his assessment of the Aces: "They're by far the best we've seen or played. There's no question about it. I think you have to go way back to someone like Ohio State when they won the national title to get a comparable team." Added Orr's assistant, Jack Lehman: "I've been looking at eastern teams for seven years and I haven't seen a team that compares to Evansville. They're the best I've seen since UCLA a year ago."

For a knowledgeable coach to even mention Evansville's Purple Aces in the same sentence as Wooden's 30–0 national champions is almost incomprehensible. The Aces were a College Division team in a state where the big-name schools were Indiana University, Purdue, and Notre Dame. Evansville wasn't even eligible for the NCAA University Division Tournament.

Lehman's comparison of the Aces to the Bruins, the defending national champions, placed Evansville at a higher level than almost every other college program in the land. Yet that is exactly what one presumably rational coach had just done.

The one thing that UCLA and Evansville had in common was that, at that point in this season, both were at 6–0. Evansville had a long way to go before the Aces could lay claim to perfection. But so far, after facing a schedule that represented the toughest competition they were likely to face all season, they had emerged victorious. Mac was not quite ready to make the claim that he would be finishing undefeated—at least, not yet. "I believe we could go on the floor with anybody in the country," he said. "I'm not saying we'd win them all, but we'd be respectable."

Respectable was what Mac always aimed for. But he was getting more than respect: he was receiving superlatives normally reserved for the game's greatest teams. And he was getting them for Evansville College, enrollment 2,500, not mighty UCLA or Ohio State or Michigan with enrollments of many times that number.

Today it is hard to imagine that a small college team could garner such accolades, but at the time the Purple Aces and Evansville took it all in stride. The Aces had been good for a while; that others were just now realizing exactly how good wasn't especially noteworthy so far as their fans were concerned. They had embraced and honored and loved the Aces, and they would continue to do so. Sure, the accolades were nice, but what Evansville fans really wanted was a repeat national title.

The Aces' success had imbued residents with civic pride, and it gave them a distinct and enviable identity throughout Indiana, where being good at basketball was just about the most important ability a Hoosier could have. The Aces' achievements were nothing short of a tonic for Evansvillians, who lived in a place so desperate for recognition it had sought to brand itself with refrigerators for crying out loud.

The Aces had given the city joy. They allowed the people of Evansville to hope and to dream, and the team had done so while adhering to the proposition that you could win without compromising your values.

The people of Evansville clutched the team to their breast and embraced them with unrestrained affection. The Aces reciprocated with superb performances on the floor at Roberts Stadium. Of course, no one yet knew just how good the 1964–65 edition of team would prove to be—it was way too early for that— but all the evidence indicated that they were very, very good indeed.

After thrashing UMass, the Aces took to the road, where they vanquished South Dakota State and South Dakota on successive evenings with performances that reminded the hometown fans in the Black Hills of Custer's Last Stand.

Humes had 26 and then 36 points in the lopsided wins, and Herb Williams grabbed 20 rebounds against the Coyotes, prompting their coach to observe that "they ought to give Williams a pilot's license. He goes up so high I bet they pick him up on radar screens."

At 8–0 after the road trip all the Aces were flying high. Even the plane carrying the team back to Evansville caught a favorable tail wind, landing an hour early and ruining Mayor Frank McDonald's planned welcome-home party.

When the regular conference season began in January, Evansville's ICC foes faced a daunting task in stopping a repeat by the champs. And none of the other members of the conference was anywhere near as good as the teams the Aces had already played.

Ball State was the first to test the Aces and failed miserably, swamped 108–92 in Muncie. Humes, facing a collapsing zone defense designed to contain him, refused to be restrained. He accounted for 48 points, eclipsing Ed Smallwood's school and ICC single-game scoring mark of 45. "We did everything we possibly could to stop Humes," Ball State's coach Jim Hinga said. "We would put three men on him around the basket, and he still got the shot off, and it would either go in, or he would get fouled." Mac, who had heard boos when he pulled Humes early in the romp over LSU, told his star, "I'm proud of the record now. You got it when it counted."

Watkins, roaming free because the Cardinals were concentrating on Larry, poured in 25 points. The Aces "have five players who can hurt you, while Michigan has only Cazzie Russell," said Hinga, whose Cardinals had already been beaten by Michigan's Wolverines, the top-ranked major college team.

The Butler Bulldogs, the team most figured had the best chance to dethrone the Aces, were next to meet Evansville, in Indianapolis. While Herb Williams, suffering from the flu, was struggling with Butler's center, 6-7 Mike Chapman, Larry continued his hot hand. He nailed 10-for-14 from the field in the first half to give the Aces a four-point cushion. In the second half the Aces were tied three times but managed to shake off each Butler challenge to eke out a 79–71 win.

Tony Hinkle joined the list of coaches pouring sugary praise on the Aces, telling reporters, "If there is anybody around who can handle Evansville, I'd be surprised."

The win over the Bulldogs was Mac's 300th victory.

When the Aces returned to Roberts, their next victim was DePauw. The Tigers tried a full-court press, but Mac's team had little trouble handling it. The crowd of 12,416 witnessed a well-coached, well-trained, well-balanced team that made just about everything it did look ridiculously easy. "We did most everything together on and off the court. On the court we knew just what everyone would be doing at all times," Herb Williams said. "We didn't have to think about it. We knew instinctively where everyone would be."[16]

The final score was 117–88, and it wasn't even that close. The Aces held a rebounding edge of 58–30, giving them second-chance opportunities that they converted with relative ease. The third string had mopped up, and Mac's starters had seen most of the second half wrapped in their robes from seats on the bench.

Even the usually reserved McCutchan was becoming impressed with the team. Of Evansville's first-half scoring splurge that sank the Tigers' chances, Mac said, "That's about the greatest eight minutes of basketball any team has ever played for me."

Even when Mac rested his starters, the Tigers got no respite. Sophomore Gary McClary had come off the bench with the third team in the waning minutes to make his varsity debut in an Aces uniform. He proceeded to hit 4-for-7 from the floor and finished with 10 points in his first game.

Indianapolis was beginning to notice what Mac had assembled in far-off Evansville. After the DePauw win, *Indianapolis Times* reporter Dick Mittman told readers, "It's quite possible this Evansville squad won't lose a single game this season. It's [*sic*] stiffest challenge through the remainder of the year comes Wednesday night when the Aces cross the Ohio to do battle with rugged Kentucky Wesleyan."

Guy Strong's current edition of the Panthers stood 5–4 for the season and lacked the depth of previous squads. Even so, Evansville was trailing by 28–22 at the 6:30 mark. Then the Aces finally caught fire and scored the next 13 straight points to take a 7-point lead at the half.

The second half began as the first had ended. The Aces reeled off nine straight points to up the lead to 44–30. When the Panthers' two big men fouled out, they were clawless and fell to the visitors 82–67.

Evansville had its twelfth win, and Strong credited Herb Williams. "We didn't think he'd hurt us that much," Strong said of his decision to leave Williams alone while he double-teamed Humes. Herb's 17 points proved Strong wrong. Despite the humiliation, Strong didn't join the chorus of those heaping accolades on the Aces. He put Southern Illinois above the Aces. "They're as good as I've seen this year, major or minor. They're good enough to beat Evansville, I know that," he averred.

Well, he'd also "known" Williams couldn't hurt him, and he had been wrong about that. Strong's latest prediction would also prove to be inaccurate, colored, no doubt, by his bitter feelings toward his main rivals from across the river.

The Aces remained undefeated with an easy win over St. Joseph's before the Salukis of SIU made the trek to Roberts. Later in the season the Aces would play the Salukis in Carbondale for the first time in four years. Evansville had long begged off trips to Carbondale because the gym held only 1,600. But now the Salukis had a new home that could accommodate 10,014 fans, and the Aces would pay a visit.

As the Salukis arrived in Evansville for the Wednesday evening clash, they boasted a 7–3 mark against a quality schedule, and coach Jack Hartman was sure his troops were good enough to test the Aces. "We think we've got a pretty good ball club," he said. "But Evansville is a good team too . . . a typical Evansville team that is better than ever because of an improved defense." Mac responded with his usual understatement. "Bit by bit, they seem equal to our team," he said. "But I'm not saying they're going to beat us."

In the throng of 12,123 was a crew from *Sports Illustrated,* at Roberts to cover the story of the small college that was drawing record crowds and knocking off the giants of the basketball world.

The magazine's interest was, in large measure, attributable to the Aces' unblemished record, but in the early going against the Salukis, that record looked to be in serious jeopardy. The Salukis had stunned the vast crowd into silence as they raced to a 14-point first-half lead. The Aces were stone cold.

Finally, after more than eight minutes Sam Watkins sank the Aces' first bucket. But SIU extended its lead to 15 points three times before the Aces bounced back. Humes and Sloan both converted steals into buckets, and Watkins cut the margin further with a jumper. When Grieger sank a layup at the buzzer, the Aces were down by only three as they headed to the locker room.

Watkins led the Aces back with two fast-break baskets to start the second half, and Evansville finally had the lead. The Salukis, though, weren't going away. The lead would change hands twelve times during the half. With just a little more than three minutes to play, Humes's two free throws stretched Evansville's lead to seven points.

But the visitors, led by their 6-1 guard David Lee, a former McLeansboro teammate of Jerry Sloan's, retaliated. Lee sank a 20-foot jumper, then converted two free throws to pull the Salukis within three points at 77–74.

Lee then stripped his former teammate of the ball and was fouled by Sloan in desperation. It was Sloan's fifth foul and he was done. But Lee wasn't. He converted the two free throws to put the Salukis within a point of the Aces. Watkins's free throw put Evansville up, 78–76. There was but 2:12 to play.

The other SIU guard, sophomore Walt Frazier, converted a steal beneath Evansville's basket into a fast-break basket, but referee Don Elser's whistle negated the bucket. Instead, he charged SIU's forward, Randy Goin, with a personal, sending Watkins to the free-throw line.

The small group of SIU faithful in the crowd was howling—and they were so irate that they had to be restrained by police after one of their number went after the referee. When order was restored, 39 seconds were showing on the scoreboard clock high above the court. Watkins made one of the free throws, giving the Aces a precarious three-point edge. Then Lee struck again. He nailed a 20-footer to pull the Salukis within a single point. Now just 12 seconds remained.

SIU's Goin intercepted Ace Ron Johnson's inbound pass, banked a short shot off the backboard, and it went in.

Nine seconds remained.

The Aces were behind 80–79, and Mac quickly called time-out.

The crowd sat in silence. The winning streak seemed all but over. They were going to see their Aces lose for the first time in front of a team of reporters from a national magazine. How could this happen? The Aces huddled around their coach and listened intently as Mac designed a play, a typical McCutchan solution to a seemingly insurmountable problem. He later described what he'd said: "I told Russ to take it out and told Ron [Johnson] to cut through in a sweep to get the Salukis to chase him and let Russ throw it to Sam. I told Sam to get it to Larry. And then I told Larry I was sure he could figure out some way to get it in there."

Classic McCutchan. With the streak in jeopardy and the game on the line in front of national media, he calmly and quietly told the Aces just what they needed to do to win. Mac may have been a math teacher, but he must have picked up some psychology somewhere along the line.

"If you got the ball on the side of the court by our bench, Mac would never yell, 'Shoot.' He always yelled, 'Make it!'" Russ Grieger remembered.[17] Maybe it seems like a small difference, but it's huge to a player on the court. No panic. No sense of urgency. Just matter-of-fact, positive reinforcement.

Years later, Larry Humes recalled what happened next: "It went exactly like he planned it. Grieger threw it long to Sam Watkins, and Sam threw it to me near the foul line. I stumbled a bit off-balance and then spun around, faced the basket, and let it go. I had to shoot over three defenders, but I got it off. It hit the back of the rim where the flange is attached to the backboard and just hung there, perfectly balanced, for a second or two. It teetered and then dropped in. I remember it like it was yesterday." [18]

A final desperation full-court shot from Frazier fell harmlessly away, and the Aces stormed the court. Carrying Humes on their shoulders, they trooped happily to the locker-room tunnel through a jubilant crowd of well-wishers who evaded police efforts to restrain them. The *Courier* photo the next day showed the shot that sank the Salukis. "I still have it in my den," Larry said. [19]

And the Aces were still perfect.

"That was the best basket I've ever made," Humes told reporters after the game. "I didn't know whether it was going in or not, the way it was bouncing around up there. That kind usually fall off, but this one didn't."

Not this year—not to this player, not to this team. Larry finished with 38 points, including the game winner.

"We knew that ball would go to Humes, but what could we do?" Jack Hartman said. "Evansville was shooting one-and-one fouls so it wouldn't do any good to foul him. We just tried to set up a defense so we could play the ball coming down the floor and maybe keep him from getting it in time." The plan was a good one, but Mac's was even better.

Hartman described the game as "one of the worst defeats of my career." Knowing that the rematch was coming up in February, he added, "This game will have them coming out in droves."

The Evansville faithful didn't wait long. "One doctor drove over here Tuesday just to make sure he could get 10 tickets," SIU's Fred Huff said. "If my mother wanted to come I don't know if I could get her a ticket."

The Aces had held up under the intense scrutiny of the national media and were rewarded with stories that were complimentary and colorful. *Time Magazine* told readers, "When visiting basketball teams arrive they get a big hello: a tour of the Museum of Arts and Science, a hearty steak dinner in the campus dining room and then they are led off to Municipal Stadium—for the execution." [20] The national newsmagazine offered a profile of Mac and his colorful attire as well as a look at just how a "small college" had done against the major powers. It was a laudatory and light-hearted look at the growing acclaim that was accruing to Evansville and their Aces.

The attention *Time* focused on the city was especially welcome. Now, thanks to the Aces, the whole nation knew what and where Evansville was. It may have taken a long time but Evansville had finally arrived. Now Evansville was "home of the Aces"—and that sure beat "home of Pablum."

But even better than the story in *Time* was what the weekly *Sports Illustrated*, the premier sports magazine, had to say. The story was by Frank Deford, one of *SI*'s gifted young writers, and it ran in the February issue under the headline *"Aces High In Evansville: Best Small College Basketball Team in the Nation."* The detailed tribute to the team and the Aces' ardent followers was written in Deford's breezy conversational style, which would make him one of the best sports writers of the era.

Deford described in humorous detail just how difficult securing a ticket to an Aces game could be: "One ticket holder died at night, and the man who owned seats to the immediate left showed up at 8:30 the next morning to request that they be passed on to him. He was denied because the seat holder on the deceased's right had the foresight to show up at 6:15."[21]

Now, as never before, Roberts Stadium was *the* place to be if you lived in Evansville or anywhere near it. All activity took second place--a distant second place--to the Aces' games.

The spotlight Evansville had sought since its founding in 1812 had caught the city in its white hot glow through the success of the Aces on the hardwood. The same spotlight that brought them recognition throughout Indiana now swung outward. With the national coverage provided by *Time* and *Sports Illustrated*, Evansville and the Aces were now inextricably bound together and known throughout the land. It may have taken over 150 years and an extraordinary college basketball team but Evansville, at long last, could no longer be ignored.

Although the Aces had whipped Ball State by 16 points in their game at Muncie, fully 12,145 fans turned out to watch the rematch at Roberts. The outcome was decided before the opening tip, but everyone wanted to be there just the same.

The Aces didn't let their fans down. They routed the visitors 117–81. A week later another 10,411 fans braved the icy wind-whipped winter air to watch Valparaiso's demise.

Gene Bartow was the new head coach at Valpo, on his first visit to Roberts Stadium.[22] He was suitably impressed and soundly whipped: "This is really an amazing place. On a night like this, you get this big a crowd. It's almost unbelievable." Bartow left Roberts like so many others before him, a believer in the Aces' dominance of their home court. The final score was 83–78.

Bob Hudson explained why he thought so many fans were turning out. "Everyone wants to see us go unbeaten. The way I have it figured, we should draw 150,000 for the season." He was not far off.

Even the opposing teams' partisans applauded the amazing Aces. In Greencastle, Indiana, after Mac had replaced his starters in a blowout over host DePauw, a crowd of 2,000 rose to give the Aces a standing ovation that didn't subside for more than a minute. Excellence was appreciated in Greencastle. "It was the greatest example of sportsmanship I ever saw," Bob Hudson said later. "They couldn't have shown more enthusiasm if it had been their own team."

Valpo fans also packed their newly renovated gym to watch the Aces demolish the Crusaders 109–88. Humes again led the Aces with 34 points, as he had done for most of the campaign. Wheaton's head coach, Lee Pfund, had been in the stands. "This is the best Evansville team I've seen in a long time," he said. "They keep the pressure on you all the time, trap you and make you work right into it." Harold Cox, who had started for the Aces in the 1959 championship season, agreed, "This is a better team than we were. We had a little more reserve strength, but this team is bigger and stronger."

Harold was right. If the Aces had an Achilles heel, it was their bench. The starting five were solid, but Mac seldom turned to any reserves other than Ron Johnson to spell the guards in tight games. Johnson, of Centralia, Illinois (Herb Williams's hometown), was a 5-10 guard who had chosen Evansville over Houston. He had scored more than a thousand points in high school. In his senior year Johnson averaged 17 points per game and scored 18 against Chicago Carver—Cazzie Russell's high school—in the state finals but lost. Johnson had offers from Loyola of Chicago, Illinois, Bradley, Cincinnati, Kansas, Drake, and New Mexico as well as Southern Illinois. No wonder Mac relied on his services.

The Aces had seldom been in enough foul trouble in close games to expose their weakness. With any luck it would remain only a nagging concern for an always-worried Mac.

When Kentucky Wesleyan arrived at Roberts in February, the army of supporters in red shirts showed the coach their appreciation. After the Aces demolished the Panthers by 20 points, the fans presented Mac with a bright red Chrysler 300. Arad McCutchan Appreciation Night drew 12, 234 mostly red-clad partisans and boosted attendance at Roberts for the season to an astonishing 140,584 with one home game remaining.

"Dad never earned more than $20,000 until the midsixties. The school just wasn't in a position to pay any more than that at the time," Allen McCutchan recalled.[23] Cognizant of the low salary Mac was receiving at Evansville, fans sought to reward him for his efforts themselves, in appreciation for all he'd accomplished.

That last game was with Indiana State, and though meaningless in the ICC standings—Evansville had already clinched the crown by trouncing St. Joseph's on the road—fully 9,132 turned out. The real battle that the fans wanted to see was between Larry Humes and Charles "Butch" Wade, for the conference-scoring crown. The 6-4 sophomore from Columbus, Ohio, trailed Larry by just seven points. In their first game, at Terre Haute, each had scored 30 points.

Mac assigned Jerry Sloan the task of stopping Wade. "I may be the most embarrassed guy around here when it's over, but I don't think he'll get 30 tonight," Sloan told reporters. Sloan's braggadocio almost came back to bite him. Wade scored 28 against Jerry despite Sloan's attempts to smother him whenever he touched the ball.

Larry Humes gave the crowd what they had come to see. He snapped Ed Smallwood's single-season scoring record on the way to a 39-point game that gave him the ICC scoring title to boot.

"I was glad to beat him, but you have to give a lot of credit to the other guys. There were a lot of people under the basket but they still gave the ball to me," Humes said in a self-effacing statement that was representative of his attitude about the game. He ended the season with an average of 33.6 points per game, besting the 26.9 set by Bob Williams and setting a new ICC record.

Since their narrow loss to the Aces, SIU had rolled over nine straight opponents. The Salukis were unbeaten at home on the year, having won all twelve contests on their own court. Now revenge was on their minds.

SIU is located in an area known as Little Egypt. It doesn't snow in Egypt, but in Little Egypt the heavens opened that night, dumping twenty inches.. Undeterred, more than 3,000 rabid fans in red shirts caravanned to Carbondale to watch the final regular season game for their undefeated Aces. They were greeted by a crowd of SIU students clad in green bowler hats and trumpeting at the top of their lungs through long alpine horns, who clearly had been communing with spirits of other than a celestial nature as the Evansville caravan arrived.

As the Evansville fans entered town, they were confronted by marquees on businesses throughout the city, from the Holiday Inn to the LBJ Steakhouse, that screamed "Beat Evansville." Most of the snow had melted by game time, but if it hadn't, the heat generated by Saluki fans would have reduced it to a puddle of slush.

WSIU-TV was televising the game live to those in Illinois who couldn't get tickets. As the telecast began, the camera panned slowly up to the rafters to a 40-foot banner proclaiming, "Beat Evansville." The Aces took the court first in their multicolored robes and were greeted by a chorus of boos that easily overwhelmed the cheers from the Evansville partisans. The Aces were followed shortly thereafter by the home team, which was greeted with a sustained roar of approval from the 10,300 in attendance.

The hosts were 16–4 on the season and were rated fourth by the AP poll and third by UPI. The Aces were, of course, first in the land, at least at the moment. Their first-place ranking and perfect season were on the line.

Normally, games that are highly anticipated fail to meet the expectations of fans. That would not be the case this evening.

The home team began the game the same way it had at Roberts, racing ahead of the Aces by hitting 12 of their first 15 attempts. Evansville, unable to get the ball down low to Humes, struggled offensively, trailing by two at the half.

The second half saw an energized Saluki squad take a 53–46 lead. The Aces' chances for perfection were growing dimmer with each passing second. A blanket of defenders was still covering Humes down low, and Sam Watkins, who had solved the Saluki defense at Roberts with long-range jumpers, was off target. But the Aces refused to roll over and die.

They fought back tenaciously with a smothering defensive effort that caused three straight SIU turnovers that the Aces converted into baskets. At the 10:18 mark the Aces tied the game at 58 on a Williams basket. A little more than six minutes remained when the Aces took the lead outright at 63–61.

Walt Frazier stole a Russ Grieger pass and scored on a driving layup to tie the game again.

A free throw by Humes put the Aces up by a point at 68–67 with a 1:07 on the scoreboard clock.

On Evansville's next possession Watkins's shot, under heavy pressure, bounced away, and SIU gained the rebound and quickly called a time-out. Only 18 seconds remained.

The SIU guards had bested Evansville all evening. Jack Hartman knew it and instructed his team to get the ball to the 6-2 Boyd McNeil for the final shot. The play he designed unwound exactly the way it should have. The inbounds pass from beneath the SIU basket went upcourt to McNeil, who took it in midstride, stopped at the top of the key, and put up the shot.

The ball bounced once, high off the back iron.

It fell harmlessly away.

The buzzer sounded.

The Aces had won. They had completed the regular season in heart-pounding fashion, but they were 24–0, and that was all that mattered.

In the dressing room after the game the five Evansville starters were subdued. The game had drained all the energy and adrenaline from their weary bodies. They had played every one of the tension-packed forty minutes without respite.

"They've got a great team," Russ Grieger told reporters after he caught his breath. "But we're that much better." He held his thumb and forefinger about an inch apart.

SIU had held Larry Humes to his lowest output of the season at 20 points. But Herb Williams had compensated by scoring 16. Sloan had 21. "We played when we had to," Jerry said.

"How many times is Williams going to hit that many against us?" asked a confounded Hartman, who had now been burned twice by Herb.

Mac was impressed with the Salukis' David Lee, who had gone 8-for-18 from the field. "Everyone tells me he's not that good, but he's beginning to convince me."

Lee's comment was indicative of the Salukis' outlook before the game: "I honestly thought we could beat them." He added: "Now, I don't know. How many times can you do so well and lose?"

Maybe he'd get his answer. The NCAA had announced its brackets for the tournament, and Evansville and SIU were in opposite brackets. If things went according to form and both teams advanced to the finals, David Lee, Mac, and everyone else would get their answer. Mac was not unaware of the possibility. "Maybe we'll meet them again and beat them by half a point," he quipped.

The Aces would not have their usual home-court advantage. Participants in past tournaments who had to play the Aces in Evansville in the early rounds had complained. Now the NCAA was sending the Aces packing to play away from their home court. They had to travel to Bellarmine College in Louisville, to begin play in the South Central Region.

Bob Hudson was beside himself. "The tickets we've been allotted will all be gone by tomorrow," he moaned. "We don't even have the tickets yet, but we have heavy orders already from people who have come by and left their money." Fifteen hundred of the faithful accompanied the Aces to Louisville for the first two rounds of post-season play. Their opening-round opponent was Florida's Bethune-Cookman College, a historically black school that had posted a record of 20–7 for the season.

The Daytona Beach school had been founded in 1904 by a determined young woman, Dr. Mary McLeod Bethune, the fifteenth child born to parents who had been slaves. Raised in South Carolina, where she toiled in the fields next to her parents and siblings, she did not attend school until she was ten. She quickly learned to read and began to realize that education was the path out of poverty. "The whole world opened to me," she told her biographer.

She became a teacher and dreamed of opening her own school. She realized that dream when she established a school for Negro girls in Daytona Beach with $1.50, four young students, and an unshakable faith.

The school eventually became a four-year college. Bethune was an active civil rights advocate in the 1930s and 1940s and led the fight against school segregation and inadequate health care for blacks. She also served as an adviser to presidents Herbert Hoover and Franklin D. Roosevelt and was elected head of the National Association of Colored Women's Clubs.[24]

If the Wildcats of Bethune-Cookman had half the spunk and determination of their school's founder, they would be a handful for the Aces. Their coach was John "Cy" McClairen, a former tight end for the Pittsburgh Steelers. He had never seen Evansville play and asked EC's advance scout, Dave Fulkerson, about Mac's team during Bethune-Cookman's own conference tournament, which Fulkerson attended.

"I asked him did they have any Negro boys up there at Evansville, and he said, yeah, they got three starting," McLairen said. "I asked him if they were any good, and he told me, 'No, they can't play a lick.' Well I just looked at that man, and I said, 'Those other two white boys must be awful good.'"

The Wildcats had their own star in the country's top rebounder, 6-9 center Carl Fuller. They also had two guards who weren't afraid to shoot from anywhere.

"We're a running team, and we fast break anytime we can," McLairen told reporters.

Well, maybe they could, but Mac's Aces could run with anyone. If the Wildcats chose to run with the Aces, they'd better be prepared for a long night. During the regular season Evansville had averaged 95 points per game and had exceeded the century mark on eight occasions. The Wildcats would have done well to heed the warning of Jack Hartman when he described the Aces' style of play earlier in the year: "They are tougher than hell in an up and down ball game." Apparently, McLairen hadn't heard that.

If running was what the Wildcats wanted, well, Evansville would be happy to oblige. The Aces were off and running from the opening tip. The score after the first ten minutes was 36–14. Humes had made five baskets and had been fouled repeatedly. He canned 10 free throws in the opening half as Evansville built the lead to 62–32 at the break.

Mac's starters played only eight minutes in the second half. Up by 35 points, Mac pulled them all and sent in his reserves, who finished off the outmanned and outrun Wildcats by 118–77. Fuller, who had scored 60 points against Fisk College only a week earlier, was held to 10 by the Aces.

Alex Groza, coach of Bellarmine College, which had survived its opener and would face the Aces in the next round, said, "This is the finest team I have seen this year. Maybe the best thing we could do is just to stay at home and not show up."[25]

Groza had been one of the players involved in the point-shaving scandals of the 1950s that had nearly killed college basketball. He had been working in a tavern in his hometown of Martin's Ferry, Ohio, when the Bellarmine job came open in 1959. Groza had jumped at the chance to get back into the sport he had once dominated. Now he and the Knights were in the NCAA Tournament. That was the good news. The bad news was that they were going to have to face the Aces.

The Knights elected to show up for the game and put up a spirited fight in the early going. They used screens on offense and an aggressive defensive job on the boards to stay close to the Aces. The Knights' big men covered Humes closely wherever he went.

Eventually, the talent level of Evansville began to assert itself. At the half the Aces held a 15-point lead. At the beginning of the second half the Knights mounted a serious charge. They made seven of their first ten shots to pull within three points of the Aces. But that was as close as they would get.

Humes canned two straight buckets, and Mac ordered the Aces to slow the pace, forcing Bellarmine, down by six, to foul. When it was over, the Aces had moved on and Bellarmine was going home. The final score of 81–74 was closer than most thought it would be and gave some hope to the Aces' next opponents.

Groza was realistic. "We might have beaten them if we hadn't made so many mistakes. But then, that's part of Evansville's success. A good team will force you into mistakes and then kill you for making them," he told reporters

Jerry Sloan was selected as the regional's MVP award winner. Larry Humes joined Jerry on the All-Tournament team. "Anytime we lose one now, it's my last game. We haven't lost one yet, and I don't aim to start losing now,' Sloan said.

The Aces had survived their exile to Louisville and would be returning to the cozy confines of Roberts Stadium for the NCAA Finals. No one was happier than Bob Hudson, whose office phone never stopped ringing. "Even before the tournament opens, we'll have a greater sale than we had last year after it was over," he beamed. On Sunday callers to GR-6-7211 had snapped up 2,000 tickets. "My mother and I both helped handle the calls for tickets," Joan Hudson Roth said. "It was a hectic and wonderful time for all of us. Our life revolved around basketball. Trying to juggle all the ticket requests gave my dad a terrible time. But he loved every minute of it."[26]

Advancing along with Evansville were three other midwestern schools, Washington University of St. Louis (21–5), Akron (21–6), and, as many had hoped or feared, Southern Illinois (18–5). Joining the field was Philadelphia Textile (24–3), which drew the unenviable task of facing the Aces in the first round. "We're just glad to be here," said the Rams' coach, Walter "Bucky" Harris, before the game.

With a record Wednesday night crowd of 9,866 looking on, Bucky got progressively less happy. The Aces tipped off at nine o'clock, after SIU had advanced by turning back Washington University in the opener. The Aces had a little trouble getting started, but they soon were firing on all cylinders and running Textile's Rams into the ground. The half saw the Aces up by 12.

In the second half an early scoring burst from Humes and Sloan put the Rams away for good. With a minute to play the regulars finally got a rest as Mac put the reserves in. The final score was 92–76. Sloan had grabbed 26 boards, and Evansville had managed to outmuscle the visitors to hold an overwhelming rebounding edge of 62–24. Humes and Sloan had combined for 57 points, and Williams added 12 despite a nasty second-half fall in which he injured both knees. "I don't think it's anything worse than a bruise," Mac said hopefully. "We're sending him downtown for X-rays just to be sure."

For the first time in all his years at Evansville, Mac had started the same five in each and every game. He didn't want to change anything now. He didn't have to, as Herb was jumping center as usual when the Aces faced off against a familiar old foe, St. Michael's College of Vermont.

Those in the crowd who could recall the 1957–58 season had reason to be concerned. They saw the decidedly unpleasant possibility of a repeat upset by the team that had foiled the Aces in that memorable season's semifinal game. Now, seven years later, the Iron Mikes again stood as the only barrier between the Aces and the championship game.

Earlier, the Salukis of Southern Illinois had held form and advanced to the final round by crushing North Dakota. The stage was set for a memorable final if—and it was a big if—the Aces advanced.

Fans concerned about a repeat of the 1958 game were soon feeling relieved. Evansville came out blazing, with Humes canning six of his first eight attempts. The Aces were ahead 35–20 after only 10 minutes of play.

At the intermission, after a Sloan tip-in, the Aces held a comfortable 51–33 lead. The second half saw Mac rest his starters early. With a little more than nine minutes to play, the reserves took over and finished the demolition job. There would be no upset this time. It was 93–70 when the final buzzer ended the Iron Mikes' misery and heralded an SIU-Aces rematch for the national title.

The Salukis had stopped the Aces twice before, in 1962 and 1963. The teams had met twice earlier in the season, and both games had been nailbiters to the very end. Evansville had managed to beat the Salukis both times, but the total margin of difference was just two points.

Two points separating two teams battling for the championship. Bob Hudson couldn't have dreamed up a better scenario if he tried.

The *Evansville Courier* that morning carried a warning from an NCAA official: "If you don't have a ticket, there's no need to come out." The highly anticipated final drew 12,797 fans, mostly clad in red. The red army had seen many memorable games at Roberts through the years but none was bigger than this one. The national title was on the line, the undefeated season was at stake. The opponent was a bitter rival that had nearly ended the Aces' streak twice before. It simply didn't get any better than this.

Allen McCutchan was off at Yale in frigid New Haven, where he was a medical student. He knew his father would be outwardly calm while hiding a major case of nerves. So he sent his father a telegram to help break the tension. Allen used biblical references he knew Mac would appreciate and a play on words describing the area of Carbondale where SIU was located.

When the telegram arrived on the day of the game, Mac opened it and a smile spread slowly across his face. His wrinkled brow relaxed as he read his son's message: SINK THE LITTLE EGYPTIANS IN A SEA OF RED.[27]

Mac's opposite number had no such tension-breaking moment. "I don't know if I can stand another [close game] or not," said Jack Hartman.

Walt Frazier had returned to action for the Salukis against North Dakota after not feeling well enough to play in the regional final. Now he was back in form, having notched 26 points in the SIU romp. "They looked real good to me," Mac had said after watching the Salukis take the Sioux. "I think they're ready."

Larry Humes thought the Aces were more than up to the difficult task of beating a team for the third time in a single season. "I don't think we played up to par in either of the other games against Southern," he said. "I think we can win one more and then take a little rest."

The crowd was in a frenzy, chanting, "We want Southern! We want Southern!" even before the consolation game had ended (North Dakota took third place). Then fans began to count down the minutes to the tip-off for the championship, interrupting themselves periodically to indulge in favorite chant: "Aces! Aces!" *Clap, clap, clapclapclap.*

The SIU-Evansville championship game was everything a college basketball fan could hope for. The Salukis had replaced the Panthers of Kentucky Wesleyan as the Aces' most bitter rival. The two teams had met in the NCAA Tournament on two other occasions, and both times SIU had spoiled the Aces' title hopes. Every contest between the two teams was a close one that could have gone either way. Now the national title was at stake.

There were no secrets. Each team knew the other's strengths and weaknesses. Each coach knew what the other was likely to do in any given situation. All that was left was to play the game.

For the twenty-ninth straight game the Aces' starters were Herb Williams at center, Larry Humes and Jerry Sloan at forward, and Russ Grieger and Sam Watkins at guard—the iron men of Evansville, whom the press had labeled the Fabulous Five. "Before the game Coach McCutchan got us all together in the locker room. He looked around at us and said, 'Have fun. We'll all have breakfast together tomorrow morning one way or another,'" Russ Grieger recalled.[28]

The game, unlike many other ballyhooed and highly anticipated match-ups that end up fizzling, lived up to its billing in every possible way. Larry Humes started the scoring with a jumper, and the two teams resumed play as if the previous two weeks had never happened. The Salukis tried to stop Humes with an aggressive man-to-man defense.

Like the two before it, the game unfolded as a back-and-forth contest, with neither team able to put much distance between it and its opponent. They were tied six times, and the lead changed hands twice in the first half as they battled toe-to-toe, seeking an advantage. At the half the Aces clung to a four-point edge.

The second half saw the Salukis come alive. The play of forwards Joe Ramsey and Boyd McNeil put SIU ahead 63–55 at the midway point in the second half. Save for a few hardy Saluki fans, the crowd at Roberts was suddenly quiet. Was it all going to end here? The unbeaten streak, the national title, all torn cruelly away by the Salukis when it was so close? Aces fans looked down at their weary team and hoped for a miracle.

The five starters had become "like a family," Larry Humes recalled. "We all knew each other's moves instinctively by now, and we trusted each other to be there when we needed them."[29] Their slim lead had evaporated. Their winning streak was in dire jeopardy. They were leg and arm weary from a long season. They could have easily given up. But these Aces didn't quit. They didn't even consider that they could lose.

They summoned an inner resolve that had been instilled in them by their coach. He never talked of losing, only of "how we will win."

The clocked showed 8:27 left to play. The Aces trailed, 67–59.

Their backs to the wall, the Aces fought back with every fiber of their being. Adrenaline rushed into aching legs and limbs. And they came back. With a vengeance.

It started, fittingly, with Larry Humes stepping up to tip in a miss. Then Herb Williams hit from near the top of the key. Suddenly, the score was 67–65, and the Aces could taste a win. The crowd was on its feet, roaring encouragement as only an Aces crowd could. The enthusiastic support was like having a sixth Evansville man, and it's hard to play with five against six.

At the 5:45 mark Larry Humes completed a three-point play, and the Aces took the lead at 68–67. But the Salukis refused to fold. They tied the game at 74 with only 1:39 to go. This game, like the other two, was going down to the last possession.

At the 1:20 mark on the scoreboard clock, the Aces were whistled for a three-second violation, and the ball went to SIU.

The crowd moaned and groaned.

Jack Hartman immediately ordered his team to stall and to play for the last shot. "That seems to be the difference between these two teams: the last basket," he had said the night before. Hartman had picked his poison.

As the clock ticked inexorably and steadily down, the Salukis set up the shot that would give them the win, and the title, if they could just make it.

McNeil took the shot from twelve feet.

The ball hit the back iron and bounced away.

The buzzer sounded.

There would be overtime.

The two teams had now played three complete games and had finished only two points apart.

Now they would play another five minutes.

For Evansville's starters another five minutes was asking a lot. They had played all but 58 seconds of the game, and then only Herb Williams had enjoyed a brief rest before returning. They would have to dig deeper than they ever had dug before. They would have to play an overtime period on guts and sheer willpower. All else had been exhausted through the long season and the tension-packed game that had not yet ended.

Would it be enough?

Herb Williams controlled the opening tip.

"He could jump out of the gym," Larry Humes said of the 6-3 center who had not lost a tip-off all season.

The Aces capitalized as Sam Watkins took the tip all the way in for a layup, putting the Aces up by two.

Then Humes put up a sweeping hook shot at the four-minute mark.

The Aces were up by four with 4:00 to play.

Boyd O'Neil countered to pull the Salukis back to within two, but Sloan's two foul shots restored the four-point Aces lead.

Humes followed with a free throw.

Aces by five, 81–76.

Little over a minute remained in overtime.

After Walt Frazier put a Saluki miss back in, the Aces' lead was down to just three.

Sam Watkins converted two foul shots as the Salukis, now desperate for the ball, promptly fouled him.

Sam coolly sank both.

SIU got the ball, but the Salukis were now down by five, and only 35 ticks remained on the clock.

Walt Frazier wasn't quite ready for the season to end. He fired from beyond the free-throw line, and the ball hit nothing but net, putting the Salukis within three.[30]

The noise inside Roberts was deafening.

Sloan was fouled immediately and stepped to the line. His two free throws could ice the game.

He missed.

SIU rebounded, and Joe Ramsey took advantage of Sloan's miss to make the layup that drew SIU within the same one point that had decided both earlier games between the two teams that season.

Seven seconds showed on the clock.

All Evansville needed to do was to get the ball inbounds and hold on. The inbounds pass from Russ Grieger went to Sloan, who was fouled. That put Sloan, who had missed a critical free throw only seconds earlier, back on the line for the Aces.

A single second remained on the clock.

SIU watched, helplessly, as Sloan, the one-time would-be Saluki, eyed the basket.

He didn't miss the first.

And his second free throw sank the Salukis' last chance for survival.

The Aces had won, 83–80.

The Aces were national champions.

They were also a perfect 29–0.

Among those 29 wins were 3 over SIU that had been decided by a grand total of just 5 points.

Mac's Aces had done the most difficult thing in college basketball. They had repeated as national champions and had done so without losing a single game. Mac now had four national championship trophies on display in the trophy case at Carson Center. No other College Division coach had as many.

On the sidelines, by the Aces' bench, the celebration was under way. Fans mobbed the players. Someone put cowboy hats on both Sloan and Humes. Jerry's wife, Bobbye, holding their infant daughter, Kathy, left the stands to join the celebration.

Sloan's career at Evansville College was over. He had ended his stay with back-to-back titles. He was a three-time selection as All-American, and his play in the tournament earned him the MVP award. Accepting the award, he told the crowd, almost all of whom had remained, "I'm glad I made two serious 'mistakes' in my life. At least people…thought I was mistaken. I'm glad I quit Illinois and came to Evansville," he said, omitting his flirtation with SIU from the chronology. "The other 'mistake' I'm most grateful for is declining the professional offer last year [in order] to finish out with the Aces."[1] With a wide sweep of his long arm around the stadium, he concluded with, "This is something money can't buy. It's something worth more than a million bucks."

Sloan would leave Evansville College after three seasons without any individual records. His floor generalship, pinpoint passing, and rebounding were all crucial to the team's success the previous two seasons. He would go on to a career in the NBA. He was a first-round draft choice of the Baltimore Bullets and played one season for them, then was traded to Chicago. Sloan played a total of eleven seasons in the NBA and was a two-time All-Star. He was a perennial choice for the NBA's all-defensive team.[32] After his playing career ended, he stayed with the Bulls as a scout and assistant coach.

He spent three unremarkable seasons as head coach of the Chicago Bulls before moving on to the Utah Jazz. He remained with the Jazz for the next twenty-two seasons, amassing 1,127 wins with the Jazz and leading his teams to the NBA Finals twice. Then he abruptly resigned partway through the 2011 season. Some things never change: only two days before he quit, Sloan had signed a contract extension to stay on through the 2012 campaign.[33]

Larry Humes still had another season to play in an Aces uniform, but he was going to miss Jerry. "Jerry and I worked well together," he said. "We were just like two old country boys out there having a good old time."[34] Jerry Sloan was equally candid in his assessment of Larry Humes: "As far as I'm concerned, Larry is better than I am. He's the best in the country." That was February 1965, and he hasn't changed his mind about Larry, at least not yet.

"Whenever Jerry is asked by people who the greatest player he ever played against is, he always answers the same way. 'Larry Humes is the best player. Period,'" Humes said.[35]

Humes had finished his junior year with a scoring average of 32.4 points per game, a school record. His 941 points had established a new single-season record as well. He was rewarded for his spectacular season by being named a small college All-American by both the AP and UPI.

Humes was quick to share the credit for his success: "Half the credit goes to my teammates. I play under the basket, and if they don't get the ball in to me, I don't score." Two of his teammates, Watkins and Williams, would be joining Humes for their senior year on the Aces.

Russ Grieger, like Sloan, had exhausted his collegiate eligibility. Russ had been a consistent and reliable back-court performer all season. He had averaged just under 10 points per game, but his strength was his ability to swipe passes on defense and to deliver timely ones to his teammates.

"I can't tell you what this means," he said. "Not many kids get to play college basketball. But to play for a team like this, before a crowd like this, and for a man like Coach McCutchan, it's just something you can't put into words."

Grieger went on to earn his master's and doctoral degrees in psychology at Ohio State University. He then joined the faculty at the University of Virginia in Charlottesville and spent a number of years in academia before striking out on his own and establishing a private psychological counseling practice. The practice covers the full range of psychological services, from substance abuse to marriage counseling. He also writes and conducts seminars for corporate clients that focus on personal responsibility and team building.

He draws heavily on his experiences as a member of the Evansville team of 1964–65 in those presentations. "That team represented, in every way, the essence of teamwork," he said. "There was not a single conflict on the team. There was no jealousy between Sloan and Humes. On the contrary, there was mutual respect. Each player knew his role, accepted it, and performed to the best of their ability for the greater good of the team. We weren't a bunch of rah-rah guys. We were all mature and self-confident. We just went about the business of winning basketball games and derived great personal pride in doing so."

Grieger describes his years at Evansville as having been "unbelievably positive," and there is no doubt at all that, as part of the perfect season team, he understands completely what it takes to become a winner.[36]

Reserves Larry Denton, Ron Eberhard, Dave Cox, and Jim Forman would also be concluding their careers at Evansville. Though they had spent many minutes of many games on the bench, they had all been part of the team's success.

The Aces' Fabulous Five—the iron men Humes, Sloan, Grieger, Watkins, and Williams—had done what Evansville had done only once before: they had repeated as national champions.

How good were they?

One man had no doubt.

Colby College coach Lee Williams, who knows a thing or two about basketball, said they were "the greatest accumulation of talent ever assembled on a college division team."[37]

They were also something else.

They were a perfect team.

(Endnotes)

1   I again want to thank Bill Bussing, who made his lengthy manuscript available to me. The detailed manuscript contains no footnotes, but when I interviewed Bussing in February 2011, he identified his sources as the *Evansville Courier* and *Evansville Press,* the two local papers at the time. Bussing's manuscript usually makes no distinction between the two, but the direct quotes are from one or the other and appear in the Bussing manuscript in quotation marks. Bussing also had access to a collection of old bound scrapbooks kept by Bob Hudson. My research assistant and I also used the scrapbooks, which are now housed in the university archives. The articles do not identify which paper they are from, much less the date and page, but I (and Bussing) assume they are from the *Courier* and *Press,* or the combined Sunday edition, the *Courier & Press.* Where no endnote appears with information crediting another source, the reader may assume that it comes from the scrapbooks and/or the Bussing manuscript.

2   "July '64: Rochester Riot Timeline," n.d., PBS.org, www.pbs.org/independentlens/july64/timeline.html; "Civil Rights Movement: 'Black Power' Era Timeline," www.shmoop.com/civil-rights-black-power/timeline.html; "New York Race Riots," Civil Rights Digital Library, http://crdl.usg.edu/events/ny_race_riots/?Welcome.

3   "Violence in the City: An End or a Beginning?" December 2, 1965, report of the Governor's Commission on the Los Angeles Riots, www.usc.edu/libraries/archives/cityinstress/mccone/part3.html.

4   Herb Williams, telephone interview by author, May 22, 2011.

5   Russ Grieger, telephone interview by author, May 22, 2011.

6   Williams interview.

7   Miller moved to Oregon State after the 1970 season and stayed there until he retired in 1989 at the age of seventy. He was the winningest active coach in the game at the time. He amassed 654 wins, ranking him seventh at that point. He was national coach of the year twice, in 1981 and 1982. He was enshrined in the Naismith Memorial Basketball Hall of Fame in 1988. He died in 2001. The court at Gill Coliseum is named after him, as is the drive in front of the building ("Hall of Famers: Ralph H. Miller," Basketball Hall of Fame, n.d., www.hoophall.com/hall-of-famers/tag/ralph-h-miller).

8   Larry Humes, telephone interview by author, April 22, 2011.

9   Larry Humes interview.

10   Reed, who played two seasons in the NBA with the Detroit Pistons, would go on to a long career in baseball as a pitcher with Atlanta, St. Louis, Philadelphia, and the Chicago White Sox. He pitched for nineteen seasons before retiring in 1985 ("Ron Reed Statistics and History," Baseball-reference.com, n.d., www.baseball-reference.com/players/r/reedro01.shtml).

11   Williams interview.

12   The Irish finished 15–12 and went to the NCAA Tournament, where they lost in the first round to Houston by a single point, 99–98.

13   Larry Humes interview.

14   Larry Humes interview.

15   Orr would coach three seasons at UMass before leaving for Michigan. He took the Wolverines to the Final Four in 1976, defeating previously unbeaten Rutgers University, before falling to fellow Big Ten power Indiana and giving Bob Knight a perfect season and national title. Orr moved to Iowa State in 1980 and retired with 466 wins in 1994 He is the winningest coach in Iowa State history, with 218 victories ("Johnny Orr," SR/College Basketball, n.d., www.sports-reference.com/cbb/coaches/o/orrjo01.html).

16   Williams interview.

17   Grieger interview.

18   Humes interview.

19   Humes interview.

20   "College Basketball: The Purple Gang," *Time Magazine*, January 8, 1965.

21   Frank Deford, "Aces Are High in Evansville," *Sports Illustrated*, February 15, 1965.

22 Bartow had compiled a record of 47–21 at Central Missouri State before taking the job at Valparaiso. He would remain there for six seasons, compiling a 93–69, record including a 21–8 season in 1966–67. He coached at Memphis State, now the University of Memphis, from 1970 to 1974 and took the Tigers to the NCAA national championship game in 1973, where he lost to UCLA. He was named coach of the year for 1973. Bartow moved on to Illinois after coaching the U.S. National team and spent only a single season in Illinois before being hired by UCLA to replace the now legendary John Wooden as coach of the Bruins. After taking the Bruins to the national semifinals in 1976, Bartow departed after the 1977 season for the University of Alabama—Birmingham, which was just starting a basketball program. There the specter of Wooden, as well as his physical presence, was nowhere to be seen. Just three seasons later Bartow took the Blazers to the NCAA tournament. He stayed at UAB until he retired in 1996. Upon retirement he had amassed 647 wins over thirty-four years. He was, at that time, one of only eighteen coaches with six hundred or more victories. Later he became an executive with the Memphis Grizzlies of the NBA. He is a member of the Alabama Sports Hall of Fame (Cary Estes, "Gene Bartow," Encyclopedia of Alabama, August 20, 2009, www.encyclopediaofalabama.org/face/Article. jsp?id=h-2404).

23 Allen McCutchan, telephone interview by author, February 11, 2011.

24 "History," Bethune-Cookman University, www.cookman.edu/about_BCU/ history/index.html.

25 Groza was part of the University of Kentucky's Fabulous Five, who won back-to-back national championships in 1948 and 1949 and an Olympic gold medal. A three-time All-American, Groza went on to play (he was a two-time All-Star) and become part owner of the Indianapolis Olympians of the NBA. His career ended when he was arrested and indicted along with his former UK teammates. He admitted he had accepted bribes to shave points in the 1949 NIT tournament. The scandal that resulted dealt a severe blow to college basketball, and the NBA barred Groza and the others for life. Groza was not elected to the Kentucky Hall of Fame until 1992 and never to the Naismith Memorial Basketball Hall of Fame. After a coaching career and involvement with other professional teams outside the NBA, he died in 1995 ("Alex Groza Obituary," *Lexington Herald-Leader*, January 22, 1995).

26 Joan Hudson Roth, telephone interview by author, January 21, 2011.

27 Allen McCutchan interview. The area was known as Little Egypt, and the SIU's team name, Saluki, is the name of a breed of Egyptian dog.

28 Russ Grieger interview.

29 Humes interview.

30 Walt Frazier led the Salukis to an NIT championship at Madison Square Garden in 1967, and his play so impressed New York Knicks managers that they drafted him. Better known to younger fans as a spokesman for a men's hair-coloring product, Frazier, with his long, fur-lined coats, fedora, and Rolls Royce, became a media star in New York. He was a main cog in the New York Knicks teams of the early 1970s, winning two NBA Championships with them. He had a thirteen-year NBA career, ten with the Knicks before finishing with three seasons with Cleveland and retiring in 1980. He was inducted into the Naismith Memorial Basketball Hall of Fame in 1987. His number 10 jersey has been retired by the Knicks ("Walt Frazier," Basketball-reference.com, n.d., www.basketball-reference.com/players/f/fraziwa01. html).

31 Actually, the team had rejected his counteroffer.

32 "Jerry Sloan," Basketball-reference.com, n.d., www.basketball-reference. com/players/s/sloanje01.html.

33 Jody Genessy, "Utah Coach Sloan to Resign," *(Salt Lake City) Deseret News*, February 10, 2011; "Jerry Sloan," Basketball-reference.com.

34 Humes interview.

35 Humes interview.

36 Grieger interview.

37 Williams was president of the National Association of Basketball Coaches in 1963–64. In 1959, while the athletic director at Colby, he established the Naismith Memorial Basketball Hall of Fame. He was the executive director of the hall from 1966 to 1985. At Colby College his teams often met major college foes. He amassed 252 wins there before retiring. He was a member of two Olympic basketball team committees and twice served on the NIT selection committee. He was honored by the Hall of Fame with its Bunn Award for outstanding contributions to college sports. He is an inductee of the Maine Sports Hall of Fame ("Lee Palmer Williams," Maine Sports Hall of Fame, 2007, www.mshof.com/index.php?p=5&s=3&id=49).

In the Beginning

Nearly five centuries before white Europeans set foot on North American soil, the area now known as Evansville was the site of the largest settlement in what would become the state of Indiana.

A tribe of Native Americans known as the Mississippians had erected a large walled city on the floodplain of the Ohio River where people had gathered since the Stone Age.[1] Later, roving bands of Shawnee, Kickapoo, and Miami Indians moved in. In the 1670s French explorers were the first white men to visit the area and to see the mighty river that flowed through the lush woodlands.[2] They knew it as La Belle Riviere (Beautiful River); Native Americans called it the O-hi-O in their language.

In 1732 the first settler, believed to have been the Frenchman Pierre Brouilette, established a crude lean-to along Pigeon Creek, which runs roughly east-west just north of the great horseshoe bend in the Ohio; there he gave the Indians trinkets in exchange for their furs. That was the same year that the first city, Vincennes, was founded just fifty miles north. Less than fifty years later, in 1779 during the Revolutionary War, the British held Fort Sackville at Vincennes, which was captured by 175 Revolutionaries in a daring midwinter raid.[3] That put the area into American hands, which spelled doom for local Native Americans.

The War of 1812 had barely ended when settlers began moving into Indiana Territory in 1814, usually arriving by the Ohio River.[4] Flatboats brought people from the Northeast and Midatlantic states, while many entering through the port of New Orleans from Germany made the trip upriver by steamboat. Still others traveled from Virginia and the Carolinas over well-traveled traces and river valleys in Kentucky and Tennessee.[5] Most ended up in the southern part of Indiana Territory. So many arrived so quickly that Indiana was admitted to statehood only two years later, in 1816.

Among the earliest settlers was Hugh McGary, whose family was closely associated with Daniel Boone. While crossing into Kentucky to court his future wife, McGary saw the geographical importance and natural beauty of the area at the great bend in the river. There the land rose sharply above the water, high enough, he figured, that any community built there would be safe from flooding.

In March 1812 McGary walked the fifty-three miles due north to Vincennes and purchased all of section 30, township 6 south, range 10 west—440 acres that today comprise much of the area now known as Evansville. McGary petitioned the territorial government for licenses to operate ferries, one across the Ohio opposite his small log house and the other across Pigeon Creek several hundred yards above its mouth. The area became known as McGary's Landing.

In its earliest days Evansville was cut off from the interior of the state by the thick forests that surrounded it. Until the first stagecoach arrived from Vincennes in 1824, the only access to Evansville had been by river.[6]

But news the next year that the Erie Canal had been completed roused high hopes in Evansville that its isolation would soon be at an end. Two years later, in 1827, Congress gave Indiana the land grant that enabled construction of the Wabash and Erie Canal, connecting Toledo and Evansville.[7]

Evansville learned that the city would be the terminus for the new canal from an announcement that arrived by stagecoach. Residents were thrilled and began planning a celebration. They held a dinner, and local dignitaries made speeches full of predictions about Evansville's great future. Said one, "She is destined ere long to become one of the great commercial emporiums of the West." It proved to be yet one more example of the locals' propensity for wishful thinking.[8]

When it opened in 1853, the Wabash and Erie Canal, linking Evansville and Toledo, Ohio, was 452 miles long, the longest in the country. But it was also obsolete. That was the same year the Baltimore and Ohio Rail Road completed construction of the first passenger railway in the United States, from Wheeling, West Virginia, to Baltimore. Railroads doomed the canal. Only two boats made it to Evansville before the canal's operating company declared bankruptcy in 1853.

Indeed, it was already possible for Evansville residents to catch a train in Vincennes. The railroads, not the canal, would become of major importance to the city on the river. By 1900 the city was served by three railroad lines. They, and the discovery of a major seam of coal in Vanderburgh County at about the time the canal became a pipe dream, "became a major spur for industrial development during the nineteenth century as the city served as a gateway between the industrialized North and East and the agricultural South."[9]

The town prospered. Someone established a gasworks, which led to illumination of the city. Others set up library associations, erected multistory hotels, and established iron, wood, and leather works. Property values increased.

Men worked in agriculture, foundries, and stores devoted to manufactured items—plows, furniture, soap, brooms—or in flour mills and breweries. The average wage was a dollar a day for a ten-hour day, and men worked six days a week.[10]

By the end of the 1850s Evansville had grown from a sleepy village at a water crossing to the second-largest city in Indiana.

By the time of the Civil War, Evansville had a population of about 12,000, nearly half of whom were conversant in German. Attracted by the myriad jobs in manufacturing, Germans had steadily made their way to Evansville. Their influence can be seen today throughout the city—the Old Vanderburgh County Courthouse, in the German baroque style; the Sheriff's Residence and Jail, modeled after Lichtenstein Castle; Wesselman Park; Reitz Home Museum; Weinbach Avenue and Burkhardt Road. The city throws a large German festival, Volksfest, in early August and the Kunstfest in mid-September.

Because of the city's strategic location on a major river that provided direct access to the Southern states, Evansville was of major importance during the Civil War. The Union took no chances, stationing large gunboats along the waterfront and batteries of cannon above it, and thus prevented any serious Southern incursions.[11] Such precautions were only sensible because residents' sympathies were sharply divided—Lincoln had barely carried Indiana in 1860, and many Evansville residents had come from across the river in Kentucky. But the city did serve as a stop on the Underground Railroad and housed a marine hospital, built by the federal government in 1853 at a cost of $73,000, that cared for both Union and Confederate wounded.[12]

The end of the war brought a period of social and economic change to Evansville. By 1870 its population had grown to 21,830, which made it the second-largest city in the state.

And it was a lively place. River commerce boomed; six or seven steamboats docked in Evansville daily. Farmers' markets abounded, the result of spiking farm production as freed slaves crossed the river to live and work. Lumber-yards, furniture plants, stove foundries, flour mills, brickyards, and tobacco manufactures sprang up all over town in the four decades after the Civil War. Streetcars appeared, and the city established a municipal waterworks that drew water straight from the Ohio. One of the best-known local businesses, Igleheart Brothers, established the first major flour mill in 1856 (by 1890 there would be eleven, producing $2 million worth of product a year); its best-known product was Swans Down Cake Flour (1895), and Igleheart is now a subsidiary of General Mills.[13]

The surrounding hardwood forests that had helped keep Evansville isolated for so long now proved to be a great source of lumber, which became an important business. One of the many German immigrants had established a sawmill as early as 1845, and as it grew, it enriched the Reitz family, whose members repaid the community with a public high school as well as a parochial school and a Catholic home for the poor and aged. (The Reitz family home is now a museum.)

The lumber business spawned cask and keg manufacturers, carriage and boat works, makers of coffins and farm implements, and, most important, furniture makers. The many skilled German cabinetmakers and woodcarvers who arrived in Evansville set up small and medium-sized shops that turned out furniture prized for its workmanship.

In the 1870s the Armstrong brothers set up a six-story factory at Seventh Avenue and Franklin Street that produced both hand-carved Victorian furniture as well as more affordable machine-made pieces.

By the 1890s Evansville was home to impressive public buildings. The massive Old Vanderburgh County Courthouse, still in use as a courthouse today, opened in 1891, and the Sheriff's Residence and Jail opened in 1890.

One day in 1891, far across the country in Springfield, Massachusetts, a young physical education teacher at the YMCA nailed two peach baskets to the wall. He decided that the young men in his charge needed some recreation in the winter months between the end of football season and the beginning of baseball season. He called his new game basketball.

Evansville, busy as ever with trade and construction, didn't notice.

Less than ten years into the new century, Evansville boasted a furniture exchange with 60,000 square feet of display space for 31 exhibitors. The city now also had a thriving brick trade. More than a dozen brickyards operated in the area, and they left their mark on the many brick homes and buildings that still dot Evansville's downtown and neighborhoods. Every month Evansville shipped 500,000 to one million bricks, mostly to the southern states.

With prosperity came gracious hotels, newer and bigger schools and theaters, and more than one brothel.

Local manners and social events reflected the southern origins of many Evansville residents. Debutante balls were lavish affairs, as were the weddings of the upper class. Afternoon teas, dinner parties, and glittering balls were heavily attended, and more than a few out-of-town guests found brides at these affairs.

Meanwhile, the poorest in Evansville suffered. Evansville's population of African Americans increased sharply after the Civil War, reaching about 5,500 by 1890. (In all of Vanderburgh County the 1840 population had been 6,250, including 114 free blacks and no slaves.) Most blacks lived in poverty, with no public sanitation. As a result, their mortality rate was high. Although they represented less than 10 percent of the population, they accounted for 20 percent of all burials.

But between 1900 and 1920 Evansville's black population fell, from 12.7 to 7.5 percent. "In this," writes Samuel W. White, "Evansville had more in common with Louisville and cities of the upper South than with other cities of the industrial Midwest. One oft-cited reason . . . is a race riot that occurred in 1903 in which eleven people died and fifty others were injured, and which forever marked Evansville as one of the least hospitable northern cities for African Americans. Another reason . . . is that job segregation became firmly established in Evansville during the decades following the Civil War. African American workers were effectively kept out of better-paying jobs and spatially segregated within the city."[14]

Still, impoverished blacks were not alone in their misery. A large population of poor white laborers inhabited shanties and shacks near Pigeon Creek and the old marine hospital grounds.

Finally, the daughter of a Methodist minister decided that she would alleviate the suffering and deprivation. Albion Bacon (1865–1933) had become aware of the poor section of Evansville after two of her children came down with scarlet fever. She joined the sanitation committee of the city's Civic Improvement Society, discovered Evansville's slums, and became a crusader for improved sanitation and housing conditions for the poorest residents. Her work led to marked improvements in all areas.[15] At her death she was remembered as "Evansville's most famous woman."

Although John McGary had believed that his site for Evansville was high enough above the river to keep his city safe from flooding, the waterway that had brought prosperity to much of Evansville also brought devastation.

The first in a series of three Ohio River floods hit the town in 1882 when the river crested at forty-eight feet. In a 1910 history of the Red Cross, Clara Barton reported that the organization's "special agent for the South" found millions of acres . . . and thousands upon thousands of homes under the waters of the mightiest of rivers—where the swift rising floods overtook alike man and beast in their flight of terror, sweeping them ruthlessly to the gulf beyond, or leaving them clinging in famishing despair to some trembling roof or swaying tree top till relief could reach and rescue them.[16]

The Ohio River flooded again the next year, again causing great damage and misery, but it had reserved its worst for the flood of 1884. Along a thousand miles of river, snow was melting rapidly that February, and Congress quickly appropriated "several hundred thousand dollars for relief, to be applied through the War Department."[17] Writing in third person, Barton, the president of the Red Cross, reported that she felt "it was incumbent upon her to visit the scene in person, to see for herself what floods were like."[18]

We quickly removed our headquarters from Cincinnati to Evansville, three hundred miles below and at the head of the recent scene of disaster. A new, staunch steamer of four hundred tons burden was immediately chartered and laden to the water's edge with clothing and coal; good assistants, both men and women were taken on board; the Red Cross flag was hoisted and as night was setting in, after a day of intense cold . . . the clear-toned bell and shrill whistle of the "Josh V. Throop" announced to the generous inhabitants of a noble city that from the wharves of Evansville was putting out the first Red Cross relief boat that ever floated on American waters.[19]

She was impressed by the generosity of the people of Evansville, noting, "Notwithstanding all the material we had shipped and distributed, so abundant had been the liberality of the people that on our return to Evansville we found our supply greater than at any previous time."[20] It is clear from her report of this flood that Evansville somehow was spared much of the fury that was visited on Cincinnati and cities downstream, especially New Orleans.

Evansville continued its affair with manufacturing, this time as maker of the noisy contraptions called horseless carriages that began to appear after the turn of the century. Prominent among the manufacturers was William Harvey McCurdy's Hercules Body Company, which made carriage bodies for shipment to Sears for its new horseless Motor Buggy. The new body works opened in 1905 within the same complex that housed the Hercules Wheel Company; the Hercules Surrey and Wagon Company, which made larger farm wagons and coaches; the Hercules Warehouse Co., which stored parts and shipped completed vehicles to their new owners; the Hercules Paint Company; and the conglomerate's own lumberyard with massive kilns and drying sheds.[21]

In 1908 McCurdy branched out into rail transportation, starting the interurban Evansville and Ohio Valley Railway Co. Hercules of course made its first passenger cars. McCurdy also helped establish Evansville's streetcar system. His rail interests grew to provide both intercity and freight service to Boonville, Fort Branch, and Mount Vernon in Indiana, as well as Owensboro and Henderson in Kentucky.[22]

Four years later Sears approached McCurdy about building engines for Sears's vehicles; by early 1914 the Hercules Gas Engine Co. was producing gas engines for a variety of retailers across the country.[23] At its peak Hercules employed 1500 workers at a plant that covered 30 acres.

Evansville, however, was not spared the ravages of World War I. On November 3, 1917, a German attack overran U.S. lines, and three soldiers attached to the American Expeditionary Force were killed. Among them was Corporal James Gresham of Evansville, who became the first American to die in combat in the Great War.

The war also brought a major social change to Evansville. The insular and proud German community tried to rally support for Germany early in the war in Europe and withdrew its support of Evansville's German American congressional representative when he backed Woodrow Wilson's sending warning resolutions to Germany. That decision ended the local politician's career. When the United States entered the war, the German American community, once conspicuous for its devotion to the fatherland, became ardently patriotic of its adopted homeland. Local schools even stopped teaching German.[24]

War news dominated conversation everywhere, and the bitter cold froze the

Ohio during the winter of 1917–18. Residents battled the influenza epidemic of 1918–19 as well as the cold. The local papers devoted increasing amounts of space to obituaries. The end of 1919 also saw a protracted labor strike after the local chamber of commerce riled everyone by calling a meeting to protest the year-old decision of city police and firefighters to unionize. The labor historian Samuel W. White notes that "the successful attack on the police and firemen's unions represented only the first in a series of events that amounted to an attack on all of organized labor in Evansville."[25] He goes on to detail how the subsequent steel strike weakened unionism within Evansville. Then a strike at a nearby auto company coincided with the early rumblings of what would become the nationwide coal strike of 1919. More than 28,000 miners were employed in southwestern Indiana. Their grievances included unsafe conditions, the high cost of safety equipment the miners had to purchase, and intermittent work during summer months.

The strike began on November 6, 1919. Three weeks later local manufacturers began to shut down and furlough their workers. Local mines tried to reopen on December 1, but the miners remained on strike and the owners' effort failed. A federal judge imposed legal restraints on nearly a hundred union leaders—having them arrested for contempt of court and levying fines against each in the thousands of dollars. Woodrow Wilson himself mediated the settlement, which was only a partial victory for the unions. Workers got a pay increase but no attention to safety issues. The strike, White says, lasted almost six weeks and "exacted a high cost in terms of public opinion, as Evansville residents joined others in condemning the actions of miners at the expense of the citizenry."[26]

The end of hostilities in Europe brought the men back home, and Evansville and the rest of the country were about to embark on a hedonistic era recalled as the Roaring Twenties. It would be yet another time of change for Evansville.

Moore's Hill Male and Female Collegiate Institute had been founded in 1854 as a Methodist institution in a small town in southeastern Indiana and first held classes in September 1856. But by 1917 the college was facing severe financial difficulties. George S. Clifford, an Evansville native who had done well in the wholesale hardware business, had a wide-ranging intellect and "became possessed of the idea that a college in Evansville would minister to [the] fundamental needs of the community."[27] Clearly, the college's financial difficulties presented Evansville with a great opportunity.

Clifford approached the Methodist Church about moving the school to Evansville. He pointed out that no college was within fifty miles of Evansville, and he managed to persuade the Methodist Conference to agree to the move. The school was relocated to Evansville in 1919 and renamed Evansville College.[28]

At about the same time, Evansville welcomed another newcomer when in 1920 the Ku Klux Klan set up shop in Evansville. Top officials of the Klan in Atlanta had tapped a man named Joe Huffington to bring the Klan to Indiana. He soon met a big-talking wheeler-dealer—D. C. Stephenson, a former socialist reporter and traveling salesman—who had moved to Evansville to take a job at a coal company. He built a wide network of contacts whom he regaled with wild stories, and he organized local veterans. He had insinuated himself into the fabric of the community, one that was already fairly overwrought with jingoistic sentiments. He soon was helping Huffington recruit for the Klan, and by 1922 had gotten himself appointed local Exalted Cyclops. He moved the state headquarters to Indianapolis and took the organization statewide.

The KKK had had no trouble attracting new members in Evansville: its rallies had attracted as many as 10,000 people. Statewide, it had a banner year in 1923, when 27,000 new members signed up, bringing total membership to 100,000 in Indiana alone and making it a force in state politics. In 1925 the Klan-supported Republican candidate for mayor won in a landslide, despite stories in the *Evansville Press* detailing the backroom dealing that had the KKK calling the shots in the Republican Party. Klan-backed Republicans also were voted into all other offices in the city.

But the Klan's foray into local politics had a swift and satisfying ending: "The Klan's influence over the population and politics of the Evansville community declined quickly. . . ." one historian reports, "[Its] political fortunes declined with those of the [Republican] administration, as it faced investigations of alleged ethical violations less than a year after winning the municipal election—a glaring contradiction to the Klan's promise to clean up local government."[29]

By now Evansville's forests were depleted and its furniture business was in decline. The popularity of gas and electricity shuttered the cast-iron stove factories. But replacing those employers were McCurdy's thriving transportation companies, which would provide local residents with jobs for forty years.

McCurdy had his fingers in yet another new industry. He had brought James Dennedy and Karl Zimmerman to Evansville sometime before 1920 to complete development of their ice machine after he bought the rights to it. In those days every home had an ice box that needed constant replenishment. Dennedy and

Zimmerman had invented a mechanism that kept the appliances cold without ice. McCurdy had recently purchased the Schroeder Headlight Company, which he now renamed the Schroeder Headlight and Refrigerator Company. Then, he reorganized his holdings and in late 1919 or early 1920, Schroeder became Sunbeam Electric Manufacturing and moved to the Hercules plant.[30]

Meanwhile, Morris Trippett, who bought buggies and cars for Sears, became enamored of refrigerators, came up with the brand name Serv-El (from the slogan "Serve Electrically"), and contracted with Sunbeam to produce the machines. By then, McCurdy was in poor health and sold "a controlling interest in Hercules Corp. to Trippett's Serv-El Corp. which was consequently reorganized as the Servel Manufacturing Co. . . . Sales of the new . . . refrigerator commenced in 1926, and within a year, Servel had cornered the market for the popular appliance."[31] By now Evansville was boasting that it was the "Refrigerator Capital of the World."

But the Roaring Twenties ended when the stock market crashed three years later. For the first two years Evansville tried to take care of its own, raising thousands of dollars to finance work relief, until Franklin D. Roosevelt was elected in 1932 and the subsequent New Deal programs kicked in. Local efforts continued thereafter, but the ever-testy local labor unions no longer were participating in community-wide programs but instead were concentrating on taking care of union members. The 1932 election also swept Democrats into almost every major elective office at any level in Vanderburgh County, completing the job of purging Republicans that had begun four years earlier.[32]

The automotive business literally drove Evansville out of the Depression. Chrysler, which had closed its Evansville truck assembly plant in 1932, reopened, renovated and expanded the plant, beginning production of 1936 Plymouths in 1935, adding Dodges in 1937.[33] But just as the area was beginning to pull itself out of the Depression, another Ohio River flood struck.

The flood of 1937 would prove to be the worst on record. The waters reached 53.7 feet and remained there for three days. The extensive damage cost more that $20 million to repair, and more than a third of Evansville's homes were flooded.

But within a year the regional economy got some very good news. In 1938 oil was discovered in nearby Kentucky and Illinois, and wildcatters poured into the tristate area in search of the next gusher. Many remained in Evansville and environs, and "oil barons . . . spent millions of dollars in the city."[34]

By 1940 Evansville's population stood at 97,000, and its manufacturing plants were providing jobs to more than 25,000 people.

Like many other cities, Evansville was transformed by the 1941 attack on Pearl Harbor, which made the city a manufacturing center for war materiel and weapons. Republic Aviation built a $16 million plant there to produce the P-47 Thunderbolt, a mainstay of the fighter force. The plant employed more than 5,000, many of them women, and its production was so high—twenty-five fighters a day—and so important that President Franklin D. Roosevelt himself visited Evansville in 1943.[35]

The riverfront became a shipyard that produced the LSTs (landing ship, tanks) that were so crucial to the war effort. At its peak the shipyard employed more than 19,000 workers, who produced two LSTs every week.[36] George Koch Sons, a long-time Evansville concern that turned out tin toys and metal floral containers and distributed Carrier air conditioners, fabricated parts for the LSTs, as well as aircraft parts and shell-case testing equipment.[37] The Chrysler plant was converted to the production of ammunition and produced more small-caliber ammunition than any other plant in the world.[38] The Briggs automotive manufacturing plant, which had been building Plymouth auto bodies, began producing wings for the navy fighter plane known as the F4U Corsair and for the Dauntless SBD bomber.[39]

When the United States entered World War II, labor unions across the country made a no-strike pledge for the duration of the war. Union leaders worked with supervisors and employers to suppress any expressions of dissatisfaction, and in return the unions gained certain powers that ensured the burgeoning of their membership. Workers in war industries set production records year after year, and year after year their employers' profits rose, yet with their no-strike pledge the unions had given up their biggest bargaining chip for securing some of those profits for their members. This is not to say that there were no strikes during the war—the 1943 national coal miners' strike is a notable exception—but organized labor sanctioned few of them. But the United States saw a rash of wildcat strikes throughout the war years, sometimes by workers unhappy about wages but more often to protest disciplinary measures, company policies, or the firing of certain employees. The labor historian Jeremy Brecher notes, "The number of such strikes began to rise in the summer of 1942, and by 1944, the last full year of the war, more strikes took place than in any previous year in American history, averaging 5.6 days apiece."[40]

When the war ended abruptly with the bombing of Hiroshima and Nagasaki in 1945, "the record of Evansville's war workers was impressive," writes historian White. "Despite a few strikes and the racial tension often related to them, the city's defense plants had won more production citations than any city of its size in the country."[41] But when the war ended, so did all that production. And the unions' no-strike pledge. In the months after the war ended, workers saw a decrease, not an increase, in their incomes as plants retooled to produce consumer goods once more. Brecher paints a vivid picture of what happened:

In September 1945, the first full month after the Japanese surrender, the number of work days lost to strikes doubled. It doubled again in October. Forty-three thousand oil workers struck in twenty states on September 16. Two hundred thousand coal miners struck on September 21 to support the supervisory employees' demand for collective bargaining. Forty-four thousand Northwest lumber workers, seventy thousand Midwest truck drivers, and forty thousand machinists in San Francisco and Oakland all struck. East Coast longshoremen struck for nineteen days, flat glass workers for 102 days, and New England textile workers for 133 days. These were but a prelude to the great strikes of 1945 and 1946.[42]

Evansville's unionized workers were no exception. The meatpackers, then the bricklayers, painters, and cement finishers struck in the first half of 1946, and national strikes by the mine workers and railroad unions that year affected life in Evansville, disrupting mail delivery and train service, which meant that local plants had difficulty shipping product and receiving parts and raw materials. But it wasn't until the summer of 1948 that Evansville saw a major union local walk out on strike.

The Bucyrus-Erie Company, a major producer of heavy construction equipment, had long been at odds with Local 813 of the United Electrical, Radio, and Machine Workers of America (UE), which represented 7,000 workers at major employers in Evansville: Seeger-Sunbean, Faultless, Servel, George Koch Sons, and Hoosier Cardinal, "quickly becoming the largest labor organization in the city."[43]

United Electrical had its eye on Bucyrus, whose president had warned before the election that if UE won, it would mean that workers would be taking orders from Moscow, and he refused to deal with the union afterward. Local 813 itself was beset by a small internal faction of rabid anticommunists. And that suited H. R. Knox, the president of Bucyrus, just fine: he conflated the union's demands on wages and benefits with communism and refused to negotiate. The National Labor Relations Board scheduled a hearing on the issues for September 22, and the company obtained a series of restraining orders of dubious legality against the union. On August 28 forty foremen tried to break through a line of one hundred picketers, which led to a riot that leaked into the adjoining neighborhood. Police arrested twenty strikers, but the local prosecutor refused a complaint that union leaders tried to press against several foremen.

There was more: three days later 140 state troopers appeared at the plant to escort workers to their jobs, and 50 more troopers stood ready to assist. Seven women appeared at the main entrance and tried to keep cars from entering. The troopers tried to push them aside, the women fought back, and 200 strikers rushed to overcome the troopers. All as a thousand people looked on.

Despite the theatrics and violence, the strike dragged into a second month as Knox did his best to marshal local, state, and federal power against the union. Ultimately, the original issues of the strike were all but lost as it devolved into a classic communist witch hunt of the period, with a local Republican member of Congress holding hearings and demanding of workers, "Do you believe in God?" and "Are you a communist?" There was plenty naming of names, the Klan and the Association of Catholic Trade Unionists—another far right-wing group—attacked some of the more outspoken union members in the city, and in the end the hearings ended the strike and fractured support for Local 813 in the city.[44]

And 1948 wasn't even over. Despite continuing tensions—and sometimes outright strife—in the industrial sector of the city, no one was willing to acknowledge the reputation that Evansville was gaining. "Conflict between workers and employers in Evansville remained constant throughout the postwar period," historian Samuel White writes.[45]

But Evansville had a lot on its mind in the years after the war. The demand for housing from returning servicemen and women, and the large number of workers who had settled in Evansville during the war, created a construction boom, and all those new homes needed refrigerators, furniture, appliances, and a car to park in the garage. Many former war production workers found jobs in construction, and the economy quickly bounced back.[46]

The returning veterans also were eager to take advantage of the GI Bill and go to college. And, thanks to the decision of Moore's Hill College to relocate to Evansville twenty-six years earlier, they wouldn't have to leave home to do it.

(Endnotes)

1   Marjorie Melvin Jones and Besse Freeman Buttle, *The Inquiring Visitor's Guide to Angel Mounds State Historic Site,* 3d ed. (Evansville, Ind.: Mission Press, 2000); Glenn A. Black, *Angel Site: An Archeological, Historical, and Ethnological Study* (Indianapolis: Indiana Historical Society, 1967), 491–530. Excavation continues under the supervision of Indiana University.

2   Howard Henry Peckham, *Indiana: A History* (Champagne: University of Illinois Press, 2003), 18.

3   "The Battle for Fort Sackville," Moment of Indiana History, n.d., www.purdue.edu/wbaa/ipbs/Scripts/010.htm.

4   4 Ibid.

5   Kenneth P. McCutchan, William E. Bartelt, and Thomas R. Lonborg, *Evansville: At the Bend in the River* (Sun Valley, Calif.: American Historical Press, 2004), 11.]

6   Ibid., 21.

7   "Historical Sketch," Wabash and Erie Canal Company Records, 1833–77, Indiana Historical Society, www.indianahistory.org/library/manuscripts/collection_guides/m0758.html#HISTORICAL; "Wabash and Erie Canal," Montezuma, Indian, History, n.d., www.montezuma.in.gov/history/.

8   McCutchan, Bartelt, and Lonborg, *Evansville: At the Bend in the River,* 21.

9   Samuel W. White, *Fragile Alliances: Labor and Politics in Evansville, Indiana, 1919–1955* (Westport, Conn.: Praeger, 2005), 11.

10 Ibid.

11 "Western Gunboat Flotilla (Operations on the Mississippi and Ohio Rivers)," BrownWater Navy.org, n.d., www.brownwaternavy.org/umiss1.htm.

12 Fred Padgett, "Marine Hospital History," Westside Improvement Association, 2011, www.westsideimprovement.org/marine_hospital_history.htm.

13 McCutchan, Bartelt, and Lonborg, *Evansville: At the Bend in the River,* 40.

14 White, *Fragile Alliances,* 10.

15 Edward T. James, Janet Wilson James, and Paul S. Boyer, eds., *Notable American Women: A Biographical Dictionary* (Boston: Radcliffe College, 1971), 77.

16 Clara Barton, *The Red Cross: In Peace and War* (Washington, D.C.: American Historical Press, 1910), 111.

17 Ibid., 115.

18 Ibid.

19 Ibid., 116–17.

20 Ibid., 117.

21 Ibid.

22 Ibid.

23 Ibid.

24 White, *Fragile Alliances,* 25.

25 Ibid., 26.

26 Ibid., 30. See White's book for a well-written and informative account of labor relations in Evansville during the first half of the twentieth century.

27 Charles Roll, "George S. Clifford," *Indiana: One Hundred and Fifty Years of American Development,* vol. 3 (New York: Lewis, 1931), http://debmurray.tripod.com/indiana/indbioref-4.htm.

28 "History," University of Evansville, www.evansville.edu/aboutue/history.cfm.

29 White, *Fragile Alliances,* 41, 49, 51–53, 57, 59, 63; overview of *Political Scandals in Indiana: Indiana Klan, Black Day of the Indiana General Assembly, Blocks of Five* (booksllc.net: Books LLC, 2010).

30 Theobald reports in "Hercules" that the reorganization occurred in 1920, but the Digest of Current Electrical Literature reported in its January 3, 1920, edition that "the Schroeder Headlight and Generator Company, Evansville, Ind., has changed its name to Sunbeam Electric Manufacturing Company." See *Electrical World: A Review of Current Progress in Electricity and Its Practical Applications,* vol. 75, January 3–June 26, 1920 (New York McGraw-Hill, 1920), 51, available through Google Books.

31 Theobald, "Hercules."

32 White, *Fragile Alliances,* 75–82.

33 W. P. Chrysler Museum, "Chrysler LLC Chronology," 2008, http://wpchryslermuseum.org/pg500chron_print.php?pageNum=0&totalRows=62&year=1930d.

34 McCutchan, Bartelt, and Lonborg, *Evansville: At the Bend in the River*, 71.

35 Bill Beck, "The Whirlpool Plant's War Record," *Indiana Business Magazine,* April 1, 1998, www.allbusiness.com/north-america/united-states-indiana/688629-1.html; McCutchan, Bartelt, and Lonborg, *Evansville: At the*

Bend in the River, 68.

36 "The Evansville Shipyard," Evansville Museum, n.d., www.emuseum.org/
    virtual_museum/evansville.shipyard/shipyard.html.

37 "Corporate Profile: History," Koch Enterprises, Inc., 2009, www.kochenter-
    prises.com/corporate/history.htm.

38 Charles Parrish, "The Louisville Engineer District," in Barry W. Fowle, ed.,
    Builders and Fighters: U.S. Army Engineers in World War II (Ft. Belvoir, Va.:
    U.S. Army Corps of Engineers, 1992), 144.

39 Darrel E. Bigham, *Evansville: The World War II Years* (Chicago: Arcadia,
    2005), 51; McCutchan, Bartelt, and Lonborg, *Evansville: At the Bend in the
    River*.

40 White, *Fragile Alliances*, chap. 4; Jeremy Brecher, *Strike!* (San Francisco:
    Straight Arrow Books, 1972), excerpts posted at libcom.org under the head-
    line "The World War II and Post-War Strike Wave," http://libcom.org/his-
    tory/world-war-ii-post-war-strike-wave.

41 White, *Fragile Alliances*, 131.

42 Brecher, *Strike!*

43 White, *Fragile Alliances*, 139.

44 I am indebted to White for his painstaking reconstuction of this strike and its
    aftermath in *Fragile Alliances*, 139–51.

45 Ibid., 162.

46 McCutchan, Bartelt, and Lonborg, *Evansville: At the Bend in the River*.

A College Town, 1917–1944

Evansville embraced its college from the beginning. After George Clifford impressed the Methodist Conference's Joint Education Commission with his research on the lack of higher education within one hundred miles of Evansville, commissioners said the college could relocate on one condition: the city had to raise $500,000.[1]

It was 1917 and a war was raging in Europe. Many felt the timing was not quite right, but Evansville's mayor was not among them. "I never want it said of me that I failed to do all in my power to provide for the boys and girls of Evansville the educational opportunities which I did not receive," Benjamin Bosse declared.

The sum needed seemed enormous. The most money Evansville had ever raised was $150,000, for the YMCA building. But Bosse's determination was matched by that of the leading citizens, and they got a much-needed assist from the *Evansville Courier*.

Coverage of the fundraising effort dominated the news. The college was on the front page for eleven consecutive days.

The *Courier*'s headline on April 23 read: "It's Taken Evansville 100 Years to Awaken to the Necessity of Having a College. . . ISN'T THAT LONG ENOUGH?"

More than 400 people participated in the effort, and money flowed in from donors large and small. Led by the indefatigable Bosse and the business community, the drive succeeded, with a pledge by Francis Joseph Reitz, a Catholic and one of the city's wealthiest men, supplying the last $50,000 needed. Evansville would get its school.[2]

Two years later the school enrolled its first 104 students at Evansville College. They attended classes in temporary quarters in the old Adath Israel Synagogue for three years while the new campus was being built on 70 acres that had been purchased for $83,000.[3]

A year and $315,000 later the new building opened and served the school's every need for the next 23 years, a period in which its enrollment never exceeded 550. The college had no electric lights until the 1930s, and a horse-drawn field mower tended the grass. Students routinely bent to the task of clearing the campus of dandelions.[4]

The administration building, a collegiate gothic structure of Indiana limestone, stood tall above the former farmland, a proud reminder of what the city had done for itself.

The school fielded sports teams—in football, basketball, track, and baseball—even in those early years. John Harmon arrived in 1923 as athletic director and coach of all sports. That first season the basketball team's record was 5–9. In football Harmon had a pool of only 160 men from which to field a team. In seven seasons his gridders, known as the Pioneers, won 18 and lost 35, with one tie.

When Harmon moved on in 1930 to get his doctoral degree at Indiana University, he left a legacy, despite his teams' undistinguished records. After his charges had beaten Louisville in a 1924–25 game, the Louisville coach had told Harmon, "You didn't have four aces up your sleeve, you had five." When Harmon related the story to Dan Scism, who covered sports for the *Courier,* both men agreed that "Aces" sounded better than "Pioneers," and it fit better in headlines, too. Because the school's colors were purple and white, the Aces soon became the Purple Aces.

Harmon's replacement was William Slyker, who had been coach at Reitz High School and had coached in Cleveland before that. He had played in the 1921 Rose Bowl for Ohio State. He had also gone to law school, but his love for athletics had sent him into coaching.

Like Harmon before him, Slyker was coach of all sports. In football he faced stiffer competition and had a record of 34–60, with nine ties, over thirteen years. Despite his own gridiron success, he could not get his football team to win a game. From 1936 until the 1938 season, his Purple Aces played twelve games without managing a single point. The basketball team fared better, compiling a record of 123–96 against better competition, when the team faced Ohio State, Indiana, Kansas State, and other big schools.

Given the woeful performance of the football team, and the school's eventual decision to abandon baseball, the basketball program inevitably became the focus of local attention. But Evansville College teams had a frustrating challenge from the beginning. They had to play their home games in a variety of venues.

In 1924 the games moved from the tiny campus gym to downtown, first to the Agoga Tabernacle, and then, in 1935, to the gymnasium at Memorial Coliseum, and eventually to the National Guard Armory near campus.[5] As interest in the program grew, the number of fans seeking to watch the games became more than the 2500 the armory could handle.

The 1933-34 version of the Aces fared better than most of its predecessors. That year the Aces were led by a farm boy from nearby Daylight, Indiana. His name was Arad, and he was born on the Fourth of July in 1912. The name was given to him by his father who, according to an old family custom, opened the family Bible and, eyes closed; put his finger on a page. The closest name to the spot he touched was Arad.

When people asked about his unique name, he would reply with a straight face: "It means 'wild ass.'"[6]

But everyone always called Arad McCutchan just Mac. He was born and grew up in Daylight, a crossroads north of Evansville. His parents operated a small farm there where they raised chickens and grew corn. There were six children, who had plenty of room to play and run around, and the large barn on the property had a basket nailed to its side where Mac and the others shot baskets. When it was time for him to go on to high school in 1926, Mac wanted to attend Bosse High School and play basketball there. But Bosse was a long drive from Daylight, and the school offered no transportation.

However, Mac's older sister Bernice was a teacher at Bosse, and his brother Owen drove a bread truck in the area. Bernice and Owen managed to get Mac to school and back every day. Mac starred on the high school basketball team, earning All-City and All-Sectional honors before he graduated in 1930.

Then he went on to Evansville College, which he attended from 1930 to 1934, and led the team in scoring three years in a row. In his final season the Aces went 15–4.

Mac McCutchan had been a good basketball player, but Gus Doerner was Evansville College's first All-America player. He played for Slyker from 1938 to 1942.

Wilfred Otto Doerner, named after his father and called "little Gus" until he outgrew his dad, grew up in a crossroads village called Buckskin, in Gibson County, north of Evansville. Buckskin was little more than a store, a church, and a post office.

Like so many others in the area, the Doerners were of German heritage and had settled in Buckskin because it reminded them of Prussia. Like Mac, Gus was raised on a small farm and learned to play basketball in a dirt barnyard with a peach basket nailed to the side of the barn.

His grade school was a one-room building for grades one to eight. Gus was naturally left-handed, but his teacher insisted that he learn to write with his right hand, an ability that later helped him on the basketball court. He enrolled at Mackey High in Gibson County, where he excelled at basketball. At 6-4 he was tall for the era and had a nose for the ball. Slyker recruited the sixteen-year-old "Mackey Marvel" to play for Evansville College.[7]

"No one in the family had ever gone to college," said his daughter Marilyn Doerner. "If it wasn't for basketball and the scholarship offer, he probably wouldn't have, either."[8]

In his senior year, 1942, Gus was Slyker's best player. "Gus had a unique way of playing," said Bruce Lomax, a former Aces player. "A lot of his game was inside. He was left-handed, and he had a great hook shot. It took an act of Congress to keep him from scoring."[9] The Aces compiled a winning record in each of Doerner's four seasons and qualified for post-season play for the first time in 1941.

On November 13, 1941, a Douglas C-47 rolled off the production line in Santa Monica, California, one of 10,500 that would be built. Its serial number would be 483. The tail of the plane was low to the ground, and the nose stood high in front. Known affectionately as the "gooney bird" by the Navy and "Dakota" by

the Army Air Corps, it became the U.S. military's workhorse during World War II, carrying men and equipment to every major battleground in Europe and the Pacific with amazing proficiency and reliability. It flew low and slow but could stay aloft with only one of its two Pratt and Whitney engines. It often suffered heavy damage in combat yet made it back to base without incident. In its later commercial incarnation it would be known as a DC-3, and many airlines used the safe and reliable craft for years.[10]

❑ ❑ ❑ ❑ ❑

During his final season, 1941–42, Gus averaged 24.4 points per game and was the third-leading scorer in the nation. After the season Doerner earned first-team All-America honors, the first player from Evansville to do so. After college he continued to play basketball for the Ft. Wayne Zollner Pistons (later to become the Detroit Pistons) and won a world championship with them in the nascent days of professional basketball.

World War II interrupted his basketball career, and he served in the Army Air Corps as a flight instructor until hostilities ended. He returned to pro ball after his discharge from the Army Air Corps in November 1945, but a broken leg curtailed his season. He then signed with the Indianapolis Kautskys for $7,800. Both John Wooden and Branch McCracken had played for the team in previous seasons. From 1945 to 1947 the team played in the National Basketball League, a forerunner to the NBA.[11] Gus Doerner was a Kautsky for one of those seasons, until he decided to enter teaching and become a basketball coach.

Following his pro career he returned to his hometown area and coached the basketball team at the high school in Ft. Branch for three years before he entered a partnership to start a sporting goods store. He was driving home from a sales trip in 1954 when he was struck head-on by a drunken driver and critically injured. The once-smooth player with ballet-like moves had a broken pelvis, and his left side was paralyzed. The doctors wanted to amputate his left leg, but Gus refused to allow it. "He told them he would fight through it," his daughter Karen said. After the doctors inserted several rods in his leg, they finally released him for rehabilitation therapy three months after the accident.

The former star was confined to a wheelchair at first, then got about on crutches, and finally was able to manage with a cane but always walked with a limp after that.[12]

But that didn't stop Gus from enjoying golf, and he remained familiar to Aces fans, whose ranks were growing, because he called many Aces games on radio.

The business partnership that had operated the sporting goods business dissolved in 1962, and Gus Doerner Sports came into existence. It would thrive for the next four decades at a downtown location and later in an outlying mall, supplying local teams with uniforms and equipment.

Doerner remained a loyal Aces fan, and whenever he appeared at a game, whether to do the radio play-by-play or to sit in his reserved seat as just another fan, he was met with applause as the crowd expressed its appreciation for the first player to bring national attention to the Purple Aces – and to Evansville.[13]

(Endnotes)

1   George Klinger, *We Face the Future Unafraid: A Narrative History of the University of Evansville* (Evansville, Ind.: University of Evansville Press, 2003), 29.

2   Ibid., 32.

3   Ibid., 35, 38.

4   Ibid., 38–40.

5   Ibid.

6   Marilyn McCutchan Disman, telephone interview by author, February 22, 2011.

7   Ron Eaton, *Local Legends: The Stories Behind The Headlines, 100 Years of Southwestern Indiana Sports History* (Evansville, Ind.: M. T. Publishing, 2008), 115.

8   Disman interview.

9   Ibid.

10   The DC-3 is still being used around the world to transport both passengers and freight. Its longevity is unequaled in aviation history.

11   The Kautskys joined the NBA in 1947 after winning the World Professional Basketball Championship. They changed their name to the Indianapolis Jets but folded after one season.

12   Karen Doerner, telephone interview by author, February 25, 2011.

13   Ibid.

Mac, 1945–1950

After he graduated from Evansville College, Mac McCutchan began teaching math at Bosse High and a year later became the basketball coach. That was in 1935. He held both positions until he entered the service in 1943, the same year Coach Slyker left the college.

Mac had met a teacher from Central High in Evansville, Claude Robinson, who had a daughter named Virginia. She had attended Evansville College for two years before transferring to Indiana State to get a degree in home economics. Mac met Virginia when he stopped by the Robinson home one day to get some materials for a class from her father.[1]

Their daughter, Marilyn McCutchan Disman, recalled that "Mom was very beautiful and intelligent. She was a city girl." She also had some pretty strong ideas about whom she would marry, telling her mother emphatically, "I will never marry a farmer, a teacher, or a coach."[2]

That strong conviction soon crumbled under siege by a farmer, teacher, and coach—with an assist from her own mother, Grace. "The first time my father called on my mother, it was in the late afternoon," Marilyn related. "Her mother had put a roast in the oven. She [Grace] became so enthralled talking to my dad that she let the roast burn."

Mac was enthralled with Virginia, and her attraction to him was immediate as well. Still, Mac wasn't taking any chances and decided to woo Virginia by winning Grace first.

"He found out [Grace] liked rhubarb," Marilyn said. "[So he] picked a bunch of it from the patch on the farm and took it to her on every visit."[3]

Soon the pretty young woman who had vowed never to marry a farmer, teacher, or coach was walking down the aisle with a man who was all three.

During World War II Mac taught navigation as a flight instructor at Pensacola Naval Air Station in Florida. He was not a pilot, but he had gotten his master's degree in math at Columbia University during summers off from school, and he taught trigonometry to navy pilots and navigators.

On September 24, 1945, the U.S. Reconstruction Finance Agency, having declared the C-47 aircraft bearing serial number 4837 to be surplus equipment, transferred ownership to General Motors Corporation in exchange for $80,000. The plane, which had been designed to carry troops and materiel, now would be retrofitted to carry corporate executives on business travel. In its new life as a corporate plane, with the designation DC-3 and with FAA registration number N51071, it would join hundreds of others like it in ferrying passengers around the globe.

When the war ended, Mac and Virginia had two children, Allen and Marilyn. Now they had to decide what they would do and where they would do it. Mac had decided while he was in the Navy that he didn't want to return to the long hours and low pay of a high school coach. He decided he would look for a job as a high school math teacher.

A friend of Virginia's was a secretary at Evansville College, and she told the McCutchans that the college was about to start looking for a head basketball coach.[4] (Emerson Henke, a former Ace, had succeeded Slyker and coached until 1946.)[5] "Because of the salary and the gymnasium situation, I had a great many doubts," Mac said.[6]

Meanwhile, Virginia's friend had been busy, telling Lincoln Hale, president of Evansville College, all about Mac's record as a successful high school basketball coach. Mac received a confidential letter from Hale, asking whether he might be interested in the job. Mac said he was interested, but declined to make a firm commitment.

At the same time the local paper was reporting on discussions about building an athletic program at the college that would feature a modern new athletic complex with a large gym to replace the antiquated armory. And the city had grand plans for a downtown athletic complex on the east side that would include a gymnasium large enough to host the state high school basketball finals.

The city's plan, complete with colorful artists' renderings, was impressive. The possibility of a great basketball facility, whether on campus or somewhere in the city, was enough to get Mac to reconsider the coaching job, although neither plan ever got off the drawing board.

Although he had already written to decline the position, before the letter arrived Mac called the college trustee who was heading the search committee for a new coach and told him, "I want it and I will be there."

The young family lived in a small house at 1041 East Chandler Avenue near the site of Roberts Stadium today, and Mac went to work almost immediately as a summer school instructor in physical education at the college he had left twelve years earlier. He would stay for more than three decades.

As he prepared for the first of what would prove to be 31 seasons at Evansville, Mac told a local reporter, "I can promise this to any boy who decides to come to Evansville College and play a little basketball along with his studies. He will get a look at the best in the business, because we're going to build the game from the bottom up."

The coach really didn't have many other choices. The Athletic Department was allocated only four scholarships, twice the number Mac's predecessor had been allowed. Mac's total budget for recruiting was $1,200 per year, a paltry sum even in 1946–47.[7] Because of the tight budget, he had to limit his search for players to the tristate area of Indiana, Illinois, and Kentucky, and hope to recruit some good players who had been overlooked by big colleges. It was the beginning of a process that would continue for years: while Mac was coach, most of Evansville's players came from the surrounding area, simply because the coach couldn't afford to recruit farther afield. Nevertheless, his formula worked wonders.

In that first year he quipped, "I've been looking all summer for a 7 foot center, some 6-10 forwards and some fast 6-4 guards but in vain."

Instead he found 43 would-be players, none of whom matched those descriptions and most of whom were returning GI's who hadn't played in several years.

Among them were a few returning players and 18-year-old freshmen.

It would take a while for the odd mix to become a team, and Mac had to change his lineups regularly: some of the older players found they couldn't juggle the academic and athletic requirements and left the team.

In that first year Mac notched his first win against Indiana Central before 2300 fans at the armory. It would be one of only seven victories that season. In one of those games, Evansville faced off against Indiana State and its young coach, John Wooden, who was also in his first year in the job. An Indiana native who had starred at Purdue University, where he earned All-America honors, Wooden had spent twelve years as a high school coach, interrupted by two years in the service, and had brought several of his South Bend Central players with him to Terre Haute.

Wooden's first season was going a bit better than Mac's when the two met in an Indiana College Conference game at Evansville. Wooden's squad was 8–6 for the season and stood 4–1 in conference play.

Despite Mac's ever-changing lineup, the Aces managed to defeat Wooden's squad by a single point, 49–48. The winning bucket came from reserve center Adren Keener with just forty seconds to play. Mac had sent in Keener and forwards Bob Kohlmeyer and Paul Kiefer to counter the Sycamores' height advantage, and the shrewd move paid off, making Mac look like a wizard.

When the Aces followed up with a win against St. Joseph's College and ran their conference record to a perfect 2–0, fans' hopes for a winning season were high. But then the team fell to Kentucky Wesleyan by a humiliating 58–23, the worst loss ever in what was already a bitter rivalry. In the Aces' next outing, against the University of Louisville, Mac sent in a reserve player, who was ejected without explanation by referee Frank Jarrel and umpire Al Unser, a former major league baseball catcher. Mac became so upset that he refused to replace the ejected player. The Aces finished the game with four players on the court and lost, 49–41.

Mac's team of grizzled vets and youngsters struggled all season, but fans embraced the team's fast-paced style and enthusiastic effort; the armory, which held only 2500 fans, was usually near capacity for their games.

Their last victory during that first season came against the Thundering Herd from Marshall College in West Virginia. Cam Henderson was the Marshall coach, and he is credited with introducing the running-game style that would later be used by many teams, including Loyola Marymount University, where the

Lions, led by Hank Gathers and Bo Kimble, set national scoring records in the late 1980s that still stand.

But Mac could employ that style as well, and in the Marshall contest his players used it to turn back Henderson's charges by 73–69, led by Andy Collins with 27 points.

Mac's first season at Evansville ended 7–15, when the Aces were trounced 91–70 by Miami of Ohio. These 91 points were the most surrendered by Mac's charges all season. Two of them came from a reserve guard, the 5-10 Ara Parseghian, who hailed from Akron South High School. He would find even more success as the football coach at Notre Dame, guiding the Fighting Irish to national championships in 1966 and again in 1973.[8]

The Aces did slightly better in Mac's second season, finishing 8–18, but in his third year, 1948–49, the squad improved to 14–11, finishing with a loss in the Ohio Valley Conference Tournament, which Evansville had joined, to Morehead State.

Because of its location in the southwestern "toe" of Indiana, Evansville had struggled for decades to carve out a niche that would attract attention to the growing city that Hoosiers to the north largely ignored. Evansville was connected politically to the rest of Indiana but it remained a place apart.

Exuberant chamber of commerce types had, through the years, made a concerted effort to establish Evansville in the minds of other state residents by touting the city's emergence as the sole manufacturing center in the tri-state area and trumpeting to all that it was in turn, "Refrigerator Capital of the World," "Plastics Capital of the World" and even "Barbeque Capital of the World."

But nothing worked.

Not even a later slogan that was, at least, accurate: "Where Northern Industry Meets Southern hospitality," it proclaimed.

Isolated, ignored and beset and divided by religion, race, culture and labor management hostility, Evansville was still a city in search of itself.

Many long-time residents describe it as "a city that feels like a small town." The description is appropriate. Residents take great pride in their homes. They manicure their lawns and keep their houses—largely modest dwellings made of local brick—in good repair.

"Neighbors look out for each other. It's a place where you never have to worry about keeping your doors locked," says Art Ayde.[9] Talk to people there, and you will hear this repeatedly, too: "Evansville is a great place to raise children."

Despite such attributes, Evansvillians were dissatisfied with accepting such a modest reputation and continually sought to stamp the place as something more than just a nice little city on the river. All such efforts to date had fallen short, and it didn't help that the one reputation the city was developing was not flattering.

Labor unrest, walk-outs, and strikes seemed to plague the industries that had established themselves there. Evansville was gaining a reputation among employers as a place with "labor problems," which did nothing to help it recover from economic setbacks.

By the time 1949 turned into 1950, the flood of 1937 was a distant memory, and new dikes had been established along the waterfront to prevent a repeat. New business entities occupied space that had been used for wartime production, and the returning vets needed housing, furniture, and jobs, keeping the plants busy. But the 1950s the population had soared by 43% to over 125,000 as many of the southerners who had come to work in the city during the War stayed on.

It should have been a good time: But the 1950's were not the best of times in Evansville.

(Endnotes)

1   Dr. Allen McCutchan, telephone interview by author, February 11, 2011.

2   Marilyn McCutchan Disman, telephone interview by author, February 22, 2011.

3   Marilyn McCutchan Disman interview.

4   Ibid.

5   Ron Eaton, *Local Legends:The Stories behind the Headlines, 100 Years of Southwestern Indiana Sports History* (Evansville, Ind.: M. T. Publishing, 2008), 104.

6   For this quote from Mac, and others in this chapter that are attributed to no other source, the reader may assume that they come from articles in the *Evansville Courier* and *Evansville Press,* the two local papers at the time. Those articles may be found in the collection of bound scrapbooks kept by Bob Hudson and now housed in the university archives and/or Bill Bussing's manuscript history of the Aces. Bussing generously made his lengthy manuscript available to me, and I have relied on it for some information especially

in the early years of the McCutchan era and in determining attendance figures. The detailed manuscript contains no footnotes, but when I interviewed Bussing in February 2011, he identified his sources as the *Evansville Courier, Evansville Press,* and the combined Sunday edition, the *Courier & Press.* Bussing's manuscript usually makes no distinction between the papers, but the direct quotes are from one daily or the other or the Sunday combined paper and appear in the Bussing manuscript in quotation marks. Bussing used Hudson's scrapbooks, as did I and my research assistant. Many of the articles do not identify which paper they are from, much less the date and page, but I (and Bussing) assume they are from the *Courier, Press, or Sunday Courier and Press.*

7   Dr. Allen McCutchan, telephone interview by author, February 11, 2011; Bussing ms.

8   "Ara Parseghian," www.pro-football-reference.com.

9   Art Ayde, telephone interview by author, January 28, 2011.

Evansville gym, 1922.

The Early Fifties (1950–1953)

In Mac's third season, his veteran squad went 14–14 and competed in the 32-team postseason, National Association of Intercollegiate Basketball tournament for small colleges. The Aces headed to Terre Haute for the four-team qualifying round. They ended up with only eight players healthy enough to play and were eliminated by Indiana State in the first round.

The Aces' local following had continued to build. By now not all of the fans who wanted tickets could buy them because the armory was so small. Two local radio stations, WIKY-FM and WGBF-AM, began to broadcast some of the games for those who couldn't get tickets.

As he watched his 1950–51 squad run laps around East Side Park, led by returning senior Bob Barnett in one of many voluntary preseason training sessions, Mac was feeling confident. And that confidence was rewarded early in the season when the Aces soundly defeated St. Joseph's of Indiana at the armory in the season's third contest. With Bob Barnett and his older brother Jim at forward; Harry Axford, only 6-1, in the pivot ("because he was well built and had a good shot from around the foul line," according to Mac); and Dude Holder and 6-3 Bob Sakel at the guard spots, the Aces toasted the winless Pumas as a blizzard roared around the armory.

The Aces racked up a 107–66 win, in the process establishing a new single-game scoring record for Evansville College. Reporter Bill Robertson of the *Evansville Press* gushed, calling the performance "one of the most amazing and spectacular shooting exhibitions in Evansville College's illustrious history."

It only got better as the season wore on.

One impressive early win came at the expense of Tom Blackburn's Dayton Flyers, a team that featured 6-7 Monk Meineke. The Aces used Mac's favored up-tempo fast-break game and limited the turnovers to just five in dispatching Dayton, then a perennial power, 60–54. "The boys played their finest game of the year," Mac said, adding that "they were alert, they handled the ball well and took full advantage of all their opportunities."[1]

That was a succinct but accurate summary of what would make Arad McCutchan's teams so formidable. "[Mac] stressed fundamentals and never stopped emphasizing them," former player Thornton Patberg said.[2]

Mac's Aces ran the floor much more than other teams of the era. "He recognized that basketball came down to very marginal differences, so he always looked for angles," his son, Allen, recalled.[3] He added that his father's mathematics background played a large part in his coaching. "He was used to problem solving. If during a game the team encountered some defense they hadn't expected, he could figure out how to solve it. He even used statistical analysis to impress his charges with the importance of each possession and the cost of each turnover based on his detailed analysis."[4]

"Mac's basic philosophy was to run, run, and run some more," said former Aces star Hugh Ahlering. "We were running from the preseason on." Their regimen would begin in the preseason in East Side Park and continue with countless trips up and down the armory's steps. "Mac always wanted us to be better conditioned than anyone else, and we almost always were," Ahlering recalled. "He drilled us in fundamentals and especially passing the ball. We would run a passing drill over and over until, in games, it was second nature to us. After a 'made basket' he wanted our big man to take the ball out and get it to the guard."

Ahlering was one of those guards. "Then we'd come up court as fast as we could go, passing the ball and almost never dribbling," he said. "The forwards would make their way up the sidelines, and we knew where they would be. They were told to make cuts at an angle for the key, and we'd hit them there for easy baskets. Many times the ball never touched the floor."[5]

Mac's teams, with their fan-friendly style of play and high-scoring offense, were fun to watch, and fans continued to pack the armory for their games.

By 1950–51, the Aces were winning a lot. They sailed through their first seven games with an unblemished record, nipping Xavier University 71–69 and facing off against the Butler Bulldogs in the Aces' sternest test to date. The Bulldogs' coach, future Hall of Famer Tony Hinkle, was someone Mac admired. Although the two schools would be bitter rivals for years, Mac and Hinkle became friends.

Hinkle enjoyed the benefits of playing in massive Butler Field House in Indianapolis where the state's high school championship game was always contested. The vast structure—it held 14,000—impressed the high school kids who played there, making Hinkle's recruiting job a lot easier. Mac's recruiting efforts, on the other hand, were hindered by the armory: it was old, dark, and small.

Butler and Evansville met after the Christmas break in the first of two back-to-back contests at the Sportscenter in nearby Owensboro, Kentucky, which could accommodate a larger crowd. "It was considered the Taj Mahal of basketball in the Midwest," Sakel said.[6]

Nearly 4,300 fans made the 45-minute trip across the Ohio River to watch the Aces easily turn back Hinkle's Bulldogs 82–61 before the largest Sportscenter crowd of the season.

"Strictly no contest," wrote Dan Scism of the *Courier.* "The Aces never got out of their cruising speed and coasted home with their flags down all the way. Few, if any, teams could have stopped the maneuvering of the Aces when in pay territory in the first half. They looked better than any professionals I ever saw and that includes the old Celtics in their better days," he gushed.

Three days later the Aces repeated their performance, using only six players to paste Hinkle's charges 52–37.

The Aces stood at a perfect 9–0, best in Evansville College's history, when the Murray State Racers arrived at the armory with their own perfect mark, 10–0. The largest crowd ever assembled at the armory, 3,000 strong, watched the Aces meet the Racers.

In a game marred by what Dan Scism termed "high school officiating," both Jim Barnett and Harry Axford were forced to the pine with four fouls in the first half, and the Aces suffered their first loss by just four points, 70–66.

For the Aces' game against Eastern Kentucky, fans packed the armory once more—fighting snowdrifts and high winds to get there. The Maroons became the Aces' tenth victim, falling 67–63.

Next, the Aces crossed the river again to meet Western Kentucky in the Sportscenter. A season-high crowd of 6,500 turned out, and the 400-station Liberty Broadcasting System made it "the Game of the Night."

A questionable charging call helped the Hilltoppers when the referee forced Harry Axford from the game with eight minutes to play. Without their center the Aces fell, 75–63.

The Aces were scheduled for eight days off before they had a rematch with Western Kentucky, and Mac used the time to good advantage. When Western Kentucky played Murray State a few nights later in Bowling Green, Mac sat quietly watching from deep in the crowd.

The Aces were ready for their rematch. In prose as purple as the Aces' shorts, Bill Robertson of the *Evansville Press* told his readers what the crowd had witnessed the night before: "A man-made tempest, conceived in deprivation and encouraged by the whipping flames of vengeance, swept Western Kentucky into temporary oblivion in a remarkable and sometimes unbelievable turn of the tide."

Sakel, who had considered Western Kentucky before deciding to enroll at Evansville, led the Aces in an easy, almost laughable, romp. He shared a nickname with the Red Sox baseball star Ted Williams: "The Splendid Splinter." Both were tall and thin.

At the end of the 1949–50 season Mac had told Sakel he would be switched to guard from his forward spot. Sakel had spent the summer honing his skills in the highly regarded summer resort league in New York's Catskill Mountains, where he was coaching hotel guests in tennis. "It was room, meals, and $20 a week," Sakel recalled. "I learned more there than I would have playing a couple years of college ball."[7]

No wonder: Among the players competing in that summer league were Cliff Hagan and Frank Ramsey of Kentucky, Sherman White of Long Island University, others from New York–area schools, and some from as far away as Illinois. The games were so competitive that they attracted gamblers. Many of those who played in the Catskills would be among those accused of fixing college games in a scandal that rocked the sport in the early 1950s (Sakel was not involved in the scandal).

Sakel, whom Scism once described as looking "harmless as a booby trap and . . . twice as dangerous," had 15 points at the half. Ahead 40–23, the Aces left the floor to a "deafening roar that fairly rocked the building," as Robertson reported.

Mac's scouting trip had paid off: the Aces went on to out-rebound the much taller Hilltoppers while using a tenacious full-court defensive scheme that held the losers to a paltry 17-for-77 from the floor.

With Sakel and Barnett leading the way, the Aces exacted revenge, 77–46.

"The Aces would have beaten any college team Thursday night," Scism told his readers. "They had carefully prepared for the game, devoting an entire week to it. McCutchan had them fired up more than I thought possible. He had perfected a defense for Western that couldn't be improved upon."

The Hilltoppers learned what many of the Aces' other foes would learn through the years. Given enough time to prepare, Mac's teams could compete with just about anybody.

People throughout the area were noticing how well the 1950–51 Aces were doing, and press coverage of the games piqued further interest in the team. That interest, however, couldn't be converted into ticket sales while the team was still playing in the outdated armory.

The Aces now were playing more of their "home" games in Owensboro's Sportscenter, which guaranteed them $1,500 against 40 percent of the gate (that is, if 40 percent of ticket sales came to more than $1,500, they would get more money). When they played there, the Aces almost always made more than the guarantee because so many fans made the trip to follow the team.

Despite the grumbling of some fans about having to trek across the river to watch their Aces, the team played in Owensboro five times that season, including a win over Tulsa. Coached by Clarence Iba, brother of Oklahoma A&M coach Henry "Hank" Iba, the Golden Hurricanes fell to the Aces 61–37, with Bob Barnett canning nine of his ten shots from the field. The next day Dan Scism compared him to "a machine in consistency."

The last seven games of the season saw the Aces go 5–2 as they prepared for the conference tournament.

Thornton Patberg had been a reserve for two seasons before deciding as a junior that he was too slow for the style Mac was playing. But Patberg was thinking about coaching after college and asked Mac if he could participate in some other way. Mac assigned him to keep statistics, and he assisted with the practices.

"I learned more in those two years helping Mac than I had in all the previous years playing basketball," he said. "Mac was a brilliant man. He loved the running game. You could never go fast enough for him. If he saw you lagging behind down court during practice, he'd fire a basketball at you to speed you up. . . . That 1950–51 team and their success was an indication of what was to come."[8]

The Aces concluded the regular season with their final home game at the armory against Morehead State. The *Evansville Courier* dubbed the game "Arad McCutchan Night" at the armory, and loyal fans showered Mac with gifts of appreciation for what he'd accomplished—and to supplement his meager salary. The players all chipped in and gave him a watch and in turn were presented with luggage from grateful boosters.[9]

Mac was humble and grateful. "I wish that I could have my father with me, and say, as I used to say, 'Look at me now, Daddy.'" The Associated Press reported the next day that McCutchan had "received practically everything from the hometown folks except the Ohio Valley Conference Championship."

As the 1950–51 Aces waited to begin the conference tournament, the pollster John McHale of Philadelphia recognized them as the twentieth-best team in the country. They were ranked thirtieth in the Associated Press poll.

Although they had dropped two games to Murray State and finished 5–4 in Ohio Valley Conference play, the Aces had ended the season at 18–4 and were made the first seed in the play-offs based on their overall record. There was even talk about the Aces' being one of thirty-six schools under consideration for invitations to the National Invitation Tournament (NIT) at Madison Square Garden.[10]

In the first round the Aces faced off against unseeded Morehead State and dumped the Eagles in a come-from-behind win. Harry Axford supplied the spark in the second half, finishing with 19 points while holding Morehead's center Jack Baker to a single bucket before he fouled out with 12:29 to play, dooming the Eagles.

Eastern Kentucky was next, and the team that had beaten the Aces once during the regular season prevailed again, 64–61, after Bob Sakel was benched with five fouls and nearly two minutes to play.

The loss put the Aces in the consolation game against Western Kentucky in a game that began just four hours later. Despite their fatigue they managed to nearly overcome a 10-point deficit with only three minutes to play, only to fall short, 72–71.

The back-to-back losses eliminated any interest from the NIT.

However, the Aces' season was not yet over. They got back to Evansville from

Louisville, where the play-offs had been held, on a Sunday and headed to Terre Haute on Tuesday to compete in the NAIB's Twenty-first District Play-offs for the second consecutive year.

The NAIB, begun in 1937 by Emil Liston of Baker College and James Naismith, along with a group of Kansas City businessmen, was the oldest tournament in the country and involved more teams than any other play-off. This grueling contest of endurance culminated in the finals, which were held at Kansas City's Municipal Auditorium before capacity crowds.[11]

Evansville's prospects looked especially bright in the spring of 1951 because the defending champion, Indiana State, was not participating—its key players were preparing for the Pan American Games. The Aces faced off against Franklin College of Indiana, marking their first meeting since 1941. Led by 5-10 guard Jerry Canterbury and Bob Sakel, who had just received word that he had been named to the third team in United Press's All-America selections, the Aces rallied from a 15-point deficit to win in overtime, 70–69.

The next day Canterbury, a reserve player, again came to the rescue, accounting for eight points as the Aces turned back Taylor College 75–68 to gain the District 21 crown.

Now the Aces were off to Kansas City and the NAIB finals with a 21–6 record that made them first seed.

In the first round they played in the last of eight opening-day games and defeated Westminster College 85–74. Bob Barnett made 27 points, including 16 in the first half on a perfect 8-for-8 from the field.

The next day the Aces were right back in action against Morningside College as 9,000 fans looked on. The game began at 10 p.m., which angered Mac.

"As the number one seed he thought we should be in prime time," Sakel said.[12]

The Aces found themselves tied at 25 at the half and facing foul trouble for three starters. A strong start at the outset of the second half carried them through to a 75–62 win, even though they had lost Axford, Sakel, and Bob Northerner to fouls.

Now only eight teams remained in the hunt for the national title.

The weary Aces—they had played eight games, all on the road, over the previous fourteen days—fell behind 36–22 at the half against Regis College, prompting the usually calm Mac to deliver an angry message that resonated with the players.

"We were sitting on a long bench in the locker room, and I was at the end of the bench," Sakel recalled. "As Mac lit into each of the starters in turn and worked his way down the bench, I was agreeing with him. When he got to me, he really blew up: 'You think you're an All-American? You didn't play like one!'"[13]

Inspired by Mac's fiery speech, the Aces clawed back into the game and drew within two points at the ten-minute mark. Led by Jim Barnett, who usually was known for his defensive play, the Aces were only one point behind Regis with 1:22 remaining. The crowd was pulling wildly for the Aces. They fought gallantly to the end but fell 70–68 when a last desperate heave from Sakel missed the mark and sent the Aces home with a 23–7 record for the season.

"Mac came up to all of us after the game and apologized for getting on us so hard," Sakel recalled. "He said he was sorry but he thought that was the only way he could snap us out of it."[14]

The 1950–51 season was marked by both the strength and the weakness of the Aces in the early McCutchan years. Mac had proved he could coach marginal players into top-flight performers. The problem was that he had no depth behind his starters. The Aces seldom played more than six players in a game, and this lack of depth hurt them.

Mac's ability to attract players from the area was growing with each passing season, but he was hampered by his lack of funding for recruiting trips. The other drawback was the armory, whose sorry state would not sway any out-of-area recruit who had other offers.

The 1951–52 season began as war once again dominated the headlines. The war-weary country would eventually turn to Dwight Eisenhower for leadership. The former Supreme Commander of Allied troops in World War II was seen as a calming, almost grandfatherly, leader who had promised to go to Korea, where American troops were fighting and dying in a war with no clear meaning for many Americans. The war, as well as the college basketball betting scandals (which never touched Evansville College), also meant that the college basketball talent pool had gotten smaller.

The few seasons following the successful 1950–51 campaign would produce only 29 wins against 35 losses. The general disaffection caused by the basketball scandals cut the number of fans vying for tickets to the Aces' games to a few hundred, and their dreary home in the armory did little to dispel the dark and gloomy mood in the arena. Although fans could buy a twelve-ticket package for home games for only $15, attendance shrank from 23,187 in 1950–51 to just 13,250 the next year. After one game in 1952, Larry Middlemas told readers of the *Sunday Courier-Post* that the crowd was "too few to keep the gym warm."

The 1952–53 campaign saw Mac experiment with a platoon system against his better judgment. "I don't fancy a two-platoon system," he told reporters. "I have always said, 'Be happy with just one good platoon.' However I have got to change things. I don't want to go on another year the way I have since I lost that good team."

Mac's strategy didn't work, but his willingness to experiment showed that he knew there was more than one way to play the game.

The 1953–54 season saw the emergence of a national phenomenon from tiny Rio Grande College in southern Ohio. His name was Bevo Francis, and he had led his team to a perfect 39–0 record the year before, only to see all the records he set, including a 116-point game against Ashland Junior College, erased from the NCAA records in what was, at bottom, a fit of jealousy.

But in 1953–54 Bevo and his teammates came back—and captivated the hearts and minds of the nation as no other team ever had. Bevo scored 113 points in a game against Hillsdale College, a record that still stands, and dominated the sports pages for the entire year while leading his small school to a 20–7 season against major college foes nationwide.

Francis and Rio Grande, and all the media attention focused on them, dispelled some of the hangover from the betting scandals, and attendance slowly began to climb again.

Mac's 1953–54 squad had a pedestrian season, 12–12, and was eliminated in the first round of the NAIB Tournament. Evansville had left the Ohio Valley Conference in 1952 and was now competing against schools similar in size and closer geographically in the new Indiana Collegiate Conference.

"President Hale felt the move, over Mac's objections, was a better fit because the schools were academically superior and were more easily (and inexpensively) reached from Evansville," Thornton Patberg recalled.[15]

During the 1954–55 season, the Aces' luck began to turn and it would bring the city something that its citizens had long dreamed of. Evansville was about to emerge from obscurity.

(Endnotes)

1   For this quote from Mac, and others in this chapter that are attributed to no other source, the reader may assume that they come from articles in the *Evansville Courier* and *Evansville Press,* the two local papers at the time. Those articles may be found in the collection of bound scrapbooks kept by

Bob Hudson and now housed in the university archives and/or Bill Bussing's manuscript history of the Aces. Bussing graciously made his lengthy manuscript available to me, and I have relied on it for some information, especially in the early years of the McCutchan era and in determining attendance figures. The detailed manuscript contains no footnotes, but when I interviewed Bussing in February 2011, he identified his sources as the *Evansville Courier, Evansville Press,* and the combined Sunday edition, the *Courier & Press.* Bussing's manuscript usually makes no distinction between the papers, but the direct quotes are from one daily or the other or the Sunday combined paper and appear in the Bussing manuscript in quotation marks. Bussing used Hudson's scrapbooks, as did I and my research assistant. Many of the articles do not identify which paper they are from, much less the date and page, but I (and Bussing) assume they are from the *Courier, Press, or Sunday Courier & Press.*

2   Thornton Patberg, telephone interview by author, January 29, 2011.

3   Ron Eaton, *Local Legends: The Stories behind the Headlines, 100 Years of Southwestern Indiana Sports History* (Evansville, Ind.: M. T. Publishing, 2008), 114.

4   Dr. Allen McCutchan, telephone interview by author, March 11, 2011.

5   Hugh Ahlering, telephone interview by author, March 11, 2011.

6   Bob Sakel, telephone interview by author, March 25, 2011.

7   Sakel interview.

8   Patberg interview.

9   Sakel interview.

10   The NIT was hard hit by the betting scandals that had dominated the headlines all season. Some schools wouldn't even consider accepting an invitation to play in the NIT because the Garden was so entwined with the point-shaving scheme that had shattered a number of major college programs. See Stanley Cohen, *Game They Played* (New York: Farrar, Strauss and Giroux, 1977).

11   Danny Stooksbury, *National Title: The Unlikely Tale of the NAIB Tournament* (Bradenton, Fla.: Higher Level Publishing, 2010), 2.

12   Sakel interview.

13   Sakel interview.

14   Sakel interview.

15   Patberg interview.

Local Products, 1953–1955

Even though he had suffered his team's hundredth loss in 1953, Mac was optimistic about the future.

He had, in fact, two reasons for not being glum: John Harrawood and Jerry Clayton. Both had graduated from Central High School in Evansville. Both had been named to the high-school all-state team by the *Indianapolis Star*.

Because he had earned several credits at his previous high school in Carrier Mills, Illinois, Harrawood had not been eligible to play during his senior year at Central. He had married while still in high school, and that had quashed Indiana University's interest in him, although both Tulane and Kentucky recruited him. John and his brother Bill had intended to go to Tulsa, where their older brother Floyd was already enrolled.

But when Texas Tech contacted the younger Harrawood brothers, they decided to enroll at the school in Lubbock. John had earned enough credits during the summer to get his high school diploma, and he arrived in time to begin practice with the Red Raiders.

But his stay in Buddy Holly's hometown was brief.

"I was the only married man on the Tech freshman team, and I didn't get along with the other players too well," he explained. He was so unhappy that he left after the fall quarter. Although he had practiced with the team, he had not played, so as soon as he enrolled at Evansville, he was eligible to play during the 1953–54 season. "Harrawood has missed a lot of work he would have normally received had he been practicing with us since October," Mac told reporters, "but he is an excellent prospect and he'll make up the lost time as he goes along."[1]

Mac was right. By January Harrawood had cracked the starting lineup of the struggling Aces. He ended the season with a 14-point average, as did Bob Wessel, who had joined Harrawood as a starter in January. Like Harrawood and Clayton, Wessel had played for Central High. All would figure prominently in Evansville's future.

On Evansville's freshman team was another player who would contribute to the Aces's success: Jim Smallins, the college's first black player. He was originally from Shelbyville, Kentucky, and had moved with his family to Evansville when he was two years old. "My dad moved up there to work in the factories," he said. "A lot of people from Kentucky had done that, and for a while I thought there were more Kentuckians in Evansville than Indianans."

Looking back on his coming of age in Evansville in the 1940s and 50s, Smallins recalls conditions in the city as being "somewhat biased." "There were a lot of good people in Evansville, but the bias was still there. I was a lifeguard at the segregated swimming pool. The majority of black families lived in an area with mostly black families in it. It wasn't really forced segregation but more that the area was the one where they could afford the housing," he said.

Still, Evansville had a "distinct southern feel" to it. "My wife lived on Elliott Street when she was growing up. On the other side of the street white families lived, and the children all played together as kids. When they got older that all stopped," he said.

One night while he was in high school (in the early 1950s), he and his girlfriend were walking home from the movies. "A police car pulled up and asked my girlfriend—who was very light colored: 'Miss, is everything OK? Is this fella bothering you?' She said, 'No. He's my boyfriend.' Then they just drove off," Smallins recalled.

Lincoln High School had no white students at all until 1952 when one white girl enrolled. She left shortly thereafter.

"Later, kids were permitted by law to attend other schools, but during my years they were still segregated. There were no blacks attending Central High School," Smallins said. "In 1952, when the law changed and we could have transferred [to Central], my girlfriend and I decided that Lincoln offered as good or better academic preparation than Central, and we stayed there."[2]

Public facilities in Evansville were also segregated. "The Community Center was off-limits to us. As blacks we weren't allowed to go there," Smallins said. "I used the negatives to build a shield around me. It made me a stronger person. I turned the negatives into positives."

After a stand-out athletic career at Lincoln, Smallins had several scholarship offers. "I was set to go to Tennessee State, an all-black college, when Mac offered me a full four-year scholarship at Evansville. I thought, Maybe I want to be the first black basketball player at Evansville," he said. "I talked it over with my mother and my girlfriend, and they said there's nothing wrong with doing that."

The scholarship came with a lot of extra benefits for Jim and the other Aces, and only one caveat from Mac. "He told me, 'Jim, you can't date white girls.' I told him, 'That's not a problem—I have a girlfriend.'" Looking back, Smallins thinks that Mac was advising him about how to avoid trouble while on campus rather than imposing any personal bias. "I, personally, feel that Coach Mac was a good man and that was just his way of looking after one of his players, just like he would have done for any one of them," he said. "I never saw any racial bias in him at all."

The benefits for being an Ace were many. "We got clothes, summer jobs, and free hair cuts," Smallins recalled. "The first time I showed up at the barbershop with some other guys on the team, the barber looked at me and said, 'I've never cut a black's hair before.'

"I told him, 'You've got four years to figure it out.' They were the best haircuts I ever had."[3]

Smallins was talented, confident, and intelligent; he knew what was and wasn't expected of him. While some may have looked askance at his presence on the team, he welcomed the opportunity to become the first black to play for Mac and the Aces.

As a senior at Lincoln, Smallins had been the city's top scorer, but he spent much of the 1953–54 season, his freshman year at Evansville, on crutches from a knee injury suffered during a preseason practice.

Mac had seen Harrawood developing as the 12–12 campaign of 1953–54 concluded, and the coach knew a healthy Smallins would make a major contribution. Fans were especially looking forward to what Smallins would do: they knew his reputation, and increasingly Evansvillians needed something to cheer for.

In 1953 Evansville had begun to lose manufacturing jobs. When the losses ended, in 1961, the city had 28,000 fewer manufacturing jobs, 25,000 of which resulted from the closings of Servel, Chrysler, and International Harvester.

In September 1956 the manager of the Chamber of Commerce produced a report on labor-management relations, insisting vehemently that labor relations were good—although he had no comparable figures from other industrial cities. Although the term *spin* had not yet taken on today's definition of changing the meaning of facts, the manager was a master of spin, insisting that Evansville's lost-time record was "exceptionally low."[4]

 But according to labor historian White, "Several strikes during the first half of the [1950s] resulted in prolonged and bitter confrontations in the city. Strikes against most of Evansville's large manufacturing firms, by various building-trades unions, and against Indiana Bell did little to ameliorate labor relations in Evansville and hastened the movement of industry away from the area during the mid-to-late 1950s."[5]

On the basketball court though, things were a little brighter. The 1954–55 season saw Mac reap a recruiting bonanza that would begin to pay dividends immediately.

Jerry Clayton, a 6-7 center for Central High School, would follow his brothers to Evansville College. Clayton was born in rural Kentucky in 1935. When he was eight years old, he, his twin brothers, sister, and parents moved to Evansville, like so many others, to be closer to the Chrysler plant where his father worked.

Clayton remembers growing up in Evansville as a pleasant experience. "Everybody went to church. It was a very religious community. I was raised in a Christian home."[6] Like Smallins, Clayton recalls Evansville as a community that had a decidedly "southern flavor to it, as a result of all the people from Kentucky and Tennessee that came up there to work." During his high school career, he set a number of school scoring records and was named to the Indiana State All-Star team. Recruiters sought him out.

"I had scholarship offers from all over—Purdue, Indiana, Kentucky—and I even got one from West Point," he recalled.[7] Dan Scism, who covered sports for the *Courier*, flatly declared in the paper in those years that Clayton was "the all-time greatest prep player I ever saw."

Despite the scholarship offers from larger schools, "the most sought-after player in Evansville history" chose to stay at home and play for Mac. "I just decided I wanted to stay close to home," he explained.

On November 1, 1954, twenty-two varsity candidates assembled before Coach McCutchan. "Mac never cut anybody," Thornton Patberg remembered. "If you came out and practiced, you were on the team. You might not make the travel squad, but you were not cut—ever."[8]

When the 1954–55 season opened against Oakland City (Indiana) College, Mac's starting lineup had more height than he had been blessed with in nine previous campaigns. In that starting group were four members of the Central High team that had played in the 1952 sectional championships.

The team that took the court was comprised of Clayton; Bob Wessel, who was 6-3; Roscoe Bivin, the 6-5 center; and guards Bob Walker (6-1) and John Harrawood (6-2).

"Don't be surprised to see Jerry in the corner while Bivin handles the post," Mac told reporters. "In there together, they'll give me plenty of height. Of course, I'll lose something on the fast break, but that's to be expected."

Through his local contacts and growing reputation (he had been named co-winner of the Indiana Collegiate Conference Coach of the Year), Mac had managed to reap a harvest of local talent that any major college program would have coveted.

Fans were so giddy at the prospects of the 1954–55 Aces that more than a hundred were turned away at the door to the armory, where Evansville was making its season debut against Oakland City College. Evansville romped past the Oaks 100–58.

The new lineup produced 53 rebounds to Oakland's 23. The Aces also took advantage of the new free-throw rule that granted a bonus shot in the one-and-one situation. That happened thirty-six times—a school record—and the Aces converted on eight of those opportunities.

But the glow from the win over Oakland wore off with the news that Bob Wessel, who had left the game in the first half, had injured his ankle. Then Bivin slipped in the shower, struck his head, and was admitted to the hospital with two black eyes and a suspected concussion.

Mac was forced to improvise.

He had Wessel's older brother John take over Bivin's spot at center, and newcomer Clyde Cox stepped into the forward spot vacated by Wessel. Cox was a 6-3 sophomore who had transferred from Tulane. Cox had attended Kokomo High School, where he had led the team to an 18–2 season and into the state playoffs before Kokomo lost to Muncie Central. After one season at Tulane, where he had seen little action, Cox had followed the advice of Virginia McCutchan's cousin Wilbur Rust, a Kokomo resident, and had transferred to Evansville.

Cox had contributed ten points in the blowout over Oakland City and followed with another ten-point performance in his first start, against Lawrence Tech. The Aces drubbed the Detroit school 108–72 before 2,100 fans.

"When you see [Cox] in action," Mac told reporters after the game, "you wonder how anybody is going to beat him out."

The 108 points established a new school record, eclipsing the mark set only recently against Oakland City.

"Several of their razzle-dazzle maneuvers wound up by the shot being missed [*sic*] and the loud 'Oh' that echoed from the fans revealed the intense appreciation of the crowd for basketball at its best," Scism told readers.

The appreciation that fans showed for Mac's talent-laden 1954–55 team by packing the armory would only grow more intense.

The Aces dropped an ICC conference game to Valparaiso University of Indiana on the Crusaders' home court by three points before rebounding against St. Joseph's of Indiana by 105–71, and then falling to the Blue Devils of Lawrence Tech 80–75.

Next they faced DePauw. Bivin, bruised but unbowed, was back in action and had regained his starting role. Reserve Frank Healy keyed a first-half rally that propelled the Aces to an 83–63 win at DePauw. The Aces followed that victory with a road win over Oakland City, 93–72.

When the 4–2 Aces returned to the armory for the first time in three weeks, they had a standing-room-only crowd for a rematch with Valparaiso, an opportunity to avenge their loss on the road. "If we lose this one, we'd be down a game and a half and somebody else would have to beat Valpo, and I don't think anybody could do it," Mac told the press. "Besides we'd have to go unbeaten the rest of the way to figure in the [Conference] title."

After the Aces built an early lead, Valparaiso's Crusaders climbed back into the game, narrowing the score to 65–63 with a little more than three minutes to play.

John Harrawood then put on a ball-handling display that drained minutes off the clock and confounded the visitors. With only four seconds remaining, the frustrated Crusaders fouled Frank Healy to stop the clock. Healy canned the second of his two charity tosses to give the Aces a 66–63 win.

"I don't believe I could do that very often and get away with it," Mac told reporters of his stalling tactics. "The fans don't want to see that type of basketball, and yet there are times when you are forced to use it."

Mac, an avid proponent of the running game, was smart enough to realize that some game situations dictate a slower pace, and he wasn't afraid to use it to gain a win. Coaching a college basketball team in a game is not that different from engaging in a chess match or a wartime battle. The victors are those who are able to see their opponent's unexpected moves and counter them effectively. With his analytical mind, Mac would become a master game coach, which elevated him from being a good basketball coach and teacher of the game to being one of the few truly great coaches.

"He was a brilliant coach," Hugh Ahlering said years later. "He always talked of *finding a way to win*."[9]

Next, the Aces crossed the river and headed to Owensboro's Sportscenter for the annual All-American City Tournament, where they returned to their running ways and dispatched the Denver University Pioneers by 96–81, despite a 32-point performance by Dick Brott that shattered the tournament scoring mark.

The win put Evansville in the semifinals against the University of Cincinnati Bearcats, who had dispatched Mississippi State in their first round and were led by future NBA star Jack Twyman. To counter the potent scoring potential of the 6-6 Twyman, Mac put his own powerhouse, 6-7 Jerry Clayton, on the Pittsburgh native.

Twyman, a senior, collected 19 points against the Evansville freshman, who managed but eight points for the night. The Bearcats prevailed 82–62.

Mac, fearful of a letdown after the loss, fired the team up for the consolation game, and the Aces responded with the greatest offensive effort by any Evansville team. Led by Clayton's 31 points and Harrawood's 28, the Aces gored the Rams of Rhode Island 115–85.

The win produced a bushel of new records by Mac's squad. The Aces put up a new school scoring record yet again, and their 47 field goals were a new record, too. Clayton disposed of the freshman scoring record that Bob Wessel and Harrawood had shared and fell just three short of Gus Doerner's thirteen-year-old school record of 34—and he had done so in just his eleventh game in an Aces uniform.

A week later Harrawood tallied 32 points in a 79–76 win over Indiana State as the Aces came from behind to prevail at Terre Haute's College Gymnasium. The win put the Aces' conference record at 3–1, tied with Valparaiso for the lead.

Ball State, with a reputation for strong defensive play, visited the armory in January. The Aces, fueled again by both Clayton and Harrawood, nevertheless took a commanding lead. Mac inserted his reserves when the lead was at 20 but put his starters back in when that margin was soon halved. Clayton scored 33 points—one short of Doerner's record—before being pulled from the game.

"Mac didn't want me breaking Doerner's record as a freshman," Clayton said. "But when the game got close he put me back in."[10] Back on the floor, he missed his first four shots. He then converted an offensive rebound, giving him 35 points and breaking the record, which had endured for 291 games.

"I always felt Gus's record would be broken in a game when we needed the points," Mac told reporters after the Aces managed a 93–80 win. "We needed them Saturday night, and Clayton got them."

Doerner, still confined to Gibson General Hospital after his near-fatal auto accident, said, "Jerry, it took me four years to score 34 points in one game, and you bettered the mark in your first year of college competition. You'll top that 35 several times before you're finished at the College."

On hand to see the record fall was Washington University coach Blair Gullion, whose team was to meet the Aces next. "That Jerry Clayton is one of the finest players I've seen this year, and that includes Big Ten, Rocky Mountain and West Coast teams," Gullion observed. "If we try to run against Evansville, they could set a new world record against us."

Despite their attempts to control the pace, Washington's Bears fell 74–60 as junior guard Bob Walker, the only Aces player to have started every game, pumped in 14 points to accompany Clayton's 28.

"It was good to see the home products displaying their wares for the home school," a reporter observed of Mac's team.

With a perfect record of 5–0 at the armory, the Aces left the comfort of their home court to make the trip to Indianapolis for a game with the Butler Bulldogs, who also had not dropped a conference game played on their home turf.

With the game tied at 73, the chess match between future Hall of Famers saw Mac opting to stall for the last-shot opportunity. The plan went awry when Mark Peterman of Butler stole the ball from Harrawood with forty seconds to play.

Butler, in possession as time ticked down, went with Bobby Plump, who on the very same court just one season earlier had sunk the shot that gave tiny Milan High School the championship that would later inspired the 1986 movie *Hoosiers*.

With time about to expire, Plump lifted a shot from fifteen feet over Clyde Cox. "I just couldn't get to it. It went right over my fingertips," Cox recalled.[11]

Swish!

Game over.

Plump had somehow duplicated his miracle, giving Butler a dramatic 75–73 win.

"The shot just swished through, no teetering on the rim. It was identical to the shot he made to beat Muncie Central in the state finals last year," Mac said, shaking his head in wonder.

The unflappable Plump finished with 28 points, three more than Jerry Clayton, who had been a teammate of Plump's in the 1954 Indiana-Kentucky All-Star game.

"I thought they had eight referees in that game," Clayton said of the contest with Butler. "Every time I took a shot, they hit my arms. They hit them so hard someone told me later that up in the stands it sounded like a shotgun going off. Finally I had to start taking shots from about thirty feet out to have any chance at all of getting one off."[12]

Despite the loss, Clayton's spectacular play lured yet another capacity crowd to the armory as the Aces returned from the disappointing loss to face Kentucky Wesleyan. It promised to be a shoot-out between Clayton and Wesleyan's Joe Roop, who had recently set his school record with 38 points against Union College.

Clayton won the battle, though there were fewer fireworks than expected. He tallied 16 points while holding Roop to just four field goals in twenty attempts and six free-throws.

The Panthers were waiting for revenge when the Aces, who had managed only one win in four tries at the Sportscenter, which served as the Panthers' home, arrived for the rematch. Sleet and snow didn't keep the fans away—the Sportscenter welcomed 3,500 that night.

The team that Evansville faced was now comprised of three former Kentucky recruits who had transferred to Wesleyan after the Wildcats were sidelined for the entire 1952–53 season by the betting scandals. Logan Gipe, Linville Puckett, and Bill Bibb were the newly arrived players. They had been recruited by Adolph Rupp, which is all you need to know to gauge their talent.

Their transfer to another conference made them eligible to play immediately and more than 600 fans had materialized for their first practice session with the new team. "The largest crowd we've had all season," coach Bullet Wilson joked.

Local fans had eagerly anticipated the transfers' first game in Kentucky Wesleyan uniforms. Mac's reaction was typical of his understated sense of humor: "I always wanted to play the University of Kentucky." That was about the last laugh the Aces had that night.

Combining for 36 of the Panthers' 38 points in the first half, the three finished with 64 as the Aces fell to the Panthers, 74–71.

Clayton was held to just two baskets in fourteen attempts, but Mac refused to pin the loss on his performance. "None of my starters were giving us much help," he said. "Jerry was a marked man and couldn't get an open shot against Wesleyan's pressing defense. John Harrawood couldn't hit, and Roscoe Bivin, Frank Healy and Bob Wessel didn't get the job done."

Mac did find one bright spot in the loss. Jim Smallins, who had gone in as a substitute, had impressed him. "The only boy out there who was really fired up," Mac said of Jim, who accounted for a career high 17 points and kept the Aces close.

Mac had scouted Jim while he was playing for Lincoln High School. Though he usually played center, his coach, Art Taylor, had shifted him to guard for the game that Mac attended in January 1953 to see Smallins in person. "Mr. Taylor wanted to prove to McCutchan that I could play any position," Smallins explained.

What Mac saw was impressive. "It seemed that everything I did that night was right," Smallins recalled. "I was in positions for open shots all night . . . and they kept coming to me."[13] He had connected on 23 of 48 field goals, added three free-throws, and blistered the nets for a record-setting 49 points for an Evansville-area high schooler, a record that still stands.

Smallins had played on the junior varsity team as a freshman when he wasn't laid up with his bum knee, and that cost him a year of college eligibility. But that year was valuable to him in a different way.

"We were playing in Kentucky, and I had a good game. There was a large group of fans that were really getting on me all during the game, shouting and directing racial insults at me. After the game was over Mac told me I wasn't going to dress for the varsity game because of the treatment I'd received. I decided, if I wasn't going to be on the bench, I would go up into the crowd and watch from there," he recalled.

But he didn't just go into the crowd. He went right into the midst of the fans that had been riding him.

"I sat down right in the middle of them all. A little girl was seated next to me with her mother. She looked at me and then said, 'Can I see your teeth?' I said sure and flashed her a big smile. The little girl turned to her mom, all excited, and said, 'Look, Mom, he doesn't have black teeth.'"[14]

This was a year before the Montgomery bus boycott and six years before the lunch counter sit-ins in Greensboro. Jim Smallins, acting on his own, was making his point in his own subtle way. And opening at least one little girl's mind.

Now his play against the Panthers had again opened Mac's eyes to his talent. "I should probably shake up my starting five," Mac told reporters.

Mac saw to it that the trail-blazing and talented Smallins would have some help navigating the still-segregated world around him. "When Jim got here, Mac knew he might have some trouble adjusting. I came from a pretty religious family, and he assigned me to room with Jim to ease the way for him," Clyde Cox said. "The city then was still pretty 'southern' in attitude and Jim came from the segregated high school. Mac felt that it would be best if I took him under my wing."[15]

"I actually wasn't aware of it. I just remember us becoming good friends," Jim said. "Mac knew I was confident but not brazen."[16]

Mac had another reason for believing that Jim would need a friend he could count on: a few players held some rather unenlightened attitudes toward Negroes. "We broke the color line together," Clyde Cox said. "That's something I'm pretty proud about."

Smallins was, of course, acutely aware of what his presence on the team would mean when the Aces traveled—difficulty finding hotel and restaurant accommodations in the Jim Crow era. But he had a sly solution afforded by his light complexion. "He told me, 'Clyde, as far as you and the rest are concerned, when we're on the road, I'm an American Indian,'" Cox recalled.[17]

The Aces would next host DePauw University, and the problem of accommodating more fans than the cramped armory could hold was solved when a local television station, WEHT, decided to televise the game. An estimated audience of 100,000—most of them comfy in their own recliners—saw the Aces prevail, 90–68, as Clayton and Frank Healy led the way.

When the Aces beat Indiana State 104–70, they assured themselves of at least a share of the ICC crown for 1955. Their chance to claim the title outright would be at home against St. Joseph's on "Gus Doerner Night" at the armory, a fund-raiser.

Released just four days before the game from Gibson General Hospital, Doerner, the once swift and agile star, arrived in a wheelchair. Bob Hudson, a driver for the local Coca-Cola bottling plant and a referee, acted as emcee for the evening. A committee of local businessmen presented a check to Doerner for $917 (about $7,400 today), donated by members of the community, to help defray the cost of a new car to replace the one in which he had suffered his crippling and near-fatal injuries.

"I'm thankful to God for being here," an obviously moved Doerner said, "and to all my teammates who helped make me an All-American."

After Ball State had defeated Butler the night before, the Aces were assured of the conference crown and easily bested the visitors, St. Joseph's of Indiana, 101–81. Harrawood tallied 23 points for the winners.

Somehow, Mac had persuaded the District 21 selection committee of the National Association of Interscholastic Athletics (NAIA) to hold the postseason play-offs in Evansville, despite the limitations of the armory.

Although Mac's teams had played in the NAIA Tournament three times, they had never enjoyed a home-court advantage.

The selection committee chair, Angus Nicoson, who was the head coach at Indiana Central, had acknowledged that "the tourney hasn't been a money-maker in the last six years, and we're interested in getting a location where the teams can at least make their expenses."

The staunch support for the Aces from the Evansville community, despite the cramped armory, had not escaped the notice of NAIA officials. It would be a distinction that the Aces would use to their decided advantage in the future.

As 1,700 fans looked on, the Aces opened the tournament with a hard-earned victory from what looked to become a rout, as the Aces enjoyed a 41–26 half-time advantage. But the Grizzlies clawed their way back in the second half to tie the game at 65 with little more than six minutes to play.

Mac turned again to Smallins, who, along with Cox, came off the bench, replacing Clayton and Bivin, to ignite a rally. Jim cashed in four of his five shots, and Cox added eight to carry the Aces to an 87–75 win.

Facing the 20–7 Anderson College Ravens next, the Aces held a 68–56 edge when Mac once again turned to his talented sophomores. Smallins and Cox responded by combining for 19 points down the stretch to dispatch the Ravens 96–79. And Clayton's 19 points in that game enabled him to eclipse Gus Doerner's single-season scoring record.

Now the Aces were, once again, bound for Kansas City and the NAIA Finals.

They left for the tournament in a three-car caravan three days before their first scheduled game. A contingent that included Virginia McCutchan, Joan Harrawood, and Peggy Bivin, along with local radio announcer Marv Bates, brought up the rear.

The trip took two days over roads that did not remotely resemble the interstate highways that President Eisenhower was planning, and after a stop overnight in Columbia, Missouri, they arrived at the State Hotel in downtown Kansas City.

Seeded fourth based on their 20–5 record, the Aces were to face the Bulldogs of Atlantic Christian College, coached by Jack McComas, a protege of the legendary Everett Case of North Carolina State. Though they had established a 22–6 record, the Bulldogs were unseeded, and it appeared, on paper at least, that the Aces would have little trouble advancing.

All that changed soon after they arrived. Jim Smallins—"the best pinch hitter Evansville ever had," according to Bill Robertson of the *Evansville Press*—hurt his knee in a morning workout. He had injured it while walking from the hotel to Kansas City's Municipal Auditorium.

"I just had turned my foot wrong and tore my cartilage a bit. Then, in the morning workout, Bivins stepped on my right foot. I tried to turn and my cartilage tore really badly," Smallins recalled. Cox got Jim back to the hotel, made him as comfortable as possible, called a doctor, and went back to the game. By the time the game began, the reliable super sub was immobilized at the hotel, his leg in a cast.[18]

The Bulldogs were big.

John Marley, who stood 6-11 and weighed 220 pounds, particularly concerned Mac. "This will be about the first time for Bivin to run into a taller center. I wonder how he'll handle it," he mused.

Not well, as it turned out. Mac watched in dismay as Bivin, who had been averaging 12 points per game, failed to produce a single basket, whereas Marley accounted for 23 points for the Bulldogs. Clyde Cox, however, managed 23 points before he collided with the brick wall named Marley, dislocated his finger, and ended up on the bench with 7:28 to play.

"They taped it up, but it was broken bad," Cox recalled, noting that the finger is still crooked today.[19]

The Aces, out-rebounded 55–31, fell to the Bulldogs 95–88.

"You would think that a team played well on offense to score 88 points," Mac told reporters after the disappointing loss. "But we didn't. And our defense never showed up."

The Aces finished the season with a record of 20–6, their second best during Mac's tenure. But as good as the season had been, there were some worrisome aspects that threatened the future. Smallins's knee had nagged him since he entered college, and doctors had told him it wasn't going to get any better as long as he played.

Another problem was Jerry Clayton's academic performance. He was spectacular on the court: first team NAIA All-America, a school record of 487 points, and an average of nearly 19 points per game. The Aces depended on him—of the thirteen games in which he led the team in scoring, the Aces had lost only one, in Kansas City, in their last contest. He was named ICC Player of the Year—the first freshman, and first Aces player, so honored. He was the only player to be a unanimous choice for the All-Conference team. In short, a brilliant player.

But his classroom performance was not nearly as impressive. He had struggled all season to maintain grades good enough to retain eligibility.

His struggles in the classroom were common knowledge in the community, thanks to a local sports editor who had publicly implored him to study harder. (Clayton was clearly not motivated by the editor's gambit. In fact, he says, he "doesn't remember reading that at all.")[20] Many worried that Clayton would lose his eligibility.

But Clayton was a reluctant student at best. He acknowledges that he mostly didn't bother with his assignments. "Mac even got me a tutor," he said. "But I wasn't much interested in studying then."[21] He finished the spring semester, but his poor academic record left him ineligible for the fall semester. He enrolled and registered for classes but soon discovered that his athletic scholarship had been revoked. So less than a week after Mac (ICC Coach of the Year) first assembled his 1955–56 squad, Clayton announced he was leaving Evansville College.

The announcement stirred the community to action. A local oil producer and contractor, Jonathan "Bus" Turner, volunteered to pick up Clayton's expenses and the 6-8 sophomore returned to campus. "I did not have the money to continue my education without a scholarship," Clayton said. "I was embarrassed when I learned that I was not officially enrolled. I really want a college education, and I prefer to get it in Evansville."

Clayton, seemingly sincere in his newfound interest in academics, was back in the fold.

(Endnotes)

1   For these quotes from Mac, and others in this chapter that are attributed to no other source, the reader may assume that they come from articles in the *Evansville Courier* and *Evansville Press,* the two local papers at the time. Those articles may be found in the collection of bound scrapbooks kept by Bob Hudson and now housed in the university archives and/or Bill Bussing's manuscript history of the Aces. Bill Bussing graciously made his lengthy manuscript available to me, and I have relied on it for some information, especially in the early years of the McCutchan era and in determining attendance figures. The detailed manuscript contains no footnotes, but when I interviewed Bussing in February 2011, he identified his sources as the *Evansville Courier, Evansville Press,* and the combined Sunday edition, the *Courier & Press.* Bussing's manuscript usually makes no distinction between the papers, but the direct quotes are from one daily or the other or the Sunday combined paper and appear in the Bussing manuscript in quotation marks. Bussing used Hudson's scrapbooks, as did I and my research assistant. Many of the articles do not identify which paper they are from, much less the date and page, but I (and Bussing) assume they are from the *Courier*, *Press,* or *Sunday Courier & Press.*

2   Indiana abolished segregation in public schools in 1949, and it is likely that the sequence Smallins describes occurred as a result of that decision. See Dwight W. Culver, "Racial Desegregation in Education in Indiana," Journal of Negro Education 24, no. 3 (1954): 296.

3   Jim Smallins, telephone interview by author, April 8, 2011.

4   "City's 'Bad Labor' Reputation Is Disputed by C. of C. Official," *Evansville Press,* September 4, 1956.

5   White, *Fragile Alliances,* 162–63.

6   Jerry Clayton, telephone interview by author, April 6, 2011.

7   Clayton interview.

8   Thornton Patberg, telephone interview by author, January 29, 2011.

9   Hugh Ahlering, telephone interview by author, March 11, 2011.

10   Clayton interview.

11   Clyde Cox, telephone interview by author, April 5, 2011.

12   Clayton interview.

13   Smallins interview.

14   Smallins interview.

15   Clayton interview.
16   Smallins interview.
17   Cox interview.
18   Smallins interview.
19   Clyde Cox, telephone interview by author, April 5,2011.
20   Clayton interview.
21   Clayton interview.

Promise Unkept, 1955–1956

In the mid-1950s Mac and Virginia moved the family a few blocks to a house they had purchased on South Boeke Road; like the place on East Chandler, it was close to both the stadium and the campus.

"It was a small two-bedroom home that someone had left, and Dad bought it for a song," his daughter Marilyn recalled.

Mac added a bedroom and bath to the unfinished upstairs and did all the work, except the plumbing, himself. Then he converted a room that had been used for coal storage for a purpose peculiar to the 1950s. "He made it into a bomb shelter," Marilyn said. "It had thick concrete walls and floor and was below ground level, so Dad thought it would be perfect for us."[1]

In Evansville and throughout the nation the mid-1950s were tension-filled and often chaotic times. Two former World War II allies squared off in the Cold War, which through their proxies, North and South Korea, soon became the Korean War and dominated the early years of the decade. The Soviets, allegedly through the efforts of Julius and Ethel Rosenberg, obtained the coveted secret to the atomic bomb that had reduced Hiroshima and Nagasaki to radioactive rubble and ended World War II.

Once the Russians had the key to the atomic bomb, they became increasingly emboldened and belligerent toward the West. Americans and Soviets weren't shooting bullets at or dropping bombs on each other, but they were playing a game of brinksmanship and using other countries as their pawns.

In the United States the fear engendered by the Cold War and the threat of nuclear annihilation led to educating schoolchildren about the need to "duck and cover" to protect themselves from the effects of radiation in the event of nuclear attack by the Russians. Yellow-and-black signs posted on the sides of most large buildings in every city and town provided directions to the fallout shelters designated by civil defense authorities as safe refuge. Stocked with government-issued rations and water, they were a constant reminder to people of the tension that pervaded their daily lives. Evansvillians knew that tension, too.

In January John Collins, head of the Evansville Civil Defense Department, announced plans to evacuate an entire section of the city in the spring in a drill to test the routes designated for evacuation in case of an attack.[2] Later that month the city council asked that Nike missiles be installed in a ring around the city as protection against any incoming missiles or bombers.

But in many other respects, Evansville plugged along as usual. In mid-July 1957 workers at the local Plymouth plants staged wildcat work stoppages after three employees in the body trim department were fired, and the company, playing hardball, sent 3,500 workers home.[3]

Jim Smallins's recollections about the fairly early desegregation of Evansville's schools notwithstanding, a federal judge was still overseeing desegregation of the city's schools in 1972. In reprimanding Evansville for its slowness to change, U.S. District Judge S. Hugh Dillin noted that in 1949 Indiana had passed legislation mandating desegregation of the schools and providing a twelve-year window in which to accomplish it. "The message," the judge noted drily, "did not reach this community as rapidly as anticipated."[4] Perhaps that should not have been surprising, given Evansville's past embracing of the Ku Klux Klan.

The city was also busily engaged in "slum clearance." The Evansville Redevelopment Commission hired a local realtor as its executive secretary in 1954 and charged him with acquiring twenty-three blocks in the Louisville and Nashville Railroad (L&N) area for "slum clearance and industrial development." Among the new director's responsibilities was seeing to the relocation of all residents dislocated by the program and then selling the property, "after it has been cleared, to private interests for industrial development." He declared: "This is an opportunity to make an industrial area out of what is now an eyesore."[5]

The city not only wanted to gussy itself up and market itself to industry, it wanted to grow bigger, and it began to study three areas it had identified as prime candidates for annexation, one of which was the L&N Yards. Annexation was part of the city's push to lure new industries to Evansville and find a way to keep existing industries from relocating to areas with lower taxes. The L&N area, according to the city's planning commission, would add about a million dollars of assessed valuation to Evansville's tax rolls "and that would make more revenue available without raising taxes."

By 1959 the annexations were largely accomplished. The city council annexed nearly sixteen square miles and 25,000 residents in several areas as of December 1, 1959, but one area, the L&N Yards, would not become part of the city until December 1, 1963.

With his family settled in the new house and secure in the knowledge that they were prepared for any eventuality, Mac got ready for the 1955–56 season. Barring a Russian bomb, he had every reason to believe the season would bring a third straight conference crown to the Aces.

Evansville fans had several reasons to be excited, not least the imminent opening of the new municipal stadium that Mayor Henry O. "Hank" Roberts had gotten built through sheer force of will. Along with other uses it would be the home court of the Purple Aces.

The energetic mayor had spearheaded a drive to finance and construct a new $2 million stadium despite opposition from political opponents, who labeled the stadium "Hank's folly" and "Hank's tank." Roberts brushed the criticism aside and told everyone a new stadium would put Evansville sports on the map. Construction of the new facility was underway as the Aces prepared for their final season at the armory.[6]

Virtually every fan of Aces basketball saw the new stadium, which would hold 7,400 fans, as a major step forward—too many had continually been frustrated in their efforts to see the Aces play in person. But the old armory, while cramped, had been a hospitable home for the Aces during Mac's tenure.[7] Mac's teams had managed to compile an impressive 64–30 record in the aging facility, including a perfect 12–0 record in 1954–55.

Fans also were excited by the strength of their basketball team. Four of Mac's starters had returned, and Smallins had recovered from an operation on his balky knee. Mac had once again fished the local talent pool of Evansville high school players and had added yet another transfer, Harry Osterman, a junior who had played sparingly at Notre Dame before leaving for two years in the Army during the Korean conflict. He had enrolled in the fall of 1954 and was eligible for play as the 1955–56 season began.

Evansville fans, of course, knew all about the talented local players from their high school days. They knew too that Mac was grooming Osterman to replace Bivin. They paid no attention at all to Hugh Ahlering, a 23-year-old veteran who had attended Bosse High School but never played high school basketball. "I was only about 5-6 and had a heart murmur and was just too small to play basketball, though I did play baseball there," he said.

After high school and a growth spurt he had taken a job at National City Bank, then served two years in the Army. After he was discharged, he rejoined the bank for a year.

"I had been playing independent basketball in the area for a year or so when Bob Hodges, brother of Brooklyn Dodgers star Gil Hodges, suggested I try to 'walk on' at Evansville. Because Hodges told me that Mac never cut anyone who came out, I decided to use my GI Bill benefits and enrolled," Ahlering recalled.[8]

Mac's veteran squad began the 1955–56 season on the road against the Pumas of St. Joseph's College in Collegeville, Indiana. With Smallins at center, returnees Clayton and Harrawood playing forward, and Walker and Healy as guards, the season began in a most uncharacteristic fashion. Mac, who had not lost an opening game since the 1947–48 season, saw the Aces drop this one 75–73 on a last-second tip-in by Pumas center Dan Fenker.

He had used only six players in the game, and the one substitute he called on did respond. After Smallins had a unproductive first half, Mac had sent in back-up Clyde Cox, who had battled Jim for the starting role in preseason games. Cox poured in a career-high 27 points in relief and was the one bright spot in an otherwise dismal start to the season.

Based on his play, Clyde Cox started at center against Louisville in the Aces' next outing in front of a crowd of 3,026 at the Jefferson County Armory. The Cardinals had an All- American center, 6-8 Charlie "The Moose" Tyra, who led a towering team that Mac described as "the strongest team Evansville College has faced since I've been coach."

But Tyra was unable to match Clayton's swift moves, and the speedy sophomore scored 24 points. Most of Clayton's shots came from beyond the present-day three-point line. However, his performance wasn't enough, and the Aces were crushed by their hosts, 98–81.[9]

Dan Scism, a vocal proponent of the new arena, told readers of the *Courier* the next day, that, unless the college upped the number and value of its basketball scholarships, the Aces' scores would be no more bedazzling in their new home:

"This score can be repeated each year . . . until . . . Evansville College has the wherewithal to recruit a few 6'6" prep cagers, one 6'8" and others of lesser height who are outstanding as ball handlers and deadly on outside shooting."[10]

Scism's criticism appeared to be dead-on when the Aces dropped their third game in a row against DePauw (81–75) in a conference game that put Evansville's conference record at 0–2.

"My team played wretched in the last quarter," Mac told reporters after the Aces saw a 16-point lead evaporate.

Winless in three starts on the road, the Aces returned to the armory to open their final season there against Valparaiso. Valpo, another tall team, was 2–4 when it took the court against Evansville and used a zone defense to encourage Evansville's long-range bombers to try to shoot over Valpo.

The move backfired when Clayton and John Harrawood combined for 41 points from outside, vanquishing the Crusaders by 87–71 and giving the Aces their first win before a crowd of 1,700.

"I always loved to play against the zone," Harrawood told reporters.

Attendance was nearly as high (1,600) for the game against NAIA foe Atlantic Christian the following night when Evansville's potent duo of Harrawood and Clayton again scored 41 points to win, 111–88. Senior guard Frank Healy, whom reporter Bill Robertson called "the nearest thing to perpetual motion that local basketball has ever seen," added 10 points and hounded the visitors on defense.

The Aces, now 2–3, traveled to the Third Annual All-America City Tournament in Owensboro, where they would face major college opponents.

But in Kentucky Jim Smallins and the other Aces ran up against an even more formidable opponent: Jim Crow.

"We were going to have our pregame meal in a restaurant, all together," Smallins said. "When we got to the front door, Clyde stopped and looked around inside. There were all white faces in there. He turned to me and said, 'If anybody asks, you're an American Indian.' After we had finished our meal without any problem, we got up to leave. As we headed to the door, there were three white, older men, standing in the doorway looking at me. I stopped, and the oldest one looked at me and said, 'Know what, nigger? You handled yourself pretty well in there. You can come back here anytime.'

"There were a few incidents like that on the road. But I never let them bother me. I feel like they made me a stronger person," Smallins says. "And on our campus, I never experienced any bias at all."[11]

In the opening round of the All-America City Tournament, the Aces easily turned back Hardin-Simmons 79–56, setting up a meeting with coach Johnny Mauer's Florida Gators. Mauer had preceded Adolph Rupp at Kentucky and had made coaching stops at Miami of Ohio, Tennessee, and Army before taking the Florida position in 1951. Now in his twenty-eighth season as a coach, he had compiled an impressive cumulative mark of 300–211, including 53 wins in 93 outings with the Gators, who were 5–0 for the season.

Mauer's squad—"big, shifty and good," according to reporter Dick Anderson—held a 42–40 edge at the half in front of 5,000 Sportscenter fans. Clayton started slowly while Harrawood kept the Aces within striking distance with 17 points, 13 of them on free-throws.

On press row Evansville College's new director of athletic operations, Bob Hudson, told writers, "We're ready. We're in the right frame of mind. We're going to get them." The optimistic Hudson had joined the college after a varied career in other endeavors: grocery store clerk during the Depression and delivery driver for Coca-Cola Bottling in the Evansville area. He loved sports and served as a referee for basketball and football in the area, as well as Big Ten football contests, and quickly made friends wherever he went. "He was a big, blue-eyed, teddy bear," his sister, Patti Hudson Kishline, said. "He knew everybody in Evansville."

Through his referee work he had gotten to know people at the college. When administrators recognized that they would need someone to manage marketing, publicity, and ticket sales once the new stadium was built, they hired Bob to do all those jobs.[12]

Bob Hudson brought with him countless relationships from his work at Coca-Cola and the many refereeing jobs he had in the area. For Evansville College those contacts would pay large dividends, and no one much cared that he didn't have a college degree. Bob was a graduate of the world of business and business relationships, and that curriculum vitae would prove more valuable than any sheepskin.

Hudson's optimistic analysis for the press proved to be correct when the Aces returned from the second half against Florida with a 13–0 run that put them up by 53–42, a lead they never lost. The final score: 85–69.

While promoters of the tournament had hoped to see Evansville face off against host Kentucky Wesleyan in the final, the meeting of local rivals was not to be. The Panthers fell to Washington and Lee, setting up a New Year's Eve finale that featured Evansville against the upstart Generals.

Despite the absence of the host team, 4,000 fans showed up in a celebratory mood to see Evansville take on its third straight major college foe. Led by senior guard Bob Walker, who began the second half with three straight buckets, the Aces defeated the Generals 86–69. Walker, Clayton, Harrawood, and Healy were named to the All-Tournament team.

Walker and Healy, the two senior guards, were not gaining the clippings that Clayton, Harrawood, and Clyde Cox were, but their leadership was an integral part of the Aces' success. After the heralded sophomore Harold Cox injured his wrist in December, putting him out for the year, Walker and Healy started and played nearly every minute of every game.

When the Aces met Indiana State in the first contest of the new year, Walker faced his former teammate from Central High, Wayne Salmon, who accounted for 21 points. But that wasn't enough—the Aces posted a road win of 94–90, with Harrawood scoring 31 points to pace the winners. His total output included 13 free throws in a row, putting his string at 27 without a miss.

When reporters asked him to explain his success, the 6-2 junior said, "No secrets, I just flip them in."

Maybe he was too flip about it, because just two nights later his free-throw streak ended in Muncie. Ball State had battled the Aces to the wire, and the game ended with a tied score, as did the first overtime period. In the second overtime, when Harrawood finally missed a foul shot, the Aces managed to escape with a 96–95 win.

Their winning streak stood now at seven in a row as they headed back to a sold-out armory to face Kentucky Wesleyan, the last team to beat them in Evansville. The Panthers arrived at the armory with a veteran squad and a 10–1 record.

In a game that reporter Dan Scism later described as one in which neither team played as though it could beat another, the visitors were whistled for 26 fouls, sending three starters to the bench and paving the way for an ugly 96–81 win by Evansville.

The Aces were the recipients of friendly whistles that had them marching to the foul line 45 times. Together Clayton and Harrawood converted on 26 of 29 attempts.

Mac had earned his 123rd win and told reporters afterward, "I don't try to change my boys' style of shooting free-throws. I make them hit six every day. Not just six now and then, but six in a row. I figure all of them should be able to put that many together."

The Aces' prowess at the free-throw line once again proved invaluable as they topped Butler on the Bulldogs' home court 82–77. This time Healy held Butler star Bobby Plump in check as the Aces fought back from 10 points down to tie the game and send it into overtime. With Harrawood and Healy scoring 20 apiece, and the Aces outscoring Butler at the foul line 18–11, Evansville managed to escape Indianapolis with another hard-fought win.

Clayton was held to 13 points, his lowest total since the first game of the year. "They really worked Jerry over," Mac told the press. The Butler crowd of 4,500 had repeatedly booed Clayton, who got into a brief fight with center Hank Foster late in the game.

The win gave the Aces a 4–2 mark in conference play, and they had improved to 9–3 overall after the shaky start.

Back at the armory they faced Ball State with a chance to set a school record of ten straight wins. With a capacity crowd of 2,700 in attendance, the Aces struggled in the first half and finished tied with the visitors at 47. Midway through the second half a 17–2 run put the Aces in command, securing their tenth straight win, 96–81.

The win came at a cost: Clayton sprained an ankle, but Clyde Cox picked up the slack and accounted for 26 points. "He has one of the greatest pair of hands I've seen in years," observer Gus Doerner said of Cox. "He's an alert and heady player. I think he should shoot more often when wide open and within the hitting zone."

Cox, aka the "Kokomo Komet," played up to his nickname in the next game against Valparaiso. Making his first six shots without a miss for 15 points in the first half, Cox led the charge as Evansville built a 59–46 lead and coasted to an 82–74 win.

Assessing his team's performance after the Aces' eleventh straight win, Mac told reporters his players had "passed the ball beautifully. I just hope they stay as sharp for Butler."

Another full house of 2,700 gathered for the Bulldogs' visit. "I had calls coming from all around these past few days," Bob Hudson told reporters. "It's too bad the stadium isn't ready—we could have filled it."

Butler was 7–7 for the season but had managed wins over both Wisconsin and Michigan of the Big Ten and, of course, had brought along Bobby Plump. The sophomore guard, unfazed by the overflow crowd, made 7-for-11 from the field, although he was hounded by Frank Healy throughout. Despite Plump's performance, Hinkle's crew fell to the Aces, 93–77. Clayton, obviously feeling better, had combined with Harrawood for 52 points to pace the Aces.

The next day reporter Dick Anderson told readers that "Hinkle had thrown the book at the Aces and it didn't have enough pages."

Despite the inauspicious season start of 0–3, the Aces had rebounded with twelve straight wins to take the conference lead. With six of their remaining conference games at home, the Aces were well positioned to secure another NAIA appearance.

Harrawood was averaging 20 points and Clayton, drawing more attention from opposing players after his sensational debut the previous season, was still able to average more than 19. Clyde Cox, "who moves with the effortless grace of a gazelle," gushed reporter Bill Robertson, was adding 16 points per game. Frank Healy contributed his defensive skills, prompting the ever-extravagant Scism to declare that the guard had "threatened to draw a life sentence for thievery." Both Bob Walker and Jim Smallins had been steady; reporter Bill Fluty remarked that Jim had "regained the form that boosted him into a prominent spot during the 1954–55 season."

Indeed, things looked so bright at this point that Scism, never one to restrain himself, predicted that "the Aces seem ready to move into the cage company that will give them national recognition."

If only their luck had held. On a Saturday in early February, Harrawood, a team leader who had paced the Aces during their string of wins, was admitted to Deaconess Hospital with abdominal pains. The next day he was rushed into surgery with a burst appendix that was causing intense pain and threatening his life. He recovered, but he was out for the rest of the season. "You can't lose a player like Harrawood without hurting yourself," Mac said, stating the obvious.

Nonetheless, the Aces turned back St. Joseph's and Regis. But then came their next meeting with Kentucky Wesleyan, a more formidable foe, and Harrawood's absence was all too apparent. The nearly 2,000 Evansville fans who had made the trek across the Ohio watched as Bullet Wilson's Panthers took advantage of the Aces' diminished firepower to avenge the Panthers' earlier loss at the armory. They convincingly snapped the Aces' 14-game winning streak, 98–79.

The Aces had incurred thirty-two personal fouls, which meant all five starters, including Bob Wessel, who was subbing for the absent Harrawood, were benched. "My boys weren't ready for a top notch effort," Mac complained. "Their mental attitude wasn't good. They heard so much about getting a bad [unfair] whistle that they expected it."

The performance of 23-year-old transfer Harry Osterman was the only bright spot in an otherwise dismal effort. He managed 18 points in only his tenth game.

Crossing the Ohio to return to the friendlier confines of the armory with Harrawood at courtside in a wheelchair, the Aces clinched at least a share of the ICC title at home as they defeated Indiana State 80–73.

But the win was marred by more bad news. The morning of the Aces' next game, against Beloit, Dan Scism told *Courier* readers, "Unless a miracle happens, Jerry Clayton will wind up his basketball career soon at Evansville College. The gifted 6'7" sophomore forward has gotten his scholastic business in bad shape. . . . One person close to the situation said Clayton had lost so much ground recently in the classroom that his case seems hopeless."

Clayton's performance off the court had Mac so concerned that he told reporters, "I'm counting on Jim Smallins, Bob Wessel, Clyde Cox, Frank Healy, and Bob Walker as my starting five, with Osterman as my sixth man."

When the 15–4 Aces took the court against Beloit before yet another sold-out crowd at the armory, no. 2, Clayton, was in the lineup. But Beloit managed an uninterrupted 18-point run that left the Aces trailing 40–28 at the half.

"Mac got on us for our performance in the first half. He reamed all of us out pretty good. [Clayton] had been one of the targets of Mac's wrath. He'd launched a few bad shots from the bleachers and, I guess, Jerry felt it was aimed at him personally," Clyde Cox recalls, adding, "Jerry had a pretty bad temper."[13]

Actually, the talented but troubled Clayton says he had been "thinking about quitting for several games. I was failing my classes and not doing what I was supposed to be doing. It had nothing to do with Mac. He had tried everything and even got me a tutor. It wasn't him, it was me. I had been cutting classes and drinking, and I just lost interest. I'd been looking for the right opportunity to quit for a few games and just felt that this was the right time to do it."

Jim Smallins recalls it somewhat differently.

"Mac had put me in to replace Clayton in the first half. When we came out of the locker room and Coach Mac announced that I was starting instead of Clayton, he exploded: 'No way you're starting Smallins over me!'"

What actually happened is not certain. What is not in doubt is that Clayton was gone.

"I quit," he announced to the stunned team, tore off his uniform, grabbed his clothes, and left.

He was a gifted athlete, only 19 years old, who had seen his lack of academic achievement splashed across the local sports pages even as he was being praised to the heavens for his court skills. He had had enough.

"I guess I was just confused," he said years later. Clayton, who would go on to attend Houston, added that being so tall "was weird back then. I guess I just couldn't handle the attention any more."[14]

Once at Houston he was forced to sit out a year. The idleness soon led to the same pattern his academic career had followed at Evansville. "I got to drinking and stuff and didn't pay much attention to my classes."

Asked years later about the choices he had made as a teenager, Clayton said, "I made a lot of mistakes when I was young. Looking back, I wouldn't do it that way again. But you can't go back and do it over. I do tell my grandchildren, though, that they need to get an education."[15]

Without Clayton the Aces lost to Beloit, 76–68.

"We really wanted to win that game to show him that we could do it without him," Clyde Cox said.[16]

Despite the loss to Beloit, Valparaiso's defeat by DePauw gave the Aces the ICC crown outright because they had the better conference record.

The championship was one thing, but the Aces' loss of first Harrawood and now Clayton left a huge hole in the lineup. In January Mac had told reporters, "I wouldn't trade my two forwards for any two in the country." Now, he was without both. Clayton and Harrawood had accounted for nearly 40 percent of the Aces' offense.

Clayton left Evansville as the seventh-leading scorer in Aces history after less than two seasons. He had averaged more than 18 points per game, scoring 841 points as an underclassman, the most ever for an Evansville player in his first two seasons. More important, he had led or shared top-scoring honors 21 times, and Evansville had enjoyed a 19–2 record in those contests.

Mac turned to Clyde Cox, shifting him from center to forward, and moved his roommate, Jim Smallins, into the pivot position. While Cox immediately justified Mac's confidence in him by pouring in 28 points in the very next game, Evansville still lost its second straight home game to Anderson, 99–91.

Next up was DePauw. It would be the last home game for seniors Frank Healy and Bob Walker and the final contest for the Aces in the armory, their friendly home since 1939. More than 2,200 showed up to see Healy and Walker off.

The visitors seemed determined to mar the send-off until Jim Smallins got in the flow of the game. He controlled the backboards, and he and Wessel and Cox accounted for 66 points as the Aces clinched their last game at the armory 97–86.

Although it was dark, cold, antiquated, and way too small, the armory had nonetheless been a hospitable abode for the Aces since they left the Coliseum. They had managed a record of 125–47 there, including a 9–2 record in 1955–56. In short, fans had learned that when the Aces played at home, chances were good that they'd win, and that in turn had propelled the need for new quarters. The Aces could only hope that their new home would be as accommodating as their former residence had proved to be.

With the regular 1955–56 season over, the revamped Aces, sporting a 16–6 record and a conference crown, journeyed to Indianapolis for the NAIA District 21 play-offs. Their first round foe was Indiana Central College, which featured an offense led by a Crispus Attucks High School graduate named Bailey Robertson, who held the Indiana collegiate scoring mark for a single season with 664 in twenty-six games (an average of 25.5 points) for the 21–5 Greyhounds.

The Aces took a first half lead of 55–51 that they built to 59–51, and Robertson responded. Pouring in 16 of his team's next 22 points Robertson led the surge that put Indiana Central into a 73-point tie with Evansville. (Later in his career Robertson would be overshadowed by his younger brother, Oscar.)

Clyde Cox remembers that, "before the game, Coach McCutchan had taken me aside and told me that they had a great scorer on their team who shoots from the outside, and he wanted me to guard him. He told me he thought I might be able to hold him down. When the game started, and Robertson started taking shots from way out beyond what would be the three-point line today, I remember thinking, 'He can't possibly hit this.'"[17]

Clyde was wrong. Robertson continued to blaze away. Robertson and teammate Dick Nyers would not miss a free-throw down the stretch as Indiana Central made 35 of 42 attempts (21 more than Evansville) on their way to a 105–102 win. "We tried to run with them, but they got us in the end," Clyde said.

Bill Robertson told readers the next day, "The 102 points which Evansville poured in against Indiana Central's uninhibited and adventurous Greyhounds not only would have won every other game the Aces played this season but, in fact, would have won every basketball game ever played by an Evansville College team in the past 35 years."

The loss of Harrawood and Clayton was simply too much to overcome.

The loss to Indiana Central also marked the end of Arad McCutchan's first decade as coach and associate professor at Evansville. Since 1946 Mac had won 131 of 256 games. While the start had been rough at times, the Aces had ended his first decade with three straight conference titles or co-titles, and Mac had been named Coach of the Year or shared the honor for the past three seasons.

Ten seasons after his arrival amid talk about a new arena, the long-delayed plans were about to become a reality. A new era of Aces basketball was just months away.

(Endnotes)

1   Marilyn McCutchan Disman, telephone interview by author, February 22, 2011.

2   Bill Greer," We'll Evacuate Entire Sections of City in Coming Civil Defense Tests," *Evansville Courier,* January16, 1955, 1. I am indebted to Clyde Cox, who generously lent me the scrapbooks he kept in college. They are rather more complete than such scrapbooks usually are, which is why the notes in this chapter are more detailed than elsewhere.

3   "Plymouth Plants Here Closed Again," *Evansville Press,* July 15, 1957.

4   "Time to Abide by Law, Says Judge Dillin," *Evansville Press,* August 12, 1972.

5   "Realtor to Direct Slum Clearance," *Evansville Press,* May 6, 1954.

6   Ron Eaton, *Local Legends: The Stories behind the Headlines* (Evansville, Ind.: M.T. Publishing, 2008), 100.

7   Eaton, *Local Legends,* 100. Municipal Stadium (later renamed Roberts Stadium in honor of the mayor) would eventually be enlarged several times to hold as many as 11,600.

8   Hugh Ahlering, telephone interview by author, February 11, 2011.

9   Ahlering interview.

10 The indispensable source for the story of Evansville and the Aces, like most sports stories, is the daily newspaper, in this case the *Evansville Courier, Press,* and combined Sunday edition, the *Courier & Press.* But not all the papers are readily available on microfiche or electronically, so the primary repository of Aces stories is the collection of bound scrapbooks kept by

Bob Hudson and now housed in the university archives. Bill Bussing generously made his lengthy manuscript history of the Aces available to me, and I have relied on it for some information, especially in the early years of the McCutchan era and in determining attendance figures. Bussing used Hudson's scrapbooks, as did I and my research assistant. What we all found was that they were often—but not always—missing much identifying information: the byline, name of the paper, the date the story ran, even the headline. We also all found that as we became familiar with the sports reporters' style, employers, and the papers' typography, we often could figure out who wrote what. I have supplied what information I have. In this case, I know that Scism wrote the story and that he worked for *Courier*, but I have neither the headline nor the date the story ran. The reader may assume that quotes and information used, when attributed to no other source, come from either the scrapbooks or the Bussing manuscript—and originally from the *Courier*, *Press, or Sunday Courier & Press.*

11   Jim Smallins, telephone interview by author, April 8, 2011.
12   Patti Hudson Kishline, telephone interview by author, March 3, 2011.
13   Clyde Cox, telephone interview by author, April 4, 2011.
14   Jerry Clayton, telephone interview by author, April 6, 2011.
15   Clayton interview. He later sobered up and is doing fine today.
16   Clyde Cox interview.
17   Clyde Cox interview.

A New Home, 1956

Throughout most of the midwestern United States, residents annually enjoy, or suffer through, four predictable seasons. But Evansville had only two: basketball season and waiting for basketball season to begin.

The 1956-57 season was easily the most anticipated in the history of Evansville basketball. With the official opening of Roberts Stadium (named after the mayor who had spearheaded the drive to get it built) in December 1956, the shining new home of the Purple Aces became the social center of the city. Basketball, always big in Evansville, was about to get even bigger.

Excavation for the new home of the Purple Aces had taken most of a year, and progress had been monitored on a daily basis by curious residents as the massive hole that would contain the stadium was being dug and footings poured. (*Stadium* is a bit of a misnomer, evoking as it does, outdoor spaces such as those devoted to football and baseball. Roberts is in fact an indoor facility, a smaller version of Madison Square Garden or the Verizon Center in Washington, D.C.)

"My dad took us down there almost every day to watch the 'big hole in the ground' grow deeper and deeper as the building progressed," said Jon Siau, who was seven at the time. "It was built almost entirely underground. The only part that you can see above ground is a wall about ten feet high and the roof."[1]

Easily reachable from anywhere in town, the stadium is right off Route 41, not many blocks from the campus, and has a huge paved parking area.

Roberts was to be used for multiple functions: concerts, trade shows, and conventions in addition to basketball. Through the years it would host annual visits from the Harlem Globetrotters, Ice Capades, and the Shrine Circus. Eventually, even NBA teams would play exhibition games on the Aces' home court. Through the years Roberts would also host appearances by leading politicians and entertainers. Ronald Reagan, Gerald Ford, and John F. Kennedy all appeared there. So did Frank Sinatra, Willie Nelson, and Elvis Presley.

But all that was in the future. In 1956, as contractors put the finishing touches on the stadium, the whole town was excited that the Evansville College Purple Aces would be playing there. Those who had long waited to see their team play and couldn't get tickets would now be able to—in a spacious new facility that had no obstructions to block the view of the court.

Seats rose high and steep. The more expensive seats on the lower levels were chairs with backs ($1.50 a ticket); higher up were bench-like bleacher seats ($1.25). No matter where you sat, the steeply angled seats made you feel like you were right on top of the court.

The phrase "packed to the rafters" is usually hyperbolic, but at Roberts it was an accurate description of a big crowd. The uppermost bleacher seats were so close to the ceiling rafters, you could nearly touch them.

The new stadium also meant more work for the college's new athletic business manager, Bob Hudson. "He asked my mom to come in and help in the office," their daughter, Joan Hudson Roth, recalled.

When Bob approached the NCAA about playing its inaugural College Division championship at the new arena in 1957, the organization, aware of Evansville's strong fan base, readily agreed.

Hudson added management of that event to his growing list of duties. He was, in turn, ticket manager, publicist, and promoter. "Our lives revolved around basketball," Roth said. "When it came time to mail the tickets to season-ticket holders, if there were too many to be mailed with a single stamp, he would ask me to deliver them in person to save the school money."[2]

Hudson told George Klinger, author of a history of the college, "My day begins at 6:00 a.m. I can get more done between six and eight than I can the rest of the day."[3]

Despite no background or degree in public relations, Hudson proved to be the consummate professional. What Colonel Tom Parker did for Elvis, Bob Hudson did for Aces basketball, in a kinder and gentler way. Aces basketball would become a passion for Hudson and would remain so for the rest of his life.[4]

He was also blessed with a creative streak. "He had life-sized cardboard cut-out figures of the players made and would convince people to put them in store windows and restaurants, even the theater lobby," Aces guard Harold Cox recalls.

One of Hudson's more popular ideas would lead to the ubiquity in Evansville of the Aces' promotional materials. "He had pictures of the team and their schedule printed up. He got almost every restaurant and tavern to use them as place mats," Bob's sister, Patti Kishline, recalled. "You couldn't go anywhere in town to eat and not see a reminder of the Aces."[5]

As the opening of that first season in Roberts Stadium drew closer, Evansville's social set adopted a new rule to which it would adhere for more than two decades. "No one planned a social event that would conflict with an Aces game. If they did, no one would show up. The Aces game became *the* place to be. It was a giant social event. Women dressed in heels and their best dresses. Men wore suits and ties. If you wanted to see someone you hadn't seen in a while, you knew you would always find them at the Aces' games," Kishline said.[6]

For years the Aces had been regular participants in the All-American City Holiday Tournament, hosted by Owensboro, Kentucky. Now the Aces would host their own holiday event.

Hudson conceived of the tournament and worked diligently to attract high-caliber teams to attend the two-day event near Christmas. He could offer the invitees much more in guaranteed appearance money than Owensboro, and the Evansville Holiday Tournament would become a must-see event.

Hudson's canny promotion exploited the pent-up ticket demand that had developed as Mac's teams improved, and the schedule would bring high-profile teams to Roberts.

The opening contest was held on December 1, 1956, with the new venue dedicated with much fanfare in pregame ceremonies. Mayor Vance Hartke, a former Aces guard, welcomed a throng of 10,500 with the words "This is a beautiful building. Let's keep it that way."[7]

The ceremony acknowledged several local dignitaries who had worked to make the building a reality. Former Mayor Roberts, whose name now graced the edifice, was among those addressing the crowd.[8]

The Aces' first opponent in the facility was Purdue University. Purdue's was a familiar, if feared, name to the Evansville fans. The Boilermakers had finished the previous season at 16–6, third in the Big Ten Conference.

"Of the three big state schools, Purdue seemed to our coaching staff to be the more natural opponent since we knew (head coach) Ray Eddy, Mackey and some of the others up there," Hudson told reporters.[9]

Initially, Hudson had sought to bring in Indiana University to christen the stadium, but it had refused the offer.[10] Purdue's appearance would mark the first meeting between the two Indiana schools since 1928–29 and would not be the last. The large seating capacity of Roberts and the increasing eagerness of local fans to fill those seats meant that the Aces would now attract opponents that would have laughed at Hudson if he asked them to play at the old armory. The lure of Roberts Stadium and its large financial guarantees would entice many major college opponents through the McCutchan era. Most would take the money and leave with a loss.

With the move of the NCAA College Division Tournament to Evansville, coupled with the Evansville Holiday Tournament, Evansville finally achieved what it had craved for so many years—an identity.

Roberts Stadium would provide the Aces with something else that never could have happened at the armory. "With those seats filled with people cheering us on, it was like a shot of adrenaline whenever you came up court," Cox recalled.[11]

In basketball, home-court advantage is not a cliché. In the indoor arenas the roar of the fans rebounds off the ceiling and washes in, wave after wave, over the court and the players. The earsplitting noise both inspires the home team and intimidates many opponents who might be superior players but are cowed into submission by the partisan crowd. And make no mistake about it: referees, supposedly neutral in their decisions, are not unaffected by the emotion-charged atmosphere. Roberts Stadium, with its low ceiling sending down a deafening din, would prove its worth many times over for Mac and his Purple Aces.

"We loved playing in that stadium," Harold Cox said.[12]

(Endnotes)

1   Jon Siau, telephone interview by author, January 30, 2011.

2   Joan Hudson Roth, telephone interview by author, February 21, 2011.

3   George Klinger, *We Face the Future Unafraid: A Narrative History of the University of Evansville* (Evansville, Ind.: University of Evansville Press, 2003), 216.

4   Patti Hudson Kishline, telephone interview by author, March 3, 2011.

5   Patti Hudson Kishline, telephone interview by author, March 6, 2011.

6   Kishline interview.

7   Vance Hartke played for the Aces in the late 1930s and graduated in 1940. He served as mayor of Evansville from 1956 to 1958. During his term in office he integrated the city's public swimming pools. A Democrat, Hartke was thirty-nine when he was elected to the U.S. Senate in 1958 and served there until 1977. See bioguide.congress.gov.

8   For this information, and other information in this chapter that is attributed to no other source, the reader may assume that it comes from articles in the *Evansville Courier* and *Evansville Press,* the two local papers at the time. Those articles may be found in the collection of bound scrapbooks kept by Bob Hudson and now housed in the university archives and/or Bill Bussing's manuscript history of the Aces. Bill Bussing graciously made his lengthy manuscript available to me, and I have relied on it for some information, especially in the early years of the McCutchan era and in determining attendance figures. The detailed manuscript contains no footnotes, but when I interviewed Bussing in February 2011, he identified his sources as the *Evansville Courier, Evansville Press,* and the combined Sunday edition, the *Courier & Press.* Bussing's manuscript usually makes no distinction between the papers, but the direct quotes are from one daily or the other or the Sunday combined paper and appear in the Bussing manuscript in quotation marks. Bussing used Hudson's scrapbooks, as did I and my research assistant. Many of the articles do not identify which paper they are from, much less the date and page, but I (and Bussing) assume they are from the *Courier, Press,* or *Sunday Courier & Press.*

9   Don Bartlett, "Evansville College Cagers to Host Purdue Saturday at Municipal Stadium," *Evansville Press,* November 30, 1956, Harold Cox scrapbook..

10   Kishline interview.

11   Harold Cox, telephone interview by author, April 6, 2011.

12   Cox interview.

The 1939–40 team plays against Franklin College.

A Glimpse of Things to Come, 1956–1957

The Purdue University Boilermakers of 1956–57 would prove to be rude guests. The team came into Roberts Stadium for the Aces' home opener with 6-6 Lamar Lundy at center and 5-7 guard Joe Campbell as its leading returnees. Purdue's other three starters were sophomores. "We may be a little green," coach Ray Eddy warned reporters.[1]

The capacity crowd got its money's worth, if not the result it wanted. Purdue escaped Roberts with a 62–60 win on a Lundy bucket with just four seconds remaining, spoiling the Aces' debut in their new home.[2]

"What I remember most about that game was that I was never hit so hard as when Lundy blocked me out in the lane," Jim Smallins said of his encounter with the massive Lundy. "I fell and slid way across the floor. When I looked up, he was still standing right there. He never moved an inch."[3]

"We were lucky," Eddy told reporters. "I was glad to get out of that one." He also got out of town with a check for $5,000.[4]

Mac used only one substitute during the game, and since the Indiana Collegiate Conference had ruled freshmen ineligible, his lineup consisted of the veterans John Harrawood and Clyde Cox as forwards and the 6-3 Smallins as center, along with sophomores Bob Wessel and Harold Cox as guards. As his first player off the bench Mac chose sophomore Hugh Ahlering, who would spell Wessel.

The Aces' first loss in a home opener since 1947–48 had Mac wondering whether he had made a mistake in conditioning his team. "We made a lot of mistakes against Purdue, but the big one was mine. The boys were dead tired at the finish, and that's what beat us," he told the press.[5] The inability to match the Boilermakers' height hadn't helped.

What fans wouldn't know for another year was that the solution to all Mac's problems was a freshman he had recruited in the off-season and who would remain ineligible to play for another year under the new NCAA rule.

"If I could have [had] that big freshman in there tonight, we'd have won by a dozen points," Mac moaned after the Purdue game.[6]

That big freshman was Ed Smallwood from Louisville, Kentucky. He had been a star at Louisville Central High School and a member of the Kentucky All-Star team that had played a two-game series against the Indiana All-Star team. Ed had shined brightest among the stars, yet neither the University of Louisville nor the University of Kentucky had tried to recruit him.

He was a great talent, but all that ability was encased in a 6-4 body that was the wrong color for schools below the Mason-Dixon line, no matter how good the player was—and Ed Smallwood was very, very good indeed.

Although he received a number of scholarship offers from Eastern schools and historically black schools in the South, the two major powers in his home state ignored him. This was only a year after Rosa Parks took a seat in the front of a bus in Montgomery, Alabama, and was arrested for not moving to the rear.

The blind prejudice of the Old South gave Mac an opportunity to recruit a talented youngster for the Aces whom the coach otherwise would not have had a chance of landing.

Mac welcomed Smallwood to Evansville in his own way. The coach called Bruce Lomax, a local booster, and asked him to set up a barbeque at his home to "welcome some Louisville boys," Mac later recounted.[7] Lomax had played basketball with Mac and now was a partner of Gus Doerner's in the sporting goods business. Just Smallwood and two other Louisville players were there; the whole idea was to make Smallwood feel welcome.

Ed had been raised by his maternal grandparents in a rough and rugged Louisville neighborhood where gangs roamed freely. The city itself was still solidly segregated in housing and education—and much else. Ed had no way of knowing what life in Evansville would be like. Mac used the relaxed dinner gathering to help assuage any fears Ed may have had about Evansville and its attitudes toward people of color.

"Racial prejudice was the only subject that I ever remember him being upset about at the dinner table," Mac's daughter Marilyn said of her usually calm father.[8]

Mac wasn't leading sit-ins, but he made his views known in subtle ways. "For years he would get a group of friends together, and they would attend the [all-black] Lincoln High School Thanksgiving Day football game," Marilyn said. "He did it to show his support for them."[9]

When Smallwood arrived on campus from Louisville that fall, he brought with him more baggage than was evident in the cheap suitcase he carried.

"I was a sophomore when Ed got here," Hugh Ahlering said. "I had a car, and Ed didn't and I offered to give him a ride someplace we were both headed soon after he got here.

"He accepted and got in the back seat of my old car. I asked him, 'What are you doing back there? Get up here in the front seat with me. 'No, I'll just stay on back here,' he told me."

"No matter how much I urged him to get up front with me, he refused and stayed in that back seat," Hugh recalled, choking as he told the story six decades later. It would be months before Ed finally felt comfortable enough in Evansville to join Hugh in the front seat.[10]

Life in Evansville, Indiana, in the 1950s and 60s, while decidedly different from the strictly segregated life Ed had endured in Kentucky, was still beset with the social attitudes of a state that once was one of the few strongholds of the Ku Klux Klan outside the Deep South.

Although Evansville was technically a northern town, conservative southern influences had long since crossed the Ohio River. The many southerners who had migrated there to seek higher wages and employment opportunities unavailable in the rural areas of Kentucky had brought with them the ingrained social attitudes of their old Kentucky homes.

Estella Moss moved to Evansville in 1942 when her father, a coal miner, developed health problems. She worked as a maid and a housekeeper, then took jobs in laundries. She joined the NAACP in the 1950s "because I felt that I could help the community. I saw injustices. More than once I walked away from a job because of the words the person used against me."

Gerald Arnold, a black pastor in Evansville who headed the local NAACP chapter for years in the 1960s, had come from Louisiana, where terrorizing blacks had been a popular sport. He remembered well the attitudes of people in Evansville in the 1950s and 1960s when blacks began to assert themselves publicly.

"Whites would come in [to a restaurant], see us, and leave. Back then, it only took one black to clean out a restaurant," he said.

Connie Clemmons, who had come to Evansville from New Jersey in 1952, suffered more than a little culture shock. "I wanted to go to eat at one of the restaurants downtown. I got told, 'Hey, no way,'" she said. "It was because of my color. I was shocked. From where I came from, you could eat at white places."[11]

Evansville experienced none of the violent confrontations that were commonplace in the South during the 1950s. In Evansville the barriers fell quietly as politicians moved to bring the community into compliance with federal law in the 1960s. Swimming pools were integrated, and restaurants served all comers. However, as noted earlier, school desegregation was overseen by a federal judge until 1972.

The Evansville to which Ed Smallwood would be moving was less than twenty-five years removed from the Klan's heyday in Indiana, but it was heading steadily, if somewhat slowly, toward complete desegregation and more enlightened attitudes. Certainly, it was a safer place to be black than Louisville was during Smallwood's college years.

Jim Smallins, who had been the first to cross the color barrier for basketball players at Evansville, soon found that Aces fans, like their coach, were color blind once a player donned an Aces uniform. The purple pants made him one of their own. They cheered him because of his talent and treated him well wherever he went.

Still, Ed Smallwood would be slow to appreciate the differences between Louisville and Evansville. "He spent a great deal of time in the black neighborhood," Jim Smallins recalled. "He didn't really go out of that area much at all."[12]

Although the Aces' season was off to a slow start, John Harrawood was now fully recovered from his appendectomy and back in form. Harrawood had tallied 23 in the loss to Purdue and did it again in a win over Central Missouri for the first Aces' win at the new stadium. He garnered 33 points when the Aces lost to Eastern Kentucky on the road, and he gained 24 points in a 71–62 win over New Mexico State.[13]

Clyde Cox was shooting well too, tallying 24 in a game against DePauw that the Aces lost, 74–85, on December 15 at Greencastle.[14] After their first five games the Aces stood at a disappointing 2–3. "But we were getting there," Harold Cox said.[15]

The crowds weren't as big as the one that had watched the Purdue opener, but they were a marked improvement over the number of spectators at the old armory. More than 4,000 were on hand when Hugh Ahlering came off the bench and scored 14 timely points to lead the Aces over previously unbeaten San Jose State, 81–73. Nearly that many watched as the Aces trounced Valparaiso 93–75 on its way to the Orange Bowl basketball tourney in Miami.[16]

"We have drawn 14,458 paying customers in our first five home games," Bob Hudson crowed. The previous season the Aces had managed to attract only 20,658 for the entire year.

Courier reporter Dan Scism was not as impressed with the numbers as Hudson was. "You'll see the day soon when no one will go just to see the new sports center. They will be drawn only by the quality of the entertainment scheduled," the sportswriter predicted.

As early as April, Hudson had promised Evansville fans that he would provide them with "the most attractive basketball schedule in its [Evansville College's] history." The city's first Holiday Tournament was proof that Hudson was going to make good on his promise.

He had convinced Denver University, Boston College, and Mississippi State to journey to Evansville and Roberts Stadium for the inaugural event just after Christmas 1956. More than 4,500 fans showed up in a holiday mood for the opening round doubleheader.

After sophomore Bailey Howell, a flashy guard, led Mississippi State to victory over the Denver Pioneers in the first game, the Aces met the Boston College Eagles in the nightcap.[17] The Aces added to the festive feeling of the evening as they easily dispatched the 4–4 Eagles, 96–76, with the 24-year-old Ahlering—whose advanced age had earned him the nickname "Old Man"—making his first start at guard. Smallins had 22 points for the game.

But as reporter Dick Anderson warned his readers the next morning, "Joy can turn to gloom in the wink of an eyelash."

And it did, because the South rose again.

When C. R. Noble, Mississippi State's athletic director, was informed that his team had played Denver when the Pioneers had two blacks on the team and that another black, Jim Smallins, was a member of the Aces, Noble ordered his coach, Babe McCarthy, to take the team home rather than face Smallins and the Aces.[18]

The news came at six o'clock on the night of the final game as the teams were having their pregame meal at the Vendome Hotel downtown. "We were all sitting there eating when the [Mississippi] coach got the call and told his players to get up and leave," Harold Cox said. "We were all shocked."[19]

As the Mississippi State players filed quickly out of the room, Bailey Howell stopped at Jim Smallins's table and said, "I'm sorry. I've never played against a black person and this was my first time. We really wanted to play you."[20]

"I believe he was being honest about it, and I accepted his apology," Smallins said.[21]

But Howell's sincere desire had been overruled by a system that was as old as the South itself. Ben Hilbun, the MSU president, huffed in a prepared statement, "We were led to believe that there were no Negroes in the tournament, that our policy would be respected. It is contrary to our policy to play against teams with Negro players on them. We have never done it before and we will never do it again as long as I can control it."

Hudson watched in disbelief as the MSU players hurried through the hotel lobby to their bus, shoes unlaced and clothes hanging from their gym bags. "I still have their check in my pocket," he told reporters of the $2,000 guarantee they left behind.

That's where it stayed.

The departure of the Aces' opponent and its ugliness left the tournament in disarray. Few could have been more shaken than Mac, who had dreamed of the Holiday Tournament for the new stadium and who hated racism with every fiber of his being. "His face was just ashen white," his daughter recalled. "He had to go and ask the other team [Denver], who had lost, to play us and ask the Boston College coach to play the consolation game against our jayvees."[22]

"Dad was never comfortable with segregation anywhere. He had a policy of not tolerating it," his son, Dr. Allen McCutchan, said. "He was forced to confront it and make decisions, and he took a stand."[23]

Somehow Mac managed to pull it off, and the tournament went on. Evansville's athletic director, Don Ping, promised refunds to any who wanted them but only thirty-one fans accepted his offer. Four thousand fans stayed for the two games.

The Aces Jayvees, cleverly named the Deuces, nearly upset the visitors from Beantown before losing 60–58.

The championship game would be even closer.

Dick Brott, Denver's star center, tipped in a miss with 40 seconds left to play to tie the Aces at 65. When Harrawood's jumper to win it missed, the game went to overtime.[24] The two teams played evenly, forcing a second overtime.

In the seesaw second overtime period the Pioneers grabbed a one-point lead with only four seconds to play. During a time-out Mac designed a play to get a clear shot for Harrawood off a screen. Instead Harrawood practically grabbed the ball from Ahlering's hands.[25]

Clyde Cox, having fouled out, had a front row seat for what happened. Harrawood was "right in front of our bench near the side line. I was sitting next to Coach McCutchan when John heaved an old-fashioned two-handed set shot right in front of me."

Mac grabbed his head with both hands in disbelief at the shot from way beyond the present day three-point line. "'Coach, it's gonna go in,' I told him. "And it did."[26]

Harrawood finished with a new school record of 36 points. The Aces had won on a play that would long be remembered at Roberts. Harrawood said later, "I could try that shot 50 more times and never make it."

Thanks to John Harrawood, the Holiday Tournament would be remembered for the sublime joy produced by the last-second shot, not for the racist ugliness of MSU.

The Aces next turned back Indiana State and then dropped a close game to DePauw, the conference leader, at home.[27]

The next two games, against Ball State and Butler, were both losses. Ball State recorded its first home win over Mac's squad in four years by blitzing the Aces with a combined 41 points from Wayne Van Sickle and Tom Dobbs, both all-conference forwards. "It was just disgusting," Mac told reporters. "We were as disorganized as a high school gym class."

Butler eked out an 89–87 win at its field house two nights later, but there was at least something redeeming about the loss.[28]

It was Hugh Ahlering's finest game thus far.

The feisty guard slashed and drove his way to the basket all night. "I went out there and stuck my hand up and the next thing I knew—zip, he's gone," said Bobby Plump. Plump would be the first in a long line of players who would be exasperated in their attempts to corral the Aces guard. "Hugh was very quick, especially his first step. He would just fly down the lane. If he didn't make the layup, he was fouled. If they fouled him, it was as good as points on the board. He was a great free-throw shooter," said Harold Cox, who had the other guard spot.[29]

Ahlering's 22 points nearly made up for an off night for Harrawood, but Hugh, Clyde Cox, and Harrawood ended up watching the game from the bench when all three fouled out. They, and the television audience tuned to WISH-TV, watched helplessly as Butler managed to pull out a two-point win. Plump again starred for the Bulldogs with 24 points, including 14-for-15 free throws.

Frank Wilson told *Indianapolis Star* readers that Ahlering had "done everything with the ball but knock the air out of it." Dan Scism, never one to mince words, told *Evansville Courier* readers the next day that "Butler should blush when it thinks of its victory," an obvious reference to the officiating.[30]

Freezing weather of 7 degrees, as well as the cold recent play of the Aces, kept the crowd down to 3,300 when Kentucky Wesleyan, which had won its own holiday tournament, visited Roberts. [31]

Harold Cox, recovered from a broken wrist that had sidelined him the previous season, was back in form and playing with his older brother, Clyde, which pleased both of them. Harold had planned to attend Purdue, but he accepted a scholarship to Evansville when another of Mac's recruits opted for Indiana University.

"The chance to play with my brother again was what made the decision easy for me," Harold said.[32] The two had starred at Kokomo High School and were now reunited for what was Clyde's senior season and Harold's sophomore campaign.

Harold's play coupled with the emergence of Ahlering provided the Aces with a potent backcourt that complemented their strong front line of Clyde Cox, Harrawood, and Smallins. The combination would prove to be successful as they slowly adjusted to each other. Eventually, they would prove to be a smooth offensive machine as well as a colorful one.

It was during this season that McCutchan decided his Purple Aces, who had been wearing orange uniforms on the road, would wear bathrobes as warm-up suits. "They were multicolored and all very bright sateen colors. He said it was to make it easier and quicker for substitutes to shed the robes than long-legged sweat pants and jackets," Clyde Cox recalled.[33]

To add to the kaleidoscope of colors at Roberts was a growing group of fans that had decided to show unity with the Purple Aces by dressing in, well, red. This habit had started when Mac had worn a pair of red socks to a game in the Holiday Tournament. After the Aces won, he kept doing it. Fans across the arena from the bench noticed the bright red socks and decided to start wearing red to the game, Marilyn McCutchan Disman said. "He had an entire dresser drawer filled with about two dozen pairs of red socks." [34]

The improbable idea of wearing red to support their Purple Aces, who were in multihued bathrobes themselves—sometimes over orange uniforms—didn't seem at all unusual to the fans. The crimson section of fans spread rapidly throughout the arena. In short measure a veritable sea of red would greet the players at each home game.

"They became known as the Red Army," Marilyn said. [35] With not a single known communist in the bunch, this horde of red wasn't to be feared—unless, of course, you were the visiting team.

The Aces started slowly in a game against Kentucky Wesleyan that Dan Scism characterized as one that would "determine the worst team."

Smallins, giving up three inches in height to Wesleyan's big men, nevertheless grabbed 18 rebounds and scored 17 points in the first half as the Aces held a 38–24 edge at the break. Kentucky Wesleyan fought back in the second half, but Evansville hung on to win, 67–64.

Smallins added another 13 rebounds to finish with 31, a school record, and Harold Cox chipped in with a career-high 18 points. [36] Harold's performance and the strong play of Hugh Ahlering led to their gaining starting assignments from Mac. The twosome would provide a spark to the Aces that would lead to a resurgence as the season wound down.

The Aces next dispatched Ball State behind Harrawood and Smallins by 103–96 and then turned back Eastern Kentucky by 91–87 with Smallins registering a career-high 29 points. When Butler visited in February, the Aces avenged their loss in Indianapolis with an 81–72 win. [37]

The newly energized Aces next turned back Beloit, 91–87, behind another 29-point performance by Smallins, who added 16 rebounds. It was their fifth straight win. [38] Heading to meet conference rivals St. Joseph's and Valparaiso, the Aces were now 4–4 in conference play.

"I fear them both," Mac told reporters before the road trip. "Especially St. Joseph's after they beat Butler by a point at Butler." [39]

He was right to be concerned. St. Joseph's turned back the streaking Aces 73–67, despite Harrawood's 36 points, as Ahlering and Harold Cox both fouled out. [40]

The Aces rebounded against Valpo 68–62, but the loss to St. Joseph's had seen their conference championship hopes all but disappear. [41]

The fans in Evansville were nevertheless buoyed by the Aces' improving play. Adding to the excitement was that the NCAA College Division Tournament would be held at Roberts Stadium. In Evansville hope was high that the host team would be playing in the postseason.

A win at the Kentucky State Fairgrounds over Bellarmine saw John Harrawood set a new Evansville scoring record of 1,357 points as the Aces romped 92–76.[42] Harrawood had become Evansville's all-time scoring leader.[43]

The Aces next easily dispatched Indiana State by 90–62.[44]

Sporting a 15–7 record, the Aces crossed the Ohio River to meet Kentucky Wesleyan at the Sportscenter before 3,500 fans. Harrawood and the Cox brothers led a second half charge that saw the Aces claw back to an 83–83 tie at the end of regulation play.

The overtime period also ended knotted as a Kentucky Wesleyan player's last-second desperation 45-footer fell short. The second extra period saw the Aces finally pull it out, led by Harrawood, who finished with a new school scoring mark of 42 points. John had managed 18 field goals, erasing Gus Doerner's record.

"He had great range and a quick release," Harold Cox said. "He would give the defender a quick jab set and then go up from the foul line extended." Harold's passes, along with those of Ahlering, led to countless Harrawood buckets.[45]

The last regular season contest at Roberts, billed by Bob Hudson as Fan Appreciation Night, saw 7,500 assemble to watch the colorful and explosive Aces. Hudson had described Ed Smallwood, the young Aces freshman, as "the greatest Boardman in Evansville history." Mac had added to the hype by saying, "He has all the equipment to be a tremendous player. He does everything right instinctively." Of course, Smallwood's talent in varsity games wouldn't be known until the next season, but the hype already was beginning.

Now the Aces would close out the 1956–57 campaign with St. Joseph's, and then all they could do was hope for an NCAA College Division bid.

Despite the uncertainty facing his team, Mac opted to give all five of his seniors a starting role. Clyde Cox, a regular, was joined by reserve Bob Wessel, with Smallins, Harrawood, and Harry Osterman in the front line.

Making his first career start in his final game, Osterman opened with the first Aces basket, and the home team was off and running. Despite 29 points from the feisty Pumas' guard Dan Rogovich, the Aces, with the seniors combining for 70 points, closed out the campaign with an impressive 86–72 win. Harrawood, with 18 in limited action, upped his own single season and career marks, to the delight of the crowd.[46]

The unflappable McCutchan told reporters, "I don't see how we can miss [an NCAA bid]. It just seems like matter of time."[47]

Mac's optimism was rewarded when his 17–7 squad received a telegram on Monday saying that they were in the field. The NCAA, though, decided to place the Aces in the Mideast region, where they would meet first-round foe Illinois Normal at Roberts.

With all five starters scoring in double figures, the Aces easily beat the Redbirds, and their 6-8 center, Tony Cadle, 108–96. The Aces would advance to the second round.[48]

The team boarded a flight at Dress Regional Airport for Buffalo, where their next foe would be the host team, which had beaten Capital College 75–62 on its home floor.

"We gave them the game," Clyde Cox recalled. "The officials were calling it differently than we were used to, and we didn't adjust." The Aces were plagued by foul trouble on Buffalo's "brown asphalt floor with black and yellow lines all across it for badminton," lost 77–75, and were eliminated.[49]

The officials, never having seen Harrawood's quick jab step, where he would go left and then back right and release a jumper, called John's patented move a "crow hop" and cited him for traveling.

When Mac asked the officials what they were doing, they said he was doing a "crow hop." "Mac asked where that term could be found in the rule book," Harold Cox said.[50] Mac never got his answer, and the close calls kept Harrawood in check as officials whistled him six times for traveling, or "crow hoping," as they saw it.

"We should have won." a frustrated Harrawood said. "Anywhere else we would have."

Go figure.

In summing up the campaign for reporters, Mac said, "I'll say this about our season, it was as successful as I could have possibly hoped for and this was my greatest team as far as spirit and team friendship goes."[51]

The disappointment over the loss to Buffalo was mitigated somewhat when Mac arranged for the team to visit nearby Niagara Falls. "He always tried to do something like that when we were traveling," Harold said.[52]

Then the team, which had hoped to return to Roberts for the finals, instead returned to Dress Regional airport, where about a hundred faithful fans greeted them. "We were pretty low—not about losing the game, but about letting everybody down and how we lost it," Mac said upon arrival.

The 1956–57 season was over, and it had not ended the way they had thought it would. Bill Robertson, reflecting in the *Evansville Press* on the 18–8 season just completed, noted that "Evansville always seems to end their seasons in defeat in enemy territory. It is always a bit depressing to be buried on foreign fields."[53]

The season saw the college careers of John Harrawood, Jim Smallins, and Clyde Cox come to an end. Harrawood finished with 1,481 points, an average of 17.2 points per contest. He became the first Evansville player to win back-to-back conference Player-of- the-Year honors. John turned down a tryout with the NBA's St. Louis Hawks and instead played with an independent team in Brownstown, Indiana.

Clyde Cox, who had played baseball at Evansville along with basketball, signed with the Philadelphia Phillies after graduation. "They sent me to their Class D team in Matoon, Illinois. I was making $300 a month," he said. "After one season the Phillies dropped me and the Dodgers picked me up. I lasted one season there and after [I had] a talk with the general manager about my prospects for advancing to the big leagues. He told me it wasn't too promising so I decided to go into teaching."

While teaching and coaching at Circleville, Indiana, he took his team to see the Aces play Butler "to watch my brother Harold against Bobby Plump. I wanted to impress them. Unfortunately, Plump got 36 points and Evansville lost, so the lesson was kind of lost on them," he laughed.

"The Evansville experience was a great one for me," Clyde said. "It really took off after I left. But you could tell my last year there that Evansville was wild about their Aces."[54]

Bob Wessel, who had seen his starting job surrendered to Hugh Ahlering, finished with 532 points as a key reserve player for the Aces. Osterman, the last to arrive on campus, departed with 119 points as a back-up pivot player.

Jim Smallins, who had battled through injuries and racial taunts to emerge as the leader of the resurgent Aces at midseason, finished his career with 688 points and a league-best field-goal average of 53 percent. The local star who had become the Aces' first black player would go on to a long career in Milwaukee as a head coach.

"I used much of Coach Mac's running style," he said. He remembered Mac as a "good and fair man and great coach."

Jim garnered two consecutive state championships in 1966 and 1967, and one consolation championship at Lincoln High School, in Milwaukee, before he retired. In 2011 he served as a part-time guidance counselor and as a volunteer assistant basketball coach at Whitefish Bay High School, in a Milwaukee suburb, when its team won the Division II state title.

Of his years at Evansville College, Jim said, "It was a fantastic experience for me, a really beautiful experience."[55]

To show just how far racial attitudes advanced during Jim's career at Evansville, when he and his fiancee were married shortly after graduation on June 8, 1957, the wedding reception was held on campus with Vance Hartke, by then a U.S. senator, and the college president in attendance.

The *Evansville Sunday Courier-Press* carried a story on the nuptials, and the headline writer apparently couldn't decide if it was a society story or a sports story: "Roberta Arnett–Smallins Wedding Kicks Off Social Season."[56]

Times had changed, and Evansville had changed, too.

(Endnotes)

1   AP, "Purdue Plays Aces in Opener Saturday Night," *Evansville Courier*, November 30, 1956, Ahlering scrapbook. Lundy also played football at Purdue. He was MVP of both the football and basketball teams and was drafted as a pro in both sports. He would go on to a long career in the NFL and was a part of the Los Angeles Rams "Fearsome Foursome" of the 1960s: Roosevelt Grier, Merlin Olsen, Deacon Jones, and Lundy (see Lundy's obituary in the *New York Times,* February 26, 2007). Campbell, a Big Ten and state golf champion, would later compete on the PGA tour for eight years and would be named Rookie of the Year by *Golf Digest* in 1959 (www.golfhousetennessee.com).

2   Bill Fluty, "Purdue Edges Aces in 62–60 Thriller," *Evansville Courier,* December 2, 1956, Ahlering scrapbook. Because the archives of the Evansville papers have not been digitized, I have relied on clippings in scrapbooks graciously lent to me by several players. Because the players seldom noted the date a story ran, I have assumed that game accounts appeared on the day after the game they describe.

3   Jim Smallins, telephone interview by author, April 8, 2011.

4   Bill Fluty, "Failure to 'Go for the Basket,' Plus Thin Bench Cost Aces Tilt," *Evansville Courier,* December 2, 1956, Ahlering scrapbook.

5   Bill Fluty, "Aces Mixing Formula Of More Speed, Subs," *Evansville Courier*, December 6, 1956, Ahlering scrapbook.

6   For these quotes from Mac, and others in this chapter that are attributed to no other source, the reader may assume that they come from articles in the *Evansville Courier* and *Evansville Press,* the two local papers at the time. Those articles may be found in the collection of bound scrapbooks kept by Bob Hudson and now housed in the university archives and/or Bill Bussing's manuscript history of the Aces. Bill Bussing graciously made his lengthy manuscript available to me, and I have relied on it for some information, especially in the early years of the McCutchan era and in determining attendance figures. The detailed manuscript contains no footnotes, but when I interviewed Bussing in February 2011, he identified his sources as the *Evansville Courier, Evansville Press,* and the combined Sunday edition, the *Courier & Press.* Bussing's manuscript usually makes no distinction between the papers, but the direct quotes are from one daily or the other or the Sunday combined paper and appear in the Bussing manuscript in quotation marks. Bussing used Hudson's scrapbooks, as did I and my research assistant. Many of the articles do not identify which paper they are from, much less the date and page, but I (and Bussing) assume they are from the *Courier, Press,* or *Sunday Courier & Press.*

7   Ron Eaton, *Local Legends: 100 Years of Southwestern Indiana Sports History* (Evansville, Ind.: M. T. Publishing, 2008), 117.

8   Marilyn McCutchan Disman, telephone interview by author, February 11, 2011.

9   Marilyn McCutchan Disman interview.

10 Hugh Ahlering, telephone interview by author, February 11, 2011.

11 "Longtime Evansville NAACP Members Share Their Recollections," *Evansville Courier Press.com,* January 15, 2011.

12 Smallins interview.

13 Bill Robertson, "Aces Club Central Missouri, 80–57, *Evansville Press,* December 9, 1956; "Eastern Kentucky Edges Aces in Last Second, 84–81," *Evansville Press,* December 11, 1956; Bill Robertson, "Evansville Rallies to Beat New Mexico Aggies, 71–62," *Evansville Press,* December 13, 1956, all in Ahlering scrapbook.

14 "Depauw Five Rips Purple Aces, 85–74," *Evansville Press,* December 16, 1956, Ahlering scrapbook.

15   Harold Cox interview.

16   Bill Robertson, "Sharp Aces Subdue San Jose State, 81–73, *Evansville Press,* December 18, 1956; Bill Robertson, "Dazzling Evansville Attack Sinks Valpo, 93–75," *Evansville Press*, December 21, 1956. both in Ahlering scrapbook.

17   Bill Fluty, "Aces Rip Eagles, 96–76, in Tournament," *Evansville Courier,* December 29, 1956, Ahlering scrapbook. Howell, a 6-7, 220-pound guard, would become a two-time All-America selection and lead the Bulldogs to a 61–14 record over three seasons and their first South Eastern Conference title. He averaged 27.1 points per game, and seventeen rebounds. He is second on the all-time MSU scoring list with 2,030 points. He later played for twelve seasons in the NBA with the Pistons, Bullets, Celtics, and '76ers. He won two NBA championships with the Celtics and is enshrined in the NBA Hall of Fame—the first from his state to be so honored ("Bailey Howell," n.d., www2.nemcc.edu/mspeople/bailey_howell.htm).

18   Most players recollect that it was a call from the governor of Mississippi to Noble that triggered the phone call ordering the team to depart.

19   Harold Cox interview.

20   Jim Smallins interview.

21   Smallins interview.

22   Marilyn McCutchan Disman interview.

23   Dr. Allen McCutchan, telephone interview by author, February 11, 2011.

24   Bill Robertson, "Aces Trip Denver," *Evansville Press*, December 30, 1956, Ahlering scrapbook.

25   Clyde Cox, telephone interview by author, April 4, 2011.

26   Clyde Cox interview.

27   "Aces Edge Indiana State, 91–85, for Second ICC Win," *Evansville Press,* January 4, 1956; Bill Robertson, "DePauw Again Trumps Aces, 70–63," *Evansville Press,* January 6, 1956, both in Ahlering scrapbook.

28   Bill Fluty, "Aces Fall to Butler, 89–87," *Evansville Courier,* January 13,1957, Ahlering scrapbook.

29   Harold Cox, interview by author, April 5, 2011, by telephone.

30   The quotes from Wilson's and Scism's stories come either from clips that I found in Harold Cox's or Hugh Ahlering's scrapbooks, which they generously lent to me, or from Bill Bussing's manuscript history of the Aces.

31   Bill Robertson, "Aces Survive Late Storm to Subdue Wesleyan," *Evansville Press,* January 4, 1957, Harold Cox scrapbook.

32 Harold Cox interview.

33 Clyde Cox interview.

34 Marilyn McCutchan Disman interview, February 22, 2011.

35 Marilyn McCutchan Disman interview, February 22, 2011.

36 Robertson, "Aces Survive Late Storm."

37 Bill Robertson, "Aces Machine Gun Ball State, 103–96," *Evansville Press*, January 27, 1957; Bill Fluty, "Evansville Gains Revenge on Eastern Kentucky, 95–80," *Evansville Courier*, January 29, 1957; Bill Fluty, "Late Surge Carries Aces to 81–72 Win over Butler," *Evansville Courier*, February 1, 1957, all in Ahlering scrapbook.

38 "Aces Shoot Down Buccaneers, 91–87," *Evansville Sunday Courier-Press*, February 3, 1957, Ahlering scrapbook.

39 Bill Fluty, "Clyde Cox' Complete Recovery Adds Fuel to Aces Attack," *Evansville Courier*, February 4, 1957, Ahlering scrapbook.

40 "St. Joe Beats Aces, 73–67, Harrawood Scores 36 points," *Evansville Press*, February 8, 1957 Ahlering scrapbook.

41 "Aces Hot, Jar Valparaiso's Hopes, 68–62," *Evansville Press*, February 9, 1957, Ahlering scrapbook.

42 "Harrawood Sets Record as Aces Rip Bellarmine, 92–76," *Evansville Press*, February 14, 1957, Ahlering scrapbook.

43 Bill Robertson, "Harrawood Scores 42 in Overtime Win," *Evansville Press*, February 21, 1957, Ahlering scrapbook.

44 Bill Robertson, "Harrawood Sets Two Marks as Purple Aces Roll," *Evansville Press*, February 17, 1957, Ahlering scrapbook.

45 Harold Cox, interview.

46 Bill Robertson, "Evansville Triumphs over Pumas, 86–72," *Evansville Press*, February 24, 1957, Ahlering scrapbook.

47 Bill Fluty, "Game Evansville Club Virtual Cinch for NCAA," *Evansville Courier*, n.d., Ahlering scrapbook.

48 Bill Robertson, "Aces Outrun Illinois Normal, 108n96," *Evansville Press*, March 4, 1957, Ahlering scrapbook.

49 Clyde Cox interview; "Buffalo Trips Aces, 77–75," *Evansville Press*, March 11, 1957.

50 Harold Cox author interview.

51 "Mac Says There Was No Room for Aces Defense at Buffalo," *Evansville Press*, n.d., Ahlering scrapbook.

52 Harold Cox interview.

53 Bill Robertson, column, *Evansville Press*, n.d., Ahlering scrapbook.

54 Clyde Cox interview.

55 Jim Smallins, author interview.

56 Jim Smallins scrap book.

Roberts Stadium, 1958.

The Big Smoke and the Old Man, 1957–1958

The loss of the veterans who had opened the first season at Roberts Stadium during the 1956–57 season, and had logged an 18–8 mark, was significant. The departing players had accounted for 1,612 of Evansville's 2,512 points that season.

But the promise that had been displayed by Hugh Ahlering and Harold Cox, coupled with the talent of Ed Smallwood, which was obvious from his play on the jayvee team, were reasons for optimism. So was the return of reserve forward Don Sheridan.

Essentially, Mac had three starting spots to fill for 1957–58 when 36 aspirants reported for the first practice. Most were, like Ahlering before them, walk-ons. "I've got six weeks to find out about those other positions," Mac told reporters, "but I don't want to take that long."[1]

Nearly everyone knew, after his successful freshman season on the jayvees, that Ed Smallwood, or the Big Smoke as he was now known for reasons that remain elusive today, would fill one of those spots. His talent was too obvious to overlook.

As practices got under way, it became apparent that 6-4 Mel Lurker, a sophomore transfer from Murray State, would fill the pivot role. Junior Harold Halbrook and 6-6 sophomore Larry Erwin were battling to join Smallwood at the other forward spot. Halbrook, who eventually got the nod, had played two years at Reitz High School in Evansville and earned All-City honors there before enrolling at Evansville College. He had seen little action the previous season, appearing in only 14 games for the Aces.

As the opening game with Louisville loomed, Mac told reporters, "I wish they were a little more ready. However, this is virtually a new ball club, and it's hard for me to tell just how far along they are."

Mac had also further upgraded his schedule. He had little trouble enticing teams to play the Aces because he could offer them guarantees that were much higher than they could get almost anywhere else. Louisville, St. Mary's, UCLA, William and Mary, and Fresno State, all major college programs, would appear on the schedule.

Almost every successful basketball team has at least one backcourt performer who "quarterbacks" the team on the floor. Evansville was blessed with two talented guards in Ahlering and Harold Cox, both of whom would become extensions of Coach Mac out on the hardwood. They would be the co-captains and team leaders.

"Our job was to make sure everyone stayed in the game mentally at all times, and to keep their spirits up when things got rough," Harold Cox recalls.[2]

Ahlering and Cox were both able not only to score but to defend. "Hugh always got to guard the best guard on the opposition. I became a better defensive player after my sophomore season, when Mac had told me if my man scores, I'm coming out of the game. If I wanted to stay out there, I knew I had to play tough defense," Harold Cox said.[3]

When the season opened on a Monday night—which, Bob Hudson moaned, "is always a bad night for us," so far as attendance was concerned—4,303 fans turned out to see the 1957–58 edition of the Purple Aces.[4] Louisville had lost its leading scorer, Charlie Tyra, to graduation, but the Cardinals, who had finished the season ranked sixth by the AP, still had Harold Andrews and they hadn't lost an opener since 1947–48.[5]

Louisville took an early lead before Ahlering and Cox led a comeback from ten points down that saw them take a 41–38 lead at the half. After a tentative start Ed Smallwood, the Louisville native who had been ignored by the Cardinals, began to get comfortable, and the Aces ran to a narrow victory over Louisville behind a career-high 25 points from Ahlering.[6]

The second of eight straight home games for the Aces was against old nemesis Western Kentucky, which arrived at Roberts with its 6-9 center, Ralph Crosthwaite, a junior from Cincinnati. The defending Ohio Valley Conference champs, coached by Ed Diddle, whose record against the Aces was an impressive 27–12, were a formidable early season test.[7]

Diddle had refused to play the Aces in the armory because of its bad lighting. And he'd soon regret playing them at Roberts Stadium, where the lighting was excellent except for the cloud of cigarette and cigar smoke that hung near the ceiling, making for poor sightlines for those in the upper-level seats.[8]

The first half went the Hilltoppers' way as Crosthwaite accounted for 24 points and 15 rebounds against the Aces. In the second half the Aces fought back, with Ed Smallwood canning 7 of 8 field goals against Crosthwaite, whom he had faced in high school. Ahlering continued to pace the Aces' attack as he repeatedly drove through the lane and brought the Aces into a tie at 94 at the end of regulation.

For the overtime Mac sent Mel Lurker to the pivot and Bob Reisinger, the latest of many talented Central High grads to play for Mac, to forward to replace Smallwood and Halbrook, both of whom had incurred fouls in regulation. Meanwhile, the Hilltoppers had lost Crosthwaite to fouls late in the second half.

Lurker made three free-throws and a field goal in overtime to lead the Aces to a 105–98 win.[9] "I had a good idea of what the others could do, but I wasn't sure about Mel," Mac acknowledged. "He sure gave me a quick answer."

Bob Hudson, pleased with the "biggest Monday in the history of the college athletic office," extended its hours to accommodate the growing ticket demand. "I had one person purchase 122 season tickets," boasted Hudson. "Another bought 40 for the UCLA game and I sold 32 for the Holiday tournament."[10]

The Aces enjoyed a nine-day respite from their two heart-thumping wins before facing St. Mary's of California, a major college foe like Louisville. The Gaels were attracted by Hudson's $2,000 guarantee and brought their zone defense to Roberts in an attempt to stop the running game of the Aces.

Winless thus far in the season, the Gaels came back from an early deficit to force the Aces into yet another overtime game. But Ed Smallwood's tip-in attempt at the buzzer spun out and the Aces dropped to 2–1. "The Aces lost the game but they didn't lose any customers," Dan Scism wrote in the *Courier*. "They got their money's worth and the Aces got a lesson in California style basketball."[11]

With most fans looking ahead to the game with UCLA, only 3,000 showed up on a rainy Wednesday to watch the Aces defeat the Crusaders of Valparaiso 72–59 in the opening ICC game.[12]

The UCLA squad that John Wooden brought to Roberts was made up of names familiar to fans both then and now: Rafer Johnson, the gifted decathlete who would go on to an Olympic gold in the event in 1960 and carry the American flag in the opening ceremonies in Rome, the first African American to be so honored; Denny Crum, who would become an assistant coach at UCLA before moving on to Louisville, where he would win two national titles and more than 600 games; Walt Torrance, 6-3 and the West Coast high-jump champion, who had cleared 6-8 the previous season; and the centers Roland Underhill, 6-5, and Ben Rogers, 6-6.[13]

The Bruins had four returned starters from a team that had finished the previous season at 22–4 but thus far in the 1957–58 campaign had struggled to a 4–2 mark. Still, they were loaded with athletic talent and guided by Wooden, a native of Indiana who would become an iconic coach. In short, the Bruins posed a stern test for the youthful Aces.[14]

Mac's team, young and inexperienced at this level of competition, was further hindered by a lack of height. Smallwood at 6-4 would be at a height disadvantage inside so Mac inserted Larry Erwin in the starting lineup. The 6-5 Erwin replaced Halbrook, who at 6-1 had been foul plagued in the first three games as he tried to guard taller players.

The move paid off.

The Aces rolled over the Bruins, to the delight of the record crowd of 8,890, many of whom were attired in red. Led by Ed Smallwood's 25 points and 10 rebounds, the Aces captured a hard-fought 83–76 win. When Mac removed Smallwood from the game with 1:49 remaining, the crowd stood and gave "The Big Smoke" a thunderous ovation.

Harold Cox added six buckets; on one he made a "beautiful play when he went past two UCLA defenders to get the twisting layup when we needed two points badly in the second half," as Mac described it.[15]

Erwin had responded to his first start with 7 points and 10 rebounds, and Ahlering, whose slashing play had earned him 15 free throws, converted on 13 of them. Mel Lurker tallied 19 points on 7-for-9 from the field and combined with Smallwood to keep the taller Bruins off the boards.[16] Erwin's play earned him a spot with Smallwood and Lurker in the now all-sophomore front line.

In all it was a concerted team effort against a major college foe—one that had earned three Pacific Coast Conference titles. "I guarded Johnson and then Crum," said Harold Cox, who held Rafer to just six points and called the decathlete "the greatest athlete I ever saw."[17]

John Wooden offered lofty praise for Mac's youngsters, saying of Cox and Ahlering, "they were the best two guards we've played against." Mac's postgame critique was not nearly so generous as the coach was dismayed by the 22 floor errors committed by the Aces. "I figure if we make 12 such errors in a full game that's the acceptable limit," he said.[18]

The Aces next prepared to host their Holiday Tournament and another field of major college foes. Hudson had lured William and Mary, Fresno State, and Murray State to Roberts for the pre-Christmas affair. The event was in direct competition with Evansville's traditional Junior League Charity Ball, a prestigious social event that was the highlight of the winter season.

The *Evansville Press* touted the coming tournament by promising fans in a headline: "Aces Favored to Win Tournament Again."[19] The team proved equal to the task and cut into the crowd at the ball by attracting 8,837 fans who chose to wear garish red instead of black tie and tux.

"For the first time I can remember, college basketball cut in on the big dance," Dick Anderson reported in the *Evansville Press*.[20] (That wouldn't happen again. According to Joan Hudson Roth, organizers of the ball and other social events would be at pains to schedule their events for dates that did not conflict with an Aces home game.)

The popularity of the Holiday Tournament and the large crowd that had turned out to see UCLA were a testament to Bob Hudson's innovative and imaginative promotion and scheduling. That, coupled with the opening of Roberts Stadium and Mac's superb coaching, produced the large crowds that meant people were, with increasing regularity, choosing an Aces game over other forms of entertainment.

Those who chose unabashed cheering over decorous waltzing saw the Aces triumph as they turned back William and Mary 83–65 and then dispatched Fresno State for the title in a thrilling 92–90 win.

The Fresno State coach, Bill Vanderburgh, noticed upon arrival in Evansville just how much of a home-court advantage the Aces would have. "The driver of the cab taking me to the hotel told me the Aces would take us," he said. "The bell boy told me the same thing at the hotel. And then the elevator operator said the Aces would beat us for sure. I should have known we would lose. Evansville people have a lot of faith in the Aces."[21]

Smallwood was becoming increasingly dominant in the Aces' running-style offense. He tallied 23 points against Fresno State and added 16 rebounds to lead the Aces to their second straight Holiday Tournament championship. Mel Lurker continued to improve both offensively and defensively, and his play against William and Mary's 6'9" center was the deciding factor in the opening-round game.[22]

In the finals Evansville struggled but prevailed, 92–90, against the Bulldogs of Fresno State, who had defeated Murray State behind 14 points from Rolland Todd. Smallwood finished with 23 points to lead the Aces, who were forced to hold the ball for the last ten seconds to preserve the win.[23]

Todd, who remembered that game well, recalled that the size and hometown advantage of Roberts were factors: "We were used to playing in our small gym on campus that held about 2,000. . . . We really enjoyed being in Evansville and the experience of playing in that tournament. But when you are on the road, you're like a stranger in town and you don't get the close calls. That game—a close one—went against us and we lost our big man and that was the difference."[24]

The 6–1 Aces now had to prepare for the conference schedule against their traditional, if less glamorous, foes. Mac welcomed his team back from the holiday break and urged them to "prepare mentally and physically to meet the tough conference schedule ahead."

In the local press Dick Anderson cautioned the coach, "Now, now, Mac, let's not expect too much." But expectations in Evansville were growing with each passing game as the youthful squad slowly but steadily matured on the court.

When DePauw, which had lost four games, came to Roberts in January, Mac was still being cautious. The Tigers were the defending ICC champs and had turned back Evansville twice the previous season, so Mac was right to be concerned despite their slow start. "They knew how to do it to us last year," he told reporters. "They want this one pretty badly."

They probably did, but they would be disappointed—the Aces ran to their seventh victory by a score of 81–71. The Tigers had held a 58–41 lead with just fifteen minutes to play, making the 6,195 fans more than a little concerned. The Aces cut away at that lead with Ahlering and Cox applying full-court pressure defense and Smallwood and Lurker hitting key shots. With six minutes to go, the Aces, who had once trailed by 17, knotted the score at 61. After DePauw's Bing Davis converted a tip-in to give DePauw the lead again, Larry Erwin hit two free throws, Smallwood finished off an old-fashioned three-point play, and the Aces never looked back.[25]

The eight-game home stand that concluded with the furious Aces' rally provoked Dan Scism to tell readers he had just witnessed "the most amazing transformation I can recall seeing made by a basketball team in, let us say, 35 years of sports writing."[26]

That the Aces were winning and doing so in style had helped them draw 42,712 fans to the first eight games.

"You can say winning has become contagious with this ball club," Mac offered as the Aces prepared for their first road trip. "When we beat Louisville the boys thought they had beaten a great ball club. That may not be true. But the point is they believed they could win and it was the same with Western (Kentucky), UCLA and the others."

It didn't hurt that they had a coach who always seemed to find a way to win. "Mac was always positive. He always told us, even when we were down in a game, 'This is the way we're going to win this,'" said Hugh Ahlering of Mac's confidence boosting style.[27]

The Aces' 7–1 start against first-rate competition earned them a Number One ranking in the first United Press poll of the 720 small colleges in the NCAA's College Division. The Aces were, for the very first time, the top team in the nation in their division. "We simply didn't have any fear at all," Harold Cox recalled. "We felt that Mac had us prepared to play any team in the country. You'd better be on the top of your game when you approach a game that way. We all got the message he was sending—that we could play with anyone—and we set our goals pretty high."[28]

Mac's coaching and motivational styles were decidedly understated. "He was a real gentleman. He could get his points across without getting in your face and yelling and cursing. He was a very smart coach and we recognized that," Hugh Ahlering said. "He ran us up and down the old armory steps and outside in the park. We ran so much when we started the season, we were sure we could outrun anyone.

"Mac definitely had his own ideas about the way things should be done but the maddest I ever saw him was when he'd stomp his foot on the floor. When he stomped his foot, we knew he was really upset with us."[29]

The principal idea that Mac disseminated was to run and run and run some more. "We'd have the big man get the ball out of bounds or off a rebound and get it to Harold or me on the fast break," Ahlering explained. "We'd take off up court as fast as we could run. We didn't dribble at all. We'd just pass the ball up, and we'd get there without the ball ever hitting the floor. Once we got there, we'd hit one of the forwards on the wings or Ed [Smallwood] in the pivot. If they weren't open, Harold could pop from outside or I would drive to the lane.

"We'd get down court so fast that the other team didn't have time to set their defense. By the end of the game they would be too tired to chase us."[30]

The system that would work so well for the Aces for the next two years was a fan-friendly frenetic style of play that the players enjoyed as much as the fans. And happy players are likely to become winning players. The key was the play of the two guards, Cox and Ahlering, who made it all go so smoothly, even if it looked, from the stands, like basketball on fast-forward.

"Harold and I meshed together. We knew instinctively after a while exactly what the other was going to do," Ahlering said of his running mate. "Hugh and I got a lot of minutes in," Harold Cox recalled. "We ran the show and never got tired. I felt sorry for the reserves that never got to play."[31]

Sitting atop the small college basketball world, the Aces headed to a meeting with Ball State in Muncie and narrowly escaped with a 78–76 win, then headed to Indianapolis for the game with Butler.

The visit to Muncie provided yet another reminder that in 1958 racial bias could still appear when you least expected it and that Mac wouldn't stand for it anywhere at any time.

"We were all in a restaurant up there, and they took all our orders," Harold Cox recalled. "When the waiters came back with our food orders, there was none for Ed Smallwood. Mac got up from his chair and said to the manager, 'If you can't serve us all, we're leaving.' When they refused, Mac told us to get up and we all went out."[32] And, just for good measure, the Aces beat Ball State.

Two days later the Aces met Butler and Bobby Plump at the Butler Fieldhouse. Three busloads of Evansville fans made the trip to support their team, but their voices were lost in the crowd of 8,700 that showed up to support the home team.[33]

The Bulldogs had been licking their chops as they waited for the Aces. "They were really ready for us," Mac said after the game. "This was the first time that it really meant something for them to beat us, and they came out on the floor as high as I've ever seen them."[34]

Now in his senior season with the Bulldogs, Bobby Plump, who had achieved instant celebrity with his dramatic game-winning shot for tiny Milan in the high school finals against Muncie Central, had been a thorn in the Aces' side forever.[35] As a freshman he had duplicated his last-second miracle shot to defeat the Aces and had played well against them in almost every meeting since.

Harold Cox drew the unenviable role of trying to stop the Butler scoring ace. "They used the pick-and-roll very effectively against us," Harold said. "They'd set the pick, and Bobby would come off it and hit his jumper from the top of the circle. He was real good from there."

That may be a slight understatement. Plump set a new Butler single-game scoring record with 41 points, including a perfect 17-for-17 from the foul line, to lead Butler's dismemberment of the Aces, 101–76.[36]

"I can always say I held him to 41," laughed Harold years after the loss.[37] Tony Hinkle, the future Hall of Fame coach, said of his star, "I've always said Bobby was the greatest basketball player in the United States. They don't make them any better than that kid."

Perhaps not, but King Kelly Coleman, of Kentucky Wesleyan, was close, at least in the minds of many in Kentucky, and he was next on the Aces' schedule.

Coleman, whom Adolf Rupp had called, "the greatest high school player who ever lived," had originally signed with West Virginia after a high school career that saw him score 4,263 points for Wayland High School in Wayland, Kentucky. He averaged more than 41 points as a senior there, including a Kentucky State tournament record of 68 points in a single game, before enrolling at West Virginia, much to the dismay of Kentucky fans. Coleman was a Mountaineer for only a short time and left after a recruiting scandal initiated by reports to the NCAA by the University of Kentucky, which he had scorned, that revealed he had accepted money and a car to enroll at West Virginia. He enrolled next at Eastern Kentucky and left there after only six weeks without ever donning a uniform. He then worked for a year in a steel mill before enrolling at Kentucky Wesleyan.[38]

Still a freshman, the 6-4, 230-pound forward was averaging 23 points and 12 rebounds a game as the Panthers hosted the Aces in Owensboro.[39] Mac had high praise for the "King." "He's kind of like Bobby Plump in trying to defense. If you concentrate on trying to stop Coleman, Wesleyan has others that will hurt you," he told reporters. Indeed, Coleman wasn't the only threat the Aces faced. Gene Minton, a 6-6 junior forward, was a potent scorer as well.

To counter the explosive offensive potential of Kentucky Wesleyan, Mac used the same full-court pressure that had worked so well against DePauw. The Aces held a 25–19 lead when Mac surprised everyone in the crowd of 5,000 by pulling all five starters.

Casting aside their long bathrobe-like robes that pooled at their feet, the bright orange–clad Aces reserves entered the game en mass at the 6:42 mark of the first half.

It was a move that Mac had seldom, if ever, made. In fact, he often played only six or seven men in a game. But against Wesleyan the creative Mac sent in the shock troops to continue to harass the Panthers all over the court. "It was a pre-planned tactic," he explained later. "We figured if we covered Wesleyan all over the floor they'd run out of gas."[40]

They didn't.

With juniors Harold Halbrook and Harold Malicoat, along with the Aces' reserves—sophomores Tom Mulherin, Larry Gates, and Don Sheridan—on the court, the Aces saw their lead evaporate. By the 4:48 mark, with the score tied at 27, the regulars were back in the game and the shock troops were again on the bench, the experiment a failure.

Behind Lurker, Cox, and Ahlering the Aces drew away from their hosts in the second half to manage a 77–71 win.

Now 9–2, the Aces easily turned back Indiana State, with Smallwood hitting for 31 points, and nipped Ball State at Roberts 86–82.

"I probably should have started my second five [players during] the second half," Mac told reporters afterward. "My second five were anxious to play, and I really believe they could have held their own. However if I started them and we blew the game I'd never live it down."[41]

A return contest with Indiana State saw Ed Smallwood explode for 31 points again as the Aces improved to 12–2 on the season.

For the second time in just ten days the Butler Bulldogs were next for the Aces. In his column in the *Courier* Dick Anderson warned readers that "if you have any idea that you are going to the Butler game on Jan. 30 you better be doing something about it. Bob Hudson tells me the joint is filling up fast."[42]

At 5–1 in ICC play the Aces could ill afford another loss to the conference leaders. In the locker room before the game Mac used some amateur psychology. "He told his assistant coaches to watch us all when he asked, 'Who wants to guard Plump?'" Harold Cox remembered. "My eyes must have opened real wide because he said, 'OK. You've got him.'" Plump had burned Harold at the Fieldhouse for 41 points, and Cox was eager to redeem himself against the Bulldogs' star.

Bob Hudson had sold 5,000 advance tickets; 5,000 more filled the bench seats and a temporary bleachers arrangement Hudson had contrived to accommodate the horde that descended on Roberts. Traffic crawled bumper to bumper into the stadium's jammed parking lot.

The sea of red that packed Roberts had the local fire marshal in a state of near apoplexy as he tried to clear the aisles and exits of fans. Even the press box was commandeered to hold fans who couldn't find any other place to sit.

They all got their money's worth and more. "The crowd really got behind me," Harold said of the rematch with Plump. "They were like a sixth man on the court. They energized me."

Using the extra adrenaline, Harold held Plump at bay. "He didn't get a shot off the first ten minutes," Harold recalls.[43] Even so, Butler managed to stay close as Hinkle calmly surveyed the court. The game was a one-point affair at the intermission with the Aces ahead, and it remained nip-and-tuck as Butler refused to fold.

Smallwood from the outside and Lurker hitting from inside (while saddled with four fouls) kept the Aces in the game. They were tied at 81 at the final buzzer. In overtime Butler grabbed a slim lead, but Smallwood and Lurker battled back, and the Aces prevailed, 89–85, to the delight of the record throng.

Harold Cox held Bobby Plump to 19 points before fouling out with 15 points. Harold also held the usually accurate Plump to a paltry 5-for-19 from the field. Harold had exacted his revenge.

Smallwood led all scorers with 29 points and 15 boards, Lurker added 15, and Hugh Ahlering chipped in with 20 while displaying a steady hand at the controls of the Aces' offense.

If you weren't able to get to the game or listen to it on the radio, you surely read about it in one of the papers. The *Evansville Courier* ran the account of the Aces' thrilling victory as its lead story on Page One of the next morning paper. *The Evansville Press* heralded the win with a bold headline: "Aces Grind Out 89-85 Vengeance over Butler."[44] If you were living anywhere near Evansville, you could not have missed the news that the Aces were winning and winning. Euphoria reached a new level throughout the city.

Beloit was the next victim of the running Aces, who triumphed 77–69 at Roberts.[45]

A road trip to meet St. Joseph's and Valparaiso followed. "We traveled in cars most of the time. Bob Hudson and assistant coach Paul Beck and coach Mac would drive. Mac always took the starters. Sometimes a booster would take us," Hugh Ahlering said. One such booster did more than drive. "Dr. Harry Whetstone was a backer that often went with us. He would pay for our meals in the hotel when we were on the road and often took us out to eat," Ahlering said.[46]

The Evansville community looked out for the Aces in other ways as well. "Mac made sure that the players from out of town had a local family there that 'adopted' us," Harold Cox said. "They would have us over for meals and do the laundry and take care of our needs in that way."[47]

The community was solidly behind the Aces, and the support continued to grow as they continued to win.

Valparaiso's Crusaders were the next victims as they fell 80–76 in a triple overtime game on the road when Larry Erwin canned six points in the waning minutes and added a crucial steal to seal the Crusaders' fate.

"It's hard to understand these kids," Mac complained to reporters after his team had squandered a 17-point half-time lead. "They don't seem to know what to do with a lead, but they can sure get the job done when the going is close." His team's penchant for winning squeakers clearly did not sit well with the coach, but he added, "As long as they do that you've got to love them."[48]

While Mac's affection for his precocious youngsters was genuine, and growing stronger, others were noticing the Aces from afar. In New York the National Invitation Tournament's selection committee was taking a long look at Mac's 16–2 Aces. The committee announced that Evansville was among twenty teams (all but the Aces from the university, or major college, division) being considered for invites to the annual NIT at Madison Square Garden.[49]

Evansville's athletic director, Don Ping, politely thanked the committee for its consideration but took the team out of the running for an invitation. Evansville was committed to the NCAA College Division's regional tournament, and Bob Hudson was working feverishly behind the scenes to have the finals held at Roberts. The latest national poll of sportswriters ranked the Aces third, and, barring a sudden collapse, they seemed assured of an at-large bid.

A return game with the Panthers of Kentucky Wesleyan at Roberts was next for the Aces, and a crowd of 8,312 jammed Roberts for the rematch on a Saturday evening.[50] The visitors came to town with an unimpressive 11–9 mark for a season in which they had upgraded their schedule to include many major college foes. The Panthers had been the previous season's national runner-up, but their poor record eliminated them from postseason consideration.

As the Panthers took the court, coach Bullet Wilson was confident. He promised Aces fans "a lot better club" than the one that had nearly beaten the Aces in their last outing in Owensboro. A slimmer King Kelly Coleman was one reason for the optimism. Kelly, who battled a weight problem throughout his career, no doubt exacerbated by his fondness for beer, was a trim 215 pounds.[51]

"We reached our peak a few weeks ago against Louisville and should have beaten them," Wilson told the press.[52]

Harold Cox drew the unenviable role of trying to dethrone the King. "Coleman had terrific range. As he came across the time line I'd think, 'I better get on him,' and by the time I got to him, he'd already let one go," Harold said.

Throughout the tight contest some of the fans at Roberts were razzing Coleman. "They were all in the front row around the 10-second line and were giving him a really rough time each time he came near. I told them, 'Quiet down! Stop that razzing! You're only making my job tougher!'" Harold said.[53]

With Mel Lurker forced to the pine with four personal fouls, the Panthers clawed back into the game. The Aces held only a two-point lead with less than two minutes to play when Mac ordered his team into a stall. "He did that a lot when we were in the lead with foul trouble," Hugh Ahlering said.

"Usually we'd blow the lead, and he'd let us go back to our normal running style," Harold Cox said. That's exactly what happened.[54]

Many in the crowd disagreed with the tactic, and at least one voiced her displeasure loud enough for Mac to hear it. After the game he told reporters what transpired: "A woman in the stands saw what we were doing and yelled, 'Why are they in a stall? Even the coach knows they can't stall. The stupid coach.'"

For whatever reason Mac had soon reversed course, and the Aces, who had lost the ball on a turnover while trying to stall, went back to their usual style. When they did, Ed Smallwood knocked down a fifteen-footer. When Ahlering followed with a driving layup, the Aces were ahead, 83–79.

But the King wasn't ready to abdicate just yet. Coleman tipped in an errant Wesleyan effort to cut the lead to two.

When Harold Malicoat, one of the Aces' reserve players, made two free throws to put the Aces back up by four, Coleman countered with a jumper from the foul line.

Then Ahlering sank two more free throws and once more widened the margin to four. Coleman promptly retaliated with another jumper to make it 87–85 as time ticked down.

When Wesleyan's reserve center Lyle Dunbar made a free throw, and it was followed by another Coleman jumper, the Panthers held a one-point lead.

Only twelve seconds remained.

Fans were on their feet and in a frenzy as yet another nail-biter played out at Roberts Stadium. This time Larry Erwin supplied the heroics. Racing up court, he took the outlet pass from Smallwood. As the clock moved relentlessly toward zero, he spotted no one in the clear. So Erwin lofted a forty-footer.

Bingo!

The crowd exploded.

Coleman took one last desperation heave after receiving the inbounds pass. After the futile heave, the King fell face down and pounded the floor in frustration as the buzzer sounded.

Aces games were not just social events anymore. They were exciting entertainment, and the fans, if not the coach, loved the high-drama wins and supercharged atmosphere.

"I knew I had it as soon as it left my hands," Erwin told reporters in the happy dressing room.

"He doesn't have to score another point all year," Ahlering said.[55]

Erwin had pinked the Panthers. It was not a usual role for him. All four of the other starters were ranked in the top fifteen in the conference in field-goal accuracy. But on this night it was Erwin's turn to pull the Aces through, and he had done so with aplomb.

After catching their collective breath the Aces dispatched DePauw 78–65, clinching at least a tie for the conference title despite only 15 points from Ed Smallwood. Five Aces scored in double figures. Mel Lurker had 21 and added eleven rebounds.[56]

They claimed the crown outright with a 78–70 win over St. Joseph's, with Ed back to his normal output, accounting for 27.

Harold Cox and Ed Smallwood were honored at halftime as co-recipients of the Kiwanis Club's Outstanding Player award before an appreciative crowd of 8,500.

The regular season finale saw the Big Smoke explode for 35 points in a losing cause as the Aces fell to Western Kentucky 100–86 behind Ralph Crosthwaite's 26 points.[57]

"We didn't aim for this one since I don't believe in Sunday practice," the pious Methodist coach McCutchan explained afterward. "About all I did was talk to the boys on Monday, and I don't think they were ready for this one." Mac took the blame for the loss.

The regular season was over, and it had proved to be a surprisingly successful one for Mac's young team. Instead of struggling through a rebuilding effort, his team had displayed a fearless competitiveness instilled in them by their coach.

"We had fun," was the explanation that Hugh Ahlering offered of the unexpected results. "We didn't have any fear," Harold Cox said.[58] Players having fun and fearing no one usually is a winning combination.

The Aces finished the 1957–58 regular season campaign with a school-best record of 19–3. They captured the ICC title with an 11–1 conference record, the best since the conference began in 1950–51.

Now they had to prepare for the postseason NCAA Tournament. In the meantime their freshman team was taking on the yearlings from Kentucky, whom Adolph Rupp had called his finest collection of recruits since Cliff Hagan and Frank Ramsey.

If the startling success of the Aces in the regular season had not alarmed their future foes, the outcome in Kentucky surely should have.

Dale Wise, who had been recruited from Kokomo by the Cox brothers, led the Evansville freshmen to a 90–88 win over the heralded future Wildcats. It looked like the Aces were going to be very good for a while longer.

In the Mideast regional held at Roberts, the Aces began play against the Little Giants of Wabash College. The game was close for most of the contest, with the home team prevailing in yet another overtime victory, the fifth in twenty-three games. Cinching the game took a driving layup by Hugh Ahlering with five seconds to play in overtime.[59]

The Akron Zips, the Aces' opponent for the final round of the regional tournament, were 20–5 for the season and had sent the Governors of Austin Peay home in the opener on Friday night. The Zips held a decided height advantage over the Aces, which wasn't unusual, but the Aces had speed to burn and Akron couldn't keep pace.

The Aces extended a 14-point lead at the half to 70–47 when Mac emptied the bench, and they coasted into the finals with an 82–70 win. Smallwood scored 30 points before being rested, Lurker had 15, and Cox had added 10. Both Smallwood and Cox were named to the All-Regional squad.[60] Next up for the streaking Aces was American University.

But Bob Hudson was disappointed by the turnout for the regionals—snow had blanketed the area and held attendance down to just 4,389. Now that the home-town team was in the Final Eight, which would also be held at Roberts, he was hopeful that the faithful would come in from the cold to watch their decidedly hot team in action.

The NCAA was pleased with the regional results, even if Hudson wasn't. The tournament, which had been a money loser at its previous locations, turned a profit at Roberts, where it had grossed $10,000, $4,000 more than what the NCAA deemed a success. And the finals, featuring the local school, promised to be a money machine for an organization that liked nothing better.

Evansville celebrated the Aces with a mayoral proclamation by Vance Hartke, and the team rode a fire truck through downtown, where the Aces were feted at a luncheon in their honor.[61]

Advance ticket sales were brisk, and a crowd of nearly 5,000 showed up to root the Aces on against American, which came into the contest having won eleven straight and was 22–5 for the season.[62]

American failed to make it an even dozen, despite its high-scoring 5-8 guard, "Wee" Willie Jones. "I guarded him, too," Harold Cox laughed, recalling his role as Mac's designated guard to take on the opposition's leading scorer. Harold, as often happened, won this one, holding Willie to a wee 12 points on a woeful 3-for-12 from the field.[63] The East Regional champions headed home losing by 82–72 to the surging Aces.

Meanwhile, the defending national champion, Wheaton College of Illinois, had advanced to the semifinals with a win over Chapman College of California, and it was beginning to look like a Wheaton-Evansville final.[64] Hudson and the NCAA tournament committee were drooling at the prospect, because of the demand for tickets.

However, a funny thing happened on the way to the finals. The wily eleventh-ranked Coyotes of South Dakota sneaked past Wheaton, eliminating the defending national champ. So there was no Wheaton-Evansville matchup for the final, but an Evansville win in the night cap would still attract a large crowd for the championship game.

The Aces trotted out in their white robes to meet St. Michaels of Vermont. St. Michaels had lost one player to measles, and another had been summarily dismissed before the game. So the matchup of Evansville and South Dakota for the finals seemed almost inevitable.

It wasn't to be.

The Aces, perhaps a bit overconfident, struggled with the Iron Mikes and held but a one-point lead at the half. Smallwood had been hobbled by a sprained ankle, limiting his effectiveness, and Larry Erwin had limped to the sidelines following a nasty collision early in the second half. He was joined shortly thereafter by Mel Lurker, who reluctantly took a seat upon his fourth foul.

Even so, the Aces managed to make a game of it. They pulled ahead 69–68 after a Smallwood jumper with little more than three minutes to play. But then St. Michael's answered with five straight points. Smallwood's two free throws cut the lead to two with less than a minute remaining, raising hopes until St. Michael's ran off five unanswered points to win, 78–70.[65]

The Aces' remarkable campaign had fallen one game short of the title match. The loss, while a blow, gained the Aces what they had been pointing toward all season long—a game with Wheaton, the defending champion.

A crowd of 4,000, not particularly interested in the South Dakota–St. Michael's title tussle, watched as the Aces met Wheaton in the consolation game. The fans arrived early for a game that really meant nothing. They were looking forward to seeing Mel Peterson, Wheaton's 6-5 forward and the MVP of the 1956–57 tournament—who had scored 26 points in the loss to South Dakota—go *mano a mano* with Ed Smallwood, the Aces' star, who had managed 19 against St. Michael's.[66]

Peterson scorched the nets for 30 points, but Smallwood and the Aces prevailed 95–93 in another thriller at Roberts. Smallwood responded to the challenge by converting 15 of 17 free throws and canning 13 buckets to finish the game with 41 points. The Big Smoke added twenty-two boards, besting Peterson by twelve, and was awarded the tournament's MVP honors.[67]

Evansville, at 23–4, finished third in the nation with its consolation win, and Ed finished the year with 635 points, an average of 23.5 per game. He was the fourth consecutive Aces performer to win the ICC Outstanding Player award, and was named to the second team of the small-college All-America squad, earning honorable mention on the AP's team.

"I don't know where I get my athletic skill," Ed told reporters. "My father never had much chance at sports because of work. He stands 5-11. My mother is of average size. I didn't start playing basketball until I was in the ninth grade."[68] He had certainly made up for lost time, turning in one of the finest performances ever by an Aces player.

Hugh Ahlering, a Kiwanis Award winner, received an honorable mention from

UPI in All-American voting. Harold Cox joined sophomore Mel Lurker as honorable mention choices on the ICC All-Conference team.

In all, the surprising Aces had turned in a remarkable performance, and Mac was name ICC Coach of the Year for the fourth time in five seasons. He deserved it. Mac had upped his record at Evansville to an impressive 172–137; with 58 wins in 85 games he was the leading winning percentage coach in the conference at 68 percent.

The 1957–58 edition of the Aces would lose only a few substitutes to graduation. When spring breezes started to waft into the city, coaxing the giant sycamores to leaf out and the tulip poplars to blossom, the city's other season—waiting for basketball season to start again—would begin.

(Endnotes)

1   For these quotes from Mac, and others in this chapter that are attributed to no other source, the reader may assume that they come from articles in the *Evansville Courier* and *Evansville Press,* the two local papers at the time. Those articles may be found in the collection of bound scrapbooks kept by Bob Hudson and now housed in the university archives and/or Bill Bussing's manuscript history of the Aces. Bill Bussing generously made his lengthy manuscript available to me, and I have relied on it for some information, especially in the early years of the McCutchan era and in determining attendance figures. The detailed manuscript contains no footnotes, but when I interviewed Bussing in February 2011, he identified his sources as the *Evansville Courier, Evansville Press,* and the combined Sunday edition, the *Courier & Press.* Bussing's manuscript usually makes no distinction between the papers, but the direct quotes are from one daily or the other or the Sunday combined paper and appear in the Bussing manuscript in quotation marks. Bussing used Hudson's scrapbooks, as did I and my research assistant. Many of the articles do not identify which paper they are from, much less the date and page, but I (and Bussing) assume they are from the *Courier, Press,* or *Sunday Courier & Press.*

2   Harold Cox, telephone interview by author, April 5, 2011.

3   Harold Cox interview.

4   Dick Anderson, column, *Evansville Press,* December 3, 1957, Ahlering scrapbook.

5 Bill Fluty, "Expect Tilt to Attract over 5,000," *Evansville Courier,* December 2, 1957, Ahlering scrapbook.

6 Bill Robertson, "Aces Open 1957–58 Season with 92–82 Upset Victory," *Evansville Press*, December 3, 1957, Ahlering scrapbook.

7 Bill Fluty, "Western, with Big Four Back, Next Foe for Aces," *Evansville Courier,* December 4, 1957, Ahlering scrapbook.

8 John Siau, telephone interview by author, January 30, 2011.

9 Bill Fluty, "Ahlering Gets 29 to Lead Sharp Attack," *Evansville Courier-Press,* December 8, 1957, Ahlering scrapbook.

10 Dan Scism, column, "Ticket Rush Gains Momentum," *Evansville Courier*, December 9, 1957, Ahlering scrapbook.

11 Bill Fluty, "Evansville Blows Big Margin," *Evansville Courier,* December 17, 1957; Dan Scism, column, *Evansville Courier,* n.d., both in Ahlering scrapbook.

12 Bill Fluty, "Slow Starting Aces Score 72–59 Victory over Valpo," *Evansville Courier*, December 19, 1957, Ahlering scrapbook.

13 Bill Fluty, "Gaels Here Monday for First Time," *Evansville Sunday Courier-Press,* December 15, 1957, Ahlering scrapbook; "Former U of L Coach Denny Crum to Join MVC Hall of Fame," Louisville Athletics, August 17, 2011, www.uoflsports.com/genrel/081711aab.html.

14 Wooden, after two seasons at Indiana State, had compiled an overall mark of 187 victories in 255 games. He would go on to become a "Wizard" after attracting top talent from around the nation to his program when a wealthy real estate tycoon and avid Bruin booster took an interest in his program. The rest is history. In twenty-seven years at the helm in Westwood he recorded 620 wins against 147 losses. His teams won ten national titles, including seven in a row and an eight-eight-game winning streak ("John Wooden: A Coaching Legend," UCLABruins.com, n.d., www.uclabruins.com/sports/m-baskbl/spec-rel/ucla-wooden-page.html).

15 Bill Fluty, "Wooden Tabs Aces Toughest UCLA Foe of Season," *Evansville Sunday-Courier Press*, December 22, 1957, Ahlering scrapbook.

16 Bill Fluty, "9,000 See Aces Upset UCLA, 83–76," *Evansville Sunday Courier-Press,* December 22, 1957.

17 Harold Cox interview.

18 Fluty, "Wooden Tabs Aces."

19 Bill Robertson, "Aces Favored to Win Tourney Again," *Evansville Press*,

December 23, 1957, Ahlering scrapbook.

20 Dick Anderson, column, *Evansville Press*, n.d., Ahlering scrapbook.

21 Dan Scism, column, "One Good Kick Is Enough," *Evansville Courier*, n.d., Ahlering scrapbook.

22 Bill Fluty, "Aces Rout William and Mary 83–65." *Evansville Courier*, December 28, 1957, Ahlering scrapbook.

23 Bill Robertson, "Roaring Aces Grab Invitational Title, 82–80," *Evansville Press,* December 29, 1957, Ahlering scrapbook.

24 Rolland Todd, telephone interview by author, April 25, 2011. Todd entered coaching after graduation and would later become head coach at the University of Nevada–Las Vegas in the pre-Tarkanian era and took that team to Roberts Stadium in 1968.

25 Bill Fluty, "Aces Rally One of Greatest in College's History," *Evansville Courier*, January 4, 1958, Ahlering scrapbook.

26 Dan Scism, column, "Aladdin Rubbed His Lamp," *Evansville Courier,* January 5, 1958, Ahlering scrapbook

27 Hugh Ahlering, telephone interview by author, February 11, 2011.

28 Earl Wright, UPI, "Evansville Is No. 1 In Nation," *Evansville Courier*, n.d., Harold Cox scrapbook; Harold Cox interview.

29 Ahlering interview.

30 Ahlering interview.

31 Harold Cox interview.

32 Harold Cox interview.

33 Dick Anderson, column, *Evansville Courier*, January 11, 1958, Ahlering scrapbook.

34 Bill Fluty, "McCutchan Says Butler 'Really Ready' For Aces," *Evansville Courier,* January 15, 1958, Ahlering scrapbook.

35 Plump's miracle shot and the huge upset it provided made him an instant hero in Indiana. His illustrious career at Butler would only add to the celebrity he had gained as a high school star. He would leave Butler University as its all-time leading scorer. His 475 free throws made are still the Butler record as are the 41 points in a single game he recorded against Evansville. (The Fieldhouse scoring record had been set in the 1953–54 season by tiny Rio Grande College's Bevo Francis. The nation's leading scorer set the record with 48 points, less than half the total he would score against Hillsdale College later that season when he scored 113 to establish the all-time record for

college players at any level. See Kyle Keiderling, *Shooting Star: The Bevo Francis Story* [Wilmington, Del.: Sport Classic, 2005], 172–75). Plump was a member of the 1958 College All-Star team and led the Bulldogs to their first-ever NIT appearance that season. He is a member of the Butler and Indiana Basketball Halls of Fame. Plump capitalized on his hoops fame to become a successful insurance agent in the Indianapolis area. He later opened a sports bar in Indianapolis that his son still operates. The popular establishment is called, appropriately, Plump's Last Shot("Bobby Plump Profile, n.d., http://butlersports.cstv.com/genrel/plump_bobby00.html).

36 "Bulldogs Set Pace All Way," *Evansville Sunday Courier-Press,* January 15, 1958, Ahlering scrapbook.

37 A few years after that game, the two old adversaries were in a game together, and Harold greeted Bobby by saying, "I held you to forty once." Bobby looked at him and said, "It was forty-one" (Harold Cox interview).

38 "'King' Kelly Coleman and the Wayland Wasps," http://city-high-flash1955-56.tripod.com/id15.html. See also Gary P. West, *King Kelly Coleman: Kentucky's Greatest Basketball Legend* (Morley, Mo.: Steward & Wise, 2005).

39 Kentucky coach Adolph Rupp described Kelly Coleman as "the greatest high school player who ever lived . . . a combination of Frank Ramsey and Cliff Hagan and all the other great stars who have ever played at Kentucky" (Billy Thompson, "Kelly Coleman Is Called Greatest Prep Basketeer in History," Lexington Herald-Leader, n.d., reproduced at www.kingkellycoleman.com/Home.html. The son of a coal miner, Kelly Coleman was the first player in Kentucky to have been honored as Mr. Basketball, in 1956. Coleman played three seasons at Kentucky Wesleyan, where he averaged 27 points per game and twelve rebounds. Drafted by the New York Knicks in the second round (eleventh overall), he played two seasons there and later went to the ABL, where he played two more seasons and was named the league's MVP in 1963 when he led the league in scoring ("Kelly Coleman," n.d., www.thedraftreview.com/index.php?option=com_content&task=view&id=500).

40 Bill Fluty, "Evansville Wins See-Saw Duel from Wesleyan, 77–71," *Evansville Courier* ,January 16, 1958, Ahlering scrapbook; Dick Anderson, column, *Evansville Courier,* January 16, 1958, Harold Cox scrapbook,

41 Bill Fluty, "Staggering Aces Hold off Ball State, 86–82," *Evansville Courier,* January 26, 1958, Harold Cox scrapbook.

42 Dick Anderson, column, *Evansville Courier,* January 26, 1958, Ahlering scrapbook.

43 Harold Cox interview.

44 Bill Fluty, "Aces Nip Butler in Overtime, 89–85," *Evansville Courier,* n.d., Ahlering scrapbook; Bill Robertson, "10,000 See Aces Win Seething OT Thriller," *Evansville Press,* January 31, 1958, Harold Cox scrapbook.

45 Bill Fluty, "Evansville Sinks Beloit's Buccaneers, 77–69," *Evansville Courier,* February 2, 1958, Ahlering scrapbook.

46 Ahlering interview.

47 Harold Cox interview.

48 Bill Fluty, "Mac Calls Larry Erwin's Steal Big Play against Valparaiso," *Evansville Sunday Courier-Press*, February 9, 1958, Ahlering scrapbook.

49 Dan Scism, column, "The Stadium Baskets," *Evansville Courier,* February 14, 1958, Ahlering scrapbook.

50 Bill Fluty, "Final Gasp 40 Footer Shades Ky. Wesleyan," *Evansville Courier,* February 16, 1958, Ahlering scrapbook.

51 West, *King Kelly Coleman.*

52 Bill Fluty, "Final Gasp 40 Footer."

53 Harold Cox interview.

54 Ahlering interview; Harold Cox interview.

55 Bill Fluty, "Aces' Erwin 'Knew I Had It,' Soon as Winning Shot Left His Hands," *Evansville Courier,* February 16, 1958, Ahlering scrapbook.

56 "Aces Belt DePauw, 78–65, Clinch Tie for ICC Crown," *Evansville Courier*, February 21, 1958, Ahlering scrapbook.

57 Bill Fluty, "Aces Tumble St. Joseph's, 78–70, to Win ICC," *Evansville Courier*, February 23, 1958, Ahlering scrapbook; Bill Fluty, "Crosthwaithe 'Beat Aces to Death' McCutchan says of Western Tilt," *Evansville Courier,* February 25, 1958, Ahlering scrapbook. At 6-9 Crosthwaite was one of Western Kentucky's greatest players. He was the all-time leading scorer upon graduation in 1959 and still ranks second with 2,076 points. His 1,309 rebounds are the best ever in the school's history. He was named to the All-America team as a senior and was drafted by the NBA's Detroit Pistons in 1958 and the Boston Celtics in 1959 (The Legends . . . Ralph Crosthwaite," n.d., http://www.hilltopperhaven.com./legends/crosthwaite.html).

58 Hugh Ahlering interview; Harold Cox interview.

59 Bill Fluty, "Aces Win Overtime Thriller, 70–68," *Evansville Courier,* March 6, 1958, Ahlering scrapbook.

60 "Aces Win Berth in National Finals," *Evansville Press*, March 8, 1958, Ahlering scrapbook.

61 Daniel Scism, "Five Big Days Are Lined Up," *Evansville Courier,* March 10, 1958, Harold Cox scrapbook.

62 Bill Fluty, "Wheaton Still Is Favorite in Tourney," *Evansville Courier*, March 13, 1958, Ahlering scrapbook.

63 Harold Cox scrapbook. Jones would lead American to three straight NCAA tournaments and retire as its all-time leading scorer. He later coached at the University of the District of Columbia and Norfolk State University (Dave McKenna, "Jones' Town," *Washington City Paper,* January 14, 2005, www.washingtoncitypaper.com/articles/29916/jones-town/).

64 Bill Robertson, "Aces to Play St. Michael's Tonight," *Evansville Press,* March 13, 1958, Ahlering scrapbook.

65 Bill Fluty, "Aces Bow 78–70 in NCAA Semi-Final," *Evansville Courier,* March 14, 1958, Ahlering scrapbook.

66 Peterson finished his career as Wheaton's all-time leading scorer with 2,542 points. www.athletics.wheaton.edu. The 1957 NCAA College Division Tournament MVP, Peterson was drafted by the Detroit Pistons in the eleventh round in 1960. He later played briefly for Baltimore in the NBA before joining Oakland of the ABA for parts of three seasons ("Hall of Honor: Mel Peterson, Class of 1960," Wheaton College Athletics, n.d., http://athletics.wheaton.edu/hof.aspx?hof=10&path=&kiosk=; "Mel Peterson," Basketball-reference.com, www.basketball-reference.com/players/p/peterme01.html).

67 Bill Fluty, "St. Mike Worn Out; Aces Top in Consolation," *Evansville Courier*, March 16, 1958, Ahlering scrapbook.

Hugh Aherling scores on the 1959–60 team.

Home of Champions, 1958–1959

Interest in the Aces had grown rapidly during the 1957–58 season. As evidence, Bob Hudson could point with pride to the burgeoning membership of the Tip-Off Club, a booster organization that members paid $100 to join.

Tip-Off Club members got choice lower seats for their money and held receptions before and after the games at Roberts in a second-level room reserved for them. There they could enjoy the only alcohol served at Roberts, and after the games Mac would mingle with the members.

"He always attended the postgame parties," said Marilyn McCutchan Disman, who often tagged along with her dad. "They would be held at Roberts and often other gatherings were held in homes and at the country club."[1]

From all accounts by those closest to him, Mac still looked more like other members of the college faculty than the mentor of a nationally ranked team. His hairline was receding, and his horn-rim spectacles gave him the look of an intellectual owl. And if there was a scintilla of hubris in Mac, it was not evident in his demeanor or attitude. He seemed to take it all in stride. "The success never changed him," Marilyn said of her dad. "He was always the same even-keeled and affable person he'd always been."

But behind the horn-rims remained a fierce competitor who sought the same perfection on the court that he sought in problem-solving exercises in the math classes he still taught.

After a preview scrimmage for the Tip-Off Club members, hopes for the 1958–

59 season were high, and everyone was talking about the rebounding prowess of Dale Wise.

Dan Scism warned his *Courier* readers, "Wise may make somebody on this veteran five give." The veterans didn't need Scism to clue them in about Wise—the Cox brothers had coaxed him to Evansville. "We had played summer pick-up games with him back home, and we knew he was going to be real good," Clyde Cox recalled. "We worked real hard on him to come to Evansville."[2]

Wise, a 6-4, two-hundred-pound forward, was a native of Texas who had moved to Kokomo. He missed all of his senior year when he married his high school sweetheart because students who married became ineligible to play sports, but he was still courted by Purdue, Oregon, Mississippi State, and Miami of Florida.[3] But the Cox brothers kept up their recruitment efforts of their Kokomo neighbor. When Mac offered Dale a scholarship, he readily accepted.

Eyeing the unusual depth Mac had assembled for this season—the returnees plus the "Big Bear," as Dale was known back in Kokomo—Scism said, "Mac could lose his five veterans and still win half the games on his schedule." Mac himself had enough confidence in his returning lettermen and newcomers alike to tell reporters, "I'll be very disappointed if we lose more than four games."

He had set the bar high.

Finally, the new season, which couldn't come quickly enough for fans, approached and season tickets were going briskly.

Twenty dollars would buy season tickets for the fourteen home games for the 1958–59 season. Roberts sold a record number of season tickets, buoying the spirits of Bob Hudson, whose promotional skills, along with a season that nearly resulted in a national title, had goosed demand.

On December 1, 1958, the Aces opened at Roberts against New Mexico A&M (now New Mexico State), the first of eight straight visitors at Roberts. A Monday night crowd of more than 5,000 assembled to watch their veteran Aces begin the season.

Heavily favored by as much as 17 points, the Aces were jolted back to reality as New Mexico A&M, led by sophomore Billy Joe Price's 32 points, took the Aces to double overtime before prevailing, 91–85.[4]

The Aggies held Ed Smallwood to 14 points on an uncharacteristic 6-for-24 attempts from the field.

The fans got their money's worth, if not the desired result.

Mac summed it up succinctly in his remarks to the press, "We didn't rebound; we didn't cut; we didn't break; and we didn't play defense. We have a lot of work to do."

Having pretty much said all that needed to be said, Mac prepared the team for its second contest, against South Dakota on Saturday night. The defending national champs had been hit hard by graduation, but Mac warned, "They're still a good defensive club, but maybe not as strong as last year."[5] As usual, he was understating the case.

The Aces rebounded from the opening loss and skinned the Coyotes by an impressive 98–72 before 5,500. Dale Wise grabbed eleven rebounds, and Ed Smallwood returned to form with 20 points.[6]

In their first poll of the season, released after the South Dakota game, UPI sportswriters had Evansville ranked second in the College Division behind Wheaton College of Illinois.

Next on the Aces' early-season schedule was Purdue, a major college power from the Big Ten. At least the Aces would have home-court advantage.

Given Evansville's UPI ranking, the Boilermakers were taking no chances. Coach Ray Eddy sent an assistant to scout the Aces. "If we lose, don't quote me right after the game," he begged reporters. "Sometimes a fellow says things he doesn't really mean."

Most sportswriters expected Purdue to contend with Michigan State for the Big Ten title that season. Led by their 6-5 center Wilson "Jake" Eison, a Gary resident who had been the best high school basketballer in Indiana in 1955, the Boilermakers had beaten Missouri and DePaul after dropping their opener to Kansas State.[7]

"We'll have to watch this Eison close," Mac said. Eison had tallied 32 against DePaul.

"I have the best balanced team I've had at Purdue," Eddy said. "But my bench isn't as strong as I expected it to be."

Eison would have the help of Willie Merriweather, a member of the legendary 1955 Indiana state high school championship team at Crispus Attucks that Oscar Robertson had led, and the 6-6 seniors Bill Greve and Bob Ferhrman. Harvey Austin of Buffalo ran the team from the point.

The Big Ten visitors, who had spoiled the Aces' grand opening of Roberts in 1956, attracted a new record crowd to the stadium—11,088—when the teams tipped off at 8 p.m. It was also the largest crowd ever to see a College Division game anywhere.[8] Sportswriter Gordon Graham of the *Lafayette Courier and Journal* noted, "Traffic snarls had fans running through the parking lots to get inside for the tip-off. Ten minutes later and there wouldn't have been room for a starved midget."

Purdue took a 44–34 cushion to the locker room at the break and stretched it to 17 early in the second half.

The game was played in "normal" Big Ten style, something the Aces were not accustomed to seeing. "Purdue was pushing and shoving us—literally—out of the way to get rebounds in the first half," Mac would complain of the rough tactics. "When we started doing the same thing, I think we matched them lick for lick." Dale Wise concurred with his coach: "You take just so much of a beating, and then you start to give it back. And it worked."

The Aces battled, literally, back into contention, drawing within four when Eison left with five fouls, with 5:51 to play after scoring 16 points. When Ed Smallwood hit a jumper with 3:39 showing on the clock, the Aces grabbed the lead at 76–75.

Once again the game would come down to the wire. With just eight seconds to play, and Purdue holding desperately on to an 83–82 lead, Mac called a final time-out. He designed a play for the Aces that would give Smallwood, who had 30 points, a chance to win it.

When Ahlering looked to inbound the ball, Purdue threw a blanket over Ed. But the Boilermakers had left Lurker open. Mel took the pass and put up a jumper from the top of the key.

Clank! It hit the front of the iron and bounced away.[9]

Purdue had survived, just barely, recording its third straight win over the Aces. "I thought we were beat, and then, pow, that ball skidded out. It was just like Christmas," Purdue's Harvey Austin said.

The Aces were not in a celebratory mood after falling again to their in-state rival in front of a large and boisterous crowd. "Let's look ahead," Mac yelled into the showers. "We can't look back. We can win all the rest now."

Tired and worn out from their near-miss effort, the dejected Aces were lifted, yet again, by positive reinforcement from their coach. "He was always that way. He never said anything negative. He always found a way to put a positive spin on things," Harold Cox recalled.[10]

Wise was rewarded with his first start when the Aces met Valparaiso, but his elevation didn't last long. After only five minutes Dale had his legs cut from under him, and he crashed heavily to the floor. A large cut over his right eye bled profusely, and he clutched his bruised elbow as he was helped off the court.

But the Aces managed to turn back the Crusaders of Valparaiso 98–82.

After the game Dale told reporters, "The last thing I remember is Hugh giving me the ball." Though X-rays proved negative, the obviously concussed Wise remained on the bench, a bandage over his right eye, when DePaul came to town. "He won't start," Mac said, "and we won't use him unless it's necessary."

Larry Erwin replaced the banged-up Wise, who watched in street clothes as the Aces faced Ray Meyers's Blue Demons. Despite a shooting demonstration from long range by Demons guard Howie Carl, a transfer from Illinois, the Aces rallied behind Smallwood, who had 24 points, to win 86–77. Nearly 6,000 fans watched him do it.[11]

"Man, you know I was going up a lot," Smallwood said afterward.

"We sure missed you out there tonight, boy," he told Wise.

"I'll be ready Friday," Dale assured his teammate.

Friday was the opening game of the Evansville Holiday Tournament, featuring Washington University of St. Louis, Tennessee Tech, and St. Mary's of California.

After the Aces rolled over Washington easily, allowing Mac to use all sixteen players in uniform, they faced off in the finals against undefeated Tennessee Tech, which had a 6-9 center, Jimmy Hagan. Coming into the game, Hagan was second in the nation in scoring behind Cincinnati's Oscar Robertson.[12] The Gaels had held Hagan to 23, well below his season average of 33.

"We needed that one," Mac said. "It gives us a chance to catch our breath."[13]

A new attraction greeted the fans for the final game of the weekend tournament. The college's Pep Band entertained spectators for the first time and added to the festive atmosphere as Christmas approached.

The other entertainment was Ed Smallwood, who erupted in a 44-point scoring orgy, setting records for both Evansville College and Roberts Stadium and leading the Aces to an easy 100–73 laugher. "That's the best ball I ever played," Ed said after the game.[14]

Neither Mac nor Smallwood had been aware that the Big Smoke was on a recording-setting pace. "All I knew was he was playing a heck of a ball game, and I wasn't going to take him out. He hit when no one else could," Mac told reporters.

Ed was named the tourney MVP and received his trophy from the tourney queen, Connie Brammer.[15] Dan Scism summed up his performance for his *Cou-*

rier readers with "Big Ed was sharp all over. He did everything but manufacture a basketball during the game."[16]

Despite their performance in the tournament, Mac's Aces were ranked third by UPI in the latest small college poll. But Dick Dunkel's ratings, which included the College Division teams with major colleges, ranked the Aces as twenty-first in the country.

Wise was back on the court, and Ed remained in form when the Aces trounced DePauw 83–61 before nearly six thousand and improved their record to 6–2. Smallwood, leading all Indiana players with an average of 25.5 points per game, had 28, and Dale added ten points and fifteen rebounds.

"It's OK, no pain anymore," Wise said.[17] Maybe not for Dale, but his rebounding definitely hurt the visitors.

In January the Aces left the friendly confines of Roberts and headed up the road to meet Ball State and Butler. They easily dispatched Ball State, then faced the Bulldogs at their fieldhouse.

Lurker had difficulty handling Butler's Bill Scott, a six-foot guard who drove repeatedly up the lane, where the slower Lurker, whose nickname was "Foots," could not contain him. Scott tallied 23 points to lead the Bulldogs to a 78–75 win in which Smallwood was held to 15 by Johnny Jones, a transfer from Gonzaga.[18] The loss was Mac's third straight at Butler.

After the game Mac said, "I know I have to go with Wise in there and possibly [Tom] Mulherin [a reserve]. After all, you've got to go with the guys who are getting the job done."

A caravan of nearly a thousand Aces fans followed the team across the Ohio to Owensboro, where Bullet Wilson's Kentucky Wesleyan Panthers awaited.

King Kelly Coleman and Gene Minton were the veterans. Bullet had added 6-10 Martin Holland, a transfer from Vanderbilt, and 6-0 Charlie Seitz, who had come over from Louisiana State to find a friendly home with Bullet's squad.

Wise had to contend with Holland for control of the boards, and the taller and heavier Panthers center repeatedly outmuscled Dale.

The Panthers opened with a 6–0 run, then widened their lead to 20 at the half, to the delight of the hometown fans who filled the Sportscenter. "They were pretty rowdy down there. They would get all over us and our fans," Hugh Ahlering said of the Aces' trips to Owensboro.[19]

Harold Cox recalled one amusing exchange with a fan. "One of their fans, sitting close to our bench, yelled at me, 'Coxie, how many years are you going to play? I've been watching you for six years now. When you gonna graduate?'

"He'd gotten me confused with my brother Clyde and thought I was the same guy he'd been seeing for all those years," Harold laughed.[20]

That was about the only funny thing about the game. Dick Anderson, covering the game for the *Courier,* told Evansville readers that the Aces were "a mess. A real mess. Mulherin couldn't go. Erwin couldn't go. Cox couldn't hit the floor with his crewcut, Big E was out there and that's about all, and Dale Wise was back up in Howard County or someplace along Route 31 north."[21]

Evansville played the final 13 minutes without the Big Smoke, whom Mac pulled from the contest when he observed that Ed "didn't seem to want to play." Ed accounted for only 4-for-10 from the floor while picking up four fouls, and he left with only 10 points. "I went with him as long as I thought I could when he didn't seem to be helping us," Mac said.

Only Ahlering, with 21 points, had shown any spark for the Aces, who lost, 85–72. Coleman, back from another recent suspension for off-court antics, accounted for 18 points for the Panthers.[22]

The Aces rebounded from the disappointing performance and turned back Ball State and Indiana State in turn, 87–69 and 86–59, with the reserves seeing plenty of minutes.

Bob Hudson announced that the stadium box office would be open from 8 a.m. to 8 p.m. to accommodate those seeking tickets for the Butler game. [23]

With their ICC record now 5–1, the Aces were greeted by 8,623 fans at Roberts when conference leader Butler arrived for their rematch. Smallwood, who was recovering from tonsillitis, picked up his fourth personal early in the second half. Butler capitalized on his absence as the Bulldogs erased a 14-point deficit to tie the Aces at 71 before taking a lead of 75–73 as time was running out.

Ahlering converted two free throws after being fouled in the lane, and the Aces' defense held off Butler to force the visitors into overtime. "I told the boys to go get them. I told them they were tired and we'd run over them or go down firing," Mac said later of his instructions for the overtime period.[24]

Lurker hit a jumper to open the extra period, followed by Hugh Ahlering with two driving layups and Harold Cox with two free throws before Butler could get on the board. The Aces held on to notch an 85–78 win, to the delight of the large crowd.[25]

With its fourth victory over a major college opponent, Evansville next faced a small college team that sported major college credentials. Ohio's College of

Steubenville arrived at Roberts with a winning streak that stretched over the two previous seasons. It had risen to the top position in the 1957–58 season's final small college poll, and Steubenville's winning streak of 13 this season gave it, at 36 straight, the longest unblemished skein in the country.[26]

Mac told reporters on the morning of the game with the Barons, "They have forgotten how to lose." Professor McCutchan would gladly teach them.

It wasn't even close.

At the half, behind Smallwood, Lurker, and Ahlering, the Aces held a comfortable 60–36 lead. The crowd at Roberts, 9,191, attracted by the appealing match-up, was roaring with delight as the Pep Band blared away.

Mac played his reserves for the early part of the second half, and they extended the lead over the hapless Barons. With little more than four minutes to play, Mac reinserted Smallwood, who finished with 32 points. Lurker added 19, and the Barons' leading scorer, John Blanda, and his mates retreated from Roberts with their first loss.[27]

Mac had let the Aces run up the score over Stuebenville. "I had seen how they had poured it on when they could, so I decided to blow them out of the gym if we could," he said after the game.

After the game all team members, along with their girlfriends and wives, were feted at a reception hosted by a group of local dentists, all of whom had dressed in red and sat together in the same row in section M.[28]

Because red was so ubiquitous at Roberts, the dentists weren't all that conspicuous. The group that really stood out arrived for each game attired in referee shirts. These fans didn't have whistles, but they made "calls" that were often at odds with the real referee's calls on the court. Just part of the party that was an Aces game.[29]

The Evansville crowd was, of course, pleased by the runaway win over the Barons. "This, of course, was to the complete satisfaction of the Evansville crowd," Bill Robertson wrote the next day, "which came to see neither clement action nor gentility. The Evansville crowd is perpetually hungry and never gets enough of its favorite commodity—overflowing baskets."[30]

Apparently gorged from their Barons bacchanal, the Aces took a trip to Rensselaer, Indiana, where the St. Joe Pumas prevailed 100–91.[31]

The Aces got back on track against Valpo as Harold Cox scored 25 to lead the Aces on an easy 84–64 win.[32]

They then had a rematch at Roberts with their cross-river foe, Kentucky Wesleyan, as full of themselves as they could be after beating the Aces earlier in Owensboro.

Welcoming Bullet Wilson's charges to the Valentine's Day party were 12,833 Aces fans, more than a thousand over the capacity of the stadium, setting a new record for a college basketball game while taxing Bob Hudson's organizational skills. "We put them in that spacious East Side press box, set chairs in that gangway on the floor, and a lot of people stood around the back and sat in the aisles," he said.[33]

The Aces had treated the visitors to a steak dinner in the school cafeteria. When the Panthers arrived at Roberts, their bus pulled into the parking area and proceeded down a paved incline that led right into the court-level area. There they were greeted by Evansville fans who handed them fruit and soft drinks. That was the last kindness they'd experience.

The Panthers strode into jam-packed Roberts with a swagger in their steps. A week earlier King Kelly Coleman, Kentucky's troubled but talented star, had scored 45 points against Florida Southern and he had told reporters that he "would score 46 against Evansville on Saturday night." Kelly's bravado no doubt helped swell the crowd that was driving the harried fire marshal to distraction.

Mac assigned Harold Cox, "Double O," as he was now known for the uniform number he wore, and Kenny Reising to guard Coleman. That left the rest of the Aces to shut down Martin Holland and Charlie Seitz. Mac was not as concerned about Panthers freshman Gary Auten as he should have been.

At the halfway point in the first half, the unheralded Auten came off the bench to drain three long set shots and a jumper, but the Aces nonetheless held a 47–40 lead at the intermission.

Coleman, who had scored 18 points in the first half, seemed determined to make his boast a reality until he picked up his fourth foul only one minute into the second half. Bullet Wilson decided to leave Coleman in, and, though he cooled off, he managed to keep the game close.

At the 5:46 mark the Aces led 76–70.

Tom Mulherin responded with a surprising offensive spurt of his own and extended the Aces' lead to 12 points, and from there the Aces went on to claim a 92–82 win.

As the second half began, Coleman had greeted Mulherin rudely. "He put up his first shot, and Coleman knocked it clear down to the other end of the court as Mulherin stood wide-eyed, watching," Hugh Ahlering recalled.[34]

But that was unusual for the King, who normally disdained defensive effort as if it wasn't his job. Tom recovered from the shock to finish 7-for-9 from the field, with most of those points coming at a critical time, and he joined five other Aces in double figures in the team effort that thwarted Coleman's brash prediction. The King ended the game with 36, ten shy of his prediction.

"You can guard him but you can't stop him," Harold Cox said of Coleman. "He doesn't need to look when he fires. He just appears to have a magic range-finder."[35]

Hugh Ahlering had seen enough of the enigmatic Kelly Coleman to know what he was capable of. "To look at him you wouldn't think he could play a lick," Ahlering said many years later. "He was usually fat and looked out of shape. He did what he wanted to do. Bullet [Wilson] couldn't control him at all. While the other players were warming up, he'd be sitting on the sidelines in a chair. But when the game started, you'd better watch out, because he could hit from anywhere."[36]

Kenny Reising, who was supposed to help Harold hold Kelly down, had found an early seat on the bench with five fouls. "I led the team in something," he quipped. "Fouls."

Harold Cox fared better against the King, and Coleman finished only 13-for-33 from the field, a tribute to Harold's defensive skills.

The Aces made the road trip to Terre Haute in high spirits after the signature win, but those spirits were soon dampened.

Indiana State played in a gymnasium on campus that was on the second floor of the physical education building.

"We were playing terrible," Ahlering said of the Aces' slow start. "At half time Mac dressed us all down pretty good. He spared none of us. But Ed [Smallwood] took it personally."[37]

"Where he grew up in a real tough Louisville all-black neighborhood, the worst thing that could happen to you there was to be disrespected by your peers," Harold Cox explained. "Ed took Mac's comments personally and felt he was being disrespected and snapped back at Mac in front of all of us."[38]

Reacting viscerally and culturally, as he had been conditioned to do, Ed crossed the line.

"That's it. You aren't dressing for the second half. Go on back to the hotel," Mac told him.

"That's it! I quit," Ed snapped.

While the rest of the team watched in shock, the Aces' star performer left the dressing room. "We didn't know if he was serious or not," Hugh Ahlering said.[39]

The Aces, absent their leading scorer, fell to the Sycamores 77–64, but Harold and Hugh were more concerned about the loss of their main scorer than the loss to the Sycamores. "He was our star. We needed him for the tournament," Harold said. "Hugh and I went to Mac and asked him if we could talk to Ed and try to get him to apologize and come back. We weren't sure if he really meant to quit or not, but as co-captains we felt it was our role to keep him on the team."

Mac agreed.

When they got to his room, the Big Smoke was still smokin'. "We told him how much we needed him and reminded him of the times we had stood up for him," Harold recalled. "'Remember the time that they wouldn't feed you in the restaurant and we all got up and walked out? We all stood with you then, didn't we?'"[40]

Stony silence.

"'And that time they were calling you every filthy name in the book, and Harold and I put our arms around you on the court to protect you and show them you were our guy,'" Hugh prompted.

"'Yeah, I remember,'" Ed said softly, eyes glistening, as he looked at the man who had shepherded him around Evansville and insisted he climb into the front seat as an equal.

"'Well, Ed, we need you now, and you're going to have to apologize to Mac and ask him to let you back on the team,'" Hugh told his friend. Their strategy worked. Smallwood was back on the team for the next game.

Was he ever.

A chastened Ed Smallwood led the Aces to a come-from-behind win at DePauw. "It was a very special game for us," Ahlering said years later. "Ed won it for us almost by himself."[41]

"That game was the turning point for us," Harold Cox said. "It helped pull us all back together."[42]

Next on the Aces' schedule was St. Joseph's, led by the diminutive Dan Rogovich, who was second in the conference in scoring behind his teammate Bob Williams. The Pumas were 11–8 as they walked into Roberts. Evansville, third in the conference behind Butler and Indiana State, stood at 14–6 and had been offered an NCAA at-large bid, which the college had promptly accepted.

The game with the Pumas was meaningful, if Mac's troops were to stand any chance at all of winning the conference race.

Bob Hudson had figured out that if 9,098 fans attended the game, the team would reach the unheard-of total of 100,000 for the season at Roberts. His hopes fell just shy of the magic number—by 359—as the Aces rolled over the Pumas 112–94, even though Williams and Rogovich each scored 22 points.[43]

The Big Smoke, suffering from stomach pains, remained around long enough to score 29 points and grab twelve rebounds. "We were feeding him Tums and some other stuff," Mac said.

The Pumas left Roberts in need of the same.

The Aces next traveled to Beloit where they defeated their hosts 93–79, then flew back to Evansville.[44]

"Dad flew scheduled airlines whenever he could," said his son, Dr. Allen McCutchan. "He'd seen an accident while in the Navy when a young pilot had crashed a PBY [a boat plane] trying to return to the ship that launched him. The pilot's body was terribly ripped up in the crash. Seeing what the force of a plane crash did to a person affected him strongly. He'd decided after that only scheduled airlines were the way to travel, and then only if you absolutely had to fly."[45]

Back in Evansville safe and sound, the Aces had finished the regular season schedule at 16–6.

The NCAA Tournament was next—the "real season," the one that Aces and fans alike had been waiting for since the disappointing ending to the 1957–58 season. First up for Evansville was a team led by a young, feisty coach whose speech and sideline antics were nearly as colorful as the Purple Aces' gaudy attire. Al McGuire had led the tiny Catholic school, Belmont Abbey, to an impressive 20–1 mark. The former Knicks and Bullets player had learned a lot on the bench in the NBA, which was where he had spent most of his three seasons in New York.

Then he'd been an assistant to Alvin "Doggie" Julian at Dartmouth and Joe Lapchick at St. John's, where he soaked up more knowledge at the side of two of the game's most respected mentors.

Not a bad way to learn the game.

McGuire had learned his lessons well.[46]

Since taking the helm at Belmont Abbey, which had an enrollment of 612, he had led the Crusaders to a 44–4 record.

Awaiting the cocky coach was the second-ranked small college team in the country. Although his Crusaders were a nine-point underdog, their coach was not cowed by the Aces.

"It seems as if everyone thinks we are going to lose at Evansville. I think we are going to beat them and win this tourney," McGuire told reporters. "We've got a young team and should be loaded for the next two years, but I don't see anything that will keep us from taking it this year."

McGuire's vision wasn't working as well as his mouth. He was a bit myopic, as it turned out.

McGuire's lineup included four sophomores and a freshman, all from New York. The Crusaders used a 2-1-2 zone to hold the Aces in check until Harold Cox caught fire late in the opening half. Exchanging his 00 jersey for number 14 hadn't impeded Cox's performance on the court. He led an Aces charge that drove McGuire to distraction on the sidelines with animated antics that delighted the crowd.

Evansville took a 45–37 lead to the locker room, while McGuire attempted to revive his players with a half-time harangue. At first, it seemed to have worked as the visitors hung close in the opening minutes.

But then Ed Smallwood's jumper set off a 13-point Evansville run that effectively doomed McGuire's charges.[47]

Sensing the futility of continuing to try to stop the Aces with his starters, McGuire sent them to the locker room in disgust and inserted his reserves as Evansville rolled to a 64–54 win.

"If I'd won, I might have something to say," the usually loquacious McGuire told reporters. "I'm vanquished. Let the victors speak."

Nearly 5,000 were at Roberts for the regional final game, and most came early to see McGuire's team in action against Southern Illinois, which had lost to Wittenberg.

At one point near the close of the Crusaders' consolation game, McGuire tore off his jacket and hurled it to the floor in disgust. Stomping to the end of the bench, the agitated McGuire saw a vendor close at hand and said, "Give me a Coke, son. Those bums are giving me nothing," he added while pointing at his team, which was struggling again on the court.

The championship would see Wittenberg try to duplicate the zone defense that McGuire had used. Wittenberg did so with more success and trailed Evansville by only one point, 29–28, at the intermission.

The second half remained close throughout and at the six-minute mark, with the Aces clinging to a one-point edge, Mac ordered a stall. The visitors watched as the Aces' guards, Cox and Ahlering, exchanged passes. When they made no attempt to defend, the officials charged them with a technical for delay of game.

Smallwood missed the free throw, but the Aces retained possession and continued to hold the ball until Mel Lurker's free throw made it 49–47. A Lurker basket and two Harold Cox free throws put the Aces up by 51–47 with only 1:47 to go.

That was as close as the visitors would get. Evansville College held on to notch a 56–50 win and moved on to the NCAA Finals.

"I saved the stall for two years," Mac said, his team's past lack of success with the tactic no doubt much in his mind.

"It wasn't a stall," Harold Cox insisted. "We wanted to take them out of that zone defense, and we weren't going to take any shots unless we had open layups. But they wouldn't come out."[48]

Wittenberg's coach told reporters, "That Ahlering wrecked us in the first half driving in. We were wary of Smallwood but he didn't hurt us as much as that other kid." That "other kid" was Dale Wise.

Wise joined Smallwood on the All-Tournament team as Mac had his second chance in two years to win it all.[49]

Now at 18–6 for the year, the Aces' first roadblock in the field of eight at the finals was a familiar old foe and one that had thwarted their chances before. St. Michael's of Vermont was the Aces' opponent on Wednesday night. The team that had stymied the Aces in 1958 stood in the Aces' path once again. This time the Aces didn't overlook the Granite State's representatives. Taking an early lead, the Aces never let up and gained sweet revenge.

Harold Cox opened the second half with three straight baskets as the Aces pulled steadily away to win 82–63.[50]

The Aces' semifinal foe was North Carolina A&T, coached by Cal Irvin, brother of New York Giants outfielder Monte Irvin. Irvin's team, described as a "fancy Negro club," was swift and dangerous.[51] The Aggies were led by Al Attles, their junior guard, and had compiled a 27–4 record thus far.

Ed Smallwood, Evansville's only black player, found himself facing a trash-talking squad that taunted him about his presence on the otherwise all-white Purple Aces. "There was a lot of talk going on," Hugh Ahlering said later. "They were getting on Ed pretty good."[52]

But Ed wasn't about to get rattled.

As Ahlering drove repeatedly up the lane, the outside opened up and Ed began to hit from there. The Aces had built a 55–46 lead at the half.

Evansville stayed in command until Ed picked up his fifth personal at the 11:35 mark. Perhaps overeager to impress the taunting Aggies, Ed had fouled out for only the fourth time in his career.

With Ed gone and the Aces leading by 76–72, the Aggies saw Mac instruct his team to slow down. The strategy had worked against Wittenberg, and Mac had to believe that his players could do it again. With Ed sitting on the bench Mac sent in Dale Wise at center. He promptly made a free throw and a tip-in to build the Aces' lead to seven points. When Larry Erwin scored on an Aces' inbounds play, the score was 81–72.

"They platooned us," Ahlering said. "They kept running five new and fresh guys in on us all night, and they were all fast."[53]

Ahlering followed with another driving layup down the lane, and the score was now 83–72.

"The Old Man," as the fans called Ahlering, played like a frisky young colt, and his success up the middle led to repeat performances. Hugh continued to drive the lane, to the frustration of the Aggies, who kept fouling him in an attempt to stop him.

Ahlering coolly converted 17 of 18 free throws, added 7-for-15 from the floor, and provided his finest performance as an Ace when his team needed him the most. "In those days if you were fouled while driving in, the referees always called the foul on the defense. They never called charging back then," Hugh said.[54]

As Smallwood watched his friend and protector from the bench, Hugh Ahlering, barreling down the lane into a forest of arms and legs, led Evansville to a 110–92 win.[55]

The Aces were one win away from the title.

"I haven't seen any teams much better than that North Carolina club," Hugh said. "I don't know how we ever beat them, and I don't know if we could have done it again."[56]

Fortunately, they didn't have to.

For the crown to be theirs, all that remained was to beat Southwest Missouri State. Although a snowstorm blanketed the area, making travel dangerous, 8,651 fans managed to make it safely to Roberts on March 13, for the final game. No blizzard was going to stop them from seeing their Aces battle for the championship.

The Aces' opponent was the best shooting and defensive team in the field. The

Bears of Southwest Missouri State had won 23 of 25 games since losing in the 1958 tournament's semifinals. Jack Israel was the Bears' top scorer.

Mac started Ahlering and Cox at the guards, and Lurker at center with Ed Smallwood and Larry Erwin as forwards.

Under their multicolored robes the Aces were sporting their orange uniforms. Mac had a message to deliver in the locker room. Years later he recalled his feelings just before the opening tip. "Before we took the floor, I told my players that none of us, myself included, thought we'd ever be in this position," Mac said. "We weren't the pre-tournament favorites, although that was a year when nobody was heavily favored."

With Ahlering scoring 11 points, the Aces raced out to an early lead and held a 44-38 advantage at the half. Mulherin started the second half and added three quick points. Lurker's basket sailed home on an in-bounds play—one of Mac's favorite ploys—and the Aces were up, 51–40.

When Ed Smallwood left with four fouls and fifteen minutes to play, the Aces were in charge by seven points, and Mac again ordered his team to stall. It had worked against the Aggies, and he asked his charges to execute it one more time.

The Aces picked their way through the Bears' heralded defense to pull steadily away. "Mac liked to use the stall to extend the floor and open up lanes for us," Ahlering said.[57]

With the Aces holding a comfortable 83–65 lead, Mac cleared the bench, and the fans stood and applauded the starters as they made their happy way to the pine. No one noticed when the Bears added two meaningless free throws as the Aces and their fans celebrated their greatest moment together.

The scoreboard read 83–67 as the horn sounded unheard amid the tumult in Roberts.

Evansville College was now, officially, the new national champion.

Smallwood had scored 24 to lead the Aces, while Lurker added 19 and Dale Wise chipped in 8.[58]

The highest praise from Mac, though, was reserved for his dynamic backcourt duo of Harold Cox and Hugh Ahlering. "They were tremendous throughout," Mac told reporters. "With them in there I didn't have to worry too much."

"We were the coaches on the floor for him," Harold Cox said of Hugh and himself. "Mac trusted us and expected us to lead the team. He gave us a lot of credit as leaders, and we kept things going on the court. We kept the guys aggressive and helped them hold their heads up when the going got tough."[59]

The two flashy guards had led their team well. They had started 56 straight games together and logged an impressive 45–11 record since becoming starters.

Mac accepted the trophy from Swarthmore's Willis Stetson, and each of the winning Aces players received a small wooden plaque to commemorate the victory.

The next morning the lead story on Page One of the *Evansville Courier* was headlined "National Champs," accompanied by pictures of the coach and team holding the trophy aloft. It was, as the attention given it clearly demonstrates, a trophy shared by the entire city of Evansville.[60]

"It has been great fun," Hugh Ahlering, the "Old Man", told reporters after the game and his career at Evansville had ended. "The Missouri boys were a great bunch of guys, probably the best I ever met."

Harold Cox spent five years at Evansville College and completed his career there with 961 points in 87 games, an average of 11 per game. The recipient of the Kiwanis Award, Harold would go on to become a high school coach. In his stay at Evansville, he had pretty much seen it all. "I played for a terrific coach who could counsel and guide you, not only to be a better player but to be a better person and help build our lives.

"The fans loved our fast break," he said of the style he and Hugh patented during their tenure. "I saw the fan support grow. From that dark old Armory to the new Stadium their support of us just kept growing and growing."[61]

Years later he would reflect: "You have to appreciate having been part of making that all happen. I had a passion for the game, and when Roberts opened we got to play some great teams in front of those fans who supported us like no others. The coach, the players, and those fans all made it happen," he said. "It was McCutchan's way in Evansville: enjoy the game and play at the highest level you can."

Later Harold would leave coaching and begin a long and successful career in telecommunications.

Hugh Ahlering, Harold's running mate at guard, completed one of the most successful careers in Evansville history with a national title plaque. At twenty-eight, the man they had dubbed on arrival as "the Old Man" would leave the Aces with a career total of 1,036 points. He was named tournament MVP and a member of the All-Tournament team.

The Associated Press named him to its first team College Division All-America squad and UPI, which named Smallwood to its first team, placed Ahlering on its second team.

Hugh would join major college stars Jerry West and Oscar Robertson on the U.S. squad for the Pan American Games coached by Fred Schaus, a ringing endorsement for a College Division player.[62]

After leaving Evansville College with an engineering degree, Hugh had a long career with a local construction firm for which he and Dale Wise had first worked in the summers while they were at Evansville.

His memories of Evansville are fond ones. "There weren't any better fans anywhere. They treated us like royalty," he recalled.[63]

Two other Aces, Harold Malicoat and Harold Halbrook, both reserves, were also graduating. Malicoat would enjoy a successful coaching career at Bosse High School, while Halbrook pursued a much different course.[64] Halbrook, who managed to score only 113 points in fifty games with the Aces, did much better off the court. He went on to Indiana University and earned his medical degree. Later he became a cardiologist and, after further study at Stanford, performed the first heart transplant in Indiana.

The Aces were feted at a large "Acclaim the Aces" banquet on April 15 at St. Benedict's. More than 600 people assembled to hear Al McGuire call the Aces "the most explosive team" his Crusaders had faced.

"They're champions of the college division. And they would have surprised a lot of people in the university tournament," said McGuire, whose Marquette Warriors would later surprise many.[65]

In his colorful New York–accented style, McGuire told a tongue-in-cheek tale about Mac and his best player, offering an example of Mac's interest in making sure his players all got passing grades to stay eligible.

"Mac asked his player Ed Smallwood a test question.

"'Ed, what's the capital of Indiana?'

"Ed thought awhile and then answered, 'Frankfort!'

"Mac looked at him and said, 'Well, Frankfort is about 30 miles from Indianapolis. And 30 from 100 is 70.

"'Ed, you pass!'"

It brought down the house.[66]

Aces fans were charmed by McGuire long before his color commentary on television entertained millions. Entertaining the banquet throng with rapid one-liners, he had promised, "If the Aces beat Belmont Abbey next season, I'll buy everyone in the stadium an ice cream cone."

But the 1958–59 season, which would be forever remembered for bringing the city its first championship, was over. Years later, when a reporter asked him to look back over his long career at Evansville, Mac would say that of all his teams there, this was the one he remembered most fondly.

His simple explanation: "They won our first one."

(Endnotes)

1   Marilyn McCutchan Disman, telephone interview by author, February 22, 2011.

2   Clyde Cox, telephone interview by author, April 5, 2011.

3   For background on Wise, I am indebted to Bill Bussing, who generously made his lengthy account of the Aces available to me. His detailed account contains no footnotes, but when I interviewed Bussing in February 2011, he identified his sources as the *Evansville Courier* and *Evansville Press,* the two local papers at the time. Bussing's manuscript usually makes no distinction between the two, but the direct quotes are from one or the other and appear in his manuscript in quotation marks. Bussing (and I) also had access to the old bound scrapbooks kept by Bob Hudson that are now housed in the university archives. The articles do not identify which paper they are from, much less the date and page, but I (and Bussing) assume they are from the *Courier* or the *Press,* or the combined Sunday edition, the *Courier & Press.* Where no endnote appears with information crediting another source, the reader may assume that the information, especially quotations, comes from the Bussing manuscript.

4   Price is a member of New Mexico State's Ring of Honor; his number 31 has been retired by the Aggies. He is their sixteenth-leading scorer and among the leaders in rebounds .He was selected in the sixth round of the 1961 NBA draft by the Syracuse Nationals..

5   Bill Fluty, "South Dakota Earns McCutchan Respect," *Evansville Courier,* December 6, 1958, Ahlering scrapbook, n.p. In this chapter all citations to articles from Evansville newspapers come from players' scrapbooks and contain no page number. In reconstructing dates, I have assumed that game accounts appeared on the day after the game.

6   Steve Perkins, "Aces Clobber South Dakota," *Evansville Courier & Press,* December 7, 1958, Ahlering scrapbook.

7   Eison had led his Roosevelt High School team to the Indiana High School

Athletic Association finals in 1955 where he scored 31 points in a loss to Crispus Attucks, led by Oscar Robertson. Eison is in the Indiana Basketball Hall of Fame. A three-time Purdue MVP, he was drafted by the Minneapolis Lakers.

8   "Largest Crowd to Watch College Game," photo caption, *Evansville Sunday Courier & Press*, n.d., Ahlering scrapbook.

9   Steve Perkins, "Purdue Tops Aces in Last Minute," *Evansville Sunday Courier & Press*, December 13, 1958, Ahlering scrapbook..

10   Harold Cox, telephone interview by author, April 6, 2011.

11   Steve Perkins, "Aces Bound Back to Bomb DePaul," *Evansville Sunday Courier & Press*, December 21, 1958, Ahlering scrapbook.

12   UPI, "Tennessee Tech's Ace Second to Oscar," *Evansville Courier*, December 22, 1958, Ahlering scrapbook.

13   Bill Robertson, "Evansville's Last Half Burst Brings 84–53 Win over Washington University's Bears," *Evansville Press*, December 23, 1958, Ahlering scrapbook.

14   Steve Perkins, "Smallwood Hits 44 for 100–73 Victory, *Evansville Sunday Courier & Press*, December 27, 1958, Ahlering scrapbook.

15   Undated photo caption, *Evansville Sunday Courier & Press*, n.p. Ahlering scrapbook.

16   Daniel W. Scism, "Aces Change Character," *Evansville Sunday Courier & Press*, December 27,1958, Ahlering scrapbook.

17   "Ed and Aces Keep Warm," *Evansville Courier*, January 3, 1959, Ahlering scrapbook.

18   Steve Perkins, "Hinkle, Hinkle, Lil' Star, Our Aces Shot by Scott," *Evansville Courier*, January 10, 1959, Ahlering scrapbook.

19   Hugh Ahlering, telephone interview by author, April 16, 2011.

20   Harold Cox interview.

21   Dick Anderson, column, *Evansville Courier*, January 14, 1959, Ahlering scrapbook.

22   Bill Robertson, "Bristling Wesleyan Riddles Aces, 85–72," *Evansville Press*, January 14, 1959, Ahlering scrapbook.

23   Steve Perkins, "Every Ace in the Deck Hit Ball State," *Evansville Sunday Courier & Press*, January 24, 1959, Ahlering scrapbook.

24   Don Bernhardt, "Mac's Final Order: 'Go Get 'Em Boys,'" *Evansville Courier*, January 29, 1959, Ahlering scrapbook.

25   Bill Fluty, "Evansville Outlasts Butler in Extra Period, 85–78," *Evansville Courier*, January 29, 1959, Ahlering scrapbook.

26   "Unbeaten Steubenville Team Risks 36 Game Win Streak against Aces at Stadium," *Evansville Courier,* January 21, 1959, Ahlering scrapbook.

27   John Blanda was the brother of Chicago Bears place kicker and quarterback George Blanda, who would have a long and illustrious career in the NFL.

28   "Unbeaten Stuebenville Team."

29   "Unbeaten Stuebenville Team."

30   Bill Robertson, *Evansville Press*, January 30, 1959, Ahlering scrapbook.

31   "St. Joe's Knocks Aces out of ICC lead, 100–91," *Evansville Courier,* February 5, 1959, Ahlering scrapbook.

32   Steve Perkins, "A Kid from Kokomo Kills Valpo," *Evansville Courier,* February 7, 1959, Ahlering scrapbook.

33   Bill Robertson, "Record Crowd Saw Evansville College Aces Solve All Their Problems Except King Kelly," *Evansville Press*, February 15, 1959, Ahlering scrapbook.

34   Ahlering interview.

35   Robertson, "Record Crowd."

36   Ahlering interview.

37   Ahlering interview.

38   Harold Cox interview.

39   Ahlering interview.

40   Harold Cox interview.

41   Ahlering interview.

42   Harold Cox interview.

43   Steve Perkins, "Aces Win with a Vengeance—112 New Record," *Evansville Courier*, February 22, 1959, Ahlering scrapbook.

44   Bob Williams, "Aces Get Tune-Up, by 93–79," *Evansville Press*, February 22, 1959, Ahlering scrapbook.

45   Allen McCutchan interview.

46   McGuire is best known to most older fans as a television analyst whose patented nicknames and phrases enlivened his college basketball telecasts on CBS with drab Billy Packer.

47   Bill Fluty, "Ohio Five Breezes by SIU, Smallwood, Cox Spark Decisive Second Half Rally," *Evansville Courier*, Ahlering scrapbook..

48   Bill Fluty, "Aces Stall Pays Off in 56–50 Win over Wittenberg," *Evansville Courier*, n.d., Ahlering scrapbook.

49   "Wise, Smallwood on All-Tourney Team," *Evansville Press*, n.d., Ahlering scrapbook.

50   Bill Robertson, "Evansville's Blazing Attack Smashes St. Michael's, 82–63," *Evansville Press*, March 2, 1959, Ahlering scrapbook.

51   Bill Fluty, "Aces Roll into NCAA Title Tilt with 110–92 Victory," *Evansville Courier*, n.d., Ahlering scrapbook.

52   Aherling interview.

53   Ahlering interview.

54   Ahlering interview.

55   Fluty, "Aces Roll into NCAA Title Tilt."

56   Ahlering interview.

57   Ahlering interview.

58   Bill Fluty, "Aces Win National Cage Title, 83–67; Ahlering Ranked Top Performer," *Evansville Courier*, March 13, 1959, Ahlering scrapbook.

59   Harold Cox interview.

60   "National Champs," *Evansville Press*, March 14, 1959, p. 1, Ahlering scrapbook.

61   Harold Cox interview.

62   "EC Has Two All-Americans in Great Basketball Year," *Evansville Press*, n.d., Ahlering scrapbook.

63   Ahlering interview.

64   According to Allen McCutchan, Halbrook narrowly avoided being kicked out of school despite being smarter than almost everyone else there. While in ROTC he had talked back to an officer and was hauled in front of a review board on charges that would have led to his dismissal if he was found guilty. Serving on the board were a colonel, a major, and Mac. After hearing testimony they had to make a decision. Mac looked at the two officers and said, "Colonel, you're a fine pilot and officer. Major, you're a great logistics man. This kid is amazingly talented. If we're ever in a shooting war again, I want this kid on my side." That statement swung the decision in Halbrook's favor.

65   Bill Fluty, "Evansville Acclaims Its National Champions," *Evansville Courier*, April 16, 1959, Ahlering scrapbook. In 1964, after Marquette's worst season in its history, McGuire took the Marquette coaching job, leaving Belmont Abbey after taking the Crusaders to five postseason tourneys in seven years. McGuire was NCAA named coach of the year in 1970 and again in 1974. After announcing he was leaving at the end of the season, he led the

Warriors to their only national championship in 1977. Al knew how to make an exit as well as an entrance. He led the Warriors to eleven straight post-season appearances and won 74 percent of the games he coached. He was elected to the Naismith Memorial Basketball Hall of Fame in 1992. After a post coaching career as an analyst, he died in 2001.

66 Harold Cox, interview by author, April 5, 2011, telephone.

Bob Hudson in his office with one of his Aces scrapbooks.

(l-r) Gus Doerner, Evansville's first All-American; Jim Smallins, the first black player
who helped bring down racial barriers with his play as an Ace. John Harrawood,
1954–57.

(l-r) Dale Wise, 1959–61; Hugh "The Old Man" Ahlering, star of the first championship team, 1959–60; Ed Smallwood, one of the stars of the 1959–60 championship team.

(l-r) The Evansville Purple Aces 1959–60 championship team; Ed Smallwood accepts the NCAA award for Division Finals MVP; the 1959–60 championship team.

(l-r) Larry Erwin, 1958–60; Ed Rolen shoots against Ohio State, 1961; Ed Zausch in action.

(l-r) Marv Pruett goes up, 1961; Wayne Boultinghouse on the floor in 1962; Buster Briley takes a jumper, 1962.

(l-r) Ed Zausch and Buster Briley, 1964; Herb Williams, 1964; Wayne Boultinghouse and Jerry Sloan, 1964.

(l-r) The 1964 championship team; Sam Watkins (1964–66) goes for the basket.; Jerry Sloan, 1961–65, later played for and coached the Chicago Bulls. From 1988–2011, he coached the Utah Jazz to more than 1,000 wins—an NBA record.

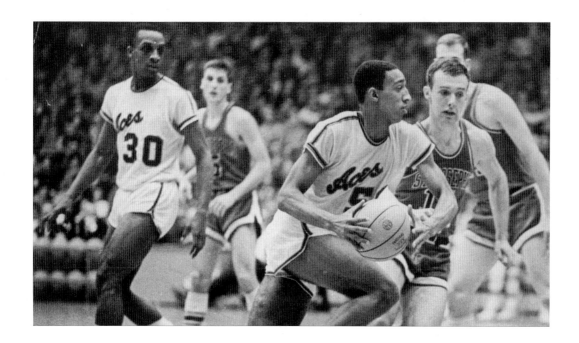

(l-r) Larry Humes, Indiana's "Mr. Basketball" in 1962, is Evansville's all-time leading scorer—a record he has held since 1966. Larry Humes scores two of his 2,236 career points; Purple Aces after a 1965 NCAA win against Southern Illinois University.

(l-r) Coach Arad McCutchan on the sidelines; Coach Arad McCutchan with his five-time-NCAA-championship smile; Don Buse, a Purple Ace from 1969–72.

(l-r) After leading Evansville's 1971 NCAA championship team, Don Buse would go on to play thirteen seasons in the ABA and NBA. The 1971 championship team celebrates; the team with the 1971 NCAA championship trophy.

(l-r) The 1973–74 Purple Aces; Mike Platt, 1977; Arad McCutchan and Harry Whetstone in 1977.

(top) Memorial Plaza, honoring the UE's men's basketball team, coaches, and support staff lost in the 1977 plane crash. (bottom) Memorial Plaza's eternal water fountain, which some call a "weeping basketball."

(l-r) Theren Bullock and Dick Walters, the coach who, in 1978–79, rebuilt the team after the crash. Brad Leaf, 1979–1982; Leaf, a member of UE's All-Time Men's Basketball Team.

(l-r) Marty Simmons charges in a game against Miami. Simmons, 1987–88, a member of UE's All-Time Men's Basketball Team, became the Ace's coach in 2007; Simmons takes a shot.

(l-r) Scott Hafner, 1987–89. Haffner shoots during his 65-point game against Dayton in 1989. Coach Crews on the sidelines.

(l-r) Evansville vs. Ohio State, 1989. Jim Crews coached at UE from 1985–2002;
Marcus Wilson, UE's 2nd-leading career scorer.

Repeat Performance, 1959–1960

As the top team in the 329-member NCAA College Division, the Aces would have a large target on their back when basketball returned for the 1959–60 season.

The Aces had lost their on-court leaders in Ahlering and Cox but would have twelve returning lettermen led by Ed Smallwood and Dale Wise, and fans were excited about the prospects for the season ahead.

Dan Scism was among the first to suggest to his *Courier* readers that the recent success of the Purple Aces made a move up to major college status a logical next step for the school. Scism's urgings attracted some support in the community, but for Mac and the administration the move was not a priority. Mac and Bob Hudson had seen to it that the Aces had enjoyed the best of both worlds since moving to Roberts. They scheduled major college teams, attracted by hefty guarantees, and supplied the Aces' loyal and growing fan base with the opportunity to see the major college powers take on their team.[1]

There was no doubt that the Aces' winning ways in the College Division were generating excitement and interest in Aces basketball at an unprecedented level. Aided by Hudson's astute marketing and Mac's scheduling of major college opponents in preconference play, Evansville College, with fewer than 2,500 students, was in the top ten in the nation in attendance, among *all* schools, major and College Division. Basketball fans had snapped up 99,641 tickets for the 1958–59 season, a testament to their pride and involvement with the Aces.[2] And total attendance at Roberts for the 1958–59 season, including the NCAA Tournament games, had exceeded 131,000 at a time when the city's population was fewer than 125,000.

In another move that proved demand for Aces basketball was growing with each passing year, Mac was to begin his own weekly television show on WEHT-TV, co-hosted by Chic Anderson. Major college coaches around the country had been doing television shows for a few years, but it was decidedly uncommon for a coach at the College Division level to gain regular access to a television audience. The station manager also announced plans to rebroadcast all Evansville games on Sunday afternoons.

Mac had added some new recruits, including two from Kokomo, and Marv Pruett from Springs Valley.

All the high hopes for the coming season were tested early when Mac's varsity barely eked out a win, 82–77, in a preseason scrimmage against the freshman team. "The old zip on the attack is gone," Mac told Dan Scism. "No one cut or drove with the fury of Ahlering or Cox. And there was no Cox back to bulldog the yearlings when they broke too fast." Mac would have to find the zip without the two players that he had relied on in the past.

"I know it can't be the same without Ahlering and Cox, but the way things are going now, I can't see how I can expect more than a 12–12 season," Mac said after the scrimmage, trying to make the hopes that swirled around his team more realistic.

Yes, Cox and Ahlering were both gone, but Iowa of the Big Ten Conference was coming back—and sooner than Mac would have liked. The Hawkeyes were the Aces' first opponents at Roberts as they began the defense of their title.

Mac filled one of the open guard positions by switching Larry Erwin from forward. He put Dale Wise, along with Smallwood and Lurker, up front. "Larry is a heady player, a good ball player, and he's not worried about scoring too much. We'll need his experience on the back line," Mac told reporters.

To fill the other open guard spot, Mac chose P. M. Sanders of Petersburg. A 6-1 guard who had attracted interest from Tennessee, Vanderbilt, Indiana, Memphis State, and Wisconsin, among others, Sanders had scored just six points in thirteen games as a reserve the previous season. Largely untested, his 13 points in the scrimmage earned him the nod. The blond with thick glasses would start against Iowa.[3]

The Aces seemed not to have missed a beat as Smallwood thrilled the largest opening-game crowd in Roberts Stadium history, 8,933 fans, by taking the Aces to an early lead. To the crowd's delight the lead built to 11–1 before the Hawkeyes got into the flow of the game.

With less than ten minutes to play in the first half, Iowa managed to bring the score to 23–22. Then reserve center Walt Deal answered with two quick baskets, and the Aces went to the locker room with a ten-point lead.

The long hoped-for win over a Big Ten foe seemed in sight until Ed Smallwood picked up his fifth foul with more than fourteen minutes to go. Ed had scored 28 points, and his offense would be sorely missed down the stretch.

Evansville still held a nine-point lead when Dale Wise followed Ed to the bench. When reserve Ken Reising left nine seconds later, things were beginning to look a little grim.

Don Nelson tied it for his Hawkeyes at 82 with 1:29 to play, and Mel Lurker joined the growing contingent of Aces on the bench.

Nelson's eleventh bucket put the Hawkeyes ahead with forty-five seconds to play. Mike Heitmann added a basket to up the Iowa lead to 86–82.

With twelve seconds showing on the clock, P. M. Sanders scored for the Aces, but Iowa held on to claim an 86–84 win.

"I think with Ed Smallwood in there all the way we might have beaten them by 20 points," Mac said after the loss. "He was as ready as I've ever seen him." Bob Carpenter, an Iowa guard who had been a high school teammate of Ed's in Louisville, agreed with Mac. "He was mighty good then and mighty good now," Carpenter said.

Iowa's head coach, Milton "Sharm" Sheuerman, at twenty-five the youngest in the Big Ten, had dreaded facing Mac's Aces so early. After the game produced a win, he told reporters, "We don't expect to play against any player this year any better than Ed Smallwood. I think Evansville would do well in the Big Ten this year. Of course they lack a big man."

Iowa's big man was 6-6 Don Nelson, and the sophomore had made his debut on the varsity a memorable one by canning 33 points. "We went into it blind as far as scouting reports go and just didn't expect a sophomore to come up with that kind of game," Mac confessed. The loss of Smallwood and then Wise had left Nelson free to fire at will from close range. Size does matter, and the Aces had no answer for the big guy.

The Aces next met Texas Wesleyan, handled the invaders easily, and got their first win, 89–73. Mac, though, still wasn't pleased with the current squad: "We were lazy. We didn't get back on defense and we made far too many mistakes."

But one player did earn an *A* for effort. Senior Ken Reising, subbing for Sanders, scored 16 points off the bench. While Lurker and Smallwood struggled, Reising, a graduate of Evansville's Mater Dei High School, was a ray of hope for Mac. He had scored only 53 points in thirty-three games while Cox and Ahlering ran things. Now Ken's play was impressive. He added 11 more points on the road as the Aces spoiled the dedication of Central Missouri Sate's new four-thousand-seat gymnasium by 81–71.

The Aces next knocked off visiting St. Mary's of California with Smallwood scoring 34 points to lead the come-from-behind Aces to their third consecutive win. Ken Reising continued to impress, adding 14 to the winning effort. "Every time I hit Ed and broke around him, I was wide open," Ken explained. The Gaels had concentrated on double-teaming Ed, repeatedly leaving Ken free for open shots.

Mac had anticipated the move and responded with a countermove that stymied the Gaels—as Ken passed the ball inside to Ed, Ken would break for the basket. Ed would then pass the ball back to Ken, who was unguarded—and right under the basket.

"It was just like Coach said," Ken marveled after the game of Mac's offensive answer to the Gaels' strategy.

When Los Angeles State arrived at Roberts in December, Ken Reising was in the starting lineup for the Aces. The game provided fans with a shootout, but the Aces were the last ones standing when it was over, managing a 109–99 victory. Wise with 22 and Smallwood with 19 were topped by reserve Walt Deal, who notched a career-best 24 points to lead the team. Deal had played for a former Ace, Thornton Patberg, at Owensville High School, where the 6-5 forward had averaged 17.2 points per game as a senior.

Mac had seen in Walt, who walked on in 1957–58, "as much potential as any high school player in the area." But Walt had failed to live up to that potential. "I goofed off last year," Walt had acknowledged after the Central Missouri State win. "I was something of a clown." Now that he was getting serious, Walt was adding depth to Mac's front line.

After an easy 87–72 win over Valparaiso, the Aces were back for their annual Holiday Tournament sporting a 5–1 record.

Others were taking notice of Mac's current squad. Wittenberg's Ray Mears told Mac his team would surely enjoy a high national ranking if the Aces were included in the major college poll after Evansville had defeated Fresno State in the opener of the Holiday Tournament before nearly eight thousand at Roberts.

Bill Vandenburgh, the Fresno State coach, agreed. "I think that Oregon is perhaps a little better all around than Evansville. But they're not as tough under the basket," he told reporters after the Aces had defeated his Bulldogs 85–77.

Another crowd of nearly 8,000 watched as the Aces met Wittenberg, which had defeated Tennessee Tech, in the finals on Monday after an unusual one-day break because of a scheduling conflict for the stadium. The Aces were not affected by the break and easily turned back the visitors 70–60. Dale Wise earned the tournament MVP award with his 24 points and twenty-four boards against Fresno State and 16 points against Wittenberg. Smallwood paced the Aces' attack with 27, while 6-5 guard Larry Erwin had sparkled on defense.

The Aces' win was the 200th of Mac's career and did nothing to hurt the Aces' number one ranking in the latest United Press International College Division poll. The win and the lofty ranking led local sportswriters to press anew for upgraded competition.

"We go along with Tony Hinkle of Butler on the Indiana Conference," Bob Hudson countered. "Hinkle said he had been in college basketball all his life, and that the ICC was plenty tough in basketball. Of course, he lines up a pre-conference schedule composed mainly of major schools. That's what we're trying to accomplish, plus a game or two with major schools during our conference play in January and February."

The Aces beat both DePauw and Ball State before Evansville made the trip to the Butler Fieldhouse. Hinkle's squad had already beaten Big Ten opponents Wisconsin, Michigan, and Purdue, as well as UCLA, before suffering recent losses to Notre Dame and Bradley.

A crowd of 9,865 turned out to watch the Bulldogs battle the Aces. Most thought that these would be the teams contending for the conference crown at the end of the season.

Mac was unfazed by the crowd and stifling heat all those bodies generated. "I felt like we had a few more horses," he said. He was right.

With Smallwood leading the offense and Lurker bottling up Hinkle's leading scorer, Ken Pennington, and holding him to just six points, the Aces had their first win at the Fieldhouse since 1956, 71–50.

"We clogged everything up inside. I believe they only got five or six baskets from inside 15 feet," Mac said after the win.

In the crowd was the new head coach at Kentucky Wesleyan, T. L. Plain. "I was impressed with Evansville's rebounding," he observed. "I also think they are better defensively than they were last year. Evansville has some players who could play anywhere."

Plain had inherited the talented King Kelly Coleman, and his Panthers were 6–4 and ranked seventh in the UPI poll. The Panthers had exceeded 100 points in their last five outings. The Aces, accompanied by about 700 rooters, were meeting the Panthers in Owensboro. "Wesleyan is rough, rugged and sharp, "Mac warned. "I don't know whether there is any answer to stop Kelly." Kelly, considered Kentucky's greatest high school player, was stoppable only when he stopped himself with off-court carousing and antics that drove his coach to distraction.[4]

As the 10–1 Aces took the floor before a standing-room-only crowd, they could only hope to stop the rest of the Panthers and that Kelly had one of his infrequent off nights.

He didn't. Led by Coleman, the Panthers raced to a 13-point lead midway in the first half before Dale Wise and P. M. Sanders brought the Aces back to within two points. Ed Smallwood, by then carrying three personals, found his range early in the second half but soon was sitting on the bench with his fifth foul. Sixteen minutes remained, and the Aces were up, 56–53.

Without their scoring leader the Aces struggled, and Coleman and Gary Auten led the Panthers to a 95–91 win. Despite Dale Wise's thirty-one rebounds, which tied Jim Smallins's school record, and the 91 points they had managed, the Aces had fallen. "They picked us pretty good," Mac said.

Sanders had shot 9-for-18 from the floor, and the performance had gotten him his starting role back. The Aces next were scheduled to play Belmont Abbey at Roberts. The Crusaders' coach, Al McGuire, had billed the game as "the world's greatest promotion," much to Bob Hudson's delight. Hudson was thrilled with McGuire's sound bites, which he knew would boost attendance.

Evansville fans, who had been entertained by McGuire's antics during the NCAA Tournament the previous year, were waiting for the colorful coach's return.

Before the game McGuire told reporters he had sent the Aces coach a "mystery gift." "It's something he can't wear. If I lose I'll take it back," McGuire said.

When Mac returned from the Kentucky Wesleyan loss, he and reporters went out to Dress Regional Airport, where McGuire's gift was waiting. It was a month-old goat, in a crate, brought to Evansville aboard an Eastern Airlines plane. Was Al trying to tell Mac he'd get his goat?

The irrepressible McGuire and his team arrived a day later. "I feel uneasy," he said upon arrival. "Everybody is being too nice to us."

Convinced, easily, by the *Evansville Courier* to write a guest column that the paper carried on the morning of the game, McGuire had used the ink to persuade Mac to use the team's orange road jerseys for the game. "Only way those refs can tell the home team is by the color of their shirts, white," he wrote. "I want my boys to wear white Saturday night."

Belmont Abbey had started its season with a 9–1 record. "I've won nine games and my boys lost one," McGuire quipped. "We're not visiting Evansville to lose, and that's no joke." Besides, all of Evansville remembered McGuire's promise to buy everyone at Roberts an ice cream cone if the Aces beat Belmont Abbey.

Bob Hudson knew a good thing when he saw one, and Al McGuire was a promoter's dream come true. Hudson had ordered the stadium's seating expanded to 10,600 for the game. When McGuire's pregame bluster became widely known, Hudson upped the seating to 12,191, which was the most it could hold.

After Evansville College student Linda Sue Bills carried Al the Goat, as he'd been named, around the concrete apron surrounding the court, the animal found a spot in front of Hudson's sister, Patti Kishline, and her husband, Al, in section D, where the kids in the crowd fed munchies to their new four-legged friend.[5]

Belmont Abbey tried to make good on McGuire's promise and stayed with the Aces until the middle of the first half, when Larry Erwin swiped a pass and drove the length of the court for a layup. The Aces never looked back.

With the Aces up 70–50, Mac inserted his reserves to finish off the Crusaders. "I didn't mean to get beat that bad," McGuire said. "I think the big crowd upset a couple of my boys." McGuire didn't have to reach into his pocket to keep his promise to Aces fans. A local company provided the ice cream on his behalf, no doubt grateful for all the entertainment he had given the city.

McGuire stayed over to appear with Mac on his Sunday television show before departing Evansville.

"I don't know exactly when we put them away, but I always felt certain we would," said Mac while munching on a McGuire-provided Booster Bar.

"Wise is tough, but Smallwood's your boy," Crusaders forward Danny Doyle said. "I played ball with Oscar Robertson and all the best this summer at a basketball camp in New York. Ed's not quite as good as Oscar, but he's just as tough as any others in the country."

Ed was not only receiving high praise, he was closing in rapidly on the school career scoring record held by John Harrawood. As the Aces took on Indiana State next, he stood just 34 points short of Harrawood's mark of 1,481.

While the Aces were pummeling the Sycamores, Ed added 30 points before being removed with little more than three minutes left to play. "I noticed the crowd gave me a buzz when I took him out, but I didn't know what it was all about," Mac said after the Aces upped their conference mark to 5–1 with the 77–61 victory. "I had no idea he was that close."

More than 6,000 gathered a week later to watch Ed break the record in a game against Ball State. They were to be disappointed—a ruptured blood vessel in his foot sidelined him for the first time in his Aces career. Mac used Walt Deal and Bob Reisinger to pick up the slack. "I didn't feel like taking a chance in a game like this," Mac said.

Without Ed the Aces still cruised past the visitors. Mac put the second team in with five minutes to play. When he sat down, Dale Wise had grabbed twenty-eight rebounds. Then Mac realized Dale was just three short of breaking the school's single game rebounding record set by Jim Smallins, so he sent Wise back in.

He did get two more but was denied the record when "Mulherin wouldn't miss one." Mulherin, who finished with a career-best 20 points, had hit five in a row at the end of the game. "I finally woke up," he told reporters later.

Tom's pronouncement had to cheer Mac's heart. With his Aces leading the conference, Smallwood recovered and Mulherin ready to go, Evansville made the road trip to St. Joseph's and Valparaiso. "This is a trip we always dread," Mac said. "St. Joseph's is always up for us and always gives us trouble."

Mac didn't have to worry. The Aces survived their meeting with their hosts at St. Joseph's 99–90.

After a practice scrimmage at Valpo, the team visited Chicago while Mac took a trip on the day off to watch Notre Dame beat Army.

Valparaiso managed to cram 2,500 fans into its tiny gym as the Aces squared off with the 6–11 Crusaders on their home court. Paul Meadows, Valpo's coach, had seen the Aces struggle against St. Joseph's zone and installed his own version to thwart the Aces. It worked—it forced the Aces to try to shoot over the tight zone defense.

They had little success and were behind by 15 points with six minutes left to play. The Aces did rally, tying the game at 71 with just thirteen seconds to play on a Larry Erwin free throw. The Crusaders inbounded the ball to their speedy

5-9 guard Fran Clements, who sped the length of the floor and drove in for a layup.

Wise, trying to prevent the game-winning shot, drew a foul. Clements coolly made both free throws to put Valpo up 73–71. Mac called a time-out and designed a play for the Aces.

Erwin inbounded to P. M. Sanders, who took an angle across the middle from the far side and launched a shot.

Too late.

The buzzer sounded before the shot left his hands.

The Aces had lost.

The game had been marred by a bench-clearing brawl with two minutes to play. Clements, who scored 29 points, including the last five for Valpo, had bumped into Ed Smallwood, and Ed drew the foul, his fifth.

As Clements offered a handshake, Ed refused, and Clements gave him a taunting bye-bye wave. Ed lunged for Clements. The benches emptied, and Valpo's Cordy Young hurled himself into Smallwood, sending him reeling.

Mac saw the incident differently.

"Clements threw an elbow at Ed, and Ed pushed him away. If anybody offered a handshake, I didn't see it," he said later. "I've never seen a crowd like that one. They really wanted blood. I actually feared for the safety of my players." He had ushered the team off the court in a group.

The Aces' next opponents were Tony Hinkle's Butler Bulldogs, who were riding a 6–1 streak and were tied with Evansville for the conference lead. The Bulldogs were coming to Roberts, and Mac was without Tom Mulherin, who had suffered a foot injury in practice.

Mac was becoming concerned about his starting five. "They seem a little dead out there," he told reporters.

Ken Pennington led Butler to a 21–16 lead before the Aces countered behind Mel Lurker to forge ahead 42–33. Smallwood had tallied 14 points in the first half, and in the opening minutes of the second half Ed continued to fire away. He hit on five of his first six attempts from the field, and when Butler crept to within five points of the Aces, he responded with five straight points.

With the crowd of more than 7,200 loudly chanting for Ed to break his own school single game scoring record of 44 points, Mac left Ed in after the game was decided.

"Smallwood!" "Smallwood!" was the chant that rose from the crowd as

Ed tipped in his own miss with twenty-eight seconds remaining and broke the record. Then he added a free throw with only eight seconds to play to give him a new record of 47 for the night. "That's about as good as I can play," the Big Smoke told reporters.

Ed's eighteen field goals tied Harrawood's school mark, and his effort established a new ICC scoring mark, erasing the forty-two set by Bob Williams, whose scoring average Ed also surpassed.

After the game, as kids surrounded Ed for autographs, someone asked him how he felt after setting the new record. "Oh, about the same, I guess," he replied. After all, he had led his Louisville Central team to the Kentucky state title as a senior and had joined the Bluegrass State's finest players on the All-Star team that faced Indiana in the annual two-game series.

Since the 1956 opening of Roberts Stadium, Evansville's support for the Aces had grown each season. The crowds put Evansville in a class reserved for major colleges in attendance figures and left them alone at the top of the heap for small colleges. The interest in the Aces had built gradually and steadily each season.

Bob Hudson had devised one marketing ploy after another to get residents involved with the Aces and to get them to attend Aces games. It didn't hurt that the Aces were scheduling name opponents and that they were winning regularly. But the community response to the championship earned by the Aces in 1958–59 was something no one could have predicted.

"In the late fifties in Evansville the economy was suffering. A number of plants had closed and moved away. The city was struggling, and the Aces were about the only good news in town," Mac's son, Dr. Allen McCutchan, said. "The success of the team diverted their attention from their problems and became the focus of their attention and a source of pride."

Until the Aces came along, Evansville had long sought to establish its identity. The city had tried just about everything, with little success. But when the Aces moved into their new and appealing stadium home, the team became the city's own. The Aces had brought home a national title, and the town, like Dorothy in the land of Oz, found right under its nose something it could be proud of, part of, and promote.

Now, as the Aces defended their national title, the community was as fully invested in the relationship as any community anywhere on the planet could be.

When the Eisenhower administration had launched its massive interstate highway program connecting the nation's major population centers both east and west, it bypassed Evansville.[6] In the euphoria over the Aces' success, Evansville barely noticed the latest snub.

Not even the optimistic Bob Hudson could have predicted the success that the Aces enjoyed. On the Saturday that Kentucky Wesleyan and King Kelly Coleman arrived at Roberts, its capacity was taxed to the limit. A record crowd of 13,913 jammed every available inch of space. That was 2,159 more than the seating capacity, but no one standing or sitting in the concrete aisles was complaining, except the harried fire marshal, who was having no success in moving people from the aisles. No one wanted to miss this matchup.

Bill Robertson marveled at the impressive turnout, which, he told his readers, "even vindicated the great architectural afterthought that was supposed to be a press box." Hung high atop the stadium, the press box was filled with high school basketball players that Mac was trying to recruit. They were squeezed in next to the working press.

The crowd was not going to be disappointed. Led by Coleman and Gary Auten, the visitors took an early lead, only to see the Aces come back when Smallwood and Dale Wise combined for 22 points near the intermission. The Aces trotted to their dressing room with a 43–38 lead and their ears ringing from the thunderous applause.

Coleman, the nation's top scorer, kept the Panthers close in the second half, and the invaders took a 50–49 lead before Ed Smallwood retaliated to put the Aces up 59–57. When Lurker and Wise combined for seven quick points, the Aces found themselves enjoying a ten-point margin, 69–59, with only three minutes to play.

Mac then ordered his team into a stall. The Aces executed it perfectly, and when time expired, the crowd roared its approval for the 93–87 win. "I knew we'd win all along," Ed Smallwood declared. "And when we still had the lead when we slowed the game up, I knew we were there."

Ed had been a large part of the reason. The Big Smoke had managed 30 points to lead the Aces in trouncing their bitter rival. His output even bested Kelly Coleman's 26, which Dale Wise had matched for the Aces. Coleman said later, "This was one of my worst games. We had a chance to break it open early, but I couldn't hit. We really wanted this one."

The King left Evansville with a closing shot—a verbal one: "I'll tell you one thing. This ranking business—it's a lot of junk. We're ranked seventh, and we're just as good as Evansville or any other college team in the country."

In less than three weeks the King's latest proclamation would be tested at the NCAA Tournament. Evansville, at 16–3, was a lock to be invited, and Kentucky Wesleyan was nearly certain to join the Aces.

But the Aces still had unfinished business in their quest for the conference crown. They were closing in on it after a two-game set against Indiana State and DePauw in which the Aces prevailed.

The final conference game was to be held at Roberts with pesky St. Joseph's. More than 8,000 fans packed the place to watch the Aces try to clinch the title. Among them was Notre Dame assistant coach Jim Gibbons, who was there on a scouting mission for the Irish. He saw the Aces run and gun their way to an easy 108–93 win, with Smallwood scoring 32 points

Gibbons had seen the Aces at their best and was suitably impressed. "They're just as good, or better, than we've been hearing," he told reporters. "I'm used to seeing Indiana, Illinois, Purdue and those type clubs in action. Evansville can run with any of them."

Such praise from Notre Dame's assistant coach was sweet to the ears of the Aces' fans. But even better would have been a game against the Irish at Roberts. Notre Dame had long been on Hudson's wish list. That was in no small measure because of Notre Dame's football dominance, but Johnny Jordan had brought respect for the South Bend, Indiana, cagers with his recent success—the Fighting Irish were at 15–7 for the season and headed to the major colleges' NCAA Mideast regional play-offs.

When Notre Dame dropped traditional rival Marquette from its 1959–60 schedule, Hudson seized the opportunity and signed the Irish to visit Roberts. "We're proud to play in Evansville," said Jordan as the team arrived at Dress Regional Airport. "This is probably the hottest basketball center in the world." He was proven right when 12,688 fans lined up for their seats.

The Notre Dame team captain, Mike Graney, who also played for Terry Brennan's football squad, said, "Everyone in Indiana knows Evansville has a really good team. But, say we got beat. People in New York would see the score and say, 'Look. Notre Dame got beat by Evansville. They must be lousy.' That's why we didn't come down here to lose."

People in New York might not have yet gotten the word on the Aces, but eventually they would. The game with Notre Dame was just a start on the road to national recognition.

The crowd, attired almost entirely in red as a result of Hudson's latest promotion, "Color Night," watched their Purple Aces gain a slight edge, thanks to Mel Lurker's strong first half when he collected 15 points. The Aces ran off the court at the half leading 47–42.

But the Irish weren't going to go down without a fight. They claimed the lead just five minutes into the second half. Then the Aces refused to fold, fighting back to take a 77–76 lead on Dale Wise's basket with more than seven minutes to go.

Mac soon ordered a slowdown. Mac and Jordan sought to find the winning combination, using numerous time-outs to strategize as the slower pace continued.

With the Aces up 88–85 Notre Dame's Don McGann traveled, and the turnover gave the Aces possession. To secure the win all they had to do was hold on to the ball, but Lurker traveled, and the Irish regained possession with just forty-five seconds left. The Aces held their defensive positions, and the Irish failed to score on their trip down court.

When Mike Bekelja fouled Ed Smallwood with about 38 seconds left, the Aces' prospects for victory looked good. Ed, usually deadly at the charity stripe, instead missed the front end of his one-and-one opportunity.

Barreling down the lane after his errant shot, he grabbed the ball and put it in. Suddenly, the Aces were holding a five-point lead. The Irish hurried down court, and McGann scored as the clock wound down. When Larry Erwin canned a bucket from under the basket with two seconds to play, Evansville had its hard-fought win over the Irish, 92–87.

The crowd had been entertained in high fashion by the close game with a nationally known foe, and Dick Anderson told readers who had missed it, "We'll probably never see a better ball game here in the Stadium. At least not one we can win."

Former Aces star Hugh Ahlering was in the crowd. "I have never seen an Evansville team play harder," said the feisty "Old Man," who played hard every minute of his career.

In the *Sunday Courier-Press* columnist Hap Glaudi called the Aces twentieth win "the most important in the history of this Indiana village's sports existence." That hyperbolic appraisal made even Dan Scism seem reserved. But there was no doubt about it: beating Notre Dame was a big deal.

In Evansville and everywhere else the victory was noticed by the millions of "subway alumni" of the Catholic school. Evansville was being noticed at last—and it wasn't for refrigerators or plastics or barbeque chips.

It was because of their Aces.

It didn't hurt the cause when coach Johnny Jordan graciously praised his hosts: "We think Evansville is the finest place we've ever come for basketball." Jordan said he rated the Aces team "as good as any" the Irish had faced. "The people are wonderful, and never have we been treated so well. Basketball in Evansville must be the greatest in the whole world," Jordan observed.

Unnoticed in the large crowd was a young man whose talents were coveted by Evansville and a number of major schools. He was from a tiny hamlet with the colorful name of Gobbler's Knob, Illinois. He watched from the press box with a half-dozen other potential recruits. He took in the festive, colorful atmosphere and large, animated crowd. He watched Mac's Aces play their furious guard-oriented fast-break style. He took it all in and, though he said little, his smile spoke for him.

Coming off the dramatic and emotional win over Notre Dame, the Aces let down against Wheaton and dropped their final regular season game 97–89.

But it didn't hurt them in the polls. The final UPI rankings kept the Aces at number one, where they had been for thirteen weeks straight. While the poll-sters ignored the Wheaton loss, the head coach from Arkansas State took some solace from it as his team prepared to play the Aces in the opening round of the 1960 NCAA Tournament. "The loss to Wheaton showed us that Evansville isn't unbeatable," coach John Rauth declared.

The NCAA College Division Mideast Regional got underway at Roberts just as a snowstorm struck Evansville. Bob Hudson, whose routine included a trip at dawn to one of the area's lakes to drop a line in the water, must have felt betrayed by Mother Nature's wrath. He hurriedly enlisted the city's help in clearing the stadium's fourteen-acre parking lot for the crowd that was making its way cautiously over snow-covered routes 66 and 41 to the exit for Roberts Stadium.

Despite the storm, almost 4,000 people made their way to the stadium to watch the Aces meet twentieth-ranked Arkansas State. The Aces soon ran the visitors into submission with a fast-paced attack and romped to an easy 91–74 win in the opening game in defense of Evansville's title.

Wabash College was next, and the Little Giants proved stubborn opponents.

Junior guard Charlie Bowerman, who had scored 53 points in a game against Butler that Wabash won only after five overtime periods, led the visitors with 19 points in the first half. With the score tied at 44, Mac was forced to revise his strategy for the second half. He put two men on Bowerman.

Sanders picked up five free throws to give the Aces some momentum, and Dale Wise and Ed Smallwood followed with two buckets, and the Aces were off and running. The Little Giants fell in front of the assault and succumbed, 89–68. The Aces held Bowerman to only four points after Mac's improvised strategy to stop him worked perfectly. It was just another example of Mac's ability to coach within a game and design an effective strategy on the fly.

Smallwood had another great outing, canning 42 points, including a perfect 12-for-12 free throws, after he'd tallied 24 against Arkansas State. For the third year in a row sportswriters honored the Big Smoke with the MVP award for the Mideast Regional.

Now 22–4, the Aces moved on to the NCAA Finals for the third straight year.

Big Ed was getting noticed by the NBA. The St. Louis Hawks, New York Knicks, and Detroit Pistons all were keeping a watchful eye on the Aces' scoring machine.

That weekend the Big Smoke was noticed by some others as well. When local police raided a local club on Canal Street, they nabbed Ed and fifty others for illegal gambling. Charged with visiting a gaming house, Ed was released on his own recognizance and ordered to return on April 7 for trial. It was only nine years since the gambling scandals that had nearly killed college basketball.

Mac, however, stood by his star, announcing, "I plan no disciplinary action. Ed is innocent until proven guilty, just like everyone else." Except everyone else wasn't the main engine in Mac's team. Everyone associated with the team would later deny vehemently that Ed had anything to do with gambling on basketball. "He was just in the wrong place at the wrong time," Harold Cox said years later.[7]

While Ed may have been guilty of not exercising good judgment in being there in the first place, he was free to play out the remainder of the season.

Mac prepared the team for the game with American University and their scoring dynamo, Wee Willie Jones. In an unusual but savvy move, Mac brought Ed's former Louisville Central teammate Bill Bradley to Evansville to practice against the Aces.

The 5-10 Bradley would attempt to mimic the moves of the 5-9 Jones in practice to prepare the Aces for the game against American. "I remember this Jones as a heck of a guard," Mac said of Wee Willie, whom the Aces had faced and defeated in 1958. "He has several clever maneuvers and can do a lot of things that hurt you."

As the Aces scrimmaged against Bradley imitating Jones, a snowstorm raged outside, the worst storm to hit the city since 1918.

Somehow the city's snowplowers cleared the parking lot the next day, and 6,541 spectators managed to make their way over treacherous roads on Wednesday for the four-game card.

Kentucky Wesleyan turned back St. Michael's College in the evening opener before the Aces took the court. To the surprise of no one, the game against American became a shoot-out between Smallwood and Jones. The two seniors fought furiously to extend their college careers, and the game saw seven ties before the Aces took a 51–49 lead into the locker room.

But American refused to yield. Down by 11, the Eagles climbed back to within five points with little more than three minutes to play as Lurker exited with his fifth foul. Tom Mulherin entered and, as he had in the past, answered the call with aplomb, nailing four free throws and a basket after Mel's departure. The Aces had escaped the pesky Jones and American University, 101–91.

Jones had finished with 54 points on 18-for-41 from the field, topping Bobby Plump's 41 in 1958 as the most points scored by an opposing player against the Aces. "That Jones is about the most confident player I've ever seen," said Ed Smallwood, who'd seen many. "He knows he's going to make them."

Ed had nearly kept pace with American's star; Smallwood put up 41 points to boost his season total to 688, a new Evansville College record. There was, however, no time to rest on his laurels. Waiting in the wings were none other than Kentucky Wesleyan and King Kelly Coleman, who entered the finals averaging more than 30 points per game.

The Wayland Wizard, as Kelly was known from his high school days, and his teammates waded through snow banks up to their knees to meet the Aces. In their minds had to be the disquieting thought that they had never managed to beat the Aces on their home court.

Before the two old and bitter rivals tipped off at 9 p.m. before a crowd of 9,947, the Aces and Ed Smallwood were greeted by two Kentucky Wesleyan students dressed as giant white dice to remind everyone of Ed's recent brush with the law.

The Aces jumped out to an early lead. Dale Wise notched six straight points to put the Aces in front 20–10. The foul-prone Wise picked up his fourth personal with 15:35 left to play and the Aces still leading.

Mac switched his team to a ball control slowdown pace, buying time until he could get Wise safely back in the game. The Aces managed to hold off the Panthers despite a last desperate barrage of buckets from Coleman and Gary Auten. When the buzzer sounded, the Aces had again turned back Kentucky Wesleyan, 76–69.

"Wesleyan was no baby game. The officials weren't calling pushing. It was like a pro game to me," said Ed, who harbored high hopes that he'd soon be joining the NBA. Smallwood and Wise had combined for 39 points to lead the Aces. P. M. Sanders had been battered and bruised in the roughhouse play and had suffered a gash over his right eye. He did manage to salvage one of the smaller versions of dice from the stands, left there by a Wesleyan fan. He presented the trophy to Ed, who shook his head and smiled.

"I'm tired," Smallwood told reporter Steve Perkins of the *Sunday Courier-Press*. "Not just today-tired. I mean all-year-tired. I'll be glad when it's over." Smallwood was suffering from a long season as the main target of the Aces' opponents, and the mental torment of his recent altercation with the law, which was widely publicized, was draining.

The loss to the Aces marked the sad end of the collegiate career of King Kelly Coleman, one of the greatest and most controversial stars Kentucky had ever produced. He would be a second-round draft pick of the New York Knicks, the ninth player selected, but he failed to make the team. Coleman later played in the American Basketball League but never fulfilled the potential he had displayed—and that had given rise to his legend—on the tiny court in the coal mining town of Wayland in the Kentucky mountains.

The Aces were now just one win away from repeating as national champs. For the Big Smoke and the five other seniors on Mac's squad, the last remaining game of their college careers was one they definitely weren't going to miss for any reason. The Aces had to play Chapman College of Orange, California, for the title. Coach Don Perkins's team had surprised Cornell College of Iowa to advance to the final game.

"We don't expect any trouble. We played the best game of the year last night against Wesleyan. Some people say Notre Dame, but we didn't have to go hard to beat them," said Ed, no doubt alienating every Irish rooter and Roman Catholic within earshot.

More than 5,000 Evansville faithful arrived at Roberts hoping to see the Aces repeat history.

As the announcer was introducing the individual starters to the crowd, Ed Smallwood didn't wait for his name to be announced. He charged out onto the court where he had enjoyed so many great moments as a thundering ovation swept down from the rafters. The crowd seemed to be saying thanks for all the thrills the Big Smoke had provided and, at the same time, giving him a vote of confidence in spite of his recent troubles with the law.

Within seconds he repaid the fans as he drilled a 15-foot jumper to put the Aces in the lead. Ed and the Aces were off and running. With Ed and Dale Wise leading the way, the Aces charged to a quick 17–9 lead. They extended the early margin to 41–25 at the half. Everything was clicking. The Aces were never really challenged and made the job of defending their crown look ridiculously easy.

Mac took his starters out with more than seven minutes to play, when the Aces were up by 22 points. But the reserves offered Chapman no respite from the attack. Tom Mulherin, Jim Nossett, and Tom Hamilton couldn't seem to miss, and the hapless visitors were thoroughly beaten, 90–69.

"I really can't say we were worried tonight," Mac told reporters afterward. "The boys were confident. And after we jumped out into a big, early lead, it was pretty enjoyable."

Since their loss in an upset to St. Michaels in 1958, the Aces had never taken an opponent for granted. Their teacher refused to allow it, and they had learned their lessons well.

The seniors of 1959-1960 had amassed a record of 69 wins in 83 games, including a school record of 25 wins. They had captured two national titles and appeared in the finals three straight seasons. Their record in the NCAA Tournament was a sparkling 14–1.

"Did I ever think I would win it twice?" Mac asked. "I never thought I'd win it once. But, when you have all these guys, you can do it. They were terrific."

Yes, they were, and their coach wasn't too shabby either.

Erwin, Mulherin, Reising, and Smallwood, along with transfers Lurker and walk-on Bob Reisinger, had seen it all. Erwin, who collected 618 points as an Aces player, would go on to become a successful coach. Mel Lurker finished his career at Evansville with 1,128 points and 844 rebounds. He too became a coach and teacher in Indiana.

The Big Smoke, who along with Hugh Ahlering and Harold Cox had put

Evansville on the track to greatness, would leave with his name firmly implanted in the minds of Aces fans. Of the Big Smoke, Mac would say with genuine affection, "He's just one of the great ones. What can you say about him that hasn't been written?"

Ed had been named ICC Player of the Year again and was named to the All-Conference first team for the third time. Ed missed only one start in three years, starting in 82 contests. He retired as Evansville College's all-time scoring leader with 1,898 points, career field goal leader with 702, and free throws made, with 494. His 730 points in his final season made him the highest single-season scorer as well. Ed's 26.1 average as a senior was also a school best, as was his 25.3 career average.

Ed Smallwood, the kid from Louisville who had survived life in the tough streets of the ghetto, had come to Evansville and won the affection and acclaim of the city that had adopted him as its very own He would again garner UPI All-America first-team honors along with the AP nod on its little All-America team. Mac selected him to join him on the Olympic Trials team of All-Stars he was coaching in Denver.

In April Ed's dream of an NBA career drew closer when the St. Louis Hawks selected him in the eighth round. "I've always wanted to play pro ball," the kid from the projects said after signing a one-year contract for $6,500. "You can't hardly beat it."

Easing Ed's mind was the news that the criminal charges he faced after his arrest had been dropped. He was free to go.

Then, suddenly and quietly, Ed Smallwood, the Big Smoke, was gone.

In early May, without finishing his classes and his graduation requirements, Ed left Evansville College. He left behind a stack of pictures of himself in Mac's office, and he failed to pick up his college yearbook, which was dedicated to the championship team of which he was such an integral part.

Like smoke on a gentle May wind, Ed Smallwood drifted silently away and disappeared.

His career in the NBA was not to be.

He was too small to play forward in the rugged NBA, and he was cut by the Hawks. He came back to Evansville and worked for a time with the Boy Scouts there. Later he was coaxed by Mac to come back as an assistant and finish his degree. He eventually worked as a handyman around town, doing small jobs from the back of his pickup.

"I think he was always embarrassed by not making it as a pro," said Hugh Ahlering, who had helped Ed make the adjustment to life in a northern town when he first arrived in Evansville, carrying the burden of a lifetime of racial oppression.

Years later, when their teammate Dale Wise lay dying from the insidious effects of Alzheimer's disease, Hugh sought Ed out again. "I found him through a guy at a cut-rate grocery store over on Elliot Street in the poor section of the inner city. I got his address and went and knocked on his door. I took him to lunch and we had a nice chat. I asked him to come with me to see Dale," Hugh said. "He was reluctant at first, but I refused to let him say no.

"We went and Dale was in very bad shape. He was dying and his eyes were closed. I spoke to him several times and finally he roused, and he opened his eyes and looked up with that vacant stare the dementia people get, and then he said, very slowly, 'Ed Smallwood.' Then he closed his eyes again." No one in Evansville, not even a terminal Alzheimer's patient, was likely to forget Ed Smallwood.

"After that Ed started to come with me to our players' reunions, and he was always welcomed at Roberts with a large ovation," said Hugh.[8]

The Big Smoke is gone now, but in Evansville, he'll never be forgotten. He was one of the greatest Aces ever.[9]

(Endnotes)

1   Bill Bussing graciously made his lengthy manuscript available to me, and I have relied on it for some information about Mac's tenure. The detailed manuscript contains no footnotes, but when I interviewed Bussing in February 2011, he identified his sources as the *Evansville Courier* and *Evansville Press,* the two local papers at the time. Bussing's manuscript usually makes no distinction between the two, but the direct quotes are from one or the other and appear in the Bussing manuscript in quotation marks. Bussing also had access to a collection of old bound scrapbooks kept by Bob Hudson. My research assistant and I also used the scrapbooks, which are now housed in the university archives. The articles do not identify which paper they are from, much less the date and page, but I (and Bussing) assume they are from the *Courier* and *Press.* Where no endnote appears with information crediting another source, the reader may assume that it comes from the scrapbooks and/or the Bussing manuscript.

2 "Men's Basketball Attendance, 1959–60," www.NCAA.org.

3 Sanders, named after his grandfather, Prentice Martin, was a high school track star at Petersburg High School as well as a basketball player. He high-jumped 6-4—three inches above his head—and as a pole vaulter cleared twelve feet. At Evansville he was a one-man track team and had to dig his own landing pit as the school lacked any facilities. Accompanied by his dad, he competed in track meets as Evansville's lone entrant. He high-jumped 6-5 as a collegian, still an Evansville school record. He continued to compete in track later in life at masters' meets and won all-America honors for his 60–64 age group. See Ron Eaton, *Local Legends: The Stories Behind the Headlines, 100 Years of Southwestern Indiana Sports History* (Evansville, Ind.: M. T. Publishing, 2008), 108.

4 See Harold P. West, *King Kelly Coleman: Kentucky's Greatest Basketball Legend* (Morley, Mo.: Steward and Wise, 2005).

5 The goat would later find a home with the Kishlines in Evansville.

6 Evansville still is not directly connected to an interstate. I-164, connecting Evansville to I-64, finally was completed in 1991. I-64, completed in the late 1970s, is the most recently constructed interstate in Indiana ("Interstate 64," *Highway Explorer—Illinois and Indiana Highway Ends*, http://highwayexplorer.com/EndsPage.php?id=3064&section=1; "Interstate 164, Indiana," AARoads Interstate Guide, August 25, 2005, www.interstate-guide.com/i-164_in.html).

7 Harold Cox interview.

8 Hugh Ahlering, telephone interview by author, February 11, 2011.

9 Ed Smallwood was sixty-five when he died in November 2002. His jersey was retired in 2009 and hung from the rafters at Roberts Stadium (Drew Bruno, "Smallwood Gets His Due as UE Will Retire Jersey," *Evansville Courier & Press*, November 20, 2009, B-1).

The 1959–60 team accepts the NCAA championship trophy.
Coach Arad McCutchan kneels in the center.

Rebuilding, 1960–1961

The champagne was still bubbly when Mac remarked, "Now I have to start rebuilding all over again."

He would be losing seven members of his championship team, and he knew that replacing performers who had been so brilliant would be difficult.

But some members of his championship squads were coming back: returning seniors included Dale Wise, Walt Deal, Jim Nossett, P. M. Sanders, and Tom Hamilton. And they would be augmented by some promising sophomores, including Dave Fulkerson, Marty Herthel, Walt Henry, and Marv Pruett from French Lick, Indiana.

Pruett, perhaps the second-greatest player ever produced by French Lick (after Larry Bird), was heavily recruited after a sterling high school career. "I received over 250 letters from colleges," he recalled. "I had it narrowed down to Indiana and Kentucky because I was from a small town and wanted to stay close to home.

"I was all pumped up about attending Kentucky when I went to Lexington. They took me to the fieldhouse where I waited for Coach Rupp. I saw all the pictures on the walls there of all his great stars and all the national championship teams. Then I met Coach Rupp. All he did was talk about bulls. He never talked about basketball at all."

Rupp's bull turned Marv off, and he next considered Indiana. "IU looked pretty big to me, coming from a small town. And they had a team that was loaded with young great players. I wouldn't have gotten to play there for a while so I looked at Evansville. They had a great tradition there under Coach McCutchan, and looking at their roster, I figured I would get to play there sooner than anywhere else." [1]

Pruett would see action at Evansville, exactly as he had figured. His development allowed Mac to start Sanders at a guard spot and use returning vets Dale Wise and Walt Deal at forward. Jim Nossett, who was 6-4, would play center.

It was a time of new beginnings for the nation as a whole, not just the Aces of Evansville College. Voters had chosen a new president in November. The dashing young John F. Kennedy had beaten seasoned Richard Nixon in a close race. Kennedy's election also put into the White House a new First Family that was young, attractive, and vibrant. Everything and anything seemed possible in those early heady days of the new administration. It was a time of promise and renewed hope in America.

In Evansville the hope was that the Aces could maintain the level of play that had brought them to the very pinnacle of success in college basketball. But for knowledgeable fans that hope was tempered by the reality of the difficult schedule that lay ahead, the toughest any Evansville squad had ever faced. It included games with defending national champions of the major college division—Ohio State, along with Iowa, Notre Dame, Utah, Purdue, and Penn State. Not a cupcake in the bunch.

"It's a difficult schedule. So difficult that even if we had last year's fine team back intact, we should expect to lose a great many more games than last year," Mac warned fans before the season started. "You don't go up to Notre Dame and win, and you don't travel way out to Utah and win there, too." Ever the optimist, Mac added, "But this December schedule can be a blessing. Get tough in December, and after January 1, you look at your opponents and ask, 'So who are you?'" [2]

The Aces opened the 1960–61 campaign against old foe Wheaton College of Illinois, and the history of their rivalry wasn't likely to instill any courage in the young Aces. Wheaton had knocked off Evansville in the last regular season game of 1959–60, before Chapman eliminated Wheaton in the NCAA Tournament.

"We just happened to catch them at the right time," the Wheaton coach, Lee Pfund, explained. "They had just beaten Notre Dame and had also won their conference and were waiting for the tournament."

Maybe it was Wheaton's turn to be done in by overconfidence—Mac's untested squad bombed Wheaton 100–68. Wise started in midseason form and scored 27 points while Deal had 17, and Pruett added 16. As a result, the Aces began the season ranked number one by UPI in the preseason poll.

"They weren't a good ball club," Mac said of Wheaton, warning the fans not to get too ebullient after the win over a smaller, overmatched team. "I'll find out for sure how good we are Saturday night."

Saturday saw the Hawkeyes of Iowa again invade Roberts Stadium looking for a fat payday and another win over Evansville. Junior center Don Nelson led the Hawkeyes, who had defeated South Dakota State in their opening game. In the preliminary game the Aces' freshmen walloped Southern Illinois behind a 39-point barrage launched by a youngster with the delightfully alliterative name of Buster Briley. Briley, alas, was not yet eligible for the varsity, which could have used him.

In front of 10,927 fans the Hawkeyes took an early lead and, despite several spirited rallies by the Aces that cut the lead to four points at one point, Iowa rolled over Evansville, 83–71.

Nelson, for whom the Aces had no answer, scored 31 on 12-for-15 from the floor. "You'll find out that Nelson is as good as any big man in the Big Ten this year," Dale Wise accurately predicted. Wise himself had grabbed fifteen rebounds, but Nelson had held him to just 5-for-24 from the floor.

"We felt we had to stop Wise, and I think Nelson did a pretty good job on him," Iowa coach Sharm Scheuerman said.

"Wise was off [his game] and that hurt," Mac said. After talking with each player in the dressing room, Mac told reporters the Aces were disappointed and "it's going to be hard to get them up."

But they would have to be up if they were to have a prayer against Notre Dame at South Bend, their next contest and the first in a three-game road trip for the Aces that would bring fans back home nothing but bad news. At the small field-house on the South Bend campus before 3,104, Notre Dame took the Aces' measure in the first varsity game of Ed "Monk" Malloy, future priest and president of Notre Dame. The final score was 83–68, not even that close.

After the Irish had taken a commanding halftime lead, Johnny Jordan had emptied his bench or the Aces would have done hard penance for their win over the Irish at Roberts the previous year. Dan Scism told *Courier* readers that the Aces' woeful performance was "a sin against basketball." And the sinners weren't about to get redemption any time soon.

Next up for the Aces was the University of Utah and 6-9 Bill "The Hill" McGill. Originally slated to attend the University of California, McGill had high school grades "as bad as his basketball was good," much to the chagrin of Pete Newell, who coveted McGill and sent him to San Francisco Junior College in an attempt to get his grades up. It didn't work.

Bill, who had grown up in poverty in Los Angeles, was recognized as one of the best players California had ever produced. When he couldn't get admitted to Cal, a Utah alum lured him to Salt Lake City, where his presence brought howls from faculty members who questioned his eligibility to enroll at the university. He was accepted on probation, and the chair of the faculty admissions committee acknowledged that "the fact that he was a basketball player didn't hurt."

McGill sold his car to pay his tuition as a freshman, and a faculty committee scrutinized his grades to ensure his progress was genuine. "I've got to be good," Bill said.[3] He was good enough in the classroom and great on the court.

Bill "The Hill" gave the Aces a mountain too high to climb. He scored at will against Evansville, which was powerless to stop him. The score at the half was 73–43. When the Redskins were up 113–62 and seven minutes remained, coach Jack Gardner began replacing his starters with reserves. That act of mercy didn't alter the result as the Aces absorbed their worst drubbing ever, 132–77. McGill had 33 points and twenty-five rebounds in the time he spent on the court, both Utah records.

Back in Indiana, Dick Anderson broke the shocking news to his *Evansville Press* readers with this comment: "I knew we'd maybe be in for some storms this season, but I didn't think it would be this bad."

Utah would go on that season to the NCAA Final Four and join Cincinnati, Ohio State, and St. Joseph's of Philadelphia as the best four teams in the land. Next up for the Aces was Los Angeles State in LA, a team that valued offensive production over defense. "They would just try to outscore you," Marv Pruett recalled. "They didn't care how much you scored against them; they just wanted the ball and they wanted to shoot."[4]

The Aces found the barn-burning pace to their liking. Although Dale Wise was out with a sprained ankle, they hung right in with the home team and trailed by only one point with less than two minutes to play before losing again, 106–103. "Tonight we played basketball," Mac said. "We looked like we knew the score." For Aces fans who stayed up late to catch the broadcast by Marv Bates on WGBF, the outcome was less than satisfying, but the improvement gave reason for hope.

When the Aces returned from their long, sad road trip, arriving home more than five hours late, they were greeted by about two hundred fans chanting, "ACES! ACES!" Among those on hand were Mayor Frank McDonald and the college president, Melvin Hyde. That reception spoke volumes about the support for the team in the community. Even though the Aces had been beaten and humiliated as never before, Evansville fans greeted them like heroes. "We were always treated like stars. Even when we were struggling, the people stayed with us," Marv Pruett recalled.[5]

The warm greeting had to have cheered the team, and Mac told the crowd, "After where we've been, I can't think of a better place to be than Evansville. We've got a team and I think things will get better."

He wasn't alone: despite the Aces' 1–4 record, UPI continued to rank Mac's team second behind Tennessee A&I in the latest poll.

Nearly 6,000 fans greeted their Aces on their return to Roberts. They would soon see for themselves just how tough a year the 1960–61 season was turning out to be. St. Mary's arrived from California and blasted the Aces 79–69. Leading the Gaels' attack was their 6-9 center, Tom Meschery, who accounted for 31 points.[6] Again, the Aces had no answer for the big man and paid the price.

Led by Marv Pruett, who scored 32 points, the Aces got back in the win column with a 105–80 victory over Valparaiso, salve for their victory-starved souls.

But it was fleeting.

Only a few days later Purdue's Boilermakers rolled into Roberts Stadium. First the Aces had faced Bill "The Hill," then Tom Meschery. Now they were going to have to try to contain an Olympic basketball champion. Terry Dischinger had earned his gold medal at the 1960 Olympics and was back in a Purdue uniform.

A roaring snowstorm greeted the visitors, holding the crowd to fewer than 3,600—those brave or crazy enough to defy the icy conditions to get to the game. The blizzard was expensive for WTVW-TV, which had agreed to a live telecast of the game and guaranteed Purdue $12,500. When the storm stunted attendance, the station was forced to make up the deficit of $5,117.87.

The telecast would prove to be less interesting than *The Frank Sinatra Show*, and many viewers no doubt switched channels as the visitors, led by Dischinger, pounded the Aces 69–60. Walt Deal had fouled out in a desperate attempt to stop Dischinger at the eleven-minute mark, and the 6-6 center finished with 43 points, tying the Purdue single-game scoring record. Afterward Mac said, "He's a great ballplayer, but the thing that really bothers me is I think we have a better ball club . . . we should have beaten them."

Purdue's coach, Ray Eddy, told reporters, "With the exception of Detroit, Evansville is the finest team we've played. I think Evansville will beat Penn State if they play the way they did tonight."

Eddy's crystal ball must have been obscured by the snow because the Nittany Lions handed the Aces their first opening-round loss in their own Holiday Tournament, 75–74, before 6,554 astonished fans. Down by 13 with little more than seven minutes to play, the Aces rallied but fell just short.

Consigned to the consolation game, the Aces found themselves facing Los Angeles State again before a crowd of only 4,660. The game was another shoot-out with the Diablos, but this time the Aces, behind Walt Deal's 30 points, bested the visitors and their 7-3 center, Bill Engesser, to gain the win, 121–115.

The Aces built on their win in their next game by dispatching visiting South Dakota State's Coyotes 87–82.

"[Evansvillians] expect too much," coach Duane Clodfelder said. "The only thing that the people here can remember is the two NCAA champs. But you can't keep the same players forever."

No, but you can harbor hope, and that's about all the season held for Aces fans as the team prepared for ICC play.

Thanks to Pruett, Herthel, and Utley, the Aces were looking a little more comfortable. Dale Wise, their rebounding leader, was proving difficult for Mac to figure out. "I have heard so many things I don't know what to think," Mac said. "I have never lost confidence in Dale, but I think it's time whatever is bothering him is resolved." Dale had managed only 87 points in the seven Evansville losses. To have any chance at all, the Aces needed his point production.

Perhaps Dale read the comments in the *Evansville Press* that morning, because that evening he answered Mac's questions with a 32-point game against Ball State in a 72–68 win. He followed that performance with a 27-point performance against Butler in a losing cause as the Aces fell to the Bulldogs 93–82 without Walt Deal, who was still nursing an ankle sprained in the game against Ball State.

But whatever hope had glimmered on the horizon was quickly blotted out by the appearance on the schedule of the Buckeyes of Ohio State University.

The game, for the first time ever, would pit the reigning NCAA University champions, against the champions of the College Division, the Evansville Aces, was held on the Indiana University campus in Bloomington. When the match-up had been announced back in November, many thought it was going to be the ultimate "dream game" of the year, a classic David-Goliath contest. Now it looked like Goliath was going to eat Evansville cupcakes. [7]

The Buckeyes were loaded with talent, including the future NBA stars Jerry Lucas, Larry Siegfried, John Havlicek, and Mel Nowell. The only good news for Evansville was that Lucas, who had broken Wilt Chamberlain's high school scoring records while at Middletown, Ohio, and went on to play on the Olympic team with Terry Dischinger, was not going to play. He had hurt his knee in a game against Illinois and was sitting it out next to a little-used substitute named Bob Knight.

The game proved a blessing for Knight, at least, as Fred Taylor's Buckeyes toyed with the Aces, allowing him to get some playing time and to score three baskets. The final score was 86–59. Goliath had spoken as the Aces fell to the second of the teams that would advance to the NCAA Final Four in March. [8]

What other College Division team would inflict such punishment on itself? Mac had always formulated a tough nonconference schedule for his Aces, and the high level of competition had helped him to a bevy of ICC titles and NCAA appearances in the past. This year, though, the Aces seemed to be coming up short of his expectations, although he was a realist and offered few excuses for the demanding schedule.

A loss to rival Kentucky Wesleyan followed before the Aces rebounded by beating DePauw. It would prove to be a season-long pattern: a win and then a loss or two. Most games were close, blow-outs were few, and the Aces became frustrated by their inability to sustain momentum.

That frustration played out on the court. Walt Deal and Dale Wise were getting into on-court tussles and confronting referees. With Deal the problem became terminal in a game against DePauw. The Aces had lost in overtime—already without Dale Wise, who had committed an intentional foul and asked to be taken out, Evansville was unable to stop DePauw. Deal had angrily berated the officials and was ejected from the game.

Mac had seen enough. The day after the one-point loss, he dropped Deal from the team. "I did everything I could with him, and I went as far as I could with him," Mac, who never cut anyone, told reporters. Dick Anderson's column the next day in the *Evansville Press* summed it up: "A fine student, Walter Deal, The Big Deal, lost the deal. But they say he deserved it."

The long and arduous season finally reached its unhappy end at Roberts where Dale Wise scored 30 and hauled down twenty-two rebounds in his last regular season game in an Aces uniform before 6,619 fans, who gave him a standing ovation when he left the game. P. M. Sanders added 16 and Nossett 15, while reserve senior Tom Hamilton contributed two buckets to the winning cause.

"I'm glad it's over," Dale told reporters. "I'm tired of the game."

The ICC's leading scorer and rebounder drew praise from Mac: "In the three years Dale Wise has played here, he's made rebounding popular. Dale proved a rebounder can be a hero, too."

In what psychotherapists would undoubtedly deem a classic case of denial, the Aces, despite their 10–15 record, clung to the hope that they could redeem themselves and the season by getting into the NCAA Tournament. Their season record at Roberts, 8–6, was the worst since the stadium had opened, and their road mark of 2–10 was abysmal for a McCutchan-led team. Yet the Aces refused to give up. "We'd have more to play for in the tournament, and we'd be a much better team," Dale Wise said.

Three weeks later the Aces, somehow extended an invitation by the NCAA selection committee, faced Lincoln College. After Wise fouled out with twelve minutes to play, the Aces' last hope for redeeming themselves died as he walked to the bench. The final score was 90–77.

An anticlimactic overtime consolation game win over MacMurray State signaled the end of a long and disappointing campaign for the Aces, who finished at 11–16.

"It was my fault we didn't have a big year this season," Wise told reporters. "Everybody looked up to me as the leader and it was something new and different for me. When we started losing, everybody asked me what was wrong. I just didn't know, and it became a mental block for me." Wise shouldered the blame bravely, but he could hardly be held accountable. Named to the UPI's second team All-America squad and selected as the ICC's MVP Award winner, Wise finished his career at Evansville with more than a thousand points and 1,197 rebounds, an average of 14.6 per game. Both rebounding marks were school records that still stand today.[9]

When the Aces' fortunes took a dive in 1960–61, so did attendance at Roberts.

The team had sold 168,361 tickets in 1959–60, which made Evansville fifth in the country for attendance. But Roberts saw the fannies of only 91,525 in its seats for the fourteen games at Roberts in 1960–61.

With the 1960–61 season at last mercifully behind them, fans looked forward to the 1961–62 edition of their Purple Aces. They had a number of reasons to be hopeful. The freshmen who would be now eligible for the varsity included a crop of talented young players. Wayne Boultinghouse was an All-State performer from Rockport, twenty miles up the river from Evansville, where he had been the first player from his school to score more than a thousand points. He had spurned offers from Kentucky, Louisville, South Carolina, and Clemson to come to Evansville.

"Evansville, being a small college team, never discouraged me. They had Aces basketball there. They had great media coverage, their games were on TV, and they had a great venue with enthusiastic supporters," he said. "The rivalry they had with Kentucky Wesleyan was as great as any in the country. I decided to follow Larry Erwin, from my hometown, to Evansville."[10]

He was joined there by a 6-4 forward, Paul Bullard, from Greensburg and 6-7 Ed Zausch from St. Louis, who, along with transfer Jim Smith, provided the height that the Aces had missed the previous season.

But the main reason for so much hope for the new season was a young man whose name and style of play would forever endear him to Aces fans.

His name was Harold Eugene Briley, but nearly everyone called him Buster. He had survived a tumultuous childhood, including the shooting death of his alcoholic father when he was just seven years old. He was raised by his mother, who worked as a waitress to support her three children. Buster was the oldest.

"She worked in a hotel, and the tips she got there are what we lived on," he said. "She raised us all on that money." Buster grew up in Madison, Indiana, a small town about 160 miles northeast of Evansville between Cincinnati and Louisville, on the Ohio River. Buster's high school in Madison had only 363 students, and their basketball coach was Bud Ritter from Bosse High in Evansville. He had played for Mac and was more than a little familiar with the Purple Aces.

Buster first polished his skills outdoors on a dirt court with a rusting iron rim. He never took the game seriously until he learned from a local businessman that basketball could provide a way to attend college. After that, he got serious enough to lead his team to two consecutive appearances in the state high school tournament's semistate round before being ousted by Indianapolis's Crispus

Attucks. In his senior season he led his team through the year undefeated until Madison met Muncie Central and its star, Ron Bonham, and was eliminated. Buster finished second to Bonham in balloting for Mr. Basketball in Indiana.

Everyone, it seemed, wanted Buster's collegiate services, and Buster was a big Kentucky fan. But then "Adolf Rupp and one of his assistants came to our high school banquet after the season. I heard him speak and afterwards said to myself, 'Wait a minute. I don't like his style,'" Buster recalled.

His next choice was the University of Maryland. "I was all set to go there. I had a summer job with Traylor Construction, and the owner was a brother-in-law to Bud Ritter, my high school coach, who got me the job. I was about to leave for Maryland when the foreman came over and told me there was someone on the job to see me. It was Mr. Traylor, who owned the company. He told me, 'I'll have an airplane here tomorrow morning to pick you up and take you to Evansville.'

"'But I'm going to Maryland,' I said. "'You're not going to Maryland. You're going to Evansville,' my boss said." Traylor was, it turned out, a big Aces booster, and he wasn't about to let his beloved Aces miss out on a prime recruit like Briley.

"When I got to Evansville I met right away with one of the college officers in admissions to find out about my scholarship. He told me, 'We don't have a scholarship for you.' Mac was away at the Olympic Trials, so I called Mr. Traylor and told him what they had said. He told me not to worry, everything would be OK. I found out later that he funded the scholarship himself."[11]

Buster Briley, a bona fide star with major college talent, had gone from Terrapin to Ace in a single day. Though the method used to lure him away from College Park might have raised a few eyebrows back in Maryland, it was a maneuver that would pay huge dividends for Evansville.

"I never wanted to go to a big school," Briley said. "I wanted to go to a small school and beat the big schools."[12] At Evansville he'd get that chance.

The young Aces were talented but inexperienced and, like the team before them, faced yet another tough schedule put together by Mac and Bob Hudson. The Aces would begin by meeting a Big Ten opponent familiar to fans at Roberts, the towering Hawkeyes of Iowa, whose star, 6-6 senior Don Nelson, was flanked by 6-6 forwards Dick Shaw and Dave Roach. That year most regarded Iowa as a legitimate challenger to Ohio State for the Big Ten title.

Evansville forward Paul Bullard drew the unenviable assignment of trying to stop Nelson. Iowa jumped out to a 26–10 lead, with Bullard seemingly baffled by Nelson's moves. Mac ordered a full-court press to try to disrupt the Hawkeyes, but that too failed. A late first-half run pulled the Aces to within four points at the break, and the 10,319 in attendance were on their feet as the Aces made their way to the dressing room.

Whatever Mac told Bullard at halftime to bolster the youngster's confidence worked. Bullard opened the second half by scoring seven of the Aces' first nine points. But Nelson proved unstoppable and singlehandedly kept the Hawkeyes in the game.

With eleven minutes to play, Boultinghouse and Briley scored on successive possessions to put the Aces ahead as the crowd urged the young team on. With all those red-clad fans pulling for them, the untested Aces managed to hold on and ran out the clock to grab an improbable win, 65–59.

"This wasn't the greatest game we've ever played, but it was, without a doubt, the fightingest," Mac said.

"This is better than winning the state championship," said a happy Buster between bites of a roast beef sandwich.

"Evansville outhustled us," Iowa's coach, Sharm Scheuerman, declared. Scheuerman, who became Evansville's first Big Ten victim in ten attempts in 1961–62, cited Mac's full-court press in the second half as the determining factor. "We were desperate going into it," Mac said. "But we had to try something to upset the flow of the game."

Nelson, bound for the NBA and later a long coaching career there, had 29 points, but it wasn't enough.[13]

Once he recovered from his jitters, Bullard had scored 17 to match Briley's output. The player the others called "Bull" had led his Greensburg high school team to the sectional finals and had averaged 12 points as an Evansville frosh. "I knew, and the team knew, he was capable of playing the way he did," Mac said. "He was just too nervous early."

The Aces, still basking in the glow of their triumph, left on a West Coast trip. Mac wanted the trip to be both educational and fun, not just a few basketball games. "He arranged for us to visit the Miramar Naval Air Station in San Diego and even took us across to Tijuana," Buster remembered.[14]

The West Coast swing proved to be a lot more fun for the 1961–62 squad than for the 1960–61 team. They swept three games on the coast and returned to Roberts sunburned and ready to play.

After turning back San Diego State and Valparaiso at Roberts, the Aces stood at 5–0 and were looking much better than anyone could have imagined for a young team. Now they were playing without any nervousness and were surprising even their mentor.

The team that Mac had described earlier as being "a year away from possibly being the best in Evansville's history" was rewarded in the polls with a second-place ranking behind Grambling.

Then Purdue came to town. Purdue was well aware of the Aces' earlier upset win over fellow Big Ten member Iowa. "We know what happened to Iowa down there," Ray Eddy said. "Arad out-sophomored them. We're not so foolish to think the same thing couldn't happen to us."

But Mac wasn't so sure that Eddy should have reason for concern. The Aces' coach was wary of their early success. "Some things have to be done yet," he said. "Like dropping on defense, sagging into a good position. And we need more offense too. We out-scramble them for the ball, and we go in. But you can't win on something like that."

As usual, Mac was right. The Boilermakers and Terry Dischinger brought the high-flying Aces back to earth. Bullard and Marty Herthel did an admirable job in bottling up Dischinger, but that left sophomore guard Mel Garland free to fire at will. He shot the Aces down, making his first six shots from long range.

Mac switched to a full-court press, the ploy that had succeeded against Iowa. It didn't work. Purdue led 41–31 at the half.

While Purdue's Golden Girl and the Silver Twins and their baton-twirling showcase were entertaining the fans during the intermission, Mac tried to come up with a strategy that would stop the relentless Boilermakers. He elected to drop the press but Purdue managed to score anyway.

After Marv Pruett and Briley had drawn the Aces to within four points with only three minutes to play, the visitors came back with six unanswered points to seal the Aces' fate. The final score was 83–77. "Every time I come down here they make it tougher for me," a relieved Eddy said after notching his fourth win without a loss against the Aces.

Evansville had outscored Purdue from the floor, but the Boilermakers had converted 29 of 30 free throws, and that was the difference. Garland led the winners with 25, and Dischinger had managed to shake free often enough to add 19 while grabbing twenty rebounds despite what he termed "dirty play."[15] "It didn't look that way to me" was Mac's answer to the charge.

The crowd of 12,611, including Los Angeles State's Sax Elliot and his team, who were next up for the Aces, had watched the game. The Diablos had already fallen to the Aces on the coast and arrived at Roberts at 1–5.

"They had really fast guards and a 7-3 center," Briley recalled. "They seemed to just want to shoot the ball. They didn't play much defense at all."[16]

It was just what a gunner like Briley wanted to see. That night he took advantage of the opportunities presented to him. And there were a lot of opportunities. Forty-three, to be exact. That's the number of shots Buster Briley lofted from all over Roberts Stadium against the Diablos.

Nothing Elliot tried, even replacing his center, worked against Briley, who hit on seven of his first nine attempts, including six in a row. Bothered not at all by a nagging cold, he finished the half with 25 points.

When Elliot switched from man-to-man to a zone defense, Buster just shot over it. He was successful with nineteen of his forty-three shots and finished the night with 42 points, just five short of the school record, in only his seventh varsity game.

When it was over, Buster's barrage of buckets had brought the Diablos down, by 94–89. "I blew too many to break the record," he said of the memorable night when he was free to do what he did best.

"How do you stop a kid like that?'" asked a perplexed Elliot, who had no clue. "He beat us by himself. He hit when he was dead tired. He hit when he was off balance. He hit from all over the floor."

That's pretty much the way Buster remembers it, too. "I just shot enough to score that many," he said, underplaying his accomplishment.[17]

Among the crowd of 6,207 on the Saturday night when Buster caught the fever was a Madison, Indiana, high school senior. Not just any high school senior but one of the most sought-after players in the state of Indiana. "Man. This is almost like home," Larry Humes said after watching the fireworks display.

"What do you mean, 'almost like home'?" demanded Briley, who also came from Madison. "This is better than home."

Whether Briley's display was enough to get the coveted high school star to join the Aces was not yet known. But Buster's breakout game certainly didn't hurt the cause.

The 6–1 Aces, who were 4–1 at home, were now ranked first in the UPI poll as their traditional Holiday Tournament approached. But their record and history of success at Roberts failed to impress their opponents from Yale University.

After all, they were playing for an Ivy League school and smart enough to ignore pregame hype.

The Bulldogs played not only smart but well. They took an early lead against the Aces and coasted home with an easy 92–83 win.

But Buster Briley was still smokin' hot, his 38 points kept the Aces in the game, but it wasn't enough. "I don't think Evansville was prepared for us" was the ineloquent appraisal offered by the Bulldogs coach, Joe Vancisin.[18]

The consolation game showed that the Aces weren't quite prepared for the Pitt Panthers, either, as they mauled the Aces 89–83. Plagued by foul trouble and the loss of Ed Zausch to the flu bug, the Aces lost both games of their signature event. "I was in mourning tonight," Mac said of the black suit he'd worn. "I don't know when I'll ever wear that red outfit again. I just might wear those blacks out."

The Aces lurched their way along as many young teams do. They would show a few flashes of brilliance and then disappear into a funk no one could figure out. Mac held team meetings and met with the players individually, which was unusual for Evansville.

Disciplinary problems surfaced and were quickly quelled. Injuries further stalled their progress. Wayne Boultinghouse suffered a fractured elbow, which put the spunky guard out of action for the season. The plucky Boultinghouse had seen action in all thirteen games at guard and forward, and his absence would be felt. "He'd been undercut against DePauw going for a rebound and landed right on his elbow. It was a terrible crash. I didn't think he'd ever be able to play again after that," Marv Pruett said.[19]

Despite all their problems and the loss of Wayne, the Aces were only a half-game behind Butler when Hinkle's Bulldogs came to Roberts to play the Aces riding a five-game winning streak. "With the right mental attitude I believe we could go all the way in the conference," Mac said before the February game.

With Briley and Bullard leading, the Aces managed to stay with Butler, and with 4:33 to play the score was tied at 81. With victory within reach the Aces began to play themselves right out of the contest. Turnover followed turnover as they struggled to cope with Butler's quickness on defense.

Despite Briley's 32 points, the Aces lost, 92–87. "We took it away and gave it right back to them," Buster said of the final few minutes.[20] The Aces' eighteen turnovers cost them the game.

Gary Auten and Kentucky Wesleyan also hung a loss on the staggering Aces.

The sharpshooting little guard burned the Aces for the third straight time, accounting for 29 points in a 78–66 win that upped the Panthers' record to 18–2 while Evansville slipped to 11–8. The fast start was a distant memory now, and the Aces would manage only two more regular season wins.

One loss though, stands out among all the games played that season by the young, eager, error-prone Aces. It was against the University of Notre Dame at Roberts Stadium in the Aces' final regular season contest.

A Notre Dame basket with only two seconds left to play put the Irish up by 99–89. Briley accepted the short inbounds pass just to the right of his own basket. Notre Dame, holding an insurmountable cushion, dropped back, and Buster, unimpeded, turned and threw the ball the length of the court.

"It was 85 feet and when it went in, it tore the net," he said.

Fewer than 6,000 saw it happen, but "people come up to me to this day and tell me that they were there the night I made it and beat Notre Dame," Buster said recently. "I never correct them. Why ruin a good memory?"[21] His buzzer-beating shot meant only that the Aces had lost by 99–91.

With the regular season over, the NCAA invited the Aces to the dance in recognition of their tough competition, despite their record of 13–10. They met North Carolina AT&T in the first round, and Briley poured in 40 from all over the floor. His 19 field goals tied his own record, and his performance helped keep the Aces alive to meet Southern Illinois.

Jim Smith had been on the bench after a flare-up of his volatile temper in practice. "He's not off the team," Mac said. "If we win the regional he can play in the Finals next week."[22]

Unfortunately, for Jim and the Aces, Evansville wouldn't be going to the finals this season. Southern Illinois, coached by Harry Gallatin, eliminated the Aces 88–83.[23] Briley and Pruett once again led the Aces, but they weren't able to offset the mistakes. The long season that had started so strong and full of promise was over at last. The progress of the team laden with sophomores, especially Briley and Pruett, gave Mac hope for the coming season. That hope was buttressed by Mac's certain knowledge that the team was going to get some help next season.

The help would be coming from a player who had taken a long and convoluted path to Evansville, but he was there and ready to play.

His name was Jerry Sloan.

(Endnotes)

1   Marv Pruett, telephone interview by author, April 25, 2011.

2   For these quotes from Mac, and others in this chapter that are attributed to no other source, the reader may assume that they come from articles in the *Evansville Courier* and *Evansville Press,* the two local papers at the time. Those articles may be found in the collection of bound scrapbooks kept by Bob Hudson and now housed in the university archives and/or Bill Bussing's manuscript history of the Aces. Bill Bussing graciously made his lengthy manuscript available to me, and I have relied on it for some information, especially in the early years of the McCutchan era and in determining attendance figures. The detailed manuscript contains no footnotes, but when I interviewed Bussing in February 2011, he identified his sources as the *Evansville Courier, Evansville Press,* and the combined Sunday edition, the *Courier & Press.* Bussing's manuscript usually makes no distinction between the papers, but the direct quotes are from one daily or the other or the Sunday combined paper and appear in the Bussing manuscript in quotation marks. Bussing used Hudson's scrapbooks, as did I and my research assistant. Many of the articles do not identify which paper they are from, much less the date and page, but I (and Bussing) assume they are from the *Courier, Press,* or *Sunday Courier & Press.*

3   "Body and Soul," *Time Magazine,* February 3, 1961.

4   Pruett interview.

5   Pruett interview.

6   Meschery, who was born in China to Russian refugees, would be drafted by the Philadelphia Warriors and played ten years in the NBA with San Francisco and Seattle. He was named an All-Star in 1962–63. A rugged player known for his aggressive play, he twice led the league in personal fouls. The player who disdained finesse on the basketball court returned to Utah for his master's in fine arts and became a poet, novelist, and teacher in Reno ("Tom Meschery," Basketball-reference.com; Jerry Crowe, "Former NBA Tough Guy Tom Meschery a Man of Rhyme and Reason," *Los Angeles Times,* November 9, 2009).

7   The game matching the two division champions was the first and last of its kind. It is not likely to ever happen again. The only sporting event that is analogous is the 1957 heavyweight championship bout between amateur champ Pete Rademacher and heavyweight champion Floyd Patterson. In his

first professional fight Rademacher floored the champ in the second round. Patterson recovered and, after knocking Rademacher down seven times, retained his crown with a TKO in the sixth round.

8   Ohio State was joined by Cincinnati, St. Joseph's of Philadelphia, and Utah. The Buckeyes, defending their title, advanced to the championship game, where they lost to Cincinnati.

9   University of Evansville Sports Information Office.

10   Wayne Boultinghouse, telephone interview by author, February 11, 2011.

11   Buster Briley, telephone interview by author, April 21, 2011.

12   Briley interview.

13   Nelson coached for more than twenty-five years in the NBA and won three Coach-of-the-Year honors.

14   Briley interview.

15   Dischinger would be a three-time All-American and lead the Big Ten in scoring three years in a row. He set a host of Purdue records, some of which still stand, and was named to its All-Centennial team in 1997. He was a member of the gold-medal-winning 1960 U.S. Olympic basketball team. In the NBA he was named rookie of the year in 1963. He played for nine years with four teams and was named an NBA All-Star three times. See "Terry Dischinger," Basketball-reference.com.

16   Briley interview.

17   Briley interview.

18   Yale would finish the year with an Ivy League title and go on to the NCAA Tournament, where the Elis were defeated by Wake Forest.

19   Pruett interview.

20   Briley interview.

21   Briley interview.

22   Bill Fluty, "Evansville Rocks A&T, 97–82, as Briley Bombs 40," *Evansville Courier*, March 9,1962, 18.

23   Gallatin would go on to succeed Bob Pettit as coach of the St. Louis Hawks in the NBA where Gallatin coached for five seasons. He was the NBA Coach of the Year in 1963 when he was with the Hawks. He was inducted into the Naismith Memorial Basketball Hall of Fame in 1991. See "Harry Galatin," Basketball-reference.com.

Arad McCutchan's daughter with the NCAA trophy.

Mac Lands a Big One, 1961–1963

He grew up in an Illinois hamlet with the colorful name of Gobbler's Knob, but on the basketball court Jerry Sloan was no turkey.

Like almost every other college basketball coach in the country, Mac had pursued Sloan and had lost his quarry to another school.

Sloan had enrolled at the University of Illinois at Urbana-Champaign. When he got to the sprawling urban campus, the country boy knew he had made a serious mistake.

He had been born on a small farm sixteen miles from the nearest town, McLeansboro, Illinois, in 1942. His father, Ralph, died when Jerry was only four, leaving to his widow, Jane, the job of tending to their farm and raising their ten children. Times weren't easy for the Sloan brood.

"We were all taught that we had to work to survive," Sloan said. "There were always chores to do, and we each had our responsibilities with the chickens, cows and hogs. But, it taught us that we weren't going to be given anything. We had to work for it."[1]

Jerry attended a one-room schoolhouse eight miles away where a lone teacher tried to give lessons to twenty kids in grades one through eight. After Jerry got home from school and finished his chores, he found time to shoot baskets outdoors in the fading twilight. He knew that to be good at something, you had to work at it. No one worked harder and few would be better.

When Jerry got to McLeansboro High School as a freshman, he didn't know if he'd be able to play on the basketball team. It wasn't his skills that gave him pause. It was his size or, more accurately, his lack thereof. As a freshman Jerry Sloan barely topped 5-6.

Fortunately for Jerry and McLeansboro High School, he sprouted eight inches, like a stalk of corn in the field, during the summer between his freshman and sophomore years. And in his second year on the team, Jerry, who eventually topped out at 6-5, began to shine.

In his junior and senior years he led the McLeansboro Foxes to the state play-offs. In the three years he played for coach Gene Haile at McLeansboro High School, the records Sloan compiled include scoring nearly 1,800 points. He scored 45 points in one game as a junior, then topped that with 52 in his final year. Selected to the All-State team, Sloan, dubbed the "Fabulous Fox" by sportswriters, was named Illinois's Mr. Basketball.[2]

More than ninety colleges, including Evansville, had pursued Jerry Sloan. "I had gotten my choice down to Illinois, where my brother Roger was; Southern Illinois; and Evansville. By June, I'd decided to attend Illinois," he said.

He arrived in Urbana-Champaign in September and was back home two months later. "I just didn't like it up there," he said.

Back at home, Jerry got a job in the southern Illinois oilfields and decided to preregister for classes at Southern Illinois University for the winter quarter. "A high school teammate, Curt Reed, had gone there, and I had played in a charity game for Coach Gallatin and liked him," Sloan said. But a day later he backed out.

"I just didn't like Southern Illinois," he said. "I liked Coach Gallatin but not the school. When I told him I'd decided not to come there, I just about bawled. If he'd been the coach almost anywhere else, I would have gone with him, that's how much I liked him." Gallatin himself probably shed a few tears and cursed his misfortune when Sloan delivered the news.

The state's most sought-after recruit and its number-one player was back home again, with no place to play. Then Jane offered her son some advice. "She told me to contact McCutchan, whom I hadn't talked with in about a year. I asked him, 'Do you still want me?' He said, 'Yeah,' and came right on over to McLeans-boro to see me," Sloan said.

Mac, leaving nothing to chance, brought along some help: Bob Hudson, prominent boosters Bruce Lomax and Dr. Harry Whetstone, and players Marv Pruett and Dave Fulkerson. The meeting lasted more than a half day. When it was over and all of Jerry's concerns had been assuaged, he was on his way to Evansville College. In March 1961 he enrolled for the spring quarter and began attending classes.[3]

For Mac and Evansville there had never before been a bigger catch. There had been Ed Smallwood and then, most recently, Buster Briley. Now Mac had in his fold both Briley and Sloan. After Jerry sat out one season, he would be eligible to play.

When school resumed in the fall, Sloan was back and Mac had him practice with the 1961–62 varsity all season. "He said he had to do it because, without Sloan guarding me, I was finding it too easy to score in practice," Briley explained.[4]

After the disappointing loss to Southern Illinois in the NCAA Tournament, the Aces and McCutchan knew that the young team had gained some valuable experience. Now they would be getting some help from the kid from Gobbler's Knob.

Mac's recruiting efforts had also landed him Gary McCary from Milltown, Indiana, a 6-4 guard, and Sam Watkins, from Louisville Central, where Ed Smallwood, his second cousin, had also gone to high school.

Sam, who was born in Alabama, had rejected offers from St. John's in New York, Iowa, Marquette, and Drake, among others, after being named to Louisville's All-City team. His coach, Edward Adams, had helped deliver Watkins to Mac, who had never seen Sam play.

"[Adams] told me he wanted very much to see me play at Evansville," Watkins said. "My parents insisted that I get a college education. Neither had gone past high school but they wanted me to get my degree."

Sam's family had moved to Louisville from Alabama when he was six years old. "There were eight children in my family. My dad served in the military during World War II and after he came home we moved to Louisville, where there was more opportunity for employment. He got a job at Ford Motor Company and became involved in the union activities at the plant," Sam said.

"I went to a segregated grade school in Louisville through the sixth grade. In middle school it was integrated, but when I entered high school, I went to Louisville Central and that was an all-black school at the time, with a great reputation for athletics. By my junior year we had one white student that came there and several more in my senior year.

"When I got to Evansville, I was more interested in winning than education, but I was the first in my family to go to college, and I knew how important my parents felt it was. They watched my grades as closely as the basketball games." Sam, who had been raised in a southern city, found Evansville to be a warm, cozy, mostly friendly place, but vestiges of the Old South were still present in the midsixties.

He'd been there only a few weeks when the turbulent outside world broke through his naive image of Evansville. "Buster Briley had a car, and he took Larry Humes and me out to a restaurant for something to eat. We sat at the bar, and we talked and laughed together. Pretty soon we noticed we weren't getting served. The manager came over and took Buster aside. Everyone in Evansville knew Buster, he was very popular and a gregarious guy. The manager told him, 'We can't serve those black guys here.'

"Buster turned to us and said, 'Let's go. We're leaving,' and led us out of there. He was really upset.

"'Can you believe this?' he said. 'That guy told me he wouldn't serve my friends.'

"My impression of Evansville was shattered after that," Sam said.[5]

But Sam found, as did Larry and other black players, that even if it wasn't an integrated community, Evansville generally was a welcoming one, if you were a member of the Aces.

A pleasant surprise for Mac in the fall of 1962 was Russ Grieger's decision to leave St. Louis University and head to Evansville. Grieger had played at Bosse High School, where he was the city's leading scorer as a senior, before going on to St. Louis.

"I had considered Evansville, Louisville, and St. Louis and after meeting the coach at St. Louis after an NBA play-off game there, I decided to enroll there," he explained.

Russ saw only limited playing time with the Billikens and after just seven games as a sophomore decided to leave and enroll at Evansville. "I'd played with Wayne Boultinghouse in the Indiana All-Star series and knew he was there," Russ said. "I considered Purdue, Indiana, and Vanderbilt before deciding on coming back to Evansville."[6]

Grieger would have to sit out one season, but then he'd be eligible for two more years.

"This is a big shot in the arm," said Mac. "We haven't done as well as we hoped this year in our recruiting." Larry Humes, Mac's most coveted high schooler, had yet to make public where he would be playing college basketball.

Mac shouldn't have been worried. Humes's high school coach was Bud Ritter, who had sent Briley to Mac. Humes also had attended a game at Roberts where he'd seen Buster, his former teammate, shoot lights out before a huge crowd and had enjoyed the show.

"Coach Ritter flew me down there in his own airplane," Larry said. "It was for a game in the Holiday Tournament, and there was a sell-out crowd. I was impressed with their fast-paced style of play and with Coach Mac. I got to see Buster score over 35 points and he seemed very happy to be there." Larry had also played his last high school game in the state tournament at Roberts, and the atmosphere of the place had made a big impression on him.[7]

Larry Humes was not just another recruit. He was Indiana's Mr. Basketball in 1962, the best player in the entire basketball-obsessed state of Indiana.

Like Buster, Larry had grown up in Madison. "I had seven brothers and one sister," Larry said. "My dad was a mechanic, and my mother took in laundry from white people, and she did the washing and ironing in our house. They liked the way she did their white shirts. She could somehow get the starch just right, and they liked that. She was always careful to put a sheet on the floor beneath her ironing board so that the shirts wouldn't get dirty if they slipped off onto the floor.

"We didn't have much but we had enough. Our clothes came from Goodwill sometimes and from the Salvation Army. Somehow we always had food on our table. We just did the best we could with what we had. You learn to appreciate what you do have that way," Larry said.[8]

Education for black students in the forties and early fifties was segregated at the grade-school level in Madison. While white students attended a modern, well-equipped, and well-staffed school, Larry and fifteen or so other black children were forced into an aging one-room schoolhouse, the Broadway School, where one teacher taught grades one through four and another taught grades five to seven. "It was totally segregated until you got to the eighth grade, and then it was integrated," he recalled.

Humes's playing career at Madison was a distinguished one. In his four years there he experienced only a single regular-season loss. He was a sophomore and teammate of Buster Briley's when the Madison High team advanced to the high school semistate round, only to lose in overtime to Muncie Central. He made two more trips, both as captain, to the state tournament. In his senior year Madison lost in the semistate round to eventual champion, Bosse High of Evansville.

After the tournament he was named Mr. Basketball and got offers from about eighty schools, including Purdue and Cincinnati, as well as Evansville. His coach kept the letters in a large box in his office and helped Larry make the decision. "He was a great man. He didn't care if you were black or white. If he saw some good in you he helped you," Larry said. "I owe most of my success to him.

"Coach Ritter talked to me about the choice of schools saying: 'Larry, Evansville College is a small school but they play Division I competition. They play in a great stadium with great fans, and you will get a good education there.'

"In our family education was the way out of poverty. It was tough to get out, but that was the only way we could escape. Coach Ritter told me to use my basketball skills to go to college. And use the college education you get to get a good job."[9]

Based on Bud Ritter's advice and counsel, Larry Humes, the best player in the state of Indiana, spurned the major college programs, some of which had made him offers that "dazed me for a while."

On July 1 he announced his decision. "The people in Evansville treated me real nice when I was down last Christmas, nicer than I've ever been treated. I think I'll be happy," he told reporters. Years later he would say of his choice, "Coach Ritter was right. Being in Evansville was like being part of a large family. I never regretted my decision, and I would do it all over again."[10]

For Arad McCutchan, landing a player with the talent and reputation of Larry Humes was like finding a diamond mine in his backyard. Well, actually, better. Now he would be fielding for Evansville Buster Briley, the runner-up to Mr. Basketball in Indiana; Jerry Sloan, Mr. Basketball in Illinois; and Larry Humes, the current top player in Indiana. Mac had struck the motherlode of basketball talent. He had gained for his College Division Purple Aces the gilt-edged services of three players whom any major college coach would have been thrilled to have.

With the 1962 recruiting season finally over, Mac prepared for the new season. Practice began in October in Carson Center, Evansville College's new $700,000 athletic complex that included an office for Mac, replacing the cramped space in the concrete block building that Mac and the other coaches had used since his arrival in 1946.

The day practice for the 1962–63 season began, Mac announced that center Marty Herthel was leaving the team because he "couldn't get into playing shape." That left an opening at the pivot position. "Herthel was a very good player. He was big and strong, but he had gotten a little rambunctious and was partying too much during preseason training," said a teammate who requested anonymity. "Mac wouldn't stand for that, and he dismissed him from the team."

Mac quickly filled the opening with 6-7 Ed Zausch, who had seen limited duty the previous year. Now a junior, Ed had come to Evansville from University City High, in a suburb outside St. Louis. He had been recruited by an Evansville alum, Dr. Chet Lynxwiler, and had arrived in 1960 with his brother, Charles, and Bob Hermeyer, another player from University City High.

"I was set to attend Oregon," Zausch recalled. "But I came down here to see the NCAA Tournament, and the place was just packed with people. I had never seen anything like that. All those people and their support impressed me. I changed my mind in a hurry."

Ed offers a good example of just how involved Evansville's business community was with the Aces. "There was not a business in town I didn't get a letter from," he said. "They said essentially, 'We'd love to have you come on by and visit us.'"[11] Indeed, the business community provided Mac with a far-flung scouting system and recruiting network, and when they got a prospect to commit, they made certain he was warmly welcomed to the city.

Ed Zausch would be filling Herthel's big shoes, and if Ed needed a new pair he knew where to go. Mac was confident in Ed's ability to fill the center position. For once Mac would have a legitimate big man he could count on. At a public scrimmage in November that more than 6,200 fans attended, Mac told reporters, "He's our big man and we expect big things from him."

Mac would start Buster Briley and Jerry Sloan at forward and have seniors Marv Pruett and Lyn Mautz at guard. The 1962–63 edition of the Aces would mark the debut of Sloan, the most highly regarded player ever to start for Evansville; and his presence gave rise to much euphoria among both fans and writers.

On Saturday, December 1, 1962, readers of the *Evansville Press* were treated to a large Larry Hill cartoon with caricatures of each Aces player; it took up all of page four. The headline read "Presenting Evansville's Basketball Aces." Typically, the Aces were newsmakers before they had played a single game.

In its September issue *Dell Sports* had described Evansville as the team "that plays the toughest schedule of any small college team in the country."[12] That was an understatement. Nobody in the College Division even came close. The schedule included games with Notre Dame, Iowa, Michigan, Tennessee, Denver, and Butler.

Mac issued his usual conservative predictions for fans and writers alike: "You can't say this team will be 20 percent better with Sloan. You just don't know. He and I both know he has never played college ball, but I know what he can do."

In his newspaper column Dick Anderson tried to temper the fans' belief that Jerry was a basketball savior in sneakers: "Jerry Sloan has been pictured as a basketball phenomenon, a basketball Moses ready to lead the blind out of the paths of defeat, a [sic] NCAA Championship, an undefeated season, and a joust in Madison Square Garden for the world's title. . . . Jerry will do his part, that's for sure and in a big way, but fans had better get hep to the idea that he's human."

As the opening tilt approached, Mac had seen enough of Sloan and his supporting cast to allow himself to dream big: "We know it's almost impossible for a team to go undefeated. But, looking ahead, there isn't anybody we think we can't beat."

Mac's vision was a bit myopic. Immediately ahead were the Hawkeyes of Iowa, the season's first opponent. The Aces had nine returning veterans from the squad that had defeated Iowa the previous season, and this year the Hawkeyes were, at last, without Don Nelson, who had left for the NBA.

For the opening game three busloads of fans from McLeansboro, Illinois, traveled to join a crowd of 11,219 to see the Sloan era begin at Roberts Stadium. But what they saw wasn't what they expected.

Iowa limited Briley to just eight points as the Hawkeyes smothered the sharpshooter with a tenacious defensive effort. Sloan, not at 100 percent since suffering a knee injury in practice, still managed 14 points and ten rebounds. But it wasn't enough. The Aces fell to the visitors from the Big Ten, 62–57.

"Our defense wasn't very good," Mac complained. "But I'll take the blame for that." Iowa's coach Sharm Scheuerman advised Evansville fans after the game to "be patient with Jerry. He's going to be a real great player. He has all the moves, and he certainly gets up for those rebounds. I'd certainly like to have him. Why, I'd trade myself or my assistant coach for him right now."[13]

Mac, not in a trading mood, headed for a postgame reception at the Evansville Country Club that promised to be a little more subdued than usual, telling reporters, "Now we come back to reality. We've had a dream going. People were saying we'd go undefeated. Now, there's no more hoping. Now, we have to get the job done."[14]

Professor Mac graded Sloan's debut performance: "I thought he played well tonight, but he'll be much better. He'll make a fine one yet."[15]

The Aces next made what was becoming their annual trek to the West Coast. This time Mac took along a travel squad that included his son, Allen, who'd made the team, though he admits, "I didn't get to play that much; we had a lot of talent on that team."[16]

On the way to the coast the Aces stopped off in Denver to pick up a win in the Mile-High City. Paul Bullard's old-fashioned three-point play capped a come-from-behind rally, and the Aces prevailed 88–84. All thirteen members of the team played.

Sloan's gimpy knee was still bothering him, and he sat out most of the first half against Los Angeles State and watched as the Aces fell behind by 11. In the second half he led a charge that brought the Aces to within four points before the rally sputtered and the Diablos earned a 74–64 win. Sloan, though still hurting, had accounted for 23 points and thirteen rebounds, both new highs.

When they got back to Evansville, Mac told reporters that Sloan's performance in Los Angeles was "one of the greatest individual efforts I've seen. I don't think I've ever had a player that tries as hard to lift a team off the floor and make it win." Marv Pruett seconded Mac's appraisal. "He's out there giving you 125 percent all the time, even when he's hurt. He's always hustling." Buster Briley offered his own succinct observation, "Sloan? He's the best I've ever seen."

In only four college games with the Aces, all of which he played on a heavily taped, bruised knee, Sloan was drawing critical raves usually reserved for upperclassmen with a body of exceptional work behind them. The big question was whether he could stay healthy and play at a high level over the course of a season.

Mac's appraisal was less flattering after Michigan's Wolverines came to Roberts and chomped the Aces behind big Bill Buntin and a huge front line. "Buntin was as strong an ox and played a very physical game," Ed Zausch said.[17]

The Wolverines had won three of four coming in. and they added another win, 71-64, at the expense of the Aces.[18] While pleased with the defensive effort against the taller visitors, Mac moaned to reporters about the poor shooting night the Aces had experienced. Pointing to Sloan and Briley, he said, "Look at these two. "You figure they would both give you 50 percent [from the field], wouldn't you?"[19]

There was some good news, provided by the team's oldest player, Jim Smith, who had spent time in the Air Force after graduating from Smethport (Pennsylvania) High School in 1955. A former Ace, Frank Healy, had coached Jim in the service, then sent him to Evansville.

Smith was a welcome addition. He was 6-3 and, now a junior, was comfortable in Mac's system. He had made the most of his minutes against Michigan, shooting 5-for-8 from the field while stealing three enemy passes that led to baskets.[20] He was rewarded for his efforts with a start against Los Angeles State.

The Diablos of LA State arrived at Roberts for the return match with a 3–2 record and a coach, Bill Sharman, who had been a star for the Boston Celtics.[21] Led by Marv Pruett's 19 points, the Aces avenged the loss they'd suffered and collected their third win against as many losses. Sloan bruised his heel with about sixteen minutes left and took a seat after scoring 13 points.

A familiar name made its appearance in the lineup that night as Dave Cox, younger brother of Harold and Clyde Cox, logged his first minutes. If he was even half as good as his brothers had been, the fans would be happy.

In December the Volunteers from Tennessee made a stop at Roberts. The Southeastern Conference (SEC) team was coming back to face the Aces for the first time since they'd been trounced 107–71 in Owensboro, in 1955. The Aces were ready and waiting.

Mac had secured a scouting report on his own team from Denver's Hoyt Browner, who'd offered it to him following their game. The report was not flattering. It said, essentially, that the Aces were horrible defensively and pointed out the weaknesses of each player. "So, I read the report, I mean the bad parts, to the team. I think it became personal. It was up to each man. We've been playing better defensively ever since," Mac said.

Whatever works.

Tennessee used the 1-3-1 zone preferred by their mentor, Ray Mears, who had used it with success while coaching at Wittenberg. The Aces attacked where they could. With little more than two minutes to play in the first half, the Vols' huge center, 6-10 Orb Bowling, sent Buster Briley bowling when he crashed into a screen set by the big center. The foul by the Vols' big man was his fourth, and he took a seat as the Aces moved in front, 34–30, at the intermission.

Pruett and Smith kept tightening the defensive screws on the Vols' guards, harassing them all over the court and forcing turnovers. Buster held the visitors' top scorer to just ten points while Sloan, Zausch, and Bullard battled for control of the boards. The intense combined defensive effort held Tennessee to just four second-half field goals. At one point, during a stretch that lasted more than ten minutes, the Vols didn't score a single point. Who said the Aces couldn't play defense?

The crowd of 7,212 was ecstatic with the 68–51 win over the SEC opponents. Gus Doerner, who was doing commentary for the game with Jerry Birge of WTVW-TV, gushed afterward, "It's the greatest game I've ever seen an Evansville College team play."

The 1962–63 edition of the Purple Aces still possessed offensive firepower, and their dazzling fast break was as effective as ever, but now they added an intense harassing-swarming defense to the mix.

It wasn't that Mac didn't emphasize defense. He did. But his style of running and fast-paced offense was often so effective that trying to keep up with the flying Aces would simply wear their opponents down.

"Mac's coaching of defense was an important part of our preseason training. He didn't like playing zone, so we concentrated on man-to-man," Zausch said. "We had drills where Mac put a net up real low over the court that we had to run under. It was designed to help keep us down low on defense. He made sure we'd be in shape to go all out for the whole game."[22]

The Holiday Tournament was next for the Aces, and they greeted Harvard with a rude 68–55 thumping. The Southern Illinois Salukis and the Aces faced off in the title game, and the Aces took command early by jumping out to a 15–3 lead. The Salukis never did recover and fell, 79–60.

Fred Huff, Southern Illinois's sports information director, told local reporters after the game that coach Jack Hartman "can't get over Evansville's defense. They always played the rest of the game well but this defense is something new." Hartman himself was impressed enough to say, "Evansville played better tonight than any team I've seen all year."[23] The Salukis were ranked second in the latest UPI College Division poll and had already upset major college powers Oklahoma and St. Bonaventure on the road.

"I wanted this game real bad," said Briley, who shared the tournament MVP award with Sloan. "We've taken too many on the chin this year." Ed Zausch, recalling the disappointing loss to Southern Illinois in the 1962 regional, said, "I think most of us thought a lot about that game before we went out there." Ed, whose parents came from St. Louis to see their son play an outstanding game, joined Sloan, Briley, and Paul Bullard on the All-Tournament team. "I'd like to have scored more, but I've never rebounded better than I did tonight," he said.[24]

With their Holiday Tournament win the Aces had accomplished the first of

Mac's three goals for them. Now they would turn their attention to the second, winning the ICC title.

The Aces had won their games against DePauw and Valparaiso when the conference-leading Indiana State Sycamores arrived at Roberts in January. Sporting a 9–1 mark, the visitors hung close throughout the first half, which ended with Evansville holding a two-point edge. The second half began with a Buster Briley–patented barrage of buckets, five straight, to put Evansville safely ahead and reward the 9,605 fans with a 67–51 win.

After a close win in a rugged game at Kentucky Wesleyan, Buster did it again a week later when another five straight bullets dropped Ball State 79–77. Buster had scored 28 and made eight of his last nine shots.[25]

A rematch the next Saturday at Roberts saw 8,444 show up to watch the streaking Aces. Playing a full-court smothering defense, the Aces contained Ball State's Ed Butler with Pruett and Zausch shadowing his every move while taking a 39–28 halftime lead.

After a 17–0 run in the second half Mac inserted a new five. "He called us the Go Team," Wayne Boultinghouse said. It was yet another example of Mac's ability to improvise. With a plethora of talent on his team, Mac found a way to both rest his starting five and give his reserves some coveted playing time. It kept the starters fresh and gave the reserves on the Go Team a sense of being an important element. "We usually went in and played as hard and as aggressively as we could for five minutes or so and then came back out," Boultinghouse said. "It was an example of Mac's coaching skill. He knew he had talent to spare, and he used it to perfection."[26]

With about three minutes to play Mac emptied the bench, and his third team finished mopping up the 81–62 win. "I'm glad I didn't pay to see that one," Tony Hinga, the Ball State coach, said after the game. "The big difference is that Sloan. He puts so much pressure on you. You've got to guard him when he's standing still."

Jerry finished with 25 points and 17 rebounds, three more than Butler had managed. Zausch and Bullard had held the Cardinals' star to just three points. Ed Zausch, whom the players called EZ for his initials, not his disposition, was emerging as a defensive force for Mac. For a change Mac had some height in the pivot position that could handle the bigger post players his teams usually struggled against. "Zausch is the one big pleasant surprise for me," Mac said. "We thought he could do it, but it's nice to have him come around."[27]

"I had a role to play on the team, and that role was to get rebounds and get the outlet pass out to the wings to start the fast breaks," Ed said. "My rebounding was critical to the success of the offense. If I could get the rebound out quickly to Sloan or Briley on the wings, they could use their speed to beat the defense down the court. We would get five or six easy layups a game that way. I wasn't expected to score. That was not my role. I was the rebounder and shot blocker. I got in a lot of foul trouble, but it was just part of the way I was playing. We backed each other up. We played hard on defense and were proud of the way it was working for us."[28]

In the next game against St. Joseph's, Ed's dominance was apparent to all. He blocked twelve shots during a 68–58 win. "All the boys have been talking about since the game is the performance of Zausch. They've been calling him Bill Russell," Mac told reporters.

Well, maybe not Russell, but Zausch was certainly an intimidating player who knew his role and relished his part in the success of the team. "I was the enforcer," he recalled. "If the other team got too physical with Buster or Jerry, I was there to even things up."

After dispatching Valpo, the Aces faced Butler and its star, Jeff Blue, who was leading the conference in field goal efficiency. The center was so important to the Bulldogs' success that Mac switched from the straight man-to-man defense to a shifting man-to-man that collapsed down toward the middle to try an limit Blue's opportunities. The strategy worked, as Blue was held to just four points, but Butler still managed to grab a 36–34 lead at the half.

The second half saw Mac abandon his altered defense and go back to his normal strategy. With Sloan and Briley hitting from the outside, Marv Pruett had a perfect 7-for 7-performance from the field to fuel the 78–60 win before 9,411 fans. "This year anybody can be the high scorer," Marv said. "One night I'm up there, the next night it might be Buster or Jerry. That's why it's everybody's game. Everybody gets his shot if he waits for it."

With the current edition of the Aces, much of the scoring burden that had been assumed by Buster in the past was distributed among the starters. Concentrating on Buster alone, as many had done the previous season, would no longer work. Others would, and could, step up to score.

In the crowd was T. L. Plain, the coach of 7–9 Kentucky Wesleyan, and he saw the Aces blow Butler away with a well-balanced offensive display. It gave the coach some pause as his Panthers were next on the Aces' schedule at Roberts.

They had narrowly lost the first game to the Aces, their traditional rivals, at Owensboro earlier in the season.

In that game Zausch had fouled out after nearly coming to blows with Wesleyan's Ed Ratliff, and Sloan had sustained a nasty gash over the eye from a flying elbow. The Aces were still smarting from the roughhouse tactics when the Panthers arrived for the rematch at Roberts.

The game drew 12,957 fans who were primed for the action between the two bitter rivals. "Everyone expected a barn burner," Marv Pruett remembered.[29] But they got little for their money.

Plain decided the only chance his team had was to keep the ball away from Evansville. That's exactly what he did. In one of the strangest games ever played at Roberts Stadium, the Panthers simply refused to play basketball. They held the ball and refused to shoot. With guards Skip Hughes and Clyde Wise passing the ball back and forth between them, the crowd rained boos down on the court. More than seven minutes had expired when Ratliff finally put up a shot and missed. The Aces raced down the court.

They managed to take a lead and hold it. The Panthers' first basket came with 5:43 to play in the initial half. As halftime approached, Pruett made a basket, and Evansville held an 11–3 lead. A late basket by Wesleyan's Doug Walsh cut the lead to 11–5 as the two teams headed to the locker rooms chased by a chorus of boos. "In the locker room Mac told us if that's what they want to do, let's teach them a lesson and hold the ball away from them. So that's what we did the second half. The crowd was really upset," Ed Zausch recalled.[30]

"Mac told us at halftime, 'Pull back' when they stood there with the ball on their hip. I finally just sat down on the court at the free-throw line. We loved to run, and I'd never heard boos like that before," Buster Briley said.[31]

When a little more than five minutes remained to play in the motionless imitation of a basketball game, Sloan found Zausch unguarded beneath the basket and fired a bullet that Ed easily converted to put the Aces up by 16–9. A few seconds later Ed returned the favor, hitting Jerry with a pass in the lane for a layup.

The Aces were up by nine.

After a Wesleyan player made a basket, Briley found Zausch, and Ed's easy basket sewed up the win. The final score was a laughably low 23–19, and Plain's strategy had failed. "I know the people here don't like that kind of basketball," he said later, "but . . . slowing it down was our only chance." If the Panthers had made their free throws, the strategy might have paid off. They had converted only 3 of 10 attempts from the line. "Sure I'd do it again," Plain said. "It's part of the freedom of basketball, and I believe in that."

Mac agreed with Plain: "It was certainly within the rules. But I feel a little sorry for the people who paid their way to get in." The second-largest Aces crowd ever had boosted the attendance at Roberts past 100,000 for the third time in four seasons.

More than 6,000 were on hand for the next game, which saw the Aces defeat DePauw. The home finale saw the Aces turn back St. Joseph's easily by 82–63, guaranteeing at least a share of the ICC crown.[32] "That Evansville team is a helluva ball club," said Jim Holstein, the St. Joseph's coach. "We just couldn't stay with them. In the end we were beat physically. I've been in this conference a long time and I saw those (Ed) Smallwood clubs, but this one is better, much better."[33]

The NCAA agreed. As the Aces prepared to take to the road for the last three regular season contests, the NCAA offered Evansville, at 18–3, the first at-large bid to the NCAA College Division tournament.

None of the last three games was easy. First, the Aces met the Sycamores of Indiana State in their new arena, which saw its second advance sell-out ever, despite treacherous winter weather. The game inside was treacherous as well. Lennie Long, the Sycamores' forward, sent Buster sprawling to the floor just minutes into the game. A pugnacious Buster came up swinging but was restrained by Zausch and escorted from the court. Buster's upper lip was split open. After he had it stitched and bandaged, he returned, looking for revenge.

With the Sycamores' partisans chanting, "Briley baby, Briley Baby," Buster retaliated the way only a pure shooter can, firing in a buzzer beater that gave the Aces a halftime lead of 40–36.

The Sycamores hung close and with two minutes to go threatened to take the lead. But Paul Bullard stole the ball from Long and converted at the other end off a Buster Briley bullet pass. Bullard's momentum carried him into the goal support and, after a quick trip to the dressing room for medical attention, he returned, and his lone free throw of the game iced the win for the Aces, 69–67.

"We don't know exactly what happened to Buster because no one really saw it," Mac said after the game. "It must have been pretty bad, but no one knows for sure."

Buster only shrugged, "Oh, it's all right. We want Butler."

He got what he wanted. But before 11,240 Bulldog fans, Butler deprived the

Aces of a perfect ICC mark. Behind by ten in the first half, the Aces, bolstered by a Buster Briley spurt of five straight baskets for the third time that season, got within two points. But the loss of Bullard and Zausch to foul trouble cost the Aces the game as they fell 79–74.

The Aces' winning streak of 17 was over. They headed to South Bend to meet Notre Dame, where "the gym was a small one and the crowd was right on top of you. It was loud and a very difficult place to play," Ed Zausch said.[34] The gym had been kind to the Irish, who were 10–1 at home that year and headed to the NCAA Tournament. Despite a late three-point play by Marv Pruett that got the Aces to within two, with the team again in foul trouble they couldn't get any closer, losing 78–72.

Their regular season was over, and the Aces, at 19–5, had already met two of Mac's preseason goals. They had won the Holiday Tournament and the ICC crown. Only one goal remained.

The NCAA Tournament began the next week in St. Louis, where the Aces, after a ten-day break, were sent to meet Concordia in the opening round of the Great Lakes Regional. Concordia brought a 13-game winning streak to St. Louis and proved a stubborn opponent for the Aces. Ultimately, Evansville's defense prevailed and the Aces had a 66–56 win.

"I guess I really didn't expect the boys to be sharp," Mac said. "It's been 10 days since we've played, and during that time the boys had to contend with examinations. The trip didn't do them any good either."

Their next opponent proved even tougher. Washington University was the hometown favorite. The team featured former University High star Sandy Pomerantz, who had transferred from Cincinnati.

"I grew up watching him play, and he was my role model," Ed Zausch said.[35] Ed had picked a good one. Pomerantz had scored 27 against Augustana in the opening round. "We'll start Zausch on him and see how it goes," Mac told reporters before the game. Ed, who was constantly in foul trouble all year, now was designated to hold down the high-scoring Pomerantz.

Washington's assistant coach Rick Meckfessel had seen Ed play at Notre Dame and told sportswriters, "Wait until you see him jump. He blocked 8 or 10 shots . . . they'd come driving in, and Zausch would come out of nowhere and slam the ball away."

In playing against his former idol, Ed may have been wound up a little too tightly. It wasn't long before he found himself saddled with three early fouls.

Paul Bullard, the Aces' sixth man all year, came in and tried to hold Pomerantz at bay. Paul proved equal to the task, banging the boards and providing 11 of Evansville's next 22 points. The Aces overcame a five-point deficit to take a four-point lead at the half when Wayne Boultinghouse's 35-footer banked in at the buzzer.

The second half followed the form of the first and ended with the two teams tied at 66. In overtime, just as time expired, Buster's 25-footer forced the teams into a second overtime period. With 1:18 to play in overtime number two and Evansville up by five, the Bears fouled Briley.

Mac called a time-out. As the players huddled around him, he started by saying, "'After Buster makes these two free throws, here's what we'll do,'" Buster recalled. "He was always positive, never negative. He never got down on you. He just had so much confidence in us, we wanted to win for him so badly."

Buster went to the stripe and said to the closest Washington player, "Hey, baby, you fouled the wrong guy this time. I'm gonna knock these two in."[36]

He did.

The Aces won, 85–76.

"Sloan did a terrific job setting up the others for baskets and Briley did his job, too, but overall I'd have to say Bullard was the man," Mac told reporters. "Bullard just murdered us," Washington's coach moaned. "He'd be in my starting lineup any time."

But on the Aces Paul had his role, like everyone else. He was the backup to Ed Zausch, and when Ed got in trouble, Paul's job was to give the Aces valuable minutes and play tough defense. Any offense he could provide was a bonus. He was a member of Mac's Go Team, which was becoming very popular in Evansville for its all-out play whenever it took the court.

Paul had relinquished his starting forward role when Sloan moved up to the varsity. "He never complained," Mac said. "All he said was, 'Coach, don't forget me down there.'" Mac hadn't, and Paul came through when he was needed the most. He had 20 points and 14 rebounds against the Bears and joined Sloan and Briley on the All-Tournament team.

Evansville advanced to the finals at Roberts Stadium. It would mark the end of the careers of Paul Utley, Lyn Mautz, Walt Henry, and Ed Rolen. Of Mac's 1959–60 freshmen, only Marv Pruett had managed to retain his starting role as the talent level had increased. As the Aces tipped off against Southern Illinois, Marv started his seventy-ninth consecutive game at guard for the Aces.

"We had beaten them pretty easily earlier in the season, but we just couldn't get going. We never gelled," Ed Zausch recalled.[37] More than 7,000 fans saw the Aces stumble right from the opening tip. They missed ten of their first twelve shots, and SIU took a ten-point lead that soon stretched to 16. The Aces managed to shave it to 12 at the half, but things weren't looking good.

After the half the Aces did cut it to six but that was as close as they could get. "We just got beat. We gave it our all, but nothing was working that night," Marv Pruett said.[38]

"When we lost, we felt like we had let the whole town down," Briley remembered. "Basketball was the whole thing to them. And when we lost at Roberts, it was just awful."[39]

The loss was a devastating one. The Salukis had ousted Evansville from the 1962 tournament and now had done it again in 1963 after the Aces had beaten them by 18 points earlier in the year.

The end was abrupt and unexpected, and the Aces fell one goal short of Mac's preseason hopes for them. "I don't know what was wrong with us," Mac said. "We weren't playing defense the first half, and we couldn't hit at all."

Sloan had led the team in rebounding and scoring, but the Salukis had shut down Buster, and that made the difference. For the durable Marv Pruett the loss was especially bitter. The lone senior starter, Marv left Evansville with 1,119 career points but no national title.

"I went there to get my education. That's what I wanted, and basketball got me there. I got my education, and they got their money's worth from me. Mac was a terrific coach who got the most out of his talent," Marv said.[40] And no one in Evansville would ever claim they hadn't gotten their money's worth from Marv Pruett.

After leaving Evansville Marv coached basketball for three seasons at Shoals Community Schools in Shoals, Indiana, before going into the insurance business and ending up back in Evansville, where he retired in 2005.[41]

With Pruett the lone graduating starter, Mac had only one spot to fill for the next season. "We're going to have more depth than we've had in years," Mac told reporters.

After seventeen seasons at the helm, Mac had compiled a record of 264–180. For his eighteenth season he would have Larry Humes, along with Briley and Sloan. The potential firepower they represented had fans drooling. Evansville would not be disappointed.

(Endnotes)

1   All quotes from Jerry Sloan in this book come from previously published articles that were collected in scrapbooks by Bob Hudson, with no notations about which paper ran the stories or when they appeared (see note 3); today the scrapbooks are held in the University of Evansville archives. Sloan was the sole former Aces player who refused to participate in my research for this book. He declined all requests for an interview, telling our intermediary, "All that I have to say about Evansville has already been reported. Tell the author that he can look that up."

2   Most of the records that Sloan established at McLeansboro still stand, including most career points, single-season points, and career rebounds. He held the single-season rebounding record until it was broken in 1984.

3   Ron Eaton, "Jerry Sloan: Simply the Best," *Local Legends: The Stories Behind the Headlines, 100 Years of Southwestern Indiana Sports History* (Evansville, Ind.: M. T. Publishing, 2008), 122–23. In piecing together the story of how Sloan ended up at Evansville College, I also relied on Bill Bussing's lengthy manuscript, which he generously made available to me. The detailed manuscript contains no footnotes, but when I interviewed Bussing in February 2011, he identified his sources as the *Evansville Courier* and *Evansville Press,* the two local papers at the time. Bussing's manuscript usually makes no distinction between the two, but the direct quotes are from one or the other and appear in the Bussing manuscript in quotation marks. Bussing also had access to the scrapbooks kept by Bob Hudson; my research assistant and I also used them. Where no endnote appears with information crediting another source, the reader may assume that it comes from the scrapbooks and/or the Bussing manuscript.

4   Buster Briley, telephone interview by author, April 21, 2011.

5   Sam Watkins, telephone interview by author, June 4, 2011.

6   Russ Grieger, telephone interview by author, May 22, 2011.

7   Larry Humes, telephone interview by author, April 29, 2011.

8   Humes interview.

9   Humes interview.

10 Humes interview.

11 Ed Zausch, telephone interview by author, May 4, 2011.

12 Larry Stephenson, "Mac Is Cheerful, Sloan Says Wait," *Evansville Sunday Courier and Press*, December 18, 1962, C-5.

13 Tom Fox, "Sharm Has High Hopes . . . for Aces," *Evansville Sunday Courier and Press*, December 2,1962, C-5.

14 Tony Chamblin, "Iowa Wrecks Aces' Happy New Year," *Evansville Sunday Courier and Press*, December 2, 1962, C-1.

15 Chamblin, "Iowa Wrecks Aces' Happy New Year."

16 Dr. Allen McCutchan, telephone interview by author, February 11, 2011.

17 Zausch interview.

18 Buntin, from Detroit, became a two-time All-American and, along with Cazzie Russell, led Michigan to the Final Four in 1964 and again in 1965. He averaged more than 20 points per game during his three seasons at Michigan. He is a member of Michigan's Hall of Fame and an award in his name is given each year to the MVP of the basketball team. Drafted by the Detroit Pistons, he played briefly in the NBA. He died of a heart attack in 1968 while playing in a pick-up basketball game. game (Bill Buntin, "University of Michigan Basketball All-Americans," University of Michigan Athletics History, April 10, 2006, www.bentley.umich.edu/athdept/baskmen/baskmaa/buntinaa.htm).

19 Tony Chamblin, "Wolves Eat Up Little Red Aces," *Evansville Sunday Courier and Press*, December 16, 1962, C-1.

20 Tom Fox, "Aces Give Arad a 'Pick Up' But a Letdown Too," *Evansville Sunday Courier and Press,* December16, 1962, C-1

21 Sharman, a graduate of USC, played eleven years in the NBA and was an eight-time All-Star. He was inducted into the Naismith Memorial Hall of Fame in 1976. He coached in the NBA and ABA for ten years, won two championships, and was twice named coach of the year.

22 Zausch interview.

23 Tony Chamblin, "'Aces Best I've Seen All Year': Hartman," *Evansville Sunday Courier and Press*, December 30, 1962, C-5.

24 Tony Chamblin, "Aces Blast SIU, 79–60, in Finals," *Evansville Sunday Courier and Press*, December 30, 1962, C-1.

25 Bill Fluty, "Aces Flatten Wesleyan, 70–67, in Rough Game," *Evansville Courier,* January 17, 1963, A-22.

26 Wayne Boultinghouse, telephone interview by author, February 4, 2011.

27 Tom Fox, "Mac Needs a Butler," *Evansville Sunday Courier and Press,* February 3, 1963, C-9.

28 Zausch interview.

29 Marv Pruett, telephone interview by author, April 25, 2011.

30 Zausch interview.

31 Briley interview.

32 Tom Chamblin, "Aces Jolt Pumas, Clinch I.C.C. Title," *Evansville Sunday Courier and Press*, February 17, 1963, C-1.

33 Tom Fox, "Evansville's Size, Depth Beat Us Physically, Says Holstein," *Evansville Sunday Courier and Press*, February 17, 1963, C-4.

34 Zausch interview.

35 Zausch interview.

36 Briley interview.

37 Zausch interview.

38 Pruett interview.

39 Briley interview.

40 Pruett interview.

41 Pruett interview.

A packed game at Roberts Stadium.

God Is Good to Evansville, 1963–1964

"Ain't God good to Indiana?
Ain't He, fellers?
Ain't He, though?"
—William Herschell

To the inhabitants of Evansville, home to more houses of worship than even the most pious of optimists could ever hope to see filled, so much talent on their very own college team must have seemed like an answered prayer.

The talent pool was so deep that any major college coach would have been ecstatic to have it, and all its denizens had somehow miraculously assembled at Evansville under coach Arad McCutchan, who was himself fast approaching saintly status in the city.

Indeed, Mac's cup ranneth over.

Evansvillians were looking forward to Thanksgiving, and the basketball season that beckoned just beyond, when the unimaginable happened in Dallas, where President John F. Kennedy had gone to shore up his support in advance of his reelection campaign. The nation watched in horror and disbelief as Walter Cronkite announced, with barely restrained emotion, the news that "President Kennedy died at 1 p.m. Central Standard Time." Americans spent the next few days mourning communally by the flicking lights of their television screens. Time crawled by, commerce stalled, and the nation grieved as one, moved anew by the pomp and ceremony of the slain president's state funeral. It was a tumultuous and emotionally wrenching time.

In Evansville the grief was no less than anywhere else, but the healing process was made somewhat easier by the imminent arrival of the new basketball season. The community used its perpetual hopes for the Purple Aces as a tonic for the gloom and depression the national tragedy had visited upon them.

For the 1963–64 season McCutchan had a new assistant coach. Tom O'Brien had been the assistant coach for the freshman team: Mac moved him up to the varsity and named him his chief recruiter.

"What I want to do is to find out where every good boy is located, seek him out and let him know we're interested. I don't care if he's only a junior. Maybe that will make our chances that much better to land him next year," O'Brien said upon assuming the job.

O'Brien's promotion paid immediate dividends when Evansville secured a commitment from Centralia's Herb Williams. His family had moved from Chicago after his father was hired as the pastor of New Bethel Baptist Church in Centralia. Herb's education in Centralia was typical of the times. "We lived one block from an elementary school. I couldn't go there, though, because it was an all-white school," he said. "I had to walk eight blocks to [the] school that was all black."

By the time he reached ninth grade, the small high school was integrated. Herb was a standout performer on the court. He amassed more than a thousand points during his career and was a two-time All-State selection.

Herb's strength was in his jumping ability. "We had a rebound drill using a ball attached to a pulley system. Our coach, Bob Jones, made us jump and touch that ball every day for fifteen to twenty minutes. We'd practice tip-ins and just grabbing the ball. He kept moving it higher and higher," Herb recalled.

During Herb's senior season several college coaches expressed interest in his services. None was stranger than Adolph Rupp of Kentucky. "We had a player on our team named Cliff Berger," Herb said. "Cliff was a good player, and he was white. One day his picture appeared in the local paper after he had a real good game. Under the picture the caption identified him as Herb Williams. Not long after that, Rupp showed up at one of our games. He told our coach he was there to see 'Herb Williams.' Rupp was a notorious racist who had no black players on his Kentucky teams. My coach looked at him and asked, 'You sure you want to see Herb Williams?' And Rupp told him, 'Yes, I came all the way up here to see him play.' Our coach didn't tell Rupp anything.

"At all of our home games they would turn out all the gym lights during player introductions and have us introduced and run out in a spotlight that would shine on us in the darkened gym. Well, when they announced 'Herb Williams,' and that spotlight beam hit me, Rupp almost had a heart attack. He rushed down to see my coach after the game. My coach said, "Well, you still want to talk to Herb Williams?'

"Rupp said, 'NO. NO. I want to talk to that big white kid.'"[1]

Williams, with offers from ninety-eight schools, considered Illinois and Oklahoma but rejected both and decided to attend Bradley. "I went to Peoria in June. I had my papers in my suitcase," the 6-3 forward recalled. "But the more I looked around, the more I didn't like what I saw. I almost signed, but my mind told me not to."

Williams, the minister's son, had been raised in a strict Christian home. "When I got out there to visit, they gave me a host . . . to show me around the campus. He took me to the biggest drunken brawl you have ever seen. That was it for me. I knew that wasn't the kind of college life I wanted."[2]

Bradley's loss would be Mac's gain. Mac had been to Williams's home once, while Chuck Osborn of Bradley was there talking with Williams and his parents. Mac's car had broken down on the way and he'd hitchhiked to get there.[3] Mac was nothing if not persistent, and now that persistence paid off. Williams decided to attend Evansville.

"I got a call from Tom O'Brien," Herb recounted. "He told me Evansville was only three hours from Centralia, and what could I lose? He said if I don't like it, I could always go home." Another call came from Jerry Sloan. "He called me and asked me if I'd ever thought about going to Evansville," Williams said. "I told him I hadn't really given it any thought. He said, 'Well, I hadn't either, but I'm glad I'm here now. You owe it to yourself to come down here and see it.'"

Williams decided to give the school a look. "My dad knew a minister in Evansville; he arranged for my dad to speak down there so I went along, and after he preached, we went to visit the school. I liked it right away. It had a real closeness and familiar feel to it. I felt comfortable there. After we got back, I called Coach McCutchan and told him I'd like to come there. He said, 'I'll be at your house tomorrow.'"

Mac arrived and offered Herb a scholarship on the spot. "My mom and I were very close, and she had suffered a heart attack, and I wanted to be close enough to come home and visit her. Evansville was only about eighty or ninety miles away, and I could get a ride home easily from there," Herb said. "I have never regretted that decision. It was the right one for me."[4]

Once again a legitimate major college prospect had spurned the larger schools and enrolled at Evansville College. In a year he'd be eligible to play.

When the 1963–64 edition of the Purple Aces debuted at Roberts in a pre-season scrimmage, more than 8,000 fans greeted the team, using the occasion to shake off the numbing trauma of the Kennedy assassination. The crowd --for a meaningless scrimmage-- was bigger than what nearly all major college schools expect for their regular season games.

In his column in the *Evansville Press* Dick Anderson compared the city and its support for the Aces to the investment by Green Bay, Wisconsin, in the fortunes of its football franchise.

"The main comparison," Anderson wrote, "is the wide awake community respect and acceptance of the product as a community asset as well as a fine entertainment feature."[5]

But fans would have to wait a little longer to see the Aces in a game that counted. They opened the season on the road, taking an Eastern Airlines flight to New Mexico when the Shrine Circus took over Roberts Stadium.[6] The starting lineup against New Mexico State had Larry Humes and Sam Watkins as the guards; Jerry Sloan moved to forward, joining Buster Briley; and Ed Zausch, who had added some pounds to his frame, was again in the pivot. Jim Smith and Wayne Boultinghouse would be the first players off the bench as subs.

Ed's weight gain had an easy explanation: "Buster and I had opened an ice cream stand called Buster and Ed's Old-fashioned Ice Cream Parlor over the summer. We had college girls working for us, and the kids would come there to get their ice cream and we'd sign autographs," Ed said. "We would sign their basketballs for them if they bought some ice cream. The place was a huge success."[7]

Buster said they were so successful they even thought of franchising the idea. He also admits to having sampled the product a little more than necessary. But once basketball season started, they shut down the ice cream stand and "got serious about basketball," he said.[8]

Sloan, now 6-6, had worked on his shooting over the summer. "I think I was pressing too much," he said, discussing his first season. "I've been through it once now, and I'm not as jumpy." As the UPI first team All-American selection prepared for his new role, Mac told reporters, "I'm not at all sure that Sloan won't be playing guard before it's all over."[9]

The road trip through the Southwest proved a successful one and gave the members of the Aces' new lineup a chance to get to know each other in their new roles on court. They cruised past New Mexico State in Las Cruces, where the Aggies played in a small high school gym, and then knocked off the University of Arizona in a 61–58 win in Tucson.

Jim Smith, the 6-3 senior who had earned a starting spot the previous season, played a large role in the second win, coming off the bench to provide help in the second half. "You have to be a competitor to make them when they count, and Smitty did a fine job," Mac said. "He was getting those rebounds, directing our stall and just playing heads-up ball."

Guard Sam Watkins agreed. "He sure knew what he was doing. He told me where he wanted me to go, and that's where I went," Sam said.[10] Watkins's twelve-foot jumper had put the Aces up 54–53 with little more than three minutes to play, and the Aces left Tucson with their second win.

Iowa assistant coach Dick Schultz attended the game, scouting the Aces before the Hawkeyes' upcoming game at Roberts. "This team has probably more potential than any of your previous ones we've played," Schultz told Evansville reporters. "They should develop into a real fine club before the season ends."

When the Hawkeyes rolled into Roberts, they were greeted by 11,715 rabid Aces fans in red shirts, who established a new opening night record. The Aces were looking to avenge the loss the Hawkeyes had inflicted the previous season, but the Aces had not acquitted themselves well against Big Ten opponents, and Iowa always seemed to find a way to win.

This year was no exception. Plagued by early foul trouble against the Hawkeyes, the Aces found themselves behind and had to play catch-up. Buster Briley's long-range bombs kept them close in the second half, and they drew even when Sloan spotted Jim Smith open beneath the basket. Smitty converted a layup and was fouled. He made the free throw to tie the game at 72. When Jimmy Rodgers, Iowa's guard, converted two free throws, the Hawkeyes regained the lead.

Sloan was called for a travel on the next Aces' possession, and with but ten seconds remaining, Watkins's fifteen-footer missed. A lone Iowa free throw completed the scoring, and the Aces again were beaten by a Big Ten visitor, for the thirteenth time in fourteen tries. The score was 75–72.

"I was bad," said Jerry Sloan, who had gathered sixteen rebounds. "Why, I don't know. I just couldn't find the basket."

Mac offered an explanation. "It might have been a case of not understanding our offense. It looked like maybe they didn't know each other too well yet," Mac guessed.

Buster, always the optimist, was not pleased to see Iowa win again. "This was 'next time,'" muttered Buster, who as a senior wouldn't get another chance to face Iowa, which had now recorded its fourth win over the Aces in five tries.[11]

That Purdue was headed to Roberts offered little to cheer Buster up. The Aces' record against Iowa was not good. It was even worse against Purdue. The Aces had yet to beat the Boilermakers in five tries since 1928–29.

Despite the Aces' dismal record against Purdue, the Boilermakers always attracted a large crowd to Roberts. And teams like Purdue, Iowa, and Notre Dame were always happy to play there because they always got a big payday. "Financially, this is the biggest money-maker Purdue plays anywhere in basketball," wrote Gordon Graham, sports editor of the *Lafayette (Indiana) Courier and Journal*.

That is, the financial reward offset the risk of defeat by a College Division team. [Of course, this simply would not be an option today, because strength of schedule is an important consideration when the NCAA Tournament selection committee is deciding who to invite to the lucrative postseason event. But in the 1960s and 1970s it was still possible to lure major college opponents to Evansville for enough money.] The local fans loved the thought of their Aces playing and beating some of the game's biggest names. Attendance always swelled when marquee opponents were in town.

This season Purdue's appearance offered an additional reason to not miss the game: Dave Schellhase, an Evansvillian. Dave had graduated from North High School, where he had been a star, averaging more than 30 points as a senior. As the leading scorer in Evansville high school history, he had received more than fifty offers and had spurned Evansville College for Purdue.

The Aces had followed their loss to Iowa with wins over San Francisco State and South Dakota State before Schellhase returned home to face the very college he had rejected.[12] The crowd, 12,437 strong, greeted Schellhase with polite applause as he made his way through the tunnel and out onto the court for the first time. It would be the last friendly gesture he would receive. When reporters asked Mac who would be guarding Schellhase—who had been averaging 21 points per game and had scored 31 against Wake Forest—Mac's answer was "Sloan. Who else?"

Purdue chose a 1-3-1 zone against the Aces, and it didn't work. Humes and Sloan shredded it repeatedly. Purdue's coach, Ray Eddy, switched to a 2-1-2 and fared little better. The Aces' offense exploded like an overheated boiler, and when Purdue finally switched to a man-to-man defense, the Aces were up by 42–31. With seven minutes left in the first half, Mac sent in his Go Team, which extended the lead to 22.

In the second half Mac sent in his reserves again, and Wayne Boultinghouse and Russ Grieger used the opportunity to their advantage. Both played outstandingly, and the Aces coasted to an easy 110–84 romp over the visitors.

"Sloan's the best man I've ever played against," said Schellhase, a bit shell-shocked after the game. "He's tough, all over you, and you can't make a move without looking him straight in the eye."

"Jerry just shut [Schellhase] down," Buster Briley recalled.[13]

"He was a marked man," Ed Zausch said of Schellhase. "The crowd was large and noisy, and they intimidated a lot of teams that came in there."[14]

With Sloan covering him like a blanket, Schellhase had managed only 14 points, and Jerry had held him to just five in the first half. Sloan managed to collect ten rebounds and said after the game, "You better believe it's great to win one like this. But, I still don't think we've reached our peak." Russ Grieger, who had combined with Boultinghouse for 32 points off the bench, said, "I think we've proven that we are good enough to take anyone on a given night. I just hope I get to help to do it."

If anything, Mac was enjoying an embarrassment of riches. While his starting five were set, he had the ability to go to his bench and insert Boultinghouse, Grieger, Jim Smith, Dave Cox, Ron Eberhard, and Allen McCutchan, all of whom could play without a noticeable dip in ability. If Ed Zausch got into foul trouble, he was spelled by Paul Bullard or Larry Denton.

"Five fresh men coming in like that can do a good job, but I don't want to get my system in a real platoon," Mac said. "I'll use individuals when I feel there is a need for them, but not particularly a whole new team."[15]

Ed Zausch recalled the Go Team as but one of Mac's many techniques for using his talent and gaining an advantage: "The five guys would come in and press all the time for five minutes or so. It was a lot like his other ideas, which he ingrained in us through repetition.

"He'd plan to get the opening tip. Get the first points. Get rebounds. Sometimes just keep the ball away. He had all the angles figured and knew exactly how and when to use them," Zausch said.[16]

As the go-go Aces prepared to host their annual Holiday Tournament, UPI placed them atop its latest poll.

Yet another Ivy League school, Columbia—5–2 for the year—had accepted an invitation to the Holiday Tournament. Even though Evansville shot poorly from the free-throw line, the Aces dispatched the Lions 96–60.

The Aces made the final, playing against the University of Arizona, which had defeated Maryland in the first round. The crowd of 9,211 was confident the Aces would prevail—after all, they'd beaten Arizona earlier in the season. But the result was far different this time.

Arizona's Bob Hensen and Al Johnson controlled the backboards, and Evansville was colder than the December weather, shooting just 33 percent from the floor. Only Larry Humes, who managed to score 12 points in the first half, prevented a Wildcat rout. When Sam Watkins made the first basket of the second half, the Aces were within four points. But that was as close as they would get. The final score was 78–61. "We got beat every way a team could get beat," Mac told reporters after surfacing from a closed-door meeting with his team.[17]

"Everybody was upset," Ed Zausch said. "It was a pretty matter-of-fact meeting. I know we didn't go away feeling good about our performance. But after that meeting things seemed to change. We got pretty ruthless after that."[18]

Buster's recollections of the game are crystal clear: "Mac was using me as a decoy. Sending me down the left side and having the ball go to the right side. After a time-out in the first half, I said to him, 'I might as well just sit if I'm just going to be standing out there.' Mac pointed to a spot on the bench next to him and said, 'Sit.' And that's where I was the rest of the game. It was just a message he was delivering to me, that we all had our roles to play, and to be successful sometimes you had to sacrifice. I got the message."[19]

The rest of the team got it as well. Loaded with talent and offensive power, the Aces would have to bury their individual egos for the good of the team. From that point on, the Aces were all on the same page of Mac's book. "We each had a role. With Humes and Sloan we weren't worried about how much we could score. If I shot from outside, it opened up the middle for Larry and Jerry to score.

If a team played a zone against us, I'd shoot over it until they came out of it," Buster said.[20]

Ed Zausch knew his role and its importance in Mac's fast-break offense: "I was to get the rebounds and get them out to the wings as fast as I could. Humes was the easiest to find. I knew exactly where he was going to be without even looking. He'd get five to six easy layups a game that way. The funny thing about Jerry Sloan was that Mac had to encourage him to shoot. He was very generous with the ball and was a pinpoint passer. You had better keep your head up when he had the ball, because he threw bullets."[21]

Whereas Buster once had carried the scoring load pretty much alone, now the load was redistributed, and it became difficult for any team to effectively shut Evansville down by concentrating on one player. Another Ace was always ready to step up and deliver.

With everyone solidly on the same page and understanding his role, the Aces reeled off a string of wins that left people wondering if they'd ever lose again. It began with DePauw, which suffered a bludgeoning 97–53 loss when Buster, eager to show Mac he'd learned something outside the classroom, hit 8-for-15 for 19 points, a season high.

"I was moving around a little better for my shots," Buster told reporters. Mac applauded Buster's moves. "We all know Buster is a great shooter," Mac said, noting that he'd added some picks and screens to give Buster some room. "It was just a matter of time before he had a night like this."[22]

Valpo was next to feel the Aces' wrath, falling 111–92 as Buster poured in 21. Humes added 29 and Sloan 21 before fouling out. "They pulled a lot of cute stuff that has no place in the game," Mac said of Valparaiso's play. "But, I was proud of my boys. They didn't retaliate. Jerry took a lot of abuse but he's getting used to it."

After being named the ICC MVP as a sophomore the previous season, Jerry Sloan had nowhere to hide. He was a marked man wherever the Aces went. The good news was that when the opponents concentrated on Sloan, other talented Aces could break free and punish his harassers. Other teams simply didn't have enough bodies to stop the deep Evansville bench.

When Indiana State concentrated on stopping Jerry in January, the Aces crushed them 123–86 while setting a new Evansville scoring record. All the reserves saw duty. The record-setting basket was made by walk-on Jim Forman, who was at Evansville because he knew Mac never cut anyone. It was Jim's very first collegiate basket—from 18 feet with 20 seconds to play—that set the new mark. He was not even listed in the game program.

"To tell the truth I couldn't even see the basket," the excited junior said later. His field goal was the Aces' fifty-first, another record, and the crowd of 11,017 loved it. ISU's coach, Duane Klueh, was impressed: "This is by far the best basketball team we've seen this year. In fact, it's probably the best team ever to represent the Indiana Collegiate Conference."[23] He wasn't exaggerating. The rampaging Aces were something to behold.

After a trip to Ball State where, behind Ed Zausch's 18 points and 15 rebounds, the Aces turned back the Cardinals 98–92 in Ball State's new 7,000-seat gymnasium and headed home.[24]

Roberts was expecting a large crowd for the Aces' next game, which was against archrival Kentucky Wesleyan. T. L. Plain had departed as coach, replaced by Guy Strong. Strong hadn't missed a beat; he had the Panthers at 12–2 when they arrived at Roberts with two freshmen who were attracting a lot of attention. Mike Redd, a 6-2 guard, had led his Louisville Seneca team to a state high school championship. Originally slated to attend Western Kentucky, Redd had opted for Wesleyan when Strong took the job. "He's not another Oscar," Mac said of Redd, "but he's a very solid player." Redd was averaging 22 points per game.

The other newcomer to the third-ranked Panthers had originally committed to Evansville, saying he wanted to be the next Ed Smallwood. But 6-6 Charlie Taylor had decided to stay at home and play for the Panthers. He was averaging 14 points and 9 rebounds per game.

Even though the game was scheduled for a Wednesday night, Bob Hudson hired ten off-duty police officers—six more than usual—to handle what he knew would be a huge crowd. Aces fans were known to also be especially rowdy at Wesleyan games. "We've been deluged with mail," a harried Hudson said. "I'd estimate that 40 percent of the people at the game tonight will be from Vanderburgh County."[25]

Strong wasn't fazed by his first trip to Roberts. "We certainly don't expect any trouble," he said. "We're not worrying about the fans. We're coming over to play basketball." The Panthers played about as well as they could in the first half. Even though Sloan was guarding him, Redd managed to hit 6-for-10 from the field to keep the Panthers close. Humes's last-second layup after a Sloan steal gave the Aces a 38–36 lead at the half.

But in the opening minutes of the second half, Redd collected his fourth personal and went to the bench. Only five minutes in, Taylor joined him there. With their big guns spiked, the Panthers were defenseless before the Aces' offensive assault. Boultinghouse, Grieger, Bullard, Smith, and Denton finished the Panthers off. The final score was 81–69.

Sloan had high praise for Redd, who went 7-for-11 from the floor and had 16 points for the game. Asked if Redd was as good as advertised, Sloan said, "You'd better believe it, and then some."

Bob Hudson had been right to expect a monster crowd: 12,541, just 147 short of the record set against Notre Dame, had attended the game. In fact, in just eight home games Evansville's attendance was 79,178, an average of just under 10,000 per contest.

Next up was Ball State, which had tested the Aces in Muncie before falling, 98–92. The Cardinals gave the Aces another battle before folding before a barrage of buckets from Humes. The final score was 90–83, but the Cardinals had made a game of it with Ed Butler, their All-Conference center, leading the way.

Mac's Go Team had played well in the first half and in the second half, with 14:31 to play, gave the Aces the lift they needed. Jim Smith made two quick jumpers, Russ Grieger added a bucket from outside, and suddenly the score was 64–55.

The Aces held on to win 90–83, but they weren't that pleased with the effort. Despite the efforts of Zausch and Bullard to stop Butler, he had managed to score 31 points. "We were lousy, and we know it," Bullard said. "We were flat," Sam Watkins explained. "We could sense it in practice Thursday and Friday, but I guess you can't cry too much as long as you win."

Ball State's coach, Jim Hinga, was not going to be sending any sympathy cards Sam's way. "You can't call Evansville a great team. You have to call them two great teams," he told reporters. "If they don't get shook against Butler, they could go undefeated in the conference," he predicted.[26] St. Joseph's and Valparaiso offered little resistance to the Aces, falling 100–72 and 79–49, respectively, as Mac's troops marched toward their meeting with Butler University.[27]

When the Bulldogs arrived for a Wednesday night showdown, the Aces were ready for them. Jeff Blue, Butler's 6-6 center, was forced to the bench with four fouls and more than nine minutes to play in the first half. The Aces exploited his absence to take a 10-point lead to the locker room. When Blue twisted his ankle on the opening tip of the second half, the Bulldogs were without his services for three more minutes. By the time he returned, the Aces had pulled away and the Bulldogs were whipped. It ended up 83–73.

"We sure as dickens have played better games this year," Mac complained in language as strong as he could muster. "Maybe we just wanted this one too much." Buster agreed. "I was really up for this game," Buster said after his 27-point performance. "I just kept thinking about last year up at Butler," when the Aces had lost.[28]

For two seasons the goal of the Aces' opponents had been to stop Buster, and in the past they could concentrate on him without too much at risk. No longer did they have that luxury. Jack Hartman of Southern Illinois figured a 2-1-2 zone might crimp Buster's style. Not a chance. Buster simply shot over Hartman's zone defense and made 12-for-19 from the field on his way to a 30-point performance as the Aces clobbered the visitors.

After voicing his displeasure with the officiating, Hartman told reporters, "I just hate to play here. It's rough."[29]

"We knew Briley could kill us if he hit his first two or three and got his head up," Hartman conceded. "We tried to keep him from doing it, but we couldn't."[30]

Buster had his own explanation for his sudden hot streak after cooling his heels next to Mac during the Arizona loss. "I just quit worrying about it," he told Bill Fluty of the *Courier*. "I decided to quit holding myself down and go out there and play. Just be natural."

Being natural meant Buster was back to doing what he did best: firing at will whenever he was open from wherever he happened to be when he got his hands on the ball. "These other teams have all been keying on Sloan, trying to stop him," Buster said. "They're not worried about me with Sloan in there, and Jerry's set me up with a lot of passes."[31] Buster was also cutting a finer figure on the court, having lost a lot of the weight he'd packed on while scooping ice cream over the summer.

United Press International had noticed the Aces and in a story that ran in most papers on February 8, 1964, touted their record and their remarkable fan support. The article, which proclaimed that "Arad McCutchan has built small college basketball's most formidable dynasty," concluded with the observation that, with Evansville's lofty national ranking, "everyone wants to beat Evansville."[32]

Mac was gaining a national reputation, and Evansville was basking in the national attention, but Mac hadn't forgotten how the Aces had reached such laudable heights. His coaching staff had a new but familiar face. Ed Smallwood had completed his stint in the Army, and Mac had coaxed him back to campus to finish his degree. Ed was serving as an assistant coach and helping Mac at practice with the more than forty players on the roster. They could hardly have had a better example to follow. Ed could still play, and he worked diligently with the young players. The Big Smoke was back and the Aces, well, they were smokin' too.

The last home game for the seniors before the NCAA Tournament was against St. Joseph's, and 9,764 showed up to see off the graduating players, including Buster Briley, who responded with 19 points. Zausch nabbed fourteen rebounds, blocked three shots, and fed the fast-breaking Humes three times. Bullard added 14 points in relief. "Arad played everybody but the janitor tonight and still beat us," quipped the Pumas' coach, Jim Holstein.

Well, that wasn't exactly true. Mac hadn't completely emptied his bench. Perched on his lap during the game was Jim Smith's two-year-old son of. "He wanted to report," Mac quipped. "But I'd put in enough subs by then." The easy win upped the Aces' record at home to 12–2, and they had won all six of their road games. Four games remained before the tournament, and all those were on the road.

Mac was a little concerned. "I don't know how well we'll play," he told reporters. Pretty well, as it turned out.

At Terre Haute they crushed Indiana State by 105–79 after rolling up a 63–35 halftime lead. The win was the Aces' nineteenth and secured the ICC crown for them. Humes with 19 and Buster with 12 led the Aces in the limited playing time they saw as the game became a romp.

"Sure it's great to have a championship." Mac said. "But the one we really want now is Butler Saturday night. If we win that we win them all, and that would put us in a class all alone." Once again Butler was the only team standing between the Aces and a perfect ICC season. Tony Hinkle hadn't forgotten Buster's 27-point performance in Evansville and decided to try putting 6-1 John Fledderjohn on him. The future Hall of Fame coach soon regretted the decision. "We didn't believe he could play guard," Mac said of Fledderjohn, "so we went after him. We were right. He couldn't."

Trying to hold down Buster and bring the ball up court proved too much for Fledderjohn, who repeatedly threw the ball away. Butler's turnovers put the Bulldogs behind 20–9, and they never recovered.

Sam Watkins took advantage of all the attention being paid to Buster and hit

7-for-14 from the field, while Humes added 9-for-12. The Aces left Indianapolis with a perfect ICC slate. Hinkle said of the Aces after the game, "This team doesn't have the scorer like Ed Smallwood, but that team didn't have as much depth. This is a much better team defensively. They do a fine job with the press."

Flush with their fourteenth straight win, the Aces headed to South Bend to meet Notre Dame. Now the Aces learned what it was like to play before a crowd heavily invested in the other team. "It was a tough crowd," Ed Zausch said. "They were right on top of us and very loud. The game was very physical, and they seemed to get all the calls."[33]

While his high school friend Cassius Clay was defeating Sonny Liston in Miami and taking the heavyweight crown from the brooding champ, Sam Watkins kept Evansville close with 16 points. But it wouldn't be enough. The Irish managed a 91–75 win, snapping the Aces' winning streak. Walt Sahm led the Irish with 29 points and twenty-five rebounds as the home team pounded the boards, out-rebounding the Aces by 71–51.

Sahm said afterward that Sloan and Humes could "both be playing for us. And you hear people criticize Briley because of his defense. I don't care what anybody says, he hurts you. He's as good a shooter as there is." Sahm may have just been feeling gracious, but his analysis of the Aces' strengths was right on. They may have been a College Division team, but any Ace could have started on any major college team in the country. They were simply that good.

Already assured of a spot in the NCAA Tournament, the Aces went to Owensboro to play their final game of the regular season against Kentucky Wesleyan, which would have liked nothing better than an upset win over their rivals. Wesleyan was 15–6 for the year and would also be going on to the postseason tournament. A win over Evansville would be a huge confidence builder for the Panthers.

The game was everything that fans had come to expect when these two rivals met. It was another cliffhanger that went back and forth from the opening tip. The Panthers managed to take a three-point lead to the locker room at the half, but that was erased at the 5:33 mark when Sloan's bucket put the Aces ahead. Wesleyan came right back, but a Humes basket at 1:58 again put the Aces on top.

Wesleyan refused to fold as the crowd, now on its feet, urged the Panthers on. Taylor's two free throws pulled Wesleyan to within one point, 71–70, when Briley was fouled. Mac called a timeout. Only six seconds remained, and Buster had a one-and-one coming that could ice the game. "After Buster makes these," Mac told his team, "pull back on defense right away."

Buster recalled the moment: "I stepped to the line full of confidence. The crowd was going nuts, but that didn't bother me. I put it up just like always—and I missed! I just stood there in shock. I couldn't believe I had missed that shot."[34]

Luckily for Buster, Redd's last-second desperation heave from 35 feet fell short. The Aces had survived, 71–70.

Finishing with the school's best season ever, 21–3, Evansville now turned its attention to the NCAA Tournament. In the first round the Aces met Jackson State and were heavy favorites despite Jackson State's recent win over the NAIA's top-ranked Grambling.

The Tigers got some help off the bench from Ed Manning when the freshman canned six baskets and hauled in nine rebounds. But the player who would father future Kansas star Danny Manning saw his team trounced by the Aces. After the Aces built a 33-point halftime lead, Mac sat the starters with nearly twelve minutes to play. Sloan and Humes each had 21 points. The final score was 97–69. "I knew they were a great team," Coach Harrison Wilson said of the Aces. "But, I didn't know they were this great."

Looming ahead for the Aces were the Salukis of Southern Illinois. If the Aces were to advance, they had to beat the team that had sent them packing in their last two encounters in the NCAA Tournament. "By this time SIU was our big rival, bigger even than Kentucky Wesleyan," Ed Zausch said. "They always seemed to get up for us."[35]

The Salukis opened in a 1-3-1 zone, clogging the middle. This defense opened the way for the Aces' sharpshooters, Briley, Sloan, and Watkins, to fire at will. Evansville built a ten-point lead, but SIU refused to fold and climbed back to within two points with just over eleven minutes to play.

At this point, after watching SIU claim control of the boards, Mac ordered his team into a stall. It didn't work. Jim Smith threw the ball away on three straight possessions. The Salukis edged ahead by 57–56 on a Paul Henry free throw with just four minutes to go. More than 7,300 spectators, the most ever assembled for a regional tournament game, sat in stunned disbelief as memories of the past two tournament defeats flashed through their minds.

Was it going to happen again?

Both teams failed to convert on their next possessions, and the Aces abandoned the stall. Then Jerry Sloan hauled in a missed shot, raced the length of the floor, pulled up at the free throw line, and nailed a jumper, putting the Aces ahead. Larry Humes followed with a tip-in off a free throw that Bullard missed. With 2:20 to play the Aces held a 60–57 lead.

The Aces' tenacious defense harried SIU all over the floor. When Bullard took a Sloan pass and banked one in with thirty seconds left, the crowd finally could let out its collective breath. The Aces had finally solved their Saluki problems. The final score was 64–59, and the Aces had survived to play again. "We ran our stuff for 38 minutes, but when we had our chance to get them, we forgot our patterns and tried to force the ball under," SIU coach Jack Hartman explained after the game.

Defensive pressure may have been the reason for the Salukis' lapses. The Aces made twelve steals with their intense full-court press. "Those steals made the difference," Mac said. Sloan led the Aces in scoring and rebounding, and he joined Larry Humes on the all-tournament team for the regionals.

The next day Jerry learned he'd been selected for the Olympic Trials. He would be the third Evansville player so honored, after Ed Smallwood and Dale Wise. "It's quite an honor, but right now I can't get too enthused over it," he said. "All I want on my mind right now is winning the NCAA championship."

Focused and prepared, the Aces headed for their fifth appearance at the NCAA finals in eight years. Cal Poly had won the Western Regional, and the visitors from Pomona, California, were big and strong. They brought a 25–3 record with them into Roberts as the two faced off. "They were very tough in the middle," Ed Zausch recalled.

Not tough enough.

"Jerry kept on me the whole game to go after rebounds," Ed said. "He'd tell me, 'Ed, just go for it. Get in there.' I did. I was really turned on."[36] The shooting of Larry Humes and the control of the boards by Sloan and Zausch doomed the Broncos. They trailed by as many as 20 points in the first half before mounting a rally when Zausch and Bullard each picked up his fourth foul.

With the lead down to just five points, Mac reinserted Buster, and the Aces reeled off nine straight points. The final was 95–73. Sloan had 14 points and as many rebounds, and Larry Humes led the Aces with 29 points.

"Evansville had us scouted very well and they seemed to know every move we were going to make," coach Bob Stull said. In fact, a former Reitz High School student who was attending Cal Poly had provided Mac with a detailed scouting report on the Broncos, and Mac had used the information to his advantage. Being prepared was just another of his strong points.

The next hurdle for the Aces was Norm Stewart and his Iowa State College team, with a record of 23–2.[37] More than 8,500 were on hand as the Aces and Panthers battled on a Thursday night. The visitors managed to stay close to the heavily favored Aces until late in the first half. Then Sloan fired a pass to Zausch, who was open underneath, for an easy basket. The Aces followed with two Humes free throws and two more by Sloan. The Panthers folded.

Up by 10 at the half, the Aces went on a 14–4 run in the opening minutes of the second half. Mac called on his reserves with more than eight minutes remaining, and they finished out the lopsided win, 82–67. Ed Zausch and Jerry Sloan combined for forty rebounds, outrebounding the entire Panthers team by five. "We just had too much muscle for them to handle," Mac told writers.

Bob Hudson and the NCAA Tournament committee were beaming as Evansville advanced to the final game. Hudson was expecting a huge crowd, and the Aces' partisans, attired in red, didn't disappoint. When the tired turnstiles stopped whirring, the house held 12,244, a full thousand more than Bob had expected.

Akron was the final opponent, and the Zips were designated the "home" team. When the Aces appeared from the tunnel in their bright orange road uniforms, the fans stood and began their rhythmic chant, "Aces! Aces!" *Clap, clap, clap-clapclap,* which washed down from the rafters and bathed the team in wave after wave of encouragement and affection.

For the seven seniors on Mac's squad this would be their last appearance in an Aces uniform. They had come to Evansville in 1959 and a season later had made their varsity debuts memorable when they upset Iowa. Buster Briley, Paul Bullard, and their teammates had started with a shocking win and now all they wanted to do was go out with a championship. It was just forty minutes away.

Fittingly, just nine seconds into the championship game the irrepressible Buster Briley opened fire fearlessly and canned a thirty-footer that brought the crowd back out of the seats. They hardly had time to settle when Buster came down the left side and lofted another thirty-footer.

Bingo!

Aces up, 4–0.

After Akron made a free throw, Buster went back at it. Another arcing jumper from thirty feet outside dove home, and the Aces took off. When Akron converted three straight free throws to draw within two points at 6–4, Buster slammed the door with his fourth straight bomb. The Buster Briley blitzkrieg, reminiscent of so many other nights when the senior star had fired at will from outside the zone defenses he encountered, was more than Akron could handle. Trailing by 10 with five minutes to go in the first half, Akron was all but finished. Buster had zapped the Zips.

In the second half the Aces' offense continued to click as Zausch made a tip-in, followed by a driving layup by Humes. Larry then hit a jumper from beyond the foul line. Zausch's basket with fifteen minutes to go upped the lead to 16, and as the Aces retreated on defense, Jerry Sloan gave Larry Humes a playful whack on the bottom, and Humes grinned from ear to ear. It was all but over, and the players knew it.

Mac substituted liberally as the clock ticked down. His seniors, including his son, Allen, and Dave Green both added free throws as the regulars stood and applauded on the sidelines. The final score was 72–59.

Evansville's Purple Aces were NCAA champions again.

"Buster was just amazing that night," Ed Zausch said of his friend and team-mate. "He had great touch and motor skills. After he made those long baskets, he'd just jump up and down with delight. It was fun to watch."[38]

"It was one of those times when I just couldn't miss," Buster recalled. "I knew we didn't want to get behind because then they would hold the ball on us. We'd played three games in three days, and I just wanted to get this one over with," which was why he opened up from long range.[39] Buster was tired but not from the three games in three days. He was coming down with the measles, though he didn't know that until the next day.[40]

Measles or not, Buster was hot, and he had quickly cooled off the Zips, allowing the Aces to clinch the title.

"Emotions kind of broke loose on the bench there at the end . . . tears, and that sort of thing," Mac said. "Some of it came from ones you wouldn't expect such things to come from. But, they wanted it, and they'd worked so hard to get it. . . . It was one of those things that builds up inside a person."

Buster closed out his career at Evansville with a team-leading 16 points and drew praise from his coach. "Old Buster really knocked them in, didn't he?" Mac grinned after the game. "We normally like to get a little more inside first, but they were giving him the shots." And Buster was making them.

For the seniors the championship was the culmination of four years at Evansville College. As a class they could point with pride to their accomplishments on the court. They had struggled to a 14–11 record as sophomores but rebounded to post 21–3 and 26–3 records. They had gone to the NCAA Tournament each year and had won eight of its ten games, advancing to the finals twice. Their ICC record was 31–5, including two conference titles and the very first perfect conference season.

Wayne Boultinghouse, who had suffered a serious elbow injury, had recovered to finish his career as a valuable asset off the bench. His elbow injury didn't keep him from becoming a bonus baby for the St. Louis Cardinals. After advancing to AA ball at Cedar Rapids, he was drafted into the Army. After his release from the service he played just one more season before accepting a job at Evansville as assistant basketball coach and head baseball coach. Later, he would become the head coach at Indiana State University (now the University of Southern Indiana) in Evansville when the school established a campus there. Wayne coached the Screaming Eagles for seven seasons and recorded 111 wins against only 79 losses there and later served as the athletic director. Of his years at Evansville, Boultinghouse said, "It was magical. The fan base, a Hall Of Fame coach—I couldn't have asked for more."[41]

Ed Zausch left Evansville College with a leather suitcase, a small plaque, a medal commemorating the national title, and a championship ring. "The St. Louis Hawks of the NBA offered me $12,000 to sign with them but it was only good if I made the team. I turned them down," he said. Instead he went into real estate development with a partner, which eventually led to a string of Bonanza Steakhouse restaurants. After acquiring and later selling a beer distributorship, he formed a company in 1979 that supplies pipe for underground utilities. The company is a leader in its field, with multiple offices, and his son now runs the business.

Ed, who became a starter when Herthel left the team, is candid about his years at Evansville: "For me the years at Evansville College turned out to be the greatest thing that ever happened to me. We were confident, we worked together, and it became easy for us. After that Arizona loss, we became a focused team. Our 26–3 record was the best ever at Evansville." Once a year, during the NCAA Tournament, Ed takes out his championship ring and wears it while watching March Madness.[42]

Allen McCutchan didn't get much playing time on the talent-laden teams he was a part of, even though he was the coach's son. He did play on the Go Team, and he is proud of his accomplishments at Evansville College: "I played with Sloan, Humes, and Briley, and it was a great experience just to be a part of all that." After graduation he attended Yale Medical School and became a doctor.

He eventually landed in San Diego at the University of California–San Diego, where he is a lead researcher in the battle against AIDS, who travels every year to African nations where the scourge of AIDS has reached epidemic proportions.[43]

Jim Smith left Evansville "both happy and sad." The oldest Ace, he went on to coach basketball in Illinois and later for two seasons in Henderson City, Kentucky.

Paul Bullard, another of the Aces' supersubs, admitted at the end of the season, "I'm glad it's over. I was getting a little tired. But even so, I know I'm going to miss it."

Buster Briley, the happy-go-lucky mad bomber from Madison, left the Aces as a huge fan favorite and the second-leading scorer in school history behind Ed Smallwood. Of his years as a member of the Purple Aces, Buster recalls vividly the fan support. "It was just mind-boggling," he said. "Whether you lived on the east side or the west side of town, where they each had separate local activities and identities, there was one thing everyone in Evansville had in common—they loved Aces basketball."

The St. Louis Hawks of the NBA offered Buster a tryout after college, but they were offering only a meager salary and those were the years when the likes of Cliff Hagan and Bob Pettit were playing for the Hawks, so he figured he wouldn't get much playing time and decided not to pursue it. Instead, he went into the insurance business where his charming personality, quick wit, and local fame as a former Ace served him well.

In the business world of the late 1960s and 1970s the two-martini lunch was pretty standard fare. Buster went to lot of business lunches. "I had my first drink as a teenager from my grandfather's still. It was white lightning," Buster said. Having started at the top of the alcohol potency scale, and with a family history of alcoholism, Buster soon became a heavy drinker. "I had a drinking problem and recognized it. I went into a rehabilitation center for fourteen days and then straight to AA meetings. I am an alcoholic, but I have been sober now for eighteen years," he said.

The player that the Evansville fans of the 1960s loved for his high-scoring splurges is still warmly greeted whenever he attends an Evansville game. The spot from which Buster launched the shot he made against Notre Dame was marked by a dowel with a golden head.

Years later he was a member of the city council when the university asked the city to replace the old floor. "We were having financial troubles at the time, and

I couldn't see how we could explain spending money on a new floor when we were laying people off," he said. "So I got the idea to saw up the floor and sell pieces to the fans to finance the new court. It worked, and the man who bought the section with the spike in it gave it to me in appreciation. "It's still right here in my den."[44]

If fans want to believe Buster's shot beat Notre Dame, well, they can continue to do so without being corrected by him. It is just one of the many happy memories Buster Briley provided for Evansville fans through the years.

Buster Briley had overcome a traumatic childhood and an addiction to alcohol that nearly destroyed him. He faced his inner demons and did what he had done as an Evansville Ace when facing a zone defense designed to stop him: he faced them down with confidence and courage and defeated them.

Buster joined Jerry Sloan and Larry Humes on the All-Tournament team.

The players who would be returning for the 1964–65 season promised to provide fans with more to cheer about. "There's plenty to look forward to. Now we want to win another one," Larry Humes said. Sam Watkins agreed. "I know how it feels now, and I want to have this feeling for the next two years," he said.

Mac, usually reserved in his comparisons of teams he had coached, offered this unusual critique of his new national champs: "Yes, I believe this is the greatest club we've ever had."

He didn't add the qualifier "so far," but he should have.

(Endnotes)

1   Herb Williams, telephone interview by author, May 22, 2011. Cliff Berger did go to Kentucky and played for Rupp. He was a member of the all-white 1966 NCAA finals team that included Pat Riley. Kentucky lost to Texas Western University, which had five black starters. After that watershed game the integration of college basketball teams in the South moved forward quickly. Today Berger is an oral surgeon in Georgia. For more on Kentucky–Texas Western see Frank Fitzpatrick, *And the Walls Came Tumbling Down* (New York: Simon and Schuster, 1999); Don Haskins and Dan Wetzel, *Glory Road* (New York: Hyperion, 2005), and the subsequent film, James Gartner, dir., *Glory Road*, DVD, Walt Disney Pictures, June 2006.

2   Williams interview.

3   Tony Chamblin, "Nobody's Perfect," *Evansville Sunday Courier & Press*, January 5, 1964, C-2.

4   Williams interview.

5   Dick Anderson, "Green Bay of Basketball ?"*Evansville Press*, n.d., Ed Zausch scrapbook.

6   Bill Schrader, "Mac Will Start Sophs," *Evansville Sunday Courier and Press*, December 1, 1963, C-2.

7   Ed Zausch, telephone interview by author, May 4, 2011.

8   Bill Fluty, "Aces on Run Again," *Evansville Courier*, December16, 1963, 14; Buster Briley, telephone interview by author, April 21, 2011.

9   I again want to thank Bill Bussing, who made his lengthy manuscript available to me. The detailed manuscript contains no footnotes, but when I interviewed Bussing in February 2011, he identified his sources as the *Evansville Courier* and *Evansville Press,* the two local papers at the time. Bussing's manuscript usually makes no distinction between the two, but the direct quotes are from one or the other and appear in the Bussing manuscript in quotation marks. Bussing also had access to a collection of old bound scrapbooks kept by Bob Hudson. My research assistant and I also used the scrapbooks, which are now housed in the university archives. The articles do not identify which paper they are from, much less the date and page, but I (and Bussing) assume they are from the *Courier* and *Press,* or the combined Sunday edition, the *Courier & Press*. Where no endnote appears with information crediting another source, the reader may assume that it comes from the scrapbooks and/or the Bussing manuscript.

10   Sam Watkins, telephone interview by author, June 4, 2011.

11   Bill Schrader, "Aces and Full House Can't Bluff Hawks," *Evansville Sunday Courier & Press*, December 8, 1963, C-1.

12   Bill Schrader, "Didn't Beat a Champ, Says State," *Evansville Sunday Courier and Press*, December 15, 1963, C-7.

13   Briley interview.

14   Zausch interview.

15   Bill Schrader, "Aces Blow Up Boiler Works, 110–84," *Evansville Sunday Courier & Press*, December 22, 1963, C-1.

16   Zausch interview.

17   Al Dunning, "Aces Fall to Arizona; Terps Chase the Lions," *Evansville Sunday Courier & Press*, December 29, 1963, C-1.

18 Zausch interview.

19 Briley interview.

20 Briley interview.

21 Zausch interview.

22 Bill Schrader, "Buster's Back, Aces Fly," *Evansville Sunday Courier & Press,* January 5, 1964, C-1.

23 Bill Schrader, "Aces Axe Sycamores in Record 123–86 Rout," *Evansville Sunday Courier & Press,* January 12, 1964, C-1.

24 Bill Schrader, "Buster 'n Ed Fired and Fumed," *Evansville Sunday Courier & Press,* January 19,1964, C-6.

25 Tony Chamblin, "Aces, Wesleyan Clash Here, Crowd Forecast Is 13,000," *Evansville Sunday Courier & Press,* January 19, 1964, C-4.

26 Tony Chamblin, "Cards Impressed, Not Aces," *Evansville Sunday Courier & Press,* January 26, 1964, C-1.

27 "12 Aces Gang Up on St. Joseph's," *Evansville Press,* January 30, 1964, 35; Don Bernhardt, "Valpo Slows the Aces to a 79–49 Waltz," *Evansville Sunday Courier and Press,* February 2, 1964, C-1.

28 Tom Tuley, "Butler Coach Hinkle Admits Mistake in Putting Small Guard on Briley," *Evansville Press,* February 6, 1964, 24.

29 Don Bernhardt, "Aces Take Salukis for a Walk, "*Evansville Courier,* n.d., Ed Zausch scrapbook.

30 Tony Chamblin, "Buster's Best Man," *Evansville Sunday Courier & Press,* February 9, 1964, C-1.

31 Bill Fluty, "Buster Briley Week," *Evansville Courier,* February 10, 1964, 10

32 UPI, "Hot Team in Basket Hotbed: Evansville," February 8, 1964, Ed Zausch scrapbook.

33 Zausch interview.

34 Briley interview.

35 Zausch interview.

36 Zausch interview.

37 Stewart would leave what is now Northern Iowa after the 1967 season and return to his alma mater, Missouri. He coached there until 1999 and amassed 634 more wins than all the other coaches at the university had managed in the previous sixty years of the program. Including his wins at Iowa State College, his record upon retirement was 731–375. His teams at Mizzou reached the Elite Eight twice, and he captured eight Big Eight Conference titles. His

best year was 1988–89, when the Tigers won twenty-nine games. He won a battle against cancer in the early 1990s that led him to help found the Coaches vs. Cancer organization, which has raised millions of dollars for cancer research. He is a member of the College Basketball Hall of Fame ("Norm Stewart Profile," n.d., *Mizzou,* www.mutigers.com./genrel/stewart_norm00.html).

38 Zausch interview.
39 Briley interview.
40 Briley interview.
41 Wayne Boultinghouse, telephone interview by author, February 11, 2011.
42 Zausch interview.
43 Allen McCutchan, telephone interview by author, February 11, 2011.
44 Briley interview.

Home of the Aces, 1965–1967

The Evansville Purple Aces had done what few college basketball teams at any level have ever done in the miraculous 1964-65 season. They swept through the entire season and post-season without a single blemish on their record. In capturing their second straight National Championship the Aces had brought national attention to the city and the city had responded with unprecedented support. Now the Aces of Evansville College had produced not one, not two, but four national championships, and the city had achieved its long-sought goal: it was "Home of the Aces."

It was also home of Arad "Mac" McCutchan, coach of those four championship teams, and the major colleges were eyeing him like a prime rib special. Not that they hadn't tried to lure him away before.

The major colleges had long come calling on Coach McCutchan. Missouri had tried hard in 1962, to no avail.

Now Clarence "Biggie" Munn, athletic director at Michigan State, had announced that Mac was among Biggie's top choices to replace Forrest Anderson as coach of the Spartans. Mac had just been selected as National Coach of the Year in the College Division for the second straight year. This time, he said Michigan State's offer was "a little tempting."[1]

"I asked [Biggie] if he knew my age. He said he was 55, two years older than me, so age didn't matter," Mac said.

Ultimately, to the great relief of Evansville College and the Aces' loyal followers, Mac, who had compiled an impressive 319–183 record in nineteen seasons, decided to stay put. "I told [them] I didn't think a move was practical. I had put so many years into building our program, it seemed impossible to get another program going in two-three years. That would have been the length of the contract," he said.[2]

With Grieger and Sloan lost to graduation Mac had three starters coming back. Williams, Watkins, and Humes would form the nucleus of the 1965–66 defending national champions, so this would be a year when recruiting was especially important.

But life at Carson Center, home of the athletic department, was in a state of turmoil that summer. Mac's assistant Tom O'Brien left to go to Bradley as assistant coach. O'Brien's departure was serious since he had become the chief recruiter for Mac.

Mac named Dave Fulkerson, who had been a student assistant, to replace O'Brien; it would take Fulkerson a while to get up to speed on the recruiting circuit. In the meantime Evansville's recruiting success was uneven.

Mac had decided to forgo a search for guards in favor of big men. One prime player he thought he had a chance to get was Alfred "Butch" Beard from Breckinridge High School in Kentucky. Beard was Kentucky's Player of the Year and had seen the Aces' games on television. His local station reran Aces games after the late evening news. "I stayed up to watch them," Beard remembered. "Man, was I sleepy at school the days after those games." When he visited the Evansville campus, Mac assigned returnees Humes, Williams, and Ron Johnson as the high schooler's chaperones. But Beard eventually signed with Louisville.

The loss of O'Brien, who had kept a watchful eye on all of Evansville's targets until they were safely in the fold, was painfully evident when Jim Bailey of Florissant, Missouri reneged on his pledge and signed with Marquette.

Mac added Clarence Hupfer, a 1964 recruit who had left school in September but returned in the spring, and Tom Niemeier, a 6-9 transfer from Purdue. Tom, a product of local Rex Mundi High, was a blue-chip player Mac had tried to get in 1963. Niemeier's recruitment had been controversial, with Indiana University and Purdue trading charges and countercharges about recruiting violations in wooing the *Parade Magazine* All-American.

A starter at Purdue as a sophomore, Niemeier had left Purdue. "I wasn't satisfied with my schoolwork," he said. Niemeier, who was married and had an infant daughter, said he also "wanted to be closer to my family in Evansville."

When practice opened in September, the new recruits were joined by another eleven walk-ons, including one from Maine and several transfers.

With three starters returning to the Aces, the rest would be competing for the two spots vacated by Grieger and Sloan. "I believe the three boys who started last year will all be better players this year," Mac said. "If we can do anything like equal our performances out of the other two, we could be better."

But better than perfect is hard to achieve.

Mac soon decided on two players from the undefeated team, Ron Johnson and Gary McClary, as tentative starters. Shortly thereafter McClary became seriously ill. He had been complaining of recurring headaches and eventually ended up in St. Mary's Hospital semiconscious and partially paralyzed. After being sent to St. Louis for treatment, he returned home after Thanksgiving.

McClary's absence caused a new battle for the fifth starting spot. Howard Pratt, the 6-6 protege of Marv Pruett, would eventually emerge the victor, and Pratt and Johnson would join the veteran trio of Humes, Watkins, and Williams when play opened against Iowa at Roberts Stadium.

Bob Hudson had guaranteed the Hawkeyes a payday of $5,000 or half the gate for their appearance. Evansville also agreed to offset $600 of Iowa's travel expenses.

Evansville's agreement with Roberts Stadium called for the Aces to pay a usage fee of 12.5 percent of the gross gate.

To pay for all that, Hudson had announced an increase in ticket prices for the new season, the first such boost in prices since the opening of the stadium in 1956. Single-game tickets went up from $1.50 to $1.75. Season bench seats were now $20, an increase of $2, and the chairbacks went for $24.50, up from $21.50.

"We don't expect to raise prices often," Hudson said. "We're not eager to do it. We feel the increase will take care of us for a long time." Besides, the timing would never be better. Hudson knew the Aces were an appealing attraction— coming off back-to-back championship seasons with their three leading scorers returning. Another factor was that, in all of college basketball in 1964–65, Evansville College, with an enrollment of fewer than 2,500, was second in total attendance. Only the University of Kentucky, with its larger enrollment and facility, had seen crowds for basketball that were larger than those that had gathered at Roberts to watch the Aces.

The increase in ticket prices didn't faze the Evansville fans at all. When the Aces opened the 1965–66 season, 12,581, the seventh-largest crowd in Roberts Stadium's history, were on hand for the game against Iowa. Joining the three veterans were Ron Johnson and Howard Pratt. Williams suffered a head injury after only eight minutes, and the Aces' best rebounder was lost for the rest of the game. Iowa dominated the boards and, despite Humes's 27 points, the Aces fell to the Big Ten visitors 80–73. Without Herb Williams, Iowa's 6-7 center George Peeples grabbed seventeen rebounds in the first half, four more than Evansville's combined total.

Darrell Adams, a 6-4 a transfer from Southeast Missouri, had started the second half in place of Johnson and had shown Mac enough to earn a starting role in the next contest, but the Aces' lack of defense was a sore spot with Mac. "They just beat us to death on the boards," he said. Peeples had grabbed twenty-two rebounds and scored 29 points, all from down low.

When the Aces rebounded against San Fernando Valley a week later, Adams, who hailed from Patoka, Illinois, added eight points and eleven rebounds. Sam Watkins led the Aces with 31 as they edged the California quintet 100–91 in a sloppy game.

Purdue, always a big attraction at Roberts, arrived with Dave Schellhase and a new coach. Ray Eddy had been replaced by George King from West Virginia University. The return of the Boilermakers and Schellhase, a Bosse High School product, drew 12,035 fans.

Larry Humes treated the crowd to a dazzling display of offense. He had struggled in the first two games after a preseason injury had slowed him down. Now back at full strength, he was the Humes of old. Larry finished with 44 points, third-most ever scored by any opponent of a Purdue team, and the Aces added the Boilermakers to the list of Big Ten opponents they had beaten.

Schellhase had finished with 36. After the game someone had shouted into the Purdue locker room, "Schellhase couldn't carry Humes's jock." The comment angered King, who demanded to know who had insulted his star in his hometown. When Aces fan Jack Willingham stepped forward, a scuffle ensued.

Mac apologized to King afterward. The incident had taken place in full view of a dressing room filled with fans, including two members of the Boston Celtics, John Havlicek and Frank Ramsey, who were congratulating Mac.

After tempers had cooled, Mac told reporters, "Purdue has the same problem we do. They don't know each other too well. I thought we had a distinct advantage on Schellhase because we know him well. And Williams did a marvelous job on him."

Schellhase was among those impressed with Larry Humes. "He makes everything look easy. He is one of the all-time greats," he said. Mac had started to use Larry in the backcourt to showcase his ball handling for the pro scouts that were watching Larry in almost every game. Humes responded to the task and continued to draw rave reviews from opposing coaches.

"Humes is by far the best we've played against," said Toledo Rockets coach Bob Nichols after Larry had scored 38 points against Nichols's charges. "He moves well and shoots well. . . . He's an uncanny jumper and shoots with the same soft, amazing accuracy whether he's inside or out."

After Kent State had lost to the Aces in the Holiday Tournament behind Larry's 34 points, Bob Doll, the Kent State coach, said, "With a guy like Humes—and I don't know if there are many others like him anywhere—you put your best man on him and figure he'll get his usual 30-some points. For a man with a bad back, Humes sure plays a good game of basketball. In his own habitat, playing inside, he's unstoppable."

Larry Humes would continue to impress and amaze opposing coaches and players all season long in what would be a record-breaking campaign for him.

But, for the Aces it would turn out to be a disappointing one. "We never really could find anyone who could fill Jerry Sloan's shoes, and that's what hurt us," Humes said.[3]

Mac had to tinker with his starting lineup all season to try to get the right combination on the floor at the same time. Try as he might, they never seemed to gel into the cohesive, smooth-running unit that had been the hallmark of the two championship seasons. Players came in and out. Some would shine for a game or two and then fade. Others would play well but inconsistently.

With his height Howard Pratt was a welcome sight in the lineup and took some of the scoring pressure off Humes, but he was a sophomore and had yet to reach his potential.

Rebounding would plague the Aces all season, and they would lose to teams with bigger, if not better, players as a result. As good as Larry Humes was, if he didn't have the ball, he couldn't score. Second-chance points were few and far between.

Larry, Herb Williams, and Sam Watkins carried the Aces as far as the three talented stars could. But they missed the rebounding and passing skills that the loss of Sloan and Grieger had brought, and no one stepped up to fill those gaps. But for Larry personally, the year was a triumph. He smashed every Evansville College scoring record in his final season in an Aces uniform.

The Aces finished the year at 17–8. They suffered two losses at the hands of Southern Illinois and split with Kentucky Wesleyan and Butler. Crowds still turned out—12,756 were at Roberts when Southern Illinois came to town and turned back the Aces. But Evansville fans, used to seeing their Aces win, found it hard to watch them struggle.

Humes's performances made up for some of the disappointment. He never seemed to fail to impress. He was simply too good to miss. So the fans continued to arrive and hope that somehow Larry, Sam, and Herb could rekindle the magic. They did their best, but this time it was just not good enough.

The Aces again went to the NCAA Tournament, but the results were far different from recent years'. After an opening round win over Lamar Tech, the Aces lost to Southern Illinois for the third time, a complete reversal of the previous year's record, and were eliminated. They had finished the year at 18–9.

Larry Humes's career at Evansville ended with numbers that were simply incredible. His marks included career bests in points (2,235); average points per game (26.3); field goals (865); and free throws (505). He had led the Aces in scoring in 66 of his 85 games. His 48 points as a junior against Ball State during the 1964–65 season was a school best.

Humes had earned All-Conference first-team selections as a junior and senior and was named ICC MVP in 1965–66. His 978 points in ICC games made him the conference's all-time leading scorer. He was named an AP and UPI All-American as a junior and again as a senior.

Later he would become the fifth-round draft choice of the Chicago Bulls of the NBA, where he survived until the final cut. He joined the Indianapolis school system and had a successful high school coaching career there, including a stint at Tech High School, where his star player was John Ed Washington, whom he advised to go to Evansville. Larry went on to the collegiate ranks as an assistant coach at the University of Indianapolis. He was there when Evansville called and offered him a similar role.

"I went down in the summer of 1977 and was working there when I got a call about an opening at Crispus Attucks High School, an Indianapolis basketball power," Larry said. "I took the job and left Evansville after three months." That was September 1977.

Humes eventually earned his guidance certificate and became a school counselor within the Indianapolis public school system. He stayed in that position until he retired in 2005. He still works part time there, helping young people.

"I have counseled thousands of youngsters through the years," he said recently. "All of them were good students, but some made bad choices. Some became doctors, lawyers, and teachers. Others became robbers, rapists, and drug pushers. Life is about choices . . . Some of them just made the wrong choices. I'm still 'Coach' or 'Mr. Humes' to all of them. I've earned their respect and that makes me feel good and satisfied inside."

Larry never forgot the man who steered him to Evansville years ago. "If it weren't for Bud Ritter, I might have made some bad decisions too."[4] But Larry Humes made the right decision. He followed Bud Ritter's advice and went to Evansville. There he found another mentor in Arad McCutchan and a community that elevated him to godlike status.

For Larry Humes, the Aces' greatest scorer, life has turned out all right. He made the right choices.

Sam Watkins also graduated. He had two championships behind him and had been acknowledged as a first-team all-ICC performer in 1966. He was also an AP and UPI honorable mention All-America. Sam had scored 1,287 points during his stay in Evansville and ranks ninth on the Aces' all-time list, just behind teammate Jerry Sloan.

Watkins returned to his roots and earned his master's degree at the University of Louisville. For the past twenty-three years he has headed a nonprofit community organization that serves low-income and disadvantaged families, helping them get on their feet and become productive members of the community.[5]

Sam has vivid memories of his years at Evansville under Coach McCutchan. "Coach McCutchan was a pioneer. He recruited black athletes at a time when it was very risky to do so. He told us we'd 'have to ignore some things,' but that he brought us here to play important roles. He wasn't just talking about basketball," Sam said. "He'd had Jim Smallins and Ed Smallwood, and [Mac] was a man that you just had to admire. He rose above the times and stood behind what he believed in. I hold him in high regard."

Today Sam is involved in urban planning, community development, and creating educational opportunities for young inner-city students.[6] His job is, in a way, the same as his role during his sophomore season at Evansville. "I had to figure out who to get the ball to," he said. "We had Buster Briley, Jerry Sloan, and

Larry Humes. They all wanted the ball. It was my job to give each of them an equal opportunity."[7]

Sam Watkins is still doing that in Louisville today.

Herb Williams's final season at Evansville, 1966–67, was anticlimactic. He and the Purple Aces struggled through a series of injuries, and the ever-changing lineups did little to help the Aces get any rhythm going.

The season started well, with back-to-back wins, but it ended badly. Mac's revamped lineup had Williams in the pivot and Howard Pratt and Dave Weeks at the forward spots, with Darrell Adams and Ron Johnson in the backcourt.

After the Aces took down Central Missouri State and Notre Dame, fans' hopes were soaring, but the Aces came to earth hard. They lost their own Holiday Tournament when they dropped successive games to William and Mary and Rutgers University. The latter featured Bob Lloyd, who poured in 29 points for the Scarlet Knights—aided by a 13-point performance from Lloyd's roommate, Jim Valvano.[8]

The losses were the fifth and sixth straight for the struggling Aces. The skein would continue as injuries and illness took their toll. The losses would continue to mount and eventually reached ten. Not even the presence of Tom Niemeier, at 6-9, who became eligible in January, could stop the bleeding.

Mac continued to experiment with players. Jerry Mattingly saw a lot of playing time with David Riggs in the backcourt, but nothing Mac tried seemed to work. It was always stifled by an injury or an illness to a key player, and the losses seemed to perpetuate themselves.

Finally, mercifully, the season came to a close. The Aces finished at 8–17, with their 4–11 mark at Roberts their worst home record since 1928–29. It was Mac's worst season since he had arrived in 1946.

The only bright spot in an otherwise dismal season was Herb Williams. Although he was plagued by a knee injury, Williams was the Aces' standout performer. He managed to score 31 against Indiana State in a four-overtime game. Herb played injured, and he played as well as he could before finally being stopped by his bad knee after making seventy-four straight starts. He came back one game later, but he was a hobbled shadow of his fleet-footed, high-leaping self.

Herb would complete his college career as a first-team all-ICC choice. He worked first as an assistant to Mac at the University of Evansville, as the school was now known, and then as a purchasing agent at the huge Whirlpool plant near the airport.[9] "I was the first black purchasing agent they ever hired," Herb said.

Then his hometown of Centralia, Illinois, offered him a high school coaching job, and Mac convinced him to take it by telling Herb it was an honor for him to be offered the opportunity. Herb stayed there as an assistant until the head job opened up; he applied and was turned down.

He left for Rich South High School in Richton, Illinois, where he was an assistant for three seasons. He eventually moved up to the head coaching post at Evanston Township High School, the biggest school in Illinois, where he coached from 1975 through 1984 and compiled a record of 189–80. His last team there was 32–1.

Jud Heathcote, the head coach at Michigan State University, hired Herb in 1985 and he stayed until 1990, when he landed the head coaching job at Idaho State. Herb served as coach of the Bengals for eight seasons and captured a Big Sky Conference title in 1994. Then he returned to Centralia and retirement—or so he thought.

Herb, an avid woodworking hobbyist, was hanging out in the lumber department at a big box store when he had a chance encounter that led to a new position. "This guy asked me if I'd consider taking over a team at Sandoval, Illinois, high school," Herb said. "The school was only ten miles away. I loved my woodworking, but this would give me a chance to coach again. What they told me later was that the school, with only 150 kids, hadn't won a basketball game in five years."

Herb Williams led little Sandoval High School to seven wins in his first season. "After we won that first game after seven tries, a huge basket of candy was placed on my desk to thank me. In church the pastor led everyone in celebrating the win," he laughed.

In his second year at Sandoval, Herb's team won eleven and in 2010–11 went 19–9. "This year will be my last," Herb said of the 2011–12 season.

Herb and his wife, Marilyn, who have been married for forty-six years, have five children, and he has a lot of wood to work at home. The player whom Mac once estimated jumped twenty inches over the rim on the court will finally put away his sneakers.

He's been back at Roberts several times. When Evansville retired Jerry Sloan's jersey, Herb asked for the microphone at center court before a packed house and re-created one the signature calls of long-time Aces radio announcer Marv Bates from a magical season long ago:

Williams controls the tip out to Watkins.

Watkins to Sloan outside.

Sloan down low to Humes.

Good! Good! Good!

One more time the crowd stood and roared for one last imaginary basket that brought back so many memories of so many others just like it, when their Aces were perfect.

Herb Williams, the son of a preacherman, had found both victory and defeat at Evansville. And he had treated those two imposters just the same.

To this day, he's never lost an opening tip-off as a player.[10]

*On May 22, 1967, General Motors donated a DC-3, tail number **N51071**, to the Michigan Technical University Development Fund. No one at the school today remembers how or if the university used the plane. Perhaps it was moth-balled until the fund could find a way to make money with it. One long-time administrator guessed that the aeronautical engineering program and sports teams used it, but he really didn't know.*

(Endnotes)

1   For these quotes from Mac, and others in this chapter that are attributed to no other source, the reader may assume that they come from articles in the *Evansville Courier* and *Evansville Press,* the two local papers at the time. Those articles may be found in the collection of bound scrapbooks kept by Bob Hudson and now housed in the university archives and/or Bill Bussing's manuscript history of the Aces. Bill Bussing generously made his lengthy manuscript available to me, and I have relied on it for some information, especially in the early years of the McCutchan era and in determining atten-dance figures. The detailed manuscript contains no footnotes, but when I interviewed Bussing in February 2011, he identified his sources as the *Evans-ville Courier, Evansville Press,* and the combined Sunday edition, the *Cou-rier & Press.* Bussing's manuscript usually makes no distinction between the papers, but the direct quotes are from one daily or the other or the Sunday combined paper and appear in the Bussing manuscript in quotation marks.

Bussing used Hudson's scrapbooks, as did I and my research assistant. Many of the articles do not identify which paper they are from, much less the date and page, but I (and Bussing) assume they are from the *Courier*, *Press,* or *Sunday Courier & Press.*

2   John Benington of St. Louis University got the job. He had two winning seasons and one NCAA tournament appearance in four seasons. He was dismissed after going 54–38 ("John Benington," SR/College Basketball, n.d., www.sports-reference.com/cbb/coaches/b/beninjo01.html).

3   Larry Humes, telephone interview by author, April 22, 2011.

4   Humes interview.

5   "History," Louisville Central Community Center, 2006, www.lcccnews.org/aboutus.html.

6   Sam Watkins, telephone interview by author, June 4, 2011.

7   Watkins interview.

8   Lloyd would go on to play for the New Jersey Nets. His brother, Dick, who was an assistant coach at Rutgers when Bob was a player there, later became head coach at Rutgers. Today Dick is the color commentator for Rutgers basketball on the Rutgers Radio Network. Valvano would gain fame when his North Carolina Wolfpack won a stunning victory over Houston in the NCAA championship game of 1983. He remained there until 1990 when a recruiting scandal forced him out. He began a new career as a popular ESPN analyst. Valvano's struggle with cancer, which he eventually lost, was dramatic and public, including an emotional plea for cancer research at the ESPY Awards shortly before his death. The result was the V Foundation for Cancer Research, whose motto is Jim's pledge: "Don't give up . . . don't ever give up." The foundation has raised move than $100 million for cancer research since its founding in 1993 ("Our Inspiration," V Foundation for Cancer Research, www.jimmyv.org).

9   On February 17, 1967, Governor Roger Branigan signed legislation that changed the college's name.

10 Herb Williams, telephone interview by author, May 22, 2011.

Herb Williams dunks, 1965.

Bounce Back, 1967–1968

Mac hit the recruiting trail hard in the spring of 1967, and this time he had better luck than usual.

Rick Smith of Oakland City, Indiana, selected Evansville over Indiana University. Smith had grown up in the Mackey-Buckskin area, right next to Gus Doerner's old house. After two years at Mackey High School, Rick had moved to Oakland City where he starred for the basketball team at a school of about 250 students. As a senior he led his team to a 23–0 record before Oakland City lost to Evansville North High School in the semistate at Roberts Stadium.

"I grew up listening to Aces basketball on the radio with Marv Bates as the announcer," Smith recalled. "I had gone a number of times with Bob Doerner, Gus's brother, to Roberts and had seen the Smallwood, Ahlering, and Cox brother's teams play."

Rick had sprouted from 6-1 as a freshman to 6-5 as a senior. He played guard and knew from watching the Aces that Mac always liked tall guards. "I had a shoebox full of college scholarship offers that my high school coach had received. When he showed them to me, it had no effect on me," Smith said. "I had decided I wanted to go to Evansville. It was close to my home, and both Mac and Gus Doerner had come to my house to talk with me. Jerry Sloan made a visit as well. He was with the Chicago Bulls at the time. I didn't and couldn't say a single word for ten minutes. I didn't really need a lot of convincing. I never considered any other place."[1]

After several years of failing to land his top choices, Mac had finally won one. He would have Rick Smith on his varsity in a year. Joining Rick would be another of Mac's prime targets. The 6-4 Bob Clayton, from Fairfield, Illinois, signed with the Aces in late April. Clayton had appeared at forward, guard, and center for his high school team. He was an All-Conference selection in his senior year.

"His finest asset may be his quickness," his high school coach, Larry Odum, said. "It helped make him a superb jumper and the best rebounder in the conference."[2] Clayton, who also played football and ran track, had been pursued by thirty schools but chose to play for Mac at Evansville.

"We used to have relatives there," Clayton said, "I always felt it was my college."

There was another reason.

"Jerry Sloan has long been an idol of mine. I got a real thrill watching him play on television when he was at Evansville, and I've tried to follow his pro career closely," Clayton said.[3]

Mac also landed John Wellemeyer, a 6-4 center from Huntingburg, Indiana, who had averaged 25 points as a high school senior. He had been named a second-team All-State choice. John had chosen the Aces over Georgia Tech, Tennessee, Florida Sate, and Louisiana State, among others.

"I think he has the ability to go just about anywhere on the court and we will just have to wait and see how he develops," Mac said.

When in late June 1967 Mac managed to convince 6-8 Jim Thompson of Newton, Illinois, to attend Evansville, the coach could stop recruiting. "I never really considered going anywhere else," Thompson said. "Evansville seems to be a real nice school and the people here have been really friendly to me." After the dismal campaign of 1966–67, it was no wonder a 6-8 basketball player received warm, effusive greetings from everyone he encountered in town and on campus.

Mac had managed to restock his larder with the high-quality talent that had eluded him after O'Brien's departure. He had only a year to wait until this crop could suit up as Purple Aces.

For most of the nation the summer of 1967 was a study in contrast, with thousands of long-haired young people in tie-dye and beads taking over the Haight-Ashbury section of San Francisco and thousands of other young people, mostly black, rioting out of fear and frustration.

Angry blacks and pot-smoking hippies rebelled in decidedly different ways, but both made the white middle class decidedly uneasy. But Evansville was largely isolated from all that; rebellion was something Evansville learned about from the media, not lived experience. But during that same summer, President Johnson ordered more troops to Vietnam, and that undoubtedly affected local families.

Still, residents and farmers were more concerned with the weather and how it would affect crops than they were about national problems. Young people in Evansville and on the campus soon sported longer hair and more colorful attire than in years past. A few presumably experimented with pot and hallucinogenic drugs. But for the most part it was a typical hot, humid, and dry summer—the major concern was the corn crop that was parching in the many fields ringing the city.

Aces fans, who had grown accustomed to winning, counted the dismal results of the 1966–67 season as an anomaly. The Aces would be back in the fall, and all would be well again in Evansville.

Even the Aces' poor performance had made little impact on attendance. The 8–17 team had still managed to draw more than 109,000, down nearly 20,000 from the last championship season but still more than respectable.

Happily, the 1967–68 edition of the Aces proved to be a resilient bunch. The Aces were now blessed with experience and some additional help. But they lost three members of the freshman team before the season even started—all had experienced academic problems and moved on to other schools. The backcourt suffered when Dave Riggs decided to leave early for dental school.

That left Mac with Tom Niemeier, the 6-9 transfer from Purdue, in the post position and Jerry Mattingly and Kae Moore at guard, with Layne Holmes and Dave Weeks at forward. Mac also returned to his use of the platoon system. The talent level between the starters and reserves was nearly equal, and Mac had enjoyed success with that system in the past.

The new name for the second squad was the Vampire Five. Starved for precious playing time, they would come in for five or six hectic minutes, out for blood. The team consisted of Howard Pratt, Darrell Adams, senior Roger Miller, junior Ron Bae, and sophomores Roger Guth and Mike Owens.

Mac's added depth enabled him to return to the successful formula of full-court pressure defense and running the fast break until the tired opponent faded with exhaustion.

The results were immediately obvious. The Aces forced thirty-nine turnovers by Sam Houston State and twenty-seven by Lamar Tech in the first two contests.

Both produced wins, and the Aces were once again off and running. "We like to think that nobody can stand out there and look at us. We're going to make them do something," Mac said.

A loss to the speedy Utah State Aggies, followed by a win over Seattle and then another against Texas Wesleyan, had the Aces at 4–1. Suddenly, the bitter memories of the previous season were replaced by new hope, and the Aces didn't disappoint. Using the depth and experience of the team to advantage, the Aces reeled off a string of impressive wins when December rolled around and the Aces returned home.

Southwest Louisiana, ranked third by UPI, fell 82–80, with Pratt and Weeks providing key buckets. "We knew Weeks could hit from way out, but we were beginning to wonder when," Mac told reporters.

Dave had gone 6-for-7 from the floor and continued his hot shooting when the Aces hosted Montana in the Holiday Tournament. He went 5-for-6 in an Aces blowout win that saw Evansville score 66 points in the second half. The final was 116–76.

The dazzling offensive display left Hugh Durham, coach of Florida State's Seminoles, the Aces next opponent, in shock. "I don't know if I just saw a basketball game or a track meet," he told reporters.[4]

Led by future NBA star Dave Cowens, a 6-9 center, the Seminoles had defeated George Washington in the first round. Nearly 7,000 were in attendance to see the Aces hang on to win 76–67 in a rough-and-tumble contest. The Vampire Five had found the going particularly rough and had allowed Florida State back in the game after the Aces' starters had bequeathed their relief a 58–37 second-half lead.

Howard Pratt had managed to hold Cowens to only 13 points, and Pratt was rewarded for his efforts by being named co-winner of the MVP award with Holmes. Mattingly had contributed 15 points against the team that had sought his services. The Aces had their eighth Holiday Tournament crown in twelve seasons and had erased the memories of the dismal showing of 1966–67.

As they faced off against 6–1 Kentucky Wesleyan, the Aces had risen to second in both wire service polls, just behind their rivals.

The Panthers had a new coach in Bob Daniels, and he had seen Evansville play. "I've seen Evansville play three times this year. They have a fine team. In fact, they have two fine teams," Daniels said before the game.

The Aces' rivalry with Kentucky Wesleyan was still capable of bringing out huge numbers of fans—11,102 were in their seats when the two teams began play. The Aces, sparked by the Vampire Team, held a 37–24 lead at the half. The second half saw the Panthers claw back to take a one-point lead with little more than nine minutes to play. But a Holmes jumper from outside restored the Aces' lead, and they went on to win 71–64.

Niemeier and Mattingly had 13 apiece, and Howard Pratt had held Panthers star Dallas Thornton to only nine points in a superb defensive effort. "Evansville's first unit may have a little more power on the boards, but I still think the second unit has the best shooters" was Daniels's appraisal of the deep and talented Aces.

Miller, Owens, Weeks, Bae, and Adams had contributed 27 points and, more important, had given the starters ample rest to maintain the running game. "It's worked so well. I see no reason to change it," Mac said of the two-platoon system.

More opponents felt the effects of the Aces' nonstop blitz at both ends of the floor. The Aces reeled off a string of wins that had begun with the Seattle contest and continued through the conference schedule. St. Joseph's, Butler, and Valparaiso all fell with barely a whimper. The Aces again put up 66 points in the second half in a convincing win against Valpo.

After the Valpo game the Aces were riding a ten-game winning streak, but they suffered a hiccup at Ball State when they dropped a 92–81 decision. Next up was the Aces old nemesis Southern Illinois.

"I don't know if we can stay with Evansville," the Salukis' coach, Jack Hartman, said before the game. "Besides being strong, they have good speed." Power and speed are a tough combination to overcome, and the Salukis' mentor was right. They couldn't stay with Evansville.

Hartman had figured that his only chance was to bring the speeding Ace express to a grinding halt. The Salukis, the defending NIT champions, tried to control the tempo as much as possible, but in the end they were simply outplayed. The final score was 52–45. The Aces' output was about half of their usual—90 points and more—but the result was still a win.

Howard Pratt had turned in another defensive gem. He held Dick Garrett, the lone returning starter for SIU, to just four baskets.

Mac credited the Aces' defensive prowess to their five-minute three-on-three drill. "I've found whenever we skip this drill in practice for a game, our defense isn't as sharp. So we work on it quite a bit," Mac said.

The formula Mac had concocted for the 1967–68 Aces was tenacious defense + depth of talent + offensive power = success. It had proved to be the correct answer nearly every time.

The offense was evident again as the Aces rolled over DePauw, Indiana State, Valparaiso, and St. Joseph's in turn. They scored 90 or more points twice and exceeded 100 during the spurt. The defense hadn't suffered, either. Against St. Joseph's the Aces' harassing gnats had forced forty turnovers. They had tasted blood and liked it.

Jerry Mattingly had emerged as the leader of the Aces. Though Niemeier continued to pace the scoring, the play of Mattingly was consistently high, and he had become the team's leader on the floor. "Maybe he isn't a spectacular scorer, but he does a lot of little things that count," Mac said. "He has lots of nerve, the way he stands in there when somebody runs him over; I don't believe that even Jerry Sloan got run over as often."

Being placed in the same category as Mac's favorite was high praise, even if it was for the willingness to take a physical beating. But Mac's praise for Mattingly included other, less potentially dangerous, attributes. "He pesters the other fellow on defense, gets more than his share of steals. He's always in the open spot when we come down on a fast break. He's a leader, even though he doesn't say much. And when he gets close to the board, he doesn't miss many shots," Mac said.

When the Aces made their annual trip across the Ohio to Owensboro to meet the Panthers of Kentucky Wesleyan, Evansville was riding high. But, as the Panthers had before, they brought the second-ranked Aces back to earth with a jolt.

Dallas Thornton paced the home team with 26 points in a tight game that went into overtime before the Panthers emerged victorious. Dave Erwin, brother of former Aces star Larry Erwin, had sunk the Aces with 6-for-7 shooting in the second half to force the overtime. "We didn't have much of a scouting report on him since he hadn't played too much, but we knew he was a good shooter," Mac said. "Maybe I didn't mention it enough to the boys." It was typical of Mac to shoulder the blame for the 87–78 loss.

The defeat at Owensboro knocked the Aces from their lofty ranking and sent them into a tumble that saw them lose consecutive conference games to Butler and Indiana State.

The loss to Indiana State was the first suffered at home all season by the Aces. Among the 11,127 fans were a number of Mac's recruiting targets, as well as

Jerry Mattingly's brothers, Randy, Mike, and Don. Don was a first-grader at St. Theresa's in Evansville, but Jerry assured everyone that his younger sibling wasn't focusing on basketball. "His game is baseball. He plays it the year round," Jerry said.[5]

Ball State provided the Aces' last home opponent, and they humbled the Aces 110–74.

The Aces limped through their last two contests on the road and dropped both. First they were beaten by Southern Illinois and then by DePauw. Injuries had started to take their toll as Mike Owens, Roger Miller, and Ron Bae all missed playing time.

The Aces finished regular season play at 18–7 and waited to learn where they would be playing in the NCAA Tournament. The answer was Southwest Missouri State in Springfield, where they would meet Lincoln College.

The Tigers had averaged 103.4 points per game. "They start shooting as soon as they come off the bus," warned one of Evansville's tournament hosts.

Mac decided against a footrace and played a more controlled tempo for the first half. The Tigers' full-court press was effective and on two occasions put them up by as many as nine points before the Aces retaliated.

Down by four at the half, the Aces got eight straight points, six coming from Niemeier, to start the second half. When they had an 11-point lead, the starters departed and the Vampire Five entered the fray. When Mac put the starters back on the court, the lead had shrunk to seven. But the regulars managed to hold on, and they advanced with a 95–80 win.

The next game gave the Aces a taste of their own medicine. For years teams had complained about their advantage in hosting the NCAA Tournament on their home court. Now the Aces were facing Southwest Missouri State on the Bears' home floor. The difference was that the Bears' gymnasium held only 3,000 fans and, try as they might, 3,000 can't make as much noise as 12,000.

The Bears were 19–5 after their first-round win over Colorado State as the two tipped off before an overflow crowd.

The Bears fielded three players that were 6-7, and, though they were taller and stronger than Evansville, the Aces were faster. The game was a battle throughout with neither team gaining a strong advantage. The Aces held a one-point lead with two minutes to play.

Darrell Adams broke the Bears' press and converted a layup with 1:42 remaining. The Bears tried a lob to forward Curtis Perry, but Holmes batted the ball away to Adams. Adams returned the ball to Holmes, who fired a fifty-foot bullet to a streaking Niemeier, who was hammered as he attempted the shot. Sent to the line, Niemeier converted both free throws and the Aces were up by four with only eight seconds to play.

Howard Pratt's two free throws completed the scoring. The Aces had won, 79–73, and advanced to the friendly environs of Roberts Stadium with their seventh regional championship in the past twelve years. Mac had abandoned the platoon in the second half, and he praised his starters for their work. "They wanted it awfully, awfully badly. This was as courageous a game as any team of mine has ever played," Mac said. Both Holmes and Pratt were named to the All-Tournament team.

Now sporting a 20–7 record, the Aces headed for home. "Come on, legs, just three more games," Niemeier begged his weary limbs as the Aces boarded their flight.

The return to Roberts boded well for the Aces, who had lost only one game in the fifteen played there that year. It seemed to the partisans that the Aces were a lock to gain their fifth title. Fans were further encouraged when they learned that the first-round opponent, Trinity College of Texas, had lost by 12 earlier in the season to Southwest Missouri State, whom the Aces had just beaten. Things looked promising for the home team, and more than 7,500 braved a swirling snowstorm to see their Aces take on the tenth-ranked Tigers of Trinity.

Notions of a sure-fire victory disappeared as fast as the asphalt parking lot in the storm as the Tigers took an early lead and turned it into a commanding one. Neither the starting five nor the Vampires could stem the tide as the Tigers roared out to a 35–17 lead after thirteen minutes. The Aces did manage to pull within 13 at the half, but the task ahead was a daunting one.

The second half began as the first had, and the Aces quickly fell behind by 17 again. Then the Aces woke up and reeled off seven unanswered points in less than a minute. A Niemeier jumper, an Adams layup off a steal, and a Holmes three-point play pulled the Aces to within ten. Another surge brought the Aces within four, with 14 minutes remaining and the crowd on its feet urging the Aces on.

When Jerry Mattingly's block of a Trinity shot was deemed to be goal tending, the rally fizzled. "We kind of fell apart after that," Mac said later. The final was 93–77. Mac said only that he was "sorry that we didn't know more about Trinity"—his scouting report had been delayed by the wretched weather.

The Aces' season was over.

The 1967–68 Aces had improved dramatically to record a 20–8 mark after suffering through their worst season in years the year before. Mac praised both Jerry Mattingly and Howard Pratt as having made the greatest improvement, adding, "Tom (Niemeier) came close to his potential and might have been a great one if we'd have had him longer than a year and a half."

Both Tom and Jerry Mattingly earned All-ICC honors. Niemeier earned second- team All-America status from the National Association of Basketball Coaches and honorable mention from UPI. Mac added him to his small college all-star team for the Olympic Trials. Howard Pratt would receive the Kiwanis Award and first-team All-ICC honors, along with honorable mention All-America honors from the AP.

Mac's surprisingly strong team had used depth and talent to rebound from adversity. But his losses to graduation would be substantial. Besides Niemeier, Pratt, and Mattingly, the Aces would lose Roger Miller and Darrell Adams, who had played great near the end of the season.

Mac would have to replace all of them. As he set out on the recruiting trail yet again, he had high hopes for his talented freshmen, who would be moving up that fall. Mac set his sights high for the recruits. He trained his efforts on guards, tall guards, if possible, in the mold he'd come to appreciate.

He wouldn't be disappointed with the results.

(Endnotes)

1   Rick Smith, telephone interview by author, April 27, 2011.
     I am indebted to Bill Bussing, who generously made his lengthy manuscript of this history of the Aces available to me. It contains no footnotes, but when I interviewed Bussing in February 2011, he identified his sources as the *Evansville Courier* and *Evansville Press,* the two local papers at the time. Bussing's manuscript usually makes no distinction between the two, but the direct quotes are from one or the other and appear in the Bussing manuscript in quotation marks. Bussing also had access to a collection of old bound scrapbooks kept by Bob Hudson. My research assistant and I also used the scrapbooks, which are now housed in the university archives. The articles do not identify which paper they are from, much less the date and page, but I (and Bussing) assume they are from the *Courier* and *Press,* or the combined Sunday edition, the *Courier & Press.* Where no endnote appears with infor-

mation crediting another source, the reader may assume that it comes from the scrapbooks and/or the Bussing manuscript.

2   Sam Watkins, telephone interview by author, June 4, 2011.

3   Bob Clayton, telephone interview by author, May 12, 2011.

4   Durham was in his second year as head coach and would finish the season at 19–8. He stayed at Florida State until 1978, when he moved to Georgia. He remained there until 1995 and enjoyed great success before finishing his coaching career at Jacksonville. Durham coached for thirty-seven seasons, won more than six hundred games, and took Florida State and Georgia to the Final Four. In all, his teams made eight NCAA appearances. The Hugh Durham Coaching Award is given annually to the top mid-major coach in Division I basketball ("Hugh Durham," SR/College Basketball, n.d., www. sports-reference.com/cbb/coaches/d/durhahu01.html).

5   Don Mattingly would become a major league baseball star with the New York Yankees. Don joined the Yankees in 1982 when he was twenty-one and played for the team through 1995. He compiled a lifetime batting average of .307 and was named an All-Star six times and a Gold Glove Award–winning first baseman nine times. After retiring he became a batting coach with the Yankees and then the Los Angeles Dodgers. In 2011 he became manager of the Dodgers. His number 23 uniform has been retired by the Yankees ("Don Mattingly Stats," Baseball Almanac, n.d., www.baseball-almanac. com/players/player.php?p=mattido01; "Don Mattingly: Biography," Mattingly Sports, n.d., www.mattinglybaseball.com/biography.html).

Troubled Times, 1968–1970

While most Americans wrestled with their shock and grief at the assassinations of Martin Luther King and Bobby Kennedy, and the riots in major cities on the heels of King's slaying, Mac had stuck doggedly to recruiting in the spring and summer of 1968.

He signed the best crop of talent in years for the University of Evansville's Purple Aces.

Rick Coffey was the first to enter the fold. He grew up as the oldest of three children in a suburb of Indianapolis called Greenwood. His father sold chemicals, his mother stayed at home.

Rick spent his junior and senior years at Center Grove High School under the tutelage of the renowned coach Larry Lindsay. "He had a great influence on me and introduced me to the Fellowship of Christian Athletes," Coffey said.

While the larger events occurring in the world outside Greenwood were tumultuous, they made little impact on Rick who, like his classmates, was "mainly concerned with basketball and my girlfriend," he said.

As a senior he had averaged 28 points per game. An All-Conference selection, he had set a school record with 260 rebounds. Mac regarded the 6-3 Coffey as a swingman.

"I was recruited by every Indiana school except Notre Dame," Coffey recalled. "I had a friend, Matt Umbarger, who had played football [at Evansville]. He convinced a local dentist, Dave Riggs, who had played for McCutchan, to try to talk me into going to Evansville."

Riggs had called his former coach about Rick. "He told Mac, 'You need to recruit this guy.' Mac asked him if I could play guard and Dr. Riggs told him no. 'Well, he's too small to play forward,' Mac said.

"Dr. Riggs told him, 'If you don't sign him, he'll be going to Ball State or Butler, and if he does, he will hurt you,'" Rick recounted. Mac was a bright man and Riggs's argument proved persuasive. Mac offered Coffey a scholarship sight unseen. Rick said he chose Evansville because of its "basketball reputation, the size of the school, and the friendliness of the people." He also knew he had friends who had enrolled there and, more important, his girlfriend had decided to attend Evansville.[1] Rick Coffey would become an Ace.

John Couch became an Ace at the urging of Bob Clayton, Couch's former teammate in Fairfield, Illinois. Couch, who was 6-6 and had averaged 18 points and eleven rebounds as a senior, was familiar with Evansville. "I had seen them on television a number of times. So I visited the campus, liked it, and decided this was where I want to play," Couch said. "Besides, it's close to home."[2]

Then there was "The Whale"—Steve Welmer from Columbus, Indiana, described by his former roommate as "the biggest man I'd ever seen. When he walked through the door to the dorm room, he obliterated all the outside light."[3] Welmer was 6-8 and tipped the scales at 240. With the signing of Welmer in May, Mac assured himself of the biggest front line in Evansville history.

Welmer, a lefty, had averaged 16 points and 18 rebounds as a senior. "I wanted to go to a small school that played big-time basketball, and that's what they have at Evansville. Besides, they have Mr. McCutchan," he said. "He's a powerful rebounder and has a real good touch around the basket," said Mac.

With his height problems seemingly solved, Mac scurried back to Evansville to try to make Don Buse (pronounced "Boozey") of Holland, Indiana, the crown jewel in this class of recruits.

Buse's family was so poor when he was growing up that there was no money to buy a basketball. He and his brothers often just wadded up some socks and used a trash can as a basket. His father, a farmer, was only 33 when he died of cancer, and Don was only three. "That left my mom a widow with eight kids to raise, and that was pretty tough," Don said. "We spent a lot of time while I was growing up on welfare. It was the only way my mom could survive. She worked some when she could, and my aunts and uncles helped out, but it was a difficult time for my mom."

Though times were tough, Don's memories of his childhood are not unpleasant ones. "We were a sports-minded family. My two older brothers both played sports, and they both taught me baseball and basketball. My older brother Rex was just two years older, and he played basketball with me. We practiced for hours together, starting when I was in second or third grade," he remembers.

Eventually, Don attended some Holland High School games in which his brother Junior was playing. "I watched him and the other players, and they were my idols. I decided then that's what I wanted to be," Don said.

Years later Don would star for Holland High under coach George "Woody" Neel. "He was a young man and a very tough disciplinarian. I was scared of him," Don said. "But he pushed me to do things I didn't believe I could do."

Neel pushed hard enough to see Buse make All-State at Holland. He also kept the letters from colleges that arrived in his office, and he and Don went through them after the season—a number of major powers were represented, including Jacksonville, Indiana, Florida State, and Oklahoma.

"I visited Alabama and Jacksonville. At Jacksonville I scrimmaged with the team and had a 'slight altercation' with one of the players there, and that pretty much made up my mind for me about that school," Buse said. At Alabama it was all too obvious that football was the favored sport. So he scratched both from his list.

Two schools fit the bill for Buse. "Both Kentucky Wesleyan and Evansville were close to home," he said. "I decided to go to Evansville because I knew about Sloan and those teams while he was there. I was in eighth grade at that time and remember listening to the games on the radio. I knew they had a great stadium, though I'd never seen it. It was also right down the road."[4]

The 6-3 Buse arrived in Evansville with gilt-edged credentials. He had averaged 22 points and 12 rebounds per game while adding 7 assists as a senior. He had set a school scoring mark when he tallied 48 points.

He was his conference's MVP, and the *Courier & Press* had selected him as MVP for its All–Southern Indiana All-Star team. *Coach and Athlete Magazine* had named him one of the top 100 prep stars in the country. "He can play with anyone in the country, bar none," declared former Ace Bob Sakel.

Bob Daniels of Kentucky Wesleyan, who had tried and failed to land Don, said, "He's the kind of player that makes a championship team." Not since Jerry Sloan had Mac attracted a player with such all-around skills and demonstrated leadership on the court.

Mac's final recruit for the year was Steve Wessel, who decided to follow his brothers to Evansville. Wessel, 6-6, had played at Bosse High, where he averaged 15 points and as many rebounds as a senior center. He'd earned All-City honors there and signed with Delaware, gone east, and made a U-turn. "I didn't like the East a much as I thought I would," he said when he arrived unexpectedly back in Evansville in September.

"I'm very encouraged with Steve as a recruit," Mac said. "He's happy to be here and I think he'll be able to help us."

But all that talent was still one season away from helping the Aces. For now Mac would have to fashion a lineup from those who remained from the 1967–68 season and the now-eligible sophomores. It would prove a daunting task.

The 1968–69 Aces were small upfront and had only largely untested guards. Jim McKissic, whom Mac had tabbed to start at guard, broke his wrist in practice, and Rick Smith, a 6-5 sophomore from Oakland City, was getting a long look from Mac in practice at Carson Center.

The freshman team scrimmaged with the varsity and won. Not a good sign. "We beat them three out of four times, and then Mac stopped doing it," Rick Coffey recalled.[5]

When South Dakota came to Roberts for an opener that was later than usual because the Shrine Circus was in town, the Aces were far from ready. The Aces struggled from the outset and had only 11 points midway through the first half. Mac inserted McKissic, who had shed his cast, and John Wellemeyer for their first varsity action. Dave Weeks canned a 19-foot jumper to give Evansville a tie at 19, and they had an 8-point lead by the intermission.

In the second half South Dakota caught the Aces at 64 with 3:15 to go. The visitors surged ahead on a baseline drive by Ed Douse of Brooklyn and then followed with another from underneath to clinch the victory with six seconds showing. The Aces had faced a towering team and had folded in the stretch. They had failed to score a single basket in the last four minutes of play, sealing their fate.

This was not the high-scoring, run-and-gun Aces of old. It was something else entirely. "I can't explain it," Layne Holmes, a lightly used Ace, said of his team's lackadaisical showing. "I thought we were up for the game, but we only played in spurts."

Another puzzled observer was the Coyotes' coach Bob Mulcahy, who had played against the Aces for Eastern Kentucky in the early 1950s: "I've never seen a McCutchan-coached team that would give you the opportunity to win like that when things got close. It was the most listless game I've ever witnessed as a coach."

"Listless" was also a term that Bob Hudson could have used to describe the attendance at the opener. Only 5,863 had appeared. The game lacked the marquee names of past openers, but the sparse attendance marked the fewest fans in red shirts since the first game of the 1958–59 campaign.

In 1967–68 attendance at Roberts had averaged 7,012. Still a healthy number for a College Division, or any major division, team, but it paled in comparison with attendance for the thrilling 1964–65 season, when the average crowd at Roberts had topped 10,600. Season ticket sales had remained high. The purchasers just weren't venturing out to the games.

Despite the 1967–68 rebound in the Aces' success, the dreadful 1966–67 season had muted interest in the team. But there was another reason, too. For many years blue-gray tobacco smoke had formed a low-hanging cloud that impaired the vision of spectators in the stands, until Roberts banned smoking for the 1968–69 season. The facility's managers had acted at the request of Mac, who had heard repeated complaints from his players about the smoke.

But probably the best explanation for the drop-off in attendance was that it was getting harder to seduce the major colleges to play at Roberts, even though the money was as sweet as ever. The problem was that the major powers now understood the risk to their post-season hopes inherent in coming to Roberts for a payday and leaving with an embarrassing blemish on their record. The major colleges that had been willing, in the past, to accept the risk in return for a large payday by playing at Roberts had now begun to build and occupy their own new and larger facilities. Purdue, Indiana, Notre Dame and Louisville no longer had any incentive to play at Evansville. They were all in their own spacious arenas.

For the first time in years no Big Ten opponent had appeared on the schedule in 1967–68. Notre Dame had stayed away, too. Wake Forest, Texas, Tulane, Xavier, Duquesne, and South Carolina had all resisted Bob Hudson's entreaties to visit Roberts. "We didn't make any attempt to make our schedule easier," Mac said. "Because so much of it is done far in advance, there's no way of knowing who'll be good and who won't."

Well, that's certainly true, but the Aces' reputation for beating big-name schools at Roberts had spread. And fans simply were not as interested in watching a game against South Dakota as they were in seeing the Aces play Purdue, Iowa, or Notre Dame. The decline in average attendance reflected that.

The quality of the opposition had fallen so low that the next two games at Roberts after the 1968–69 opener were against tiny Cal Western and winless Cal Poly of San Luis Obispo. While they were known for academic excellence, they were hardly glamour names in college basketball, and the Aces handily beat both. Attendance for those games had slipped to 4,800 and 3, 900, respectively.

The Aces' annual western swing proved disastrous, which did nothing to improve the mood of the fans. Losses to both Arizona and New Mexico State by 14 and 35 points, respectively, were followed by the Aces' return to Roberts for the annual Holiday Tournament.

The University of Massachusetts entered with an eleven-game winning streak carried over from the previous season, but only 3,941 fans were on hand as the Aces snapped the streak and won, 93–73. The finals matched the Aces with New Mexico State, which had thrashed Evansville earlier. Only 5,448 showed up in red to see the rematch.

Lou Henson's Aggies were ranked fifteenth by the AP and twelfth by UPI. They were undefeated on the year and had dominated the Aces in their first meeting, grabbing seventy-two rebounds in their brand new Pan-American Center. "We had a real good game in that one, and Evansville just had a sub-par night," Henson told reporters. "The Aces can perform much better than that." Henson had led the Aggies since leaving Hardin Simmons after the 1962–63 season. He had fashioned 46 wins in 63 games since taking over the program.[6]

Mac told reporters his team was looking for some payback: "Let's just say my boys have been looking forward to this game. They thought they had disgraced themselves out there."

But the change in venue did nothing to change the ultimate result. The Aces lost by 11 instead of 35, but that was little consolation to the fans and players. Mac took some solace from his team having stood up to the towering Aggies, who were fielding two future NBA draft choices, Sam Lacey and Jimmy Collins, that year. "At least we're not going to be afraid of anybody we play from now on," Mac said.

While Mac may have been correct about the Aces' mind-set, fearlessness couldn't overcome the lack of height and experienced backcourt players. Fearlessness is best mixed with equal portions of talent and skill. General George Armstrong Custer was fearless, and we all know how that turned out.

The annual grudge match against Kentucky Wesleyan attracted the biggest crowd to attend a game at Roberts that season. The Aces would be facing the

Panthers for the thirty-seventh time in their rivalry, which dated to the 1947–48 season. This year the visitors were 8–0 and were ranked first in the country.

Ron Bae, who had gained a starting role, paced the Aces, who were again facing a taller team. Bae's play kept them in the game. With 1:59 to go Bae's fifteen-footer pulled the Aces to within a basket of the Panthers.

Then a free throw by the Panthers' George Tinsley, who would grab twenty rebounds, gave Wesleyan a three-point lead.

Only forty-one seconds remained when Dave Weeks, Evansville's leading scorer, canned his sixth field goal. Now the Aces trailed by only one, and the crowd was on its feet urging them on. Layne Holmes and Weeks trapped the Panthers' guard on the next possession, forcing a turnover and giving Evansville the ball.

Mac called time-out and designed a play for the Aces.

Only ten seconds left.

The play Mac diagrammed, which assumed they'd be facing a zone defense, called for Weeks to take the shot from the baseline. But Weeks found himself smothered, and Bae came open on the left. He took the jumper from twenty-one feet.

Bingo!

Tinsley grabbed the inbounds pass and took off down court. He threw up a last desperation heave from thirty feet. The ball bounced high off the back iron and fell away.

The buzzer sounded. The Aces had won.

The crowd erupted and then charged the court, lifting Bae onto their shoulders.

Later, in the dressing room Bae told reporters, "I'm not used to all this. It feels kind of funny, because it hasn't been so long ago that I was sitting way down there on the bench, and no one was interested in me at all." Funny how winning changes people's perceptions.

McKissic was also off the bench and in the backcourt for Mac as the coach probed for the right combination to get the Aces on the winning track. The Aces had four capable guards but still lacked height and strength underneath. It was a serious deficiency that couldn't be hidden and one that opponents would exploit all year.

With a 5–4 mark the Aces had remained in the polls, but they dropped out soon after the game against Wesleyan and would never reappear. The 1968–69 Aces never found the right combination to put on the floor. Lacking an inside game, they struggled all season, eventually finishing at 12–14.

Southwest Missouri State, tall and athletic, hung a 101–74 loss on the Aces at Roberts to mark the worst defeat by Evansville at home. It was all downhill from there. There weren't many more blowout losses, but the Aces never figured out how to deal with taller teams or those that were quicker.

The team did manage to grab the conference crown in a smaller, weakened league—several teams had moved on to different conferences—giving Mac his tenth title. And he had one other consolation. His freshmen had gone through their schedule with ease, and all were eligible for the varsity next season.

He turned once again to the recruiting process. Although both Don Buse and another guard would be moving up from the freshman team, Mac sought to add more backcourt players. "When you play the style of play we do you can't get by with just two guards—not the way we pressure the opposition," he explained as he continued his search.

He snared Gregg Martin, from Earlington, Kentucky, and another guard, 6'1" Mike Stiffler from Brazil, Indiana. Martin's high school coach declared, "He can play anywhere . . . with any college team in the country. He has all the tools, and he should be good enough to start as a sophomore."

Mac reached farther than usual to land Bob Keegan, the first player from talent-laden New Jersey to play for the Aces. A native of South Amboy, Keegan had attended Frederick Military Academy for one year and had averaged 17 points per game. He was 6-3 and quick. Just the kind of guard Mac liked. "I heard about Evansville when they were a power. Anyway I wanted to attend a small school," Keegan said. Both Mac and Keegan got what they wanted.

The preseason scrimmage with the varsity of 1969–70 facing the freshmen turned out the way it should have this time. The veteran Aces—Mike Owens and Kae Moore as the forwards, Layne Holmes in the pivot, and converted center John Wellemeyer and Jim McKissic at guard, tromped the yearlings 52–14. Both Don Buse and Bob Clayton played as reserves at guard and forward, respectively.

The biggest recruit Mac had ever landed, at least in terms of size, was still holding down the bench. Welmer "the Whale" had returned to school in the fall of 1969 looking more like his nickname than ever. Mac was not particularly happy about this. "He started out way behind [in conditioning] and it's taking time for him to catch up. And that's natural for a man of that size. When he's ready, we may be hard to handle."

While awaiting Welmer's return to a more mobile condition, Mac elected to play Kae Moore, a natural forward at 6-2, in the pivot. Small, agile pivot players had long been a favorite ploy of Mac's. It had worked in the past with Clyde Cox, Mel Lurker, and Herb Williams, all undersized for pivot players but quick and great leapers. Mac hoped Moore would be another one.

After 7,184 fans saw the Aces trounce Whittier, alma mater of the newly elected president Richard Nixon, the Aces headed west, where Mac's experiment with Moore proved flawed. With their inside size and quickness Rolland Todd's Rebels of the University of Nevada, Las Vegas, manhandled the Aces 109–98. Three Aces had fouled out while trying to run with the Rebels.

Colorado was next to welcome the Aces. They did so rudely, pounding Mac's team. Colorado, the Big Eight defending champion, dominated from the outset. Coach Russell "Sox" Walseth took the starters out when they had a 82–44 lead. It didn't stop the slaughter. His reserves finished off the hapless Aces 97–66. Cliff Meeley, the Buffaloes' 6-8 junior, led the home team with 24 points while playing less than half the game.

Mac went back to basics. The Aces returned from the disaster out west and began working on defensive drills. It seemed to have done some good when they met St. Joseph's of Philadelphia at Roberts. The defending Middle Atlantic Conference champions, the Hawks were a veteran five who threatened to hang another blowout loss on the Aces.

But the home team responded this time, and with seven minutes to play and trailing by seven, the Aces mounted a comeback. Layne Holmes tied it at 71, with just seventeen seconds to go. Then St. Joe's scored to go ahead, and Mike Owens knotted it at 73.

The Hawks put up a final shot, but the ball bounced away and out of bounds. One second remained. Buse, off the bench, tried a long pass down court to a streaking Holmes. St. Joe's deflected it out of bounds before the clock started.

Now only one second remained, but this time Buse was under his own basket. He threw it high to Holmes, who stepped backward and let fly.

Good!

The 5,482 in attendance swarmed the court in celebration. Bob Clayton lifted Holmes aloft and carried him through the tunnel. "If I ever hit a bigger basket in my life, I can't remember when it was," Holmes said.

The Aces should have been carrying the timekeeper with the slow index finger, but, hey, a win is a win.

Holmes, a 6-5 swingman who had confounded Mac with his poor attitude on and off the court for the past three seasons, now drew some praise from his coach. "There's been a marvelous change in the boy. He's trying very hard to be a good boy, and he's doing a wonderful job. And I think it's obvious that in the process he's become our leader," Mac said. Holmes, from Avoca, Indiana, had starred for Needmore High School, where he averaged 25 points and 20 rebounds in his senior year. Considered by his high school coach to be "as good as anyone in the state," Layne had scored 43 points and grabbed 45 rebounds, both school records, in a game against Fayetteville. "He was recommended by every coach I asked about him," Mac said.

Mac had been expecting Welmer and Couch to step into starting roles and provide some much-needed muscle underneath. But Welmer was still trying to get into playing shape, and Couch was recovering from a broken nose. Mac would have to wait a little longer for his beef to be ready.

Buse was seeing only reserve duty, and Coffey was getting splinters on the bench while Mac stuck with his veterans. The two highly touted recruits watched from the pine as the Aces' upperclassmen sought a solution to their problems.

Purdue proved that a name opponent could still sell out Roberts when the Boilermakers came to town and 12,823 redshirts showed up. Rick Mount, their All-American forward, was injured and would not play, but the presence of a Big Ten team in Evansville was still a compelling reason for fans to brave the chill winter air. The fourth-largest crowd in regular season history saw what they had come to see. As had happened so often before, the presence of a name opponent stirred the competitive juices of the Aces.

The visitors took an early lead before McKissic was inserted into the lineup. Jim began shooting before his long robe hit the floor. He nailed four straight baskets to pull the Aces within one all by himself. The rest of the team fed off Jim's scoring surge and moved ahead at last, at 34–33. The half ended with the surprising Aces trailing by only a single point, 41–40.

McKissic and Wellemeyer kept the Aces in the contest with timely buckets, and the two teams fought down to the wire. Evansville grabbed a two-point lead at 78–76 before Purdue retaliated, tying it with 1:19 to play. The din in Roberts was deafening.

With fifty-five seconds remaining, Mac had the Aces holding on for the final shot when Purdue stole the ball from Buse, who was finally starting. Purdue waited to call a time-out with just ten seconds to play. Now the Boilermakers would get the last shot.

The inbounds pass came to Weatherford, who was guarded by Buse, who stole the ball back. The Aces quickly called time-out, and Mac designed a play on the sideline.

Just four ticks remained. Mac decided to reinsert Layne Holmes, who had been on the bench in a state of exhaustion. And he instructed Buse to inbound the ball to McKissic. Don got the pass to Jim, who turned and threw a strike to Wellemeyer, who dribbled twice and fired. He launched from just short of the half-court line, and the shot looked to be well short.

Purdue's Bill Franklin leaped high to grab the ball. Without a moment's hesitation the referee, Tom Balaban from the Big Ten, blew the whistle. He gave the signal for goal tending. The basket was good.

The twelfth-ranked Boilermakers were stunned as they stumbled off the court toward the tunnel, while Wellemeyer was mobbed at center court.

Wayne Boultinghouse, Mac's assistant coach, saw the whole play unfold. Franklin "caught the ball above the rim. They had to make the call because it was so obvious," Boultinghouse said. Mac added his explanation, noting that a shot like that "doesn't have to be a sure thing—just have a chance to go in." Then he added honestly, "It looked a little off line."

Purdue's George King wasn't saying anything about why his team had suffered a stunning last-second loss. Tight-jawed and sullen, he answered every reporter's question by muttering "No comment," and headed back to Lafayette with his third-straight loss at Roberts Stadium.

The 1969 Holiday Tournament was next for the Aces. Still basking in the glow of victory, they knocked off Fordham in the first round. That win got the Aces a game with Jacksonville for the tourney title. It wasn't the kind of thing you enjoy getting.

Jacksonville arrived from Florida with a gifted 7-2 giant who could do just about anything you can imagine with a basketball and make it look easy. His name was Artis Gilmore.[7] They called him the "A-Train," and he was definitely an express.

Gilmore was coupled with 7-0 Penbrook Burrows. Together they formed the tallest front line in all of college basketball. Also returning to Roberts with the high-leaping Dolphins was Rex Morgan. The former Ace had been unhappy at Evansville and spent one year at a junior college. He joined Jacksonville in 1967–68 when he was tenth in the nation in scoring with an average of 26.7 per game.

Morgan took the opportunity to take a swipe at his former university. Morgan told UPI reporter Charles Aldinger about his Evansville experiences: "On road trips we took along a brown sandwich bag filled with a bunch of junk. That's not much of a way to run a program. They make enough basketball money at Evansville to treat you first class."

Bob Hudson bristled at Morgan's remarks, firing back: "We do the same as the other school does when we're on a plane. We order box lunches for the players. That way we're not waylaid an hour and a half so they can go to a restaurant and eat. It makes a difference as far as getting back to class the next day."

For the second time the Aces played surprisingly well against a much more talented team. This time, though, there would be no last-second miracle. They were down only four at the half, even though 6-2 Kae Moore was trying to hold down Gilmore. Moore had told reporters, "I'll just have to try to gain position on him. He can't bend over me or he'll draw a foul."

Gaining anything on Gilmore, who towered a foot above Moore, wasn't an easy task. With the score 81–56 and less than nine minutes to play, Mac surrendered and sent in the reserves.

Buse had limited Morgan to five points, but Rex opened up on the reserves and finished with 14.[8] Gilmore scored 37 points and grabbed 13 rebounds. He was named the MVP of the tournament. The Dolphins had won by 30.

Mac joined those coaches who had been run over by the A-Train. "Gilmore may be the best college basketball player in the country," Mac said.

The Aces finally found someone their own size and beat American International but then began to slide. Losses in their next three games were offset only by a lone forfeit win they were awarded late in the season over DePauw, which had beaten Evansville in Greencastle while using an ineligible player.

As Mac searched for answers among his talented sophomores, he started using Welmer. As the 1969–70 season played out, though, he was reluctant to bench the veterans and move the youngsters up for some valuable experience.

One decision on playing time was made for him when the fiery Layne Holmes was suspended by the school on the eve of Michigan's first visit to Roberts since 1962–63. "I won't take him back," said Mac. "We'll have only the SIU game left when he returns and I feel he should have heeded the warnings." Mac, always fair with his players, had seen enough.

Holmes had averaged 13 points per game, although he was plagued by foul trouble and prone to fistfights. His offense production would be hard to replace.

Mac chose to use Bob Clayton. He had been injured the previous season and had seen limited action thus far. Now he was to start against Michigan. Mac told reporters he considered Clayton to be "the best jumper on the team."

He'd better be.

Michigan came to Roberts with 6-8 Rudy Tomjanovich. He was averaging 25 points per game and had scored 48 against Indiana. He also was pulling down 15 rebounds a game.[9] The Aces faced another stern test.

Michigan's new coach was Johnny Orr, who had been to Roberts before, with UMass. "I told Bob Hudson I'd get a big job someday, and when I did, I'd bring my team to Evansville," Orr said. Hudson's warm hospitality won him many friends in college basketball through the years. He treated them all well and was respected by those he brought to Roberts. Many remembered and repaid him when they could. Orr was just the latest of many.[10]

Welmer moved over into the pivot to try to contain Tomjanovich, and he played well, as did the Aces. Despite having Tomjanovich, the Wolverines struggled offensively, and the Aces once more rose to the occasion, literally playing above their heads. The game went down to the final seconds. With 6,423 on hand and yelling their support, the Aces clung to a 73–71 lead.

Michigan's Rick Bloodworth put up a shot with thirty-nine seconds left. Buse, guarding him closely, went up with him and took the ball away. Don fired a strike to Wellemeyer, who converted the layup—Evansville had won, 78–73.

Buse had been playing hurt for some time after damaging his wrist against Kentucky Wesleyan. "That was a fabulous performance for a cripple," Mac quipped. Buse, bad wrist and all, had recorded 20 points, 14 rebounds, and 8 steals, and had dished out 5 assists.

When the Aces were awarded the forfeit win over DePauw, they still had a chance to salvage the season as the last few ICC conference games approached. If they could beat St. Joseph's in Renesselaer, they'd move from 2–3 to 3–3 with two more conference games to go.

It was close throughout. But this time no buzzer beater saved them. The Pumas managed to defeat the Aces in Renesselaer for the first time since the 1958–59 season. The Aces' conference hopes were dashed, and the remaining games meant nothing in the standings.

Butler arrived for coach Tony Hinkle's last game at Roberts. Butler had forced him into retirement, and fans feted Hinkle in pregame ceremonies honoring the future Hall of Famer. Then Hinkle's Bulldogs bit the Aces. Buse, Clayton, and

McKissic played well in spurts, but the Aces looked uninspired. After Butler won, 98–87, Mac shook his head and told reporters that his Aces had "just quit." Never before had he uttered those words, even if he'd thought them.

The 1969–70 season had been a frustrating one. "He was never able to bring himself to write it off and give the sophomores a chance to gain some experience," Rick Coffey said. "He held on to the end with a mix of veterans and younger players. The mix never gelled."[11]

Losses to Ball State and Indiana State were followed by a win over Valpo and then a final loss to Southern Illinois in a game that had lost all its appeal.

At last the year was over. The Aces, with the forfeit converting a loss into a win, finished again at 12–14.

But some progress was discernible. Buse had showed just how good he could be on defense, and Clayton had gained valuable experience, and so did Welmer and Couch.

Only Rick Coffey had become discouraged with the view from the bench. "Mac just never had any confidence in me. He had never seen me play in high school, and when I got there he saw me as a forward," Coffey said. "I really thought about leaving after the season. I wanted to get more playing time."[12] But Rick's friends talked him into staying put. Buse, junior Rick Smith, Bob Clayton, and Couch would all be back.

They all looked ahead to next year, only eight months away.

Things were going to be different.

On June 10, 1970, Michigan Technical University sold the DC-3 bearing tail number N51071 to Sellstrom Manufacturing Canada Ltd. of Montreal. On August 3 Sellstrom leased the plane to Barrington Optical, of Cook County, Illinois. The lease, which gave Barrington an option to buy the plane, was for three years at $10,800 per year. The plane was insured for $35,000.

(Endnotes)

1   Rick Coffey, telephone interview by author, May 26, 2011.

2   For this quote from Couch, and others like it that are attributed to no other source in this chapter, the reader may assume that they come from articles in the *Evansville Courier* and *Evansville Press,* the two local papers at the time. Those articles may be found in the collection of bound scrapbooks kept by

Bob Hudson and now housed in the university archives and/or the Bussing manuscript. Bill Bussing graciously made his detailed manuscript of the history of the Aces available to me. It contains no footnotes, but when I interviewed Bussing in February 2011, he identified his sources as the *Evansville Courier, Evansville Press,* and the combined Sunday edition, the *Courier & Press.* Bussing's manuscript usually makes no distinction between the papers, but the direct quotes are from one daily or the other or the Sunday combined paper and appear in the Bussing manuscript in quotation marks. Bussing also had access to Hudson's scrapbooks, as did I and my research assistant. Many articles do not identify which paper they are from, much less the date and page, but I (and Bussing) assume they are from the *Courier, Press, or Sunday Courier & Press.*

3   Coffey interview.

4   Don Buse, telephone interview by author, May 18, 2011.

5   Coffey interview.

6   Lou Henson would coach for New Mexico State, his alma mater, until 1975. He led the Aggies to the NCAA tournament six times, including five straight from 1966 to 1971. The Aggies appeared in the Final Four in 1970. In 1975 he moved on to Illinois, where he remained for twenty-one seasons. He had the Illini in the NCAA tournament on twelve occasions, including a trip to the Final Four in 1989. He retired from Illinois in 1996 and rejoined his alma mater the next year. After he was diagnosed with non-Hodgkins lymphoma, he retired in 2005, after forty-one seasons at Division I with 779 wins, sixth most among coaches at the time. He is one of only eleven coaches to take two different programs to the Final Four. The basketball court at the Pan-American Center has been named Lou Henson Court ("Lou Henson Retires as Aggie Men's Basketball Head Coach," NMStatesports.com, January 22, 2005, www.nmstatesports.com/ViewArticle.dbml?&DB_OEM_ID=1900&ATCLID=105846&SPID=602&SPSID=9966).

7   Gilmore would lead Jacksonville into the 1970 NCAA Tournament title game that was won by UCLA. He went on to play in the ABA with Kentucky and later with the NBA's Chicago Bulls, San Antonio, and Boston. His career as a professional spanned seventeen seasons. He shot 59.9 from the field as a pro, the all-time best. He was elected to the Naismith Memorial Basketball Hall of Fame in 2011. He is a public speaker and serves as a special assistant to the president of Jacksonville University (www.actionnewsjax.com).

8   Drafted by the Boston Celtics, Rex Morgan played two seasons in the NBA. He became a high school coach in Jacksonville and coached for Arlington Country Day School there for fourteen seasons, winning five state titles. In 2010 he announced he'd been diagnosed with throat cancer and would begin radiation treatment. The announcement came just three days after he and the other members of the Jacksonville 1969–70 team were honored by the school (Jeff Elliott, "Arlington Country Day's Rex Morgan Begins a New Fight," *(Jacksonville) Florida Times-Union,* February 17, 2010, http://jacksonville.com/sports/high_school/2010-02-17/story/arlington_country_days_rex_morgan_begins_a_new_fight).

9   Tomjanovich played eleven seasons in the NBA with San Diego and Houston. He later coached in the NBA for thirteen seasons, winning two titles with Houston. He is probably best remembered, though, as the player whom Kermit Washington punched, and nearly killed, in a game in 1977 at the Forum in Los Angeles. Tomjanovich's face was fractured, and he lay in a pool of blood as trainers assisted him. The attack prompted the NBA to take action against violence, which had been steadily increasing. Tomjanovich went through five surgeries before recovering (David Leon Moore, "New Star from Old Wounds," *USA Today,* November 28, 2002). See also John Feinstein, *The Punch* (Boston: Little, Brown, 2002).

10 Joan Hudson Roth, telephone interview by author, February 22, 2011.

11 Coffey interview.

12 Coffey interview.

One More Time, 1970–1971

The memories of the dismal 1968–69 and 1969–70 campaigns had begun to fade as autumn returned to Evansville. The sycamores and tulip poplars blazed into a final burst of color as they shed their leaves for the winter and the fans and players traded their tans and flip-flops for sweatshirts and warm shoes.

Mac had been very disappointed with the past two seasons. Mike Owens, Roger Guth, and Kae Moore had graduated. Attendance at Roberts had hit its low point in 1968–69—fewer than 100,000—but had rebounded some in 1969–70, to 104,219. The Purdue game alone had drawn more than 12,000.

With Wayne Boultinghouse on his staff, Mac had someone who could go on the recruiting trail and talk to potential players about his own experiences. Wayne also was invaluable in coaching individual players in skills they were lacking.

Rick Coffey was one of the beneficiaries of Wayne's help. "I really lacked the foundation for playing good defense. I had always been a scorer. Wayne stayed with me for hours after practice, working with me just on defense," Rick said.[1]

The Aces' most pressing need wasn't at guard. They had a surplus of talent there. Jim McKissic, Don Buse, Monte Stebbins, and Curt John, who had arrived on campus in January 1970 after transferring from Tennessee, were all capable performers in the backcourt.

Welmer was back, but Mac needed some more big men upfront. Jerry Conrad, 6-5, was the first to sign with the Aces. Mac and his assistant Wayne Boultinghouse hit the recruiting trail once again. At first they seemed to have made great progress but all too soon their early smiles vanished as players they had hoped to land signed elsewhere, transferred or left school shortly after arriving. The net results would prove to be disappointing.

Steve Welmer, whom Mac had threatened to hold out for a year if he didn't slim down, sprained an ankle after a four-day fast that he had endured to reach 240 pounds. He couldn't complete Mac's mandatory two-mile run on his gimpy ankle. Newcomer 6'5" Chaundice Pullom showed up with a balky knee that not would let him run either. Then John Couch sprained an ankle and joined Welmer and Pullom on the sidelines. Don Buse was there, too—he had returned from the Olympic Trials camp in Colorado Springs with a cast on his ankle.

Defections mounted. Given the way the Aces had played recently coupled with the injuries and defections, the fans, players and coaches were all on edge.

After two losing seasons, Mac didn't need a squad that was devastated by injuries and depleted by defections. But that was exactly what he had.

In coaching, as in life, you have to play the hand you are dealt. There is no wild card coming along to save you. Mac's 1970–71 Aces, battered, bruised, and limping around, were what he had. He'd have to make the best of his cards.

Buse recovered quickly and joined Rick Smith, now a senior, in the backcourt as the Aces' varsity took on the freshmen in a scrimmage.

"There were times last year when I thought he was ready," Mac said of Smith, "but it never quite worked out. This year, though, he's playing well and hitting."

Rick was at last at the position he favored. "Mac played me as a small forward the past two years. That's the way he saw me. But, I wasn't really equipped to play there. I only weighed 170 pounds and it wasn't my natural position. I wrote a letter to Mac over the summer asking him to give me a chance to play guard. I told him, 'I think we have a chance to have a great year. I have been a winner all my life and I would like a chance to play guard again and help the team become winners again,'" he said.[2]

When practice opened in the fall of 1970, Mac came over to Rick and said simply, "Smitty, you're going to play guard."[3] All Rick had to do was show Mac he could team with Buse to make the Aces' attack run smoothly and efficiently. The job was his if he could hold it. John Wellemeyer and Bob Clayton were at the forwards, and Steve Welmer was in the pivot.

The lineup was experienced, Welmer gave them some height inside, and Buse and Smith provided defensive pressure. It proved enough to beat the freshmen, which relieved a lot of anxiety, and it was the lineup for the season opener.

The 1970–71 season opener before 7,319 at Roberts was against Rolland Todd's Rebels from the University of Nevada, Las Vegas. The Aces faced a taller, quicker team, and the Rebels managed to escape with an 87–82 win. Gregg Martin, in his first season on the Evansville varsity, came off the bench to add four straight baskets in the first half, and eight buckets in all, to keep the Aces close.

Martin was only 6-2 and had played in place of Wellemeyer at forward. He'd had to guard a 6-9 Rebel, Toby Houston. Mike Whaley led the Rebels with 24 points; Houston and Odis Allison both had 19.

The Aces would face an even bigger team the next week when Kentucky Wesleyan came to Roberts. Like so many other games between the two schools, it was a rough-and-tumble game that would be decided on the final possession.

The Aces lost both Welmer and Clayton to fouls, forcing Mac to shift Rick Smith to center with 4:29 to play. Then Monte Stebbins, playing guard in relief, also fouled out. With just thirty-two seconds remaining, the Panthers held a one-point lead, 83–82. They had possession and called time-out. They set up an inbounds play that Jim McKissic foiled, forcing a five-second call. Only eleven seconds remained when McKissic tipped the jump ball to Gregg Martin. Martin passed to Buse, who threw a bullet to Wellemeyer, who laid it up—and in, just as time expired.

The Aces had won 84–83.

Rick Coffey had come off the bench and played well. "Mac never really believed in me until I started to prove it on the court," he recalled.[4]

Mac took his team east for a two-game series against American International and Assumption College. The trip provided the Aces with a chance to see New York. Bob Hudson arranged a four-hour tour of the city that had the Aces staring wide-eyed at the towering skyscrapers in the city's canyons.

They also made a stop at the Naismith Memorial Basketball Hall of Fame in Springfield, Massachusetts. There they soaked up the history of the game. Though they couldn't have known it at the time, that history would someday include their coach's accomplishments and would place him among the game's immortals.

The trip produced mixed results. After easily turning back American International, 96–62, with Coffey adding a 6-for-7 performance after the game was decided, the Aces headed to Worcester, Massachusetts, to face Assumption before 2,000 fans.

The Aces were as cold as a New England winter. They didn't score a single field goal until nearly seven minutes had gone by. They never did catch up, and lost, 106–91.

Mac scheduled a scrimmage when the team returned to Evansville. "Sometimes you shoot well in one game, the next game you stand around looking for the shot," he told the local reporters. But standing around looking for shots was not what Mac's teams were known for.

Eastern Illinois visited Roberts next, and the scrimmage must have had a positive effect, because the Aces tromped the visitors 97–84. Coffey had played only 19 minutes in the game off the bench but had scored 19 points. He had caught the eye of the local sportswriters with his play. "The papers wrote it up. They asked, essentially, 'With a team that is struggling again for the third year in a row, why isn't that kid playing?'" Coffey recalled. "I had outscored everyone in the second half."[5]

Northeastern arrived from Boston with a 2–2 record and left at 3–2 after recording a 71–56 win.

Minnesota arrived at Roberts with a 4–2 record for the Gophers' first view of Evansville's home court. "Playing a Big 10 team was something we liked to do. We liked it even more when we could beat them. It was a real feather in our caps when we did that," Don Buse said.[6]

The Gophers must have liked what they saw because they left with a hefty check and their fifth win. The Aces played well in spurts, but "we let it get away," Coffey recalled.[7]

He was right. Behind by five points at 73–68 with only 2:09 to go, the Gophers fought back. They cut the Aces' lead to three on a twenty-footer from Jim Brewer, who then made a free throw, putting only two points between the teams.

At 1:39 Ollie Shannon's two free throws brought Minnesota even.

Shannon spotted Gerry Pyle open underneath, and Pyle converted his fourth basket.

After Stebbins missed the front end of a one-and-one, Roger Arnold intercepted an Evansville pass and scored to give Minnesota a 77–73 win.

The crowd of 6,515 sat in stunned silence. The Gophers had rallied to score nine points and steal the win.

"This was a top-flight club. It was better, I think, than the Don Nelson-Iowa teams we played in the early sixties," Mac said after the stinging loss, which was the Aces' fourth, against only three wins.

There comes a point when talent becomes apparent to everyone. Mac finally admitted to himself that he might have had Coffey wrong all along. He had been playing out of position and spending most of his time on the bench. The team, with Welmer in the lineup, lacked quickness. The Aces were struggling, and Mac needed to do something before another losing season resulted.

Mac moved Clayton, who was 6-4, into the pivot position in place of Welmer and put Coffey in the starting lineup at forward. And the whole chemistry of the team changed. "With Clayton, who could jump out of the gym, down low, and with bigger, quicker guards in Smith and Buse, we were a different team," Coffey said. "Wellemeyer was a great scorer and the defense was solid. All of the players were now more comfortable in their roles and it began to show."[8]

"Those moves made a big difference, especially on our fastbreak," Buse said. "With Clayton, who was fast and a great leaper upfront, it all just seemed to click. Wellemeyer was great on the fastbreak. I'd get the ball out to him on the wing, and he was as good as anyone I've ever played with at finishing off the fastbreak."[9]

The Aces were now a quicker, faster team. They were more athletic than they had been. They were also better on defense, long a strong point of Mac's really good teams of the past. "Buse could pick your pocket at the ten-second line anytime he wanted to," Coffey said.[10]

The revamped 1970–71 Aces debuted at Roberts in the Holiday Tournament against Portland University, and the changes paid immediate dividends. The Aces rolled over the 1–6 Pilots 91–70 in front of 4,718 fans.

That win pitted Evansville against Weber State in the finals as the Aces sought their ninth tournament crown. The visitors brought with them 6-8 Willie Sojourner, who had blocked eight shots in the first-round win over Eastern Kentucky. Sojourner had scored 28 points and grabbed 16 rebounds. He was a formidable presence on the court.[11]

"A boy like Sojourner is bound to make a difference in any game, not only for scoring, for there are some things we can do to try and stop that. But I don't know what we can do about his blocking shots. Maybe we'll just have to shoot from the center of the floor," Mac quipped.

That might not have been a bad idea. Sojourner had grabbed twenty-five boards earlier against West Texas State and as a human obstacle intimidated more than one opponent just by his physical presence in the pivot.

Fortunately for the Aces, he was human. He came down with the flu and was slowed noticeably by its effects. He didn't record a basket until late in the first half. Even so, Weber State managed to take a 32–31 lead to the locker room.

Willie used the intermission to recover his strength, and he and Brady Small led Weber State in the final half, and they held on to win 70–65. The loss put the Aces at 4–5 for the year and in a precarious spot.

Mac was exasperated. "We've got to establish that we're winners," he said. "We've got to look forward to getting our record up to where we can be invited to the NCAA tournament. We've found out you can't get an invite with a .500 record regardless of whom you play."

Ball State was due in town the next day. The visitors had left the ICC to move up to the university division in 1968. The move had not provided many wins. Coming in, Ball State was 1–6.

Mac's lineup changes were still too recent to have the desired effect. "We were still struggling and still trying to believe in one another," Rick Smith said.[12]

But the Aces trounced Ball State 97–85, and Evansville's confidence level moved up a notch. The Aces had finally managed to put their heads on the plus side of .500, and they stayed there as they vanquished Butler and Valparaiso by 91–73 and 77–73, respectively.

Rick Smith remembers the lessons of the earlier Ball State win: "Our guards had to fight like crazy to keep the ball from going down inside. If [opponents] got it down low, our smaller front line couldn't stop them. We had to prevent them from getting around us and getting it down low. At 6-4 and 6-5 we could often intimidate the other guards with our size and speed."[13]

Buse had shut down Butler's Billy Shepherd, a former Mr. Basketball, holding him to a season low of 11 points and forcing 7 turnovers. "Buse is the only player who is able to stay in front of him," Mac said of Shepherd.

The Aces had used a switching man-to-man defense. "We switched when they crossed the ten-second line. Buse and I both shared the responsibility for holding down Shepherd," Rick Smith said.[14]

Against Valpo, Buse scored 25 points to go along with his harassing defense, which produced 5 steals to lead the Aces. He held Harold Green, Valpo's leading scorer, to just 8 points, 11 below his season average.

When Southern Illinois University came to Roberts, only 6,127 showed up to watch the game with the rival that had often produced heart-stopping finishes. This time foul trouble forced Buse to the bench with four personals in the first half, but the Aces managed to hold on to a one-point lead at the intermission, 54–53. Curt John, the Tennessee transfer, started the second half for Buse and promptly drilled two long jumpers.

Buse, Coffey, Wellemeyer, and Smith, all plagued by fouls, returned together at the fourteen-minute mark. SIU went into a zone defense, but the Aces shot over it, adding two more baskets. Curt John had contributed 4-for-5 from the floor in relief, including two late layups. "The big thing tonight, was we found we could use Curt John," Mac said after the game. John's emergence added depth to the Aces' front court to go along with their strong guard play. The final score was 104–90.

The Aces took to the road against Indiana State in Terre Haute late in December. "We got crushed," Rick Smith remembered. "Coffey got injured and we lost our confidence. We didn't shoot well at all up there."[15]

At Muncie the Aces came back and thrashed Ball State. They faced a zone defense and tore it to shreds. John Wellemeyer scored 37 after Ball State's center Ike Caudill was forced to the bench with foul trouble. Welmer off the bench provided 14 as the Aces romped, 107–98.

They followed by cruising to a win, 102–72, over Southwest Missouri State when Wellemeyer continued his hot hand with 27. The beat went on as the new lineup was solving Mac's vexing problems. DePauw also went down to defeat as the Aces surpassed the century mark again, winning 113–95.

But at Kentucky Wesleyan they faltered. The 14–3 Panthers out-rebounded the Aces 67–29, and the result was a not-surprising loss to the Panthers by 102–81.

While the Aces were not big upfront with their two 6-3 forwards, they usually made up for the lack of height with speed and agility. Both Wellemeyer and Coffey could score. In fact, since Coffey joined the starting lineup, the Aces had won eight of eleven games. Rick was averaging 13.5 points. Against Wesleyan, Coffey and Wellemeyer together had accounted for 20 points.

Mac's estimation of Rick's ability had done a 180-degree swing. "If I had only one shot left, I'd just as soon see Rick take it as anyone," Mac said. Wellemeyer was also proving his mettle. He had evolved into a slashing, fearless driver down the lane, something that the Aces fans hadn't seen since the glory days of Hugh Ahlering. "The Aces haven't had a player with more speed and power and uninhibited daring than Wellemeyer when he goes to the basket," gushed Bill Robertson in the *Evansville Press*.

"John won't back off from anyone," Mac said of Wellemeyer. "Give him an inch and he'll say, 'Let's go,' and see if he can beat the guy to the basket." Wellemeyer couldn't quite explain the transformation. "I don't know what's happened to me. For one thing, I guess, I'm getting a lot more points on fast breaks, thanks to the help and great passes from Buse."

St. Joseph's and Valparaiso were next to fall to the rampaging Aces, who had now found their natural rhythm and were feeling their oats. Against Butler at the Bulldogs' Fieldhouse, Rick Smith scored 18 points, a career high for him, and the Aces again topped one hundred points, winning 102–90. "Their coach asked after the game, 'Who is that guy?'" said Smith, who hadn't scored in the Bulldogs' earlier game in Evansville.[16]

The season was winding down, but all the Aces were clicking now. The win at Butler meant they'd get at least a piece of the ICC title. Still perfect in conference play, they clinched the crown outright as they rolled over DePauw 101–74 at Roberts.

The Aces were no longer new to one another. Everyone was on the same page, and the team worked smoothly, mowing down foe after foe with precision. Speed and devastating defense, coupled with great shooting, was their sure-fire formula for success. Don Buse was the undisputed defensive leader, but Don could also provide scoring punch. He was averaging more than 21 points per game while creating havoc all over the court on defense.

When Indiana State came to Roberts, the Aces were looking for revenge. "We wanted to get them after the loss in Terre Haute when we were still struggling," Rick Smith said.[17] They got what they wanted.

In front of the season's largest crowd—9,748 had turned out to honor retiring assistant coach Paul Beck—the Aces avenged the earlier loss, winning 90–83. Buse played what Mac described later as "his best game." Don went 10-for-14 from the field for 26 points, 10 rebounds, and 8 assists. He was nearly a one-man wrecking crew. But he had plenty of help.

"Our defense, while we don't change it much, is pretty complicated." Mac said. "And it takes guts to play it right, because we are getting in front of people and chasing and battling."

When the Aces trounced St. Joseph's by 91–78, they were starting to feel invincible. Then an old nemesis came along, punctured their high-flying balloon and brought them back down to earth.

"Southern Illinois was the final game of the regular season, and we were starting to think no one could touch us," Rick Smith said. "We learned a valuable lesson at just the right time."[18]

The game was typical of past contests between the two foes. It was close throughout. The Aces were looking for their seventh straight win to close out the regular season and held a two-point advantage at the half. But the game was being played in Carbondale on SIU's home court.

With 1:39 left, the Aces were up 98–89, and the crowd from Evansville that had traveled with the team was starting to party. But it was a case of premature celebration. The Salukis got a three-point play from L. C. Brasfield, then swiped a pass that Brasfield converted, cutting the Aces' lead to just four.

When Marv Brooks made two baskets in a row for SIU, the game was tied at 89, and Mac called a time-out.

When the Aces returned, they promptly threw the ball away.

Fifty seconds remained. The game was still tied.

The Salukis had the ball. Brooks tore through the lane amid a forest of arms and put it in. He was also fouled in the act of shooting. He converted the free throw, and that clinched the win. Evansville was out of time and out of luck. The final was 101–98. "It was a wake-up call for us," Don Buse said.[19]

"We had them beaten and we just fell apart," Rick Smith said. "It may have been just what we needed. Though at the time no one believed that."[20]

"We had begun to think we were unbeatable," Rick Coffey recalled. "The loss got us refocused. And it came at an opportune time, just as we were starting the NCAA Tournament."[21]

The regular season had ended on a down note, but it had produced another conference crown and an undefeated conference schedule, the first since 1964–65's perfect season. The Aces would be happy if they could continue to duplicate the efforts of that squad.

Mac was awarded the ICC Coach-of-the-Year title for the ninth time. "It takes a super effort for us all the time, but when we're ready to play, I believe we can go with any of them," Mac said. "Of course when we're not ready, about anybody might beat us."

The team had compiled a 17–8 record entering tournament play. They wanted to keep playing. All they needed to do was to keep winning.

Ashland College of Ohio provided the first-round test, and the Aces passed with flying colors. They rebounded with a flawless performance and turned the visitors away 82–74. Bill Musselman was the Ashland coach, and he was impressed with what he saw. His team played a great game, hitting 30-for-48 from the field, and lost.

Leading the way for the victorious Aces were Coffey with 24 and Wellemeyer with 23.

After the game Musselman told reporters that the Aces "will not play a better team than the one they played tonight."[22] Mac could only hope he was right.

The win got the Aces a date with Central Michigan's Chippewas, which the Aces won easily, 78–60, with the reserves seeing some needed playing time. The Aces had taken a 41–23 lead at the half and were never really challenged. Coffey with 14, Buse with 13, and Steve Welmer off the bench with 12 paced the Aces.

With the win the Aces advanced to the finals, where they would face Hartwick College on Wednesday night in the first quarterfinal game. "We were in final exams at the time, and we were playing the last game that night," Rick Smith recalled.[23]

It made no difference to the Aces, who were up by 15 at the half and continued to pull away in the second half. "Everyone got to play," Smith remembered. Wellemeyer, with 20, Buse with 18, and Coffey with 16 were joined by Welmer, who came off the bench to score 13 points. The starters played little in the second half, and the rest was a welcome one. The final score was 105–69, Evansville over hapless Hartwick.

The Aces were looking invincible, but they would be tested by the nation's top-ranked team, the University of Southwestern Louisiana. The Ragin' Cajuns featured a high-scoring offense whose centerpiece was a guard named Dwight "Bo" Lamar. Lamar had scored 62 points in a game against rival Northeast Louisiana University. He had taken most of those shots 25 feet or more from the basket.

He was the type of guard who thought about shooting as soon as he got to center court and wouldn't hesitate to put one up. But Bo had yet to meet Don Buse. "I had a knack for anticipating passes and moves that came naturally to me," Buse said. And when the two did meet early in the game, Buse knocked Lamar's first two shots away.[24]

The game was a classic, with the Aces battling furiously on defense to stay in it. "They took us lightly," Rick Smith recalled. "It looked like David versus Goliath out there when we lined up for the center jump. Lamar was only 6-1, but they had another player, Roy Ebron, who was 6-8. The Cajuns looked a little intimidating to us."[25]

Buse remembered "watching their semifinal game with two of our reserves. They looked at each other and then at me and said, 'There's no way we can beat these guys.' I didn't see that at all. Maybe that's why they weren't starting."[26]

Once the ball went up, any intimidation quickly evaporated. "We hit two in a row, they missed two, and they panicked," Rick recalled.[27]

For the Aces it was a total team effort, as it had to be. The front line played great against the bigger, heavier Cajuns. "After everyone had counted us out, we surged at the end," Smith said. Buse and Smith alternated on Lamar, with Smith crediting Buse for taming Lamar. "We all played really good that game," Buse said. "They tried to run with us and couldn't.[28] In the end Lamar had taken 34 shots but had connected with only 9.

When the Cajuns made a move in the second half after trailing 47–33, the Aces found an answer to their prayers in Bob Clayton. "He played the game of his life," Rick Coffey said.[29]

Clayton was athletic and could score. He did so when he was needed the most. Bob scored 20 points and grabbed 19 rebounds against 6-8 Ron Ebron to pull the Aces ahead. In the end the Ragin' Cajuns wilted and fell 92–74. "I've never seen Evansville play a better game in my life," said Bob Hudson, who'd seen a lot of games.

"It was a real shock," Rick Smith said. "We were just a bunch of small country boys and we smashed them."[30]

The game was a real old-fashioned shooting match. The Aces had taken seventy-five shots and had hit forty. The Cajuns were able to convert only thirty-one of ninety attempts.

The Aces had knocked off the top-ranked team and had their fifth national title in sight. Only a single obstacle remained: the Monarchs of Old Dominion. "We felt there wasn't a team in the nation, small or large, who could beat us now," Rick Coffey said.[31] Confidence, affirmed by results, is hard to beat.

Buse harassed Old Dominion's guards into mistake after mistake.

Coffey had scored 20 points in the first half to put the Aces comfortably ahead. In the second half Mac gave him a rest after three or four minutes and put Gregg Martin in. Gregg caught fire, and Coffey remained on the pine. "Mac just forgot about me," Rick said.[32]

To have such an abundance of talent on one team was a blessing that allowed Mac the luxury of forgetting a player who had scored 20 points in the first half. But that was the way the 1970–71 team had evolved.

They were talented, tough, tenacious, and fearless. Everyone did what he was supposed to do when called upon. "Mac had a way of getting the maximum out of each player so that they played up to their ability. He saw what other coaches often overlooked when evaluating talent. He had a special knack for that," Buse said. "The changes he'd made in the lineup made us a better team. We all liked each other, and we all wanted to win. We were all very unselfish on the court."[33]

But Old Dominion was no pushover. The Monarchs, paced by Dave Twardzik, had played their way into the Finals and deserved to be there. As usual it was

Don Buse's task to stop the opposition's best player, and he seldom failed to accomplish his mission. "I had watched them play an earlier game and saw that Twardzik was very quick in getting the ball upcourt. I decided I needed to slow him down," Buse recalled.[34]

"Don was a scorer, but he was also a defender, which is a rare combination," Rick Smith said. "He was a gifted athlete, with the quickest hands and feet I've ever seen. He's the best defensive player I have ever been around. He just stayed in Twardzik's face all night long."[35]

The game was much closer than most expected it to be. Old Dominion raced out to a 6–0 lead. Wellemeyer missed his first four attempts from the floor. At that point Coffey nailed a jumper to make it 6–2, and the Aces were "just trying to hang in," he said.[36]

Facing a zone defense, the Aces found themselves down by 19–12 and were struggling. Then Old Dominion made a mistake. "They tried to match up with Coffey and Wellemeyer and left the top of the key open," Rick Smith remembered. It was all the Aces needed.

Smith hit a wide-open twenty-footer from the top of the key. On his next possession Twardzik's pass was stolen by Smith, who fired to Wellemeyer, who converted to make the score 19–16. Two free throws by Rick Coffey and the Aces were within one at 19–18.

Old Dominion responded, taking the score to 21–18 in the Monarchs' favor. Then they left Smith alone again, and he fired again.

Good.

Now the score was 21–20.

Old Dominion brought the ball up, and the Monarchs were just short of the center court line when Buse struck. Don swiped the ball, fired ahead to Rick Coffey, and, just like that, it was 22–21, Aces.

With eleven minutes remaining, the Aces lost Wellemeyer when he sprained an ankle. Mac inserted Gregg Martin for Wellemeyer, who left with just two points, and Martin rose to the occasion. "He had the game of the year," Rick Smith recalled.[37]

Martin picked up 11 points in the half. Rick Coffey had 20 points, and the Aces took a 51–40 lead to the locker room. Wellemeyer had his ankle injected with cortisone and returned to play in the second half. He seemed no worse for wear and finished with 16 points for the game.

The Monarchs never recovered from the first half blitz and succumbed to the Aces' relentless onslaught, 97–82.

The 1970-71 Aces had completed an amazing turnaround by capturing the national championship once again. Mac's fifth title had to have been especially sweet. It had taken some time and patience, but he'd finally managed to fit all the pieces together in just the right order. They weren't perfect, like the 1965 team, but they were a team that worked for everything together and had made the most of their talent.

After Buse became an NBA star, it would be remembered as Buse's team, but it was truly a team effort that brought the crown back to Evansville in March 1971. Without a single starter taller than 6-5, they had won it all. "This one is the sweetest of them all, because it was less expected," Mac told reporters.

The players received Bulova watches and a medallion paperweight with the NCAA logo to commemorate their win. The university's board of trustees authorized the purchase of rings, and all the players received NCAA championship rings with a purple stone set in the center and *National Champions* engraved on the sides along with the player's name. "I still wear it today," Rick Coffey says.[38]

At the University Division championships, played the following week in Houston, coach Press Maravich of Louisiana State walked up to Mac and said, "Arad, your Evansville team could beat any one of these four teams here." Mac said nothing, but a shy smile of contentment spread across his face.[39]

A fifth championship trophy joined the other four in the trophy case at Carson Center. No other College Division coach had ever won more.

John Wellemeyer, Rick Smith, and Bob Clayton all ended their careers with a championship. Wellemeyer earned a degree in engineering, then added a master's. He went to work at Whirlpool in Evansville as an industrial engineer. After three years he joined Bristol Myers and worked for there for thirty-three years, eventually heading pharmaceutical manufacturing operations at the Evansville plant. He retired in 2008 and still attends Aces games.

Evansville fans remember Wellemeyer for his role as a member of the Aces' championship team. "In Evansville, people never forget you if you've been a member of the Aces," he says.

"For me, the championship was great, but the life lessons I learned while playing on that team for Coach McCutchan were far more important than winning basketball games. The concepts of teamwork and discipline and problem solving that I took from that experience have been things that I have taken with me throughout my life. . . those things . . . are more important to me than the season itself was."[40]

Bob Clayton's memories of the championship year are pleasant ones, although his recollections of playing a key role in the game against the University of Southwestern Louisiana are "mostly a blank. I was so focused on doing my job against their big men, I don't really remember much of anything about it."[41]

The rest of his teammates have no such amnesia. They declare it the best game of Clayton's career. But he is self-effacing about his considerable contributions to the championship. "We were all just basically small-town kids who had a shared work ethic and desire to succeed," he said. "We all knew our roles, and there were no ego problems at all. Mac was a cerebral coach, and he prepared us so completely, all we had to do was execute. He was a great strategist who understood the subtleties of the other team's offense and could design a defense to stop it. And we could run with anyone in the country, and they could never keep up with us."[42]

When he finally convinced Mac to play him at guard, Rick Smith had teamed with Buse to provide the sparks that ignited the late season run that blazed into a championship.

It was Rick Smith who formed the group called Mac's Boys to "keep the memories alive" of the McCutchan era. They now count about sixty members and meet every September to renew acquaintances and relive the glory years at Evansville.

In 1989 Rick was diagnosed with thyroid cancer, underwent treatment, and has been fine for twenty-two years. Rick and his family participate in the organization of the Floyd County Relay for Life. He is doing well.

"My dad was a coal miner, and I became the first person in my family to attend college. The scholarship was the only way I could go. Mac gave me the chance to play guard in the stadium I'd always dreamed of playing in. I felt I contributed to the championship. It was the highlight of my career," he said.[43] His other dream while growing up and playing basketball on asphalt playground courts was to win a national championship.

Sometimes dreams do come true.

(Endnotes)

1   Rick Coffey, telephone interview by author, May 22, 2011.

2   Rick Smith, telephone interview by author, May 2, 2011.

3   Smith interview.

4   Coffey interview.

5   Coffey interview.

6   Don Buse, telephone interview by author, May 28, 2011.

7   Coffey interview.

8   Coffey interview.

9   Buse interview.

10 Coffey interview.

11 Sojourner is fourth all-time in scoring at Weber State and holds the all-time rebounding record there. He played four seasons in the ABA with Virginia and New York ("Willard Sojourner," Basketball-reference.com, n.d., www.basketball-reference.com/players/s/sojouwi01.html).

12 Smith interview.

13 Smith interview.

14 Smith interview.

15 Smith interview.

16 Smith interview.

17 Smith interview.

18 Smith interview.

19 Buse interview.

20 Smith interview.

21 Coffey interview.

22 After the season Musselman left Ashland for Minnesota, where he stayed until he left for the pros after the 1975 season. After his departure the NCAA placed Minnesota on probation and cited the university for more than one hundred violations. Musselman remained in the pro coaching ranks with various teams until he returned to the college ranks to coach South Alabama in 1995. He left again for the pro ranks in 1997 as an assistant with the Portland Trailblazers, where he remained until his death in May 2000 ("Bill Musselman: Basketball Was His Life's Passion," *Minneapolis Star-Tribune*, May 6, 2000).

23 Smith interview.

24 Buse interview. Bo Lamar led the Ragin' Cajuns' move to Division I the

next year. They advanced to the NCAA Tournament in each of his final two seasons. It had taken a restraining order to get the team onto the court after recruiting violations were alleged. Lamar's college basketball career was marred by allegations that he received improper benefits after the NCAA found 125 rules violations by the university. He later played professionally with a number of ABA and NBA teams. He returned to Louisiana and does color commentary for the school's radio broadcasts ("Dwight 'Bo' Lamar," Louisiana Sports Hall of Fame, n.d., www.lasportshall.com).

25   Smith interview.

26   Buse interview.

27   Smith interview.

28   Buse interview.

29   Coffey interview.

30   Smith interview.

31   Coffey interview.

32   Coffey interview.

33   Buse interview.

34   Buse interview. Twardzik was a two-time All-American at Old Dominion. He averaged 20 points and ten rebounds a game while there. He played in the ABA with Virginia and later with the Portland Trailblazers where he was a member of the 1976–77 championship team. His number 13 has been retired by the Blazers. He was inducted into the Virginia Sports Hall of Fame in 1995. He continued in the NBA after his playing career as an assistant coach and scout ("Dave Twardzik (1995)," Virginia Sports Hall of Fame, n.d., www.vshfm.com).

35   Coffey interview.

36   Coffey interview.

37   Smith interview.

38   Coffey interview.

39   Mike Blake, telephone interview by author, February 2, 2011. UCLA, Villanova, Kansas, and Western Kentucky were the four teams. UCLA defeated Villanova in the final game. Villanova's appearance was later vacated by the NCAA when it determined that Howard Porter of Villanova, who had been named MVP, had signed with an agent during the season. Western Kentucky was also ordered to vacate its third-place finish for similar violations committed by Jim McDaniels.

40 John Wellemeyer, telephone interview by author, May 30, 2011.
41 Bob Clayton, telephone interview by author, May 29, 2011.
42 Clayton interview.
43 Smith interview.

Sam Watkins (1964–66) goes for the basket.

Playing On, 1971–1977

Now Mac turned to the task of trying to duplicate the unexpected success of the 1970–71 season.

Rick Smith, Bob Clayton, and John Wellemeyer had graduated, but he still had Don Buse and Rick Coffey, key members of his 1970–71 championship squad. He also had Steve Welmer at center and could use Curt John at guard with Buse, and Gregg Martin at forward. Welmer, John, and Martin had performed well in reserve roles and seemed ready to step up.

The team, of course, would be constructed around Buse. He was a player, like Sloan before him, whom Mac could count on in every game.

Reporters and fans alike seemed to think that another repeat as NCAA champions was a distinct possibility. Once more, hope abounded in Evansville as the entire city waited for basketball season to come around. "We all felt with Don we were going to have a real good team," Rick Coffey recalled.[1]

While the Aces had a nucleus of vets and managed to win as many games as they had during the championship season, they were "just not that quick," Don Buse recalled.[2]

The Aces started the 1971–72 season with two easy wins and then dropped two on the west coast, to Seattle Pacific and Weber State. The Weber State game was marked by numerous fouls. When the Aces were whistled for another of the 27 fouls assessed against them, Mac finally had seen enough. He complained to the referee and was assessed a technical foul. The Aces' evening of woes wasn't over. As they were driving through a snowstorm from Ogden to Salt Lake City, they narrowly avoided an accident involving four other vehicles.[3]

Four straight wins followed, including a drubbing of Pepperdine when Buse had an off night, but Rick Coffey caught fire and led the Aces with 18 points, 11 rebounds, 4 assists, and 5 steals.

Once again the Aces won their Holiday Tournament, turning back Seattle and Murray State. The two-day attendance totaled 17,177, a new record.

In their next game after the Holiday Tournament, the Aces lost by one point, 80–79, to Utah State, when Curt John's shot at the buzzer rimmed out. The loss ended the Aces' eighteen-game winning streak at Roberts.[4]

The season saw the Aces, led by Buse and Coffey, turn back Kentucky Wesleyan before 7,614 fans at Roberts in the midst of a five-game winning streak that reminded fans of the 1970–71 season. Against Wabash in January, Mac used 19 players as the Aces rolled to a 105–70 win.[5]

Fog at the Evansville airport meant a 90-minute delay in the Aces' charter flight to St. Louis to play St. Louis University. Because they arrived so late, Mac had to cancel a tour of a brewery that he had arranged. The Aces got a hangover anyway: the Billikens won, 94–81. Buse had 26, but Coffey and Welmer were held to a combined 11 points.[6]

The loss to St. Louis University would be the last of the regular season as the Aces, spreading the scoring burden around, rolled off eleven straight wins.

On January 26 at Roberts, Don Buse scored 34 points as the Aces romped over Southwest Missouri State, 91–70. That night Don passed Gus Doerner, Dale Wise, and John Wellemeyer in career points scored by an Ace.[7] Then the Aces stomped DePauw in the midst of a seven-game winning streak to clinch Mac's twelfth ICC title.

In the next-to-last regular season game against St. Joe's, Buse passed fan favorite Buster Briley to move into third place on the Aces' single-season scoring list.[8] The Aces' strong finish, including a win in the final game over Southern Illinois, had fans hoping for another NCAA title.

The Aces easily made the NCAA Tournament, and the defending champs won the first-round meeting with Wittenberg 59–55 before advancing to meet Eastern Michigan.

George Gervin was Eastern Michigan's star, and the future pro was a formidable opponent. The Aces simply had no answer for the 19-year-old who would later earn the nickname "The Ice Man." "We just couldn't handle him.

We weren't quite as strong as last year. They had a very talented team, and we just couldn't stop them," Rick Coffey said.[9]

"It was a good game," Buse said. "I thought we could beat them."[10]

The Aces didn't stop fighting, even though they went for more than four minutes without making a shot in the first half. They rallied from a 70–59 deficit to close to within two at 75–73, but the Hurons held on, and ultimately the Aces fell short by just five points.[11]

The Ice Man had cometh, and the Aces were leaving. There would be no repeat. The Aces' season was over.

"After the last game Buse and Curt John and I took off for Florida," Coffey recalled. "We thought we had let the town down, and we wanted to get away and commiserate together."[12]

Don Buse would go on to become a professional after graduation. He was drafted by Phoenix of the NBA and the Virginia Squires of the ABA and signed with the Squires, who then traded his rights to the Indiana Pacers; he signed with them for a $3,000 bonus. He would embark on a career that spanned 14 seasons with four different teams. A two-time NBA All-Star, he was a defensive specialist who was named to the defensive All-Star team seven times earning an ABA championship in 1973 with the Pacers.[13]

At Evansville Buse shot .497 from the field and still ranks among the top ten in that category for his career. His average of nearly 17 points per game places him ninth all-time at Evansville. He finished with 1,426 points, third best at the time and currently thirteenth best in Aces history.

Of his time at Evansville Don has only fond memories. "Mac was a great coach and a great person. He wanted you to get an education there and to do things right," Don said. "Welmer and I went down there and didn't do much more than we had to in class. Mac found out, and we had to go to his house and get tutored by his wife. It wasn't just basketball that mattered to Mac. He wanted to let us know that there was more to college and life than basketball."

Don served as an assistant coach in the NBA for two seasons after his playing days ended in 1985. He moved back to Evansville and opened a bar and restaurant business and owned a small stable of thoroughbred racehorses. He began coaching again at Southridge High School in Huntingburg, Indiana, in the 1990s, serving as an assistant to the varsity coach there. He is still coaching, still has the restaurant and the racehorses. The man who grew up so poor that the family was on welfare said, "It's been a good life."[14]

With a recommendation from Mac, Rick Coffey got a job coaching in New Harmony, a small town about 30 miles from Evansville. Using many of the lessons he had learned from Mac, Rick coached his team to a big win over North Posey in 1973. New Harmony had never before beaten North Posey, a large consolidated school, and to celebrate the victory "the whole town turned out. They had fire engines lead a parade. It was a great feeling," he said.

Of his time as an Ace he said, "We were recognized everywhere we went and appreciated by the people of Evansville. Basketball was in its heyday there then . . ."[15]

1972-73

In March of 1971, Mac underwent hernia surgery he had needed but ignored for some time. While recovering from the surgery he looked ahead. "My hope remains for Jerry Sloan to become the next University of Evansville basketball coach. I'd like to coach a little while longer, although I don't think I want to go until I'm 65," he told reporters.[16] He was then fifty-nine.

Sloan was enjoying a successful career in the NBA, and coaching was the last thing on his mind. But Jerry had always been a special person in Mac's eyes, and Mac's stated desire to see the player he had coached succeed him, coming as it did on the heels of the Aces' latest appearance in the NCAA Tournament, was revealing.

Mac had been at Evansville since 1946. He'd captured five national titles in 26 seasons and now had revealed his retirement plans. If Mac was to be believed, he would be retiring after the 1976–77 season. That was still five seasons down the road, but he had set the stage for his departure and annointed a successor.

When reporters asked Mac about his choice, Jerry Sloan, who displayed no signs of slowing down as a pro and had never expressed the desire to become a college coach, Mac brushed the question aside. "We'll just cross that bridge when and if we come to it," he said.

The preseason got off to a shaky start. Three players, including veteran Curt John, failed Mac's two-mile-run test. John had one of the more unusual excuses Mac had ever heard for flunking the timed run: he had become a candidate for Vanderburgh County recorder and had been on the campaign trail all summer. The young Democrat had been running hard for office but not for basketball conditioning.

"It's been a strain," Curt said. "I start off every day at 5 a.m. going out to factories talking to voters. Then around noon I have two or three coffees, and then we practice basketball from 3:30 to about 6. Then the coffees start again, and I'm on the road until midnight."[17]

While John was eating his way through the rubber chicken circuit, Gregg Martin, one of the other returning starters, came down with a queasy stomach and sprained ankle. Neither lasted long, but both slowed his progress considerably. John lost his race for recorder, but the Democratic Party rewarded his effort with an appointment as deputy county auditor, and he relinquished his scholarship.

Mac used 6'3" junior Mike Meyerrose to fill in for Gregg as the Aces opened against Southwest Missouri State on the road. The course of the season was pretty much set in the opener. The Aces came up short against the Bears and lost, 57–53.

When the Aces returned to Roberts, they couldn't manage to find the winning way, even at home with 6,042 on hand for their first look at the 1972–73 Aces. It wasn't a pretty sight. The visitors from Weber State stunned the crowd and the Aces with a 76–71 win.

The West Coast trip that followed provided some sunshine in California but failed to produce a single win. Fresno State eked out a two-point win, and the University of the Pacific took the measure of the Aces by 10.

Returning to Roberts had always proved a sure remedy for ailing Aces teams in the past, and the magic elixir again proved effective as the 0–4 Aces managed to upset unbeaten Kentucky Wesleyan and then stung Seattle Pacific by a single point. The Wesleyan game saw a crowd of 7,614, but that number would be hard to match as the season wore on.

Another win over St. Louis University followed, and then the annual Holiday Tournament arrived. It drew the fewest fans since the second installment back in 1957.

After the Aces dropped the opener to Boston University by blowing an 18-point lead to lose in overtime, they faced the Seton Hall Pirates of coach Bill Raftery in the consolation game. The crowd was the smallest at Roberts Stadium since December 20, 1956. That was too bad, because the Aces hung a loss on Raftery's Pirates in a thrilling 74–72 win. The sideline antics of the fiery Seton Hall mentor, as he urged his team on and pleaded with the officials, were well worth the price of admission.[18]

But the Aces never proved able to sustain themselves as they made their way through the year. Even a wholesale midseason switch to the reserves failed to ignite them. They would put on a great performance and then fall flat for two or three games.

The season came to a close with a surprising win over Southern Illinois, but it was too little, too late. The NCAA would not proffer an at-large invitation to the 14–12 Aces. It marked the first time they were left out of the field in three years. Gregg Martin and Curt John were graduating. The season was a bitter pill for the two seniors after earning a championship only two years earlier.

On March 19, 1973, Barrington Optical transferred ownership of the DC-3 bearing tail number N51071 to Joseph Fontana of Kingsford, Michigan, for $35,000. Fontana placed the aircraft into service in his charter business, Fontana Aviation, housed at Ford Airport in Kingsford, Michigan.

1973–74

The Aces started the 1973–74 campaign without rising senior Irvin Graves. Mac had suspended him in a disciplinary move the previous season, and no one was sure if he was coming back. The losses of Martin and John to graduation were going to hurt—despite his political appointment and schoolwork, John had averaged eight points a game; Martin had averaged ten.

The returnees were Jerry Conrad, Don Wheeler, Mike Meyerrose, and Roger Duncan, all forwards and guards. Keith Huff, who could play both forward and guard, and center Mark Helfrich were also returning. All had seen action the previous season.

The fortunes of the Aces improved when Graves returned, apologetic and eager to play after talking with George McGinnis of the Indiana Pacers, who had advised him to finish college.

From the outset it was apparent that Mac was once again in possession of more talent than he could put on the court at one time.

The Aces began the year with a convincing win over outmanned Pepperdine at Roberts, led by Jerry Conrad and Mike "Bubbles" Platt, a 6-1 guard from Kokomo Haworth High School who had turned down Butler and Wisconsin. The Aces followed with another win over hapless Roanoke, with Conrad scoring 25 as Evansville stomped the Maroons 90–79. Mac used 10 players and impressed Roanoke's coach Mel Hankinson with the Aces' depth. "You have to admire the tremendous consistency of Evansville's 10 players," he said.

The Aces extended their winning streak by thrashing Southwest Missouri State 88–66 behind Platt's 16 points.

A trip to Kentucky Wesleyan produced a narrow loss, the season's first, when Graves's last-minute shot from 18 feet fell away. Panthers coach Bob Jones said of the Aces, "The most impressive thing about them is their bench. They have a lot of help there and this early in the season that will be an advantage."

The Aces moved on to Texas for the Sun Bowl Invitational tournament. In the opening round the Aces defeated Lamar and then faced host Texas El Paso and Don Haskins in the finals. The coach who had pulled off a miracle win over Kentucky in the 1966 NCAA championship game used the same deliberate pace and suffocating defense against the Aces that he had used to tame Rupp's Wildcats—and tamed the Aces. The final score was 60–57.

The slow pace had unnerved the Aces, who preferred an up-tempo game. "Playing a team like this really makes me mad," Jeff Frey said. "You fly all the way out here, and then they play a game like this. It's like saying, 'We can't beat you in basketball, so we'll do this.'" He must have missed Haskins's signature win. It was the hallmark of his career; he was one of the best in the country at controlling the tempo of a game.

Frey himself was no slouch. The 6-7, 210-pound forward-center had been an All-State performer at Jeffersonville (Indiana) High School. Former Ace Kae Moore, an assistant coach there who had since joined Mac's staff, had steered Frey to Evansville over Indiana, Purdue, and Louisville. When Frey signed with the Aces, Mac said, "I think we have one of the five best players in the state."

Frey and the rest of the team found their own Holiday Tournament more satisfying than the road trip had been. Their first-round opponent was Kent State University. An overtime buzzer-beater thrilled the crowd of red shirts as Keith Huff intercepted a pass with five seconds to play and put up an awkward-looking hook shot that somehow found its way into the basket. The Aces won, 67–65, in overtime.

Next they faced the Long Beach State 49ers, coached by future Hall of Famer Lute Olson. Ranked ninth by the AP and twelfth by UPI, Long Beach was a serious threat to the Aces' title hopes.[19] Olson's suffocating zone defense produced a 75–67 win for the invaders from the West Coast, and they took the trophy with them to California.

The crowds had returned to Roberts, not in the numbers that had been there in the championship seasons but larger than those that had shown up in the recent past. The total attendance of 12,236 for the Holiday Tournament was well shy of the record 17,177 in 1971 but a huge improvement over the sparse 8,083 of 1971–72.

The crowd swelled as usual when rival Kentucky Wesleyan, first in the polls for College Division teams, arrived at Roberts. The stands held 11,706 as the two archenemies faced off in an atmosphere that evoked their battles of the early and mid-1970s.

The Aces didn't disappoint, knocking off the nation's top team 103–79. "We were just soundly beaten," Bob Jones said. "Evansville is better than we are right now."

The win propelled the Aces to the top of the polls, and they appeared to the press and the fans to be capable of producing yet another championship for Mac.

Jerry Conrad was optimistic. He'd been a freshman when Evansville last ruled the division, in 1971. "We're closer together than that team. There are more of us. Only six or seven guys got a lot of playing time then, whereas we have twelve who play a lot," he reasoned.

There is no denying that the Aces were deep. And their depth allowed Mac to return to the running style he loved. He had them all fit enough to play pressure defense for 40 minutes, a formula he had used with great success in the past. Why shouldn't it work again?

When a reporter asked Mac to compare the potential of the current club with the undefeated 1965 championship team, he said, "This team can do a lot of things better than that 1965 bunch. We have many more good players. That 1965 team was kind of thin. We have the strength and ability to stay with people."

But did they have the heart and soul of the 1965 team, the intangibles and the special chemistry that had produced perfection? It was still early but others seemed to think so.

After his St. Joseph's team was nipped by the Aces 82–79, coach John Weinert said, "In the eight and a half years I've been in coaching, this is the best team I've seen." Further kudos came from Indiana State's Gordon Stauffer, whose team was trounced by the Aces 107–86 at Roberts. "They're better than Purdue," he told reporters.

When Southern Illinois fell to the Aces 77–63, the Salukis' coach, Paul Lambert, declared, "They are the best bump-and-run team in basketball." Praise was pouring in as Butler came to town. The Aces were 6–1 in the ICC, and 8,586 showed up to see whether the Aces could avenge their only conference loss.

Behind Jerry Conrad, Irvin Graves, and Ed Shelby, the Aces raced out to an early lead and held a 47–28 edge at the half. When Conrad picked up his fourth foul, Jeff Frey and Roger Duncan picked up and the Aces didn't miss a beat, winning easily, 93–60. "It's awful nice to be able to substitute a Frey or a Duncan and not lose a thing," Mac crowed.

Frey was rewarded for his play with a start against Wabash and responded with a 30-point performance as the Little Generals surrendered to the Aces 109–101. That win gave Evansville the ICC title outright. It was Mac's eleventh conference crown.

But Mac had seen something that wasn't quite right. "We didn't play a bad basketball game; Wabash played well. We do, however, have to get our defense back together. We've given up too many easy ones the last few games," he said. But Snowy Simpson of Wabash was a believer, telling reporters, "Evansville plays just one way—hard and to win. I hope they win the whole (NCAA) championship."

The Aces were a sure qualifier for the new NCAA Division II tournament, as the old College Division was now called.

Maybe they were looking ahead when their eyes should have been front and center. Maybe they believed the rave reviews. Maybe they weren't as good as everyone claimed they were. Or maybe Mac's concerns about their defensive shortcomings were warranted.

The next three games on the regular season schedule had everyone searching for answers.

The Aces traveled to St. Joseph's and were blown out, 80–68. They followed that embarrassment with a loss to Southern Illinois at home, followed by a trip to Indiana State's new arena, where they delighted the Sycamores crowd by losing 73–71 when Mike Platt's last-second layup was waved off by officials.

The Aces had staggered in the home stretch. They finished at 18–8 but were running on fumes as they prepared for the NCAA Tournament.

"Frame of mind—that's what I've been working on," Mac said. "But one thing: it sure is nice to be home." He had reason to be happy. The Aces were 13–2 at Roberts for the year. And his teams had won all eight of their previous first-round NCAA tournament games played at Roberts.

They opened against Wittenberg, a team they had defeated in the opening round in 1971–72. All the stars seemed to be aligned. Then the game started. Wittenberg fell behind early, and all seemed to be going according to plan. Then the Tigers clawed back and erased a ten-point deficit. Mac ordered a slowdown as Wittenberg switched to a zone defense and brought the score to 48–47 with eleven minutes remaining.

The Aces had shot poorly, and a stall seemed a logical move to bring the Tigers out of their zone. It didn't work. Wittenberg stood patiently, watching Evansville pass the ball lazily back and forth as the minutes melted away. The crowd of 4,393 started to boo loudly, but still the Tigers refused to yield to temptation. Finally, they tied the game at 53 on an Eddie Ford shot from the corner.

Just a few scant seconds remained when Jerry Conrad put up a 22-footer—and missed.

Overtime.

The Aces' poor shooting continued in the extra period, and Wittenberg took advantage. They held on to win, 59–55, eliminating the Aces.

The Aces had shot themselves right out of it. The numbers tell the story. For the game the Aces made just 3 of 8 free throws while Wittenberg made 15 of 21. Evansville had scored just 19 points in the second half and had taken only three shots in the last 11 minutes while trying to force the Tigers out of their zone. It hadn't worked and the Aces paid dearly. "We were looking for the shot, but Wittenberg was able to meet all the requirements on defense and not leave us any opening," Mac explained.

A meaningless consolation win over Wisconsin–Green Bay closed the 1973–74 season. In the end the Aces had failed to sustain the promise they had shown during their midseason run. All the comparisons with the 1965 team proved premature and now looked to have been merely wishful thinking.

On March 19, 1974, the DC-3 bearing tail number N51071 was transferred from Joseph Fontana, operating as Fontana Air of Kingsford, Michigan, to his son, Mark Fontana, for $30,000. Mark Fontana secured a loan from Community Federal Credit Union for that amount.

A month later, on April 16, 1974, the plane was again transferred, this time to Bernie Junior of Edgewood Lane, Oshkosh, Wisconsin, for $30,000. Junior had obtained a loan from the American Bank, which now held a lien on the plane.

At the end of the 1973–74 season Wayne Boultinghouse, a former Aces player and Mac's chief assistant coach, announced he was leaving. Mac's announcement a year earlier, that he hoped Jerry Sloan would succeed him, had made his decision easy. Wayne had been on Mac's staff since 1969. He had assumed the key role as the Aces' chief recruiter and mined more than a few gems for the team. He had served as assistant athletic director and head baseball coach, in addition to his basketball duties. His willingness to work after practice to help players with their game had been selfless and had made the Aces a better team. But he wanted to be a head coach.

"I would have to assume if they're looking for a successor to Coach McCutchan, they're not looking in my direction. At least, I've never been given any indication, any encouragement in that direction," he said.

He landed at the newly established Indiana State University–Evansville, where he became head basketball coach and athletic director, positions he held until 1981 when he became vice president of development. He led the team to the NCAA Division II tournament in 1977 and compiled a 111–79 record before stepping down. In 1986 he moved across the river to Kentucky Wesleyan University as associate head basketball coach. He became head coach in 1990 and took the team to three conference championships, four NCAA Sweet Sixteen appearances, and was named Coach of the Year in 1995. He won 74 percent of his games with the Panthers before leaving in 1996 for an assistant principal position at South Spencer High School in his hometown of Rockport, Indiana, where he also coached girls' basketball.

In thirteen seasons as a head college coach, he won 240 games while losing only 124, a 66 percent winning percentage, which ranks him among the leaders in Division II with at least ten years' experience. He is a member of the Hall of Fame at the University of Southern Indiana, as the school is now known.

Boultinghouse's departure was followed by that of Kae Moore, Mac's other assistant, who took a high school coaching position in Greenburg, Indiana. Short-handed as a result of their departures, Mac began recruiting himself to replace starters Conrad and Graves and reserves Huff and Meyerrose. Once more he took to the road, but the effort produced only one real gem, after a former Ace came to his aid.

Larry Humes had coached a junior high team in Indianapolis a few years earlier and while there he'd discovered a talented youngster who had developed into a star at Arsenal Technical High School. **John Ed Washington** had received offers from Purdue, Oklahoma State, LSU, and Wyoming, among others. The 6-3 left-hander was capable of playing both forward and guard, and could shoot and play defense. He was exactly the type that Mac coveted for his guards.

As a senior John Ed had averaged 17 points and 9 rebounds to lead Tech to the city championship. Larry Humes sold John Ed on the University of Evansville. "I got him a scholarship to go there. I felt it would be a great place for him to play, and I told him about Mac and the support from the fans there," Larry recalled.[20]

John Ed's high school coach, Ernie Cline, described his star for Evansville reporters when the signing was announced in June 1974. "John Ed is a different kind of player. He can take his defensive man inside—use his size and long arms to out power him. He doesn't have Irvin Graves' speed or [all] out-shooting ability, but he is strong and maneuverable," Cline said.

John Ed's friend Rory Hennings said, "John Ed wanted the challenge of playing major college basketball. He had the biggest hands in the world and a great wing span. When he grabbed a basketball, it looked like he was holding a tennis ball."[21]

John Ed became a member of the Purple Aces upon the recommendation of one of the best ever to play there. Because freshmen were now eligible to compete at the varsity level, he would be eligible to play for the team in 1974–75.

And because several of his former players had followed Mac's lead and entered the high school coaching ranks, Mac and the Aces had recruiting help all across the area.

Former Ace Rick Smith had tipped Mac off about another player, **Tony Winburn**, a 5-8 guard from Jeffersonville, where Smith was teaching and coaching. "Tony had gone first to Indiana University–Southeast in New Albany. He wasn't happy there and when he told me, I recommended him to Mac," Rick said. "He was a great player, and I thought he would fit well in the Evansville system."[22]

Tony was the second of Jim and Edna Winburn's five sons to attend college. "He was well liked," Edna Winburn said. "On one of his birthdays, when he was still little, he got five birthday cakes."

He had been recruited by a number of schools, including Indiana, and Bob Knight had visited the Winburn home. "We liked him but we left the decision up to Tony," Edna Winburn said. "He had a girlfriend, Sheila Sanders, and the two of them planned to get married after college. Tony worked as a teller and trainee at a bank here in Jeffersonville and planned to go into banking."[23]

Winburn had been captain of both the football and basketball teams at Jeffersonville. He led the basketball team to a 58–11 record during his three varsity seasons, including a trip to the state finals in 1972. He was a natural leader and an avid pocket pool player. Tony was sensitive about his height, or lack thereof, but compensated by always being the best and most sharply dressed guy in the crowd.[24]

"Tony fit right in here," Rory Hennings said. "He and John Ed were a lot alike.

Both were down-to-earth kind of guys. [John Ed] . . . helped Tony adjust."[25]

Because he had played for Indiana University–Southeast in New Albany, Winburn would have to sit out a year before becoming eligible for the 1975–76 season.

On September 24, 1974, the DC-3 plane bearing tail number **N51071** *changed ownership yet again, when Hawkeye Airlines of Ottumwa, Iowa, bought it, along with another DC-3 and other equipment, for a total purchase price of $300,000. Union Bank and Trust Company of Ottumwa provided the loan and secured its interest with a lien. DC-3* **Number N51071** *was placed into charter service.*

1974–75

The Aces of 1974–75 dearly needed help and found it in John Ed Washington.

After starting the season with a loss to Mississippi State, which outrebounded the Aces, they struggled on the boards in their next contest against Southwest Missouri State at McDonald Arena on the SMS campus in Springfield. Mac inserted John Ed for Don Wheeler, who was plagued by a circulation problem in his left shoulder that hindered his mobility. John Ed came off the bench to contribute five baskets that helped the Aces come back from a deficit to overtake their hosts 74–64.

Mac liked what he saw, and John Ed got his first start in the home opener for a crowd of 5,023 when Southern Colorado arrived at Roberts in December. Once again John Ed proved to be a catalyst when he accounted for 13 points and 6 rebounds in the 87–62 victory.

"He picks up scraps, doesn't he? Gets one here, tips one in there, does things so quickly that they don't know what's happened," Mac told reporters in praising his freshman's hustle and desire.

When they asked John Ed about his stellar play, he replied, "College ball is a much faster game than high school, and it's got a lot of fundamentals to it. There's a lot of concentration involved, and you just can't do what you want to do." Clearly, John Ed had been paying attention to Mac's lessons and was learning quickly how to play at the collegiate level.

When the Aces went on the road to Virginia, John Ed spurred the team on to a win over Roanoke after the Aces had lost to Old Dominion. With the Aces down by a point, he intercepted a Maroons pass with forty seconds to play, John Ed found Tim Skinner and fired a pass that Tim converted to give the Aces a 99–98 win.

The Holiday Tournament saw the Aces defeat Portland and then fall to Miami of Ohio in the title tilt. A subsequent loss to Indiana State, followed by a win over Kentucky Wesleyan, and then two straight losses to Southern Illinois and Butler at Roberts had Mac scratching his head. His wocs seemed to have accelerated the retreat of his thinning hairline.

"Up to now, I've stuck up for them and said they would be a good team," Mac said after the Butler loss. "But it's a little hard to keep that attitude after their performance Saturday. It just seems that we don't have what it takes to get together and go."

Mac had seen enough basketball to recognize when a team had the right mix of talent and chemistry to make it go, and he knew after the Butler loss that this edition of his Aces didn't possess the right formula.

He was, of course, right. The Aces struggled all season and would finish with three straight losses, first to Butler in overtime, then to Indiana Central and Southern Illinois with uninspired play, even though SIU was headed to the NIT.

The Aces' 13–13 record would bring them no postseason bid. For the second time in three years Evansville would not be appearing at the NCAA championship.

"I'm glad to get this one over with," Mac sighed. "Now it's time to go hunting."

Though the .500 season was a disappointment, it had produced one positive note. John Ed Washington had shown his coach he could play at the collegiate level. He had progressed and matured as he saw action in all 26 games. He finished with a scoring average of nine points per game and recorded 47 assists. But the intangibles distinguished his play. He constantly hustled and harassed players on defense and brought some spark to a listless offense when needed.

John Ed would be back next season, a year older and with a year's experience behind him.

1975–76

Mac and Gary Bliss, the new assistant coach who had joined the Aces in July from Snow College, a two-year school in Utah, were out on the hunt.

Because Bliss was a licensed pilot they could extend their range. While Mac was driving the back roads and highways of Indiana, Kentucky, and Illinois, Evansville's usual recruiting grounds, Bliss could wing his way over a larger area in pursuit of recruits. Both of them scoured the high school and junior college landscape in search of a big man.

It was Mac's first priority and he found what he was looking for in New Albany, Indiana. **Steve Miller** was a 6-8 product of New Albany High School, where he had led his team to a sectional title in 1975. He was tall, athletic, and mobile. He had demonstrated an ability to block and alter shots. He had set a school record by blocking 53 shots as a senior while averaging 16 points and 15 rebounds per game. Miller, whose father owned the New Albany newspaper, had chosen Evansville over Wake Forest, Clemson, Ball State, Virginia Tech, and Kent State.

Mac and Thornton Patberg, now Evansville's vice president for student affairs, had gone to see Miller play in the first round of the Seymour Regional tournament. Then Pat spoke with his dad, Don, extolling the virtues of attending Evansville while Mac chatted with New Albany's athletic director, Stan Sajko, hoping to gain his support in securing a commitment from Steve.

Patberg and Mac made an impression on the senior Millers as well as on Steve, who had played at Evansville during his high school career and was familiar with the city. In May the university announced his signing. "We feel that Steve can help us both inside and outside," said Mac.

New Albany assistant coach Lou Jensen told Evansville reporters and fans about their latest catch: "Steve can play forward or guard, is a good leaper, has good hands, and he's intelligent. He's a good team player too, and can take the ball down the floor." To hear Jensen tell it, the red shirts could expect to be cheering for a combination of Larry Humes, Jerry Sloan, and Don Buse, all wrapped up in one 6-8, 18-year-old body.

Still, Miller was, without question, a great addition to the team. He was tall, rangy, and could jump—and he could handle the ball. He would be a versatile player and would be an immediate help to the Aces as he would be eligible in the fall.

A late addition to the recruiting class of 1975 had a name that was very familiar to Aces fans, one that reminded them of the days when the Aces were winning consistently. He was Scott Doerner, son of Aces legend Gus Doerner. Scott, who was 6-2, had played forward at Evansville North as a senior and had averaged 12 points per game. "I think Scott's a late bloomer," said Mac, who was planning to move him to guard in college. "I expect him to mature and grow. He makes things happen. He gets the offense going, and he's a good rebounder."

But Miller and Doerner alone could not help Mac and Bliss avoid another lackluster campaign. They turned their attention to junior college players and to those collegians looking for a new home. Mike Smith, a star at Alameda (California) Junior College, was a late find, and he would prove to be a valuable addition to the team.

But the junior college transfer often is someone who landed at a two-year school because of problems -- usually poor attitude, poor grades, or both. These players may be talented on the court, but their value must be measured against their baggage.

Bliss, a former junior college coach, should have known that. Yet he would cast an increasingly wide net in the following year to bring in an inordinately large number of "Juco" players and transfers. Mike Smith would be a success, but Bliss's recruiting strategy would cause other vexing problems.

Evansville quickly inked three more recruits. Two were guards who had played juco ball in California. They had grown up in Oakland, California, a poor city that was troubled by gang-related violence. Evansville was in a different world.

Bryan Taylor, from Tell City, Indiana, was transferring from the University of Louisville. Transfers from four-year institutions, in contrast to those from juco programs, had consistently proved to be valuable assets for Mac. Taylor had starred at Tell City, where he led the Marksmen to a 20–4 record as a high school junior in 1973–74 and a 21–4 mark as a senior. As a junior who had averaged 17.5 points per game, he had been named to the first team all-area squad of the *Evansville Sunday Courier & Press*. He had upped his average to 22 points per game in his senior season, when he was again a first-team all-conference selection and was named player of the year by the *Courier & Press* for 1974–75. During his career at Tell City he had scored 1,206 points.

Taylor, 6-5 and 210 pounds, had chosen Louisville from a host of major colleges seeking his services. But after only one season he had decided Louisville wasn't the place to be. Fortunately for Mac, his high school girlfriend was a nursing student at Evansville. Jennifer Kuster had spotted Bryan Taylor when they were in the seventh grade, and she "wondered where the dreamy boy had been hiding." Their romance blossomed in high school. He was a basketball star, and she was a pert and pretty cheerleader. Just like in the storybooks.

Shortly after he decided to join Jennifer at Evansville, the two got engaged. Marriage would wait until after graduation, but at least now they were together.[26] He would have to sit out one basketball season, but he would be eligible to play as an Ace in 1976–77.

As returning Aces, Mike "Bubbles" Platt and Jim Frey provided some semblance of stability, and both performed well in the early going against North Dakota State in the opening win of the 1975–76 season, which the Aces followed with a romp over Southwest Missouri State. On a trip to the East Coast the Aces lost to Dave Gavitt's Providence Friars, but Frey racked up 30 points.[27] The Aces completed the trip east by swamping Assumption College.

The Aces had six Division I schools on their schedule for December. Because of the drop in attendance at Roberts, Bob Hudson had beefed up the schedule, hoping to bring the fans back. The 1974–75 season had seen attendance at Roberts plummet to an average of only 4,505 per game, the lowest since the opening season in 1956–57.

But for a number of reasons Hudson was continuing to find it increasingly difficult to find teams willing to make the trip to Evansville. The Aces' reputation as giant killers at Roberts was one. The advent of many new conferences was another. The conferences required teams to play on each other's home court, leaving little room on the schedule for nonconference games.

The other reason for the declining attendance was the competition supplied by the new college in town. Indiana State University–Evansville had established a new campus in the city in 1965. It too played Division II basketball, and with lower tuition costs and less rigorous admissions standards, it had siphoned off much of the local talent that had formerly gone to Evansville.

But the Aces had a winning tradition and a long-term love affair with the city in their favor. All they needed to do was to return to their winning ways and the community would embrace them.

Mike Platt would have his greatest game, as Mac described it, when the Aces turned back Division I Mississippi State 85–73 behind Mike's 26 points at Roberts.

John Ed Washington told reporters after the game about the reception he, as an African American, had received on the court from the visitors.

"There were a lot of people got called a lot of names out there. Usually when they start talking like that, I don't say anything back, I just keep my mouth shut. But I was doing some talking out there tonight myself," he acknowledged. Clearly, Mississippi State's racial attitudes were little better than they'd been back in 1956 when the MSU coach had pulled his team out of the inaugural Holiday Tournament rather than have his players mix it up with a team that fielded black players.

Both John Ed and Steve Miller were getting plenty of playing time. The Aces had committed thirty-one fouls against Mississippi State. When Frey picked up his fifth, Miller replaced him. Steve responded with two tip-ins and a key jump ball, and he controlled the boards, which opened Mac's eyes to Miller's defensive capabilities.

"I don't consider it a gamble at all . . . because he's demonstrated that if we need defense and rebounding, we can go with him," Mac said.

Steve's play against Mississippi State earned him a promotion to the travel squad when the Aces, 4–1, met Ohio State. The game ended in controversy, but John Ed Washington played especially well. He had key baskets to lead the Aces back from a late deficit, and he stole a Buckeye pass that he converted for a layup to cut the Buckeyes' lead to just one point with 10 seconds left.

After a rebound by Scott Johnson of an errant Ohio State shot, John Ed was knocked to the floor. The clock showed 7 seconds remaining when the referee's whistle signaled a foul. The clock operator ignored the whistle and allowed the last seconds to tick away. The Aces never got the chance to shoot the free throws and lost, 79–78. Mac confronted the referee, to no avail. "He said he heard the horn before he saw the foul," Mac told reporters. It was no use arguing—it wouldn't change a thing.

The Aces next met the University of Pittsburgh at the Civic Arena in the Steel City and, though again facing foul trouble, managed to hold on for a 62–61 win over the Panthers. John Ed Washington had his best game, nailing 17 points and 7 rebounds to lead the Aces. He had tallied 19 against Ohio State, and his play off the bench was a great pick-me-up for the Aces.

The Holiday tourney drew more than 6,900 as the Aces met Mercer College. The game was tight throughout. With Evansville trailing by one, John Ed Washington put up a shot from the base line that bounced away. Frey rebounded the miss and fired it out to Platt, whose 20-footer at the buzzer fell just short.

The consolation match with Austin Peay produced another loss, putting Evansville at 5–4.

When Mac replaced the unproductive Don Wheeler with Steve Miller, the offense immediately improved. Steve's two late baskets produced a win over Southern Illinois, and against DePauw he grabbed 12 rebounds and scored 9 points in an Aces victory. "Actually, playing this much is really a surprise," Miller said. "I never anticipated I'd play, but Coach just gave me the breaks to prove myself."

John Ed Washington had returned to the starting lineup against St. Joseph's—
he'd been in and out as a starter early in the season. The 6-3 sophomore scored
16 of UE's last 22 points to lead the Aces to a 77–71 win. Against Kentucky
Wesleyan he tallied 17 points and grabbed 14 boards in an Aces win.

Mike Smith, the Bliss recruit from Alameda Junior College, paced the Aces as
the season wound to a close. He played well against Valparaiso, St. Joseph's, and
Butler, all Evansville wins. And in beating Butler the Aces clinched a share of the
ICC title in front of 6,613 fans.

"Smith was 6-6 and he played the point," Mike Platt said. "He was able to
jump like a gazelle. He could reach the top of the box above the rim. He was a
jumping jack that could run like crazy, and he made everything easy for me. The
other teams had to concentrate on him, and that left me wide open."[28]

Platt, Washington, Miller, and Smith all were playing well, and the results
reflected the improvement. As the wins mounted and the season neared its end,
fans had renewed hopes for postseason play. Then the Aces went on the road
and dropped a game to Indiana State 87–79, with Mac trying a platoon system
that failed.

Even so, the Aces secured an invite to the NCAA Tournament and were placed
in the Great Lakes Regional. They would meet Wright State University of Dayton, Ohio, in the opener. The Raiders used a 2-3 zone to try to stymie the Aces'
offense, and the plan worked as the two teams stayed even through most of the
game.

In the end Evansville pulled away as Jeff Frey, Mike Platt, and John Ed Washington hit key buckets to give the Aces an 85–73 win. The victory put them in the
regional final against Eastern Illinois, which came in riding a 13-game winning
streak.

"We fell behind early by about 15 points and spent the rest of the game trying
to catch up," Mike Platt said.[29]

When Jeff Frey and Mike Platt got untracked in the second half, the Aces drew
even at 67 with 4:24 to go. The Aces trailed by only a single point with seven seconds to play. Then Eastern Illinois missed a free throw, and John Ed Washington
grabbed the rebound and quickly called a time-out.

It was a smart move by John Ed, but there was just one problem. Evansville
had exhausted its allotted time-outs, and John Ed's error caused a technical foul,
giving EIU two free throws and possession.

It was all over. The final score was 75–73.

The season had produced a 20–9 record and another NCAA appearance but in the end seemed to have been a disappointment if measured by attendance. The Aces had drawn only 73,222 at home, up from the previous season, when just 63,066 had shown up, but far below expectations. The season ticket price had gone to $35 the year before, but that wouldn't explain it. Fans love winners and not even the memories of the good old days, when national titles were an expectation, could rekindle interest in the most recent editions of the Aces.

The unbeaten season a decade before had produced more than twice as many fans—149,713. Back then the Aces were riding a string of winners and were playing the likes of Iowa, Northwestern, Notre Dame, and LSU at Roberts. No such name opponents were making the trek to Evansville anymore.

"I sold 3,000 season tickets this year," Bob Hudson said. "I hate to admit it but 2,000 didn't show up when we played Wabash. I don't want to mention names but that happened when we played two other teams too."

Wabash wasn't Notre Dame, not even close. The lack of marquee names, the proliferation of conference affiliations by teams seeking the automatic NCAA Division I bid that was awarded to a conference champion, the establishment of new and modern arenas, and a competing basketball program in Evansville had all contributed to the decline. And since the 1971 season the performance by the Aces had been, with the exception of the 1975–76 season, less than inspiring.

There was also constant talk about the Aces' joining the exodus of Division II schools to the Division I level. This produced much debate among residents and fans. Was it better to be a big fish in Division II or should the Aces move up? It was a question that the press in Evansville kept posing, and sports columnists were decidedly in favor of the move.

Wallace Graves, who had arrived in Evansville to become president of the University of Evansville in 1967, was among those in favor of the move. His opinion carried substantial weight, and at the end of the 1975–76 season the move seemed to be inevitable, if not universally popular.

The declining attendance at the NCAA Division II tournament had led the organization, always in search of more revenue, to announce that it would be moving the finals from Evansville to Springfield, Massachusetts, in 1977. Attendance at the finals at Roberts had slipped dramatically, from a high of 36,084 in 1965, when the Aces repeated as champions, to just 8,448.

The absence of the Aces from the finals had been a factor in the decline. Since the 1971 championship season the Aces had twice failed to make the tournament field, and on the three occasions when they did get in, they had failed to advance past the regionals. During that time the Aces had faced 56 Division I schools and defeated only 23. Of those wins, 17 came at Roberts.

The dismal showing caused many to question the move up to the Division I level. College basketball now had 59 conferences, all requiring that the teams play each other on their home courts, which left Evansville with the prospect that only lower-level Division I opponents would be willing to take the money to appear at Roberts and risk losing to the Aces with no chance for revenge.

Further, the NCAA had passed a rule requiring that the Division I schools play at least 75 percent of their games against other Division I opponents. The move reduced the number of dates that the Aces could fill with other contests that fans would pay to see.

Butler, Indiana State, and Southern Illinois all had already moved up to Division I from Division II which the former College Division was now called. Defections from the ICC also had created problems when Wabash became the latest school to leave the conference.

Graves believed the move to Division I was a prudent one for the Aces. "This is not an affair of the heart," he said. "We have looked at the costs around the country [to field a Division I program]. We think we've given it a fair look."

Thornton Patberg recalled that "a faculty committee had been formed to study the move. It was comprised of the athletic director, an alumni representative, three faculty members, and I was also on it. President Graves was the driving force behind it, and after much discussion we decided to make the move after the 1976–77 season. There was only one dissenting vote."[30]

Graves was convinced that the move would boost attendance. He had seen the program win the championship in 1971. He'd also seen the decline in attendance since that season and felt that something needed to be done.

"After Indiana State had established a branch campus here, I decided I needed to do something to differentiate between the two schools. I knew you couldn't have two schools in the same area offering the same programs at the same prices. A private institution needs to act like a private school," he said. "Basketball was also coming on strong at the Indiana State–Evansville school, and we couldn't keep dividing the Division II audience between us. There was no future in that. The basketball program here was carrying all the other sports, and we needed it to be successful.

"I believe the decision to make the move was a popular one. I know some felt uneasy about it and that there was some trepidation, but it wasn't communicated to me."[31] Bob Hudson believed the move would add about $17,000 a year to the operating costs of the program. The additional expenses would come from increases in recruiting costs and from adding another assistant coach to the staff.

Travel costs, according to Hudson, might actually decline. He thought that using a charter airline service, instead of commercial flights, which Mac preferred, might reduce that expense.

"We had started using a charter carrier in 1975–76 that Bob Hudson had found through his contacts at other Indiana schools," Mike Platt said. "It was a company called Indiana Air out of Indianapolis. We flew for the games that were two hours or more away by car. Mac wanted to make sure we didn't miss much class time. We had flown to Georgia and to other games with them. I remember once, when we were still on the tarmac after a game at St. Joseph's, we had been hit by another plane. It was pretty scary."[32]

On March 15, 1976, Hawkeye Airlines Inc., sold the DC-3 bearing tail number N51071 to National Jet Services Inc., of Indianapolis, Indiana. The charter air company added the aircraft to its fleet, which provided service for a number of colleges and universities in Indiana. The plane, now thirty-one years old, would have its fuselage repainted. When the job was completed, DC-3 N51071 would bear the name of Indiana Air.

In April, Evansville decided to try to form a new league along with Valparaiso, Xavier, Butler, and Loyola of Chicago. They hoped to add DePaul, Dayton, and Detroit. But when the latter three declined to join and Loyola backed out, the plan fell apart.

The Aces' future plans were still in a state of confusion as the 1976–77 season began.

1976–77

In preparing for the new season, Mac found his recruiting efforts squeezed by the limits of the scholarship program. The Aces had only one spot available under the NCAA scholarship rules.

One player left the basketball program, forfeiting his scholarship, and Scott Doerner, who had been ill, decided to forgo basketball for baseball, opening one more slot. He'd continue with the team as a student assistant coach.

Keith Moon, a 6-8 center from Kettering, Ohio, was the first new recruit to decide to join the Aces. He had been the outstanding player during the summer of 1976 at the fabled Five Star Camp in Pennsylvania's Pocono Mountains that attracted the nation's best players.

He had starred at Fairmount West High School, where he had led his team to a 40–20 mark over three years. Moon had earned all-conference honors as a senior when he averaged 15 points and 15 rebounds per game. He had been named to the Dayton All-Stars and Midwestern All-Star team and had gained honorable mention All-America status as a senior. He had been sought by Oral Roberts, Jacksonville, the Virginia Military Institute, and Bentley but decided to become a member of the Aces.

Tall, swarthy, and possessed of an infectious smile and a head of dark curly hair, Keith planned to become a coach. "He was a really good kid with a lot of potential," Mike Platt said.[33]

A junior college transfer with a lot of promise on and off the court was **Kevin Kingston,** the son of Evansville alumnus Donald Kingston. Kevin had starred at Eldorado, averaging 15 points and 7 rebounds as a senior, before attending John A. Logan College in Carterville, Illinois, where he had earned his associate's degree. Bob Brown, who coached Kevin at Eldorado, said, "He was just a great young man. He was the kind of guy that if you were hanging off a cliff, you'd want him on top holding the rope."[34]

"He was a diamond in the rough," Mike Platt said. "You could see that he was going to be real good."[35]

The roster contained all five starters from the previous season, plus transfers with good numbers, at least on the basketball court. And all the transfers who had arrived in the fall of 1975, including Bryan Taylor, would be eligible to play.

But when the 1976–77 team assembled at Carson Center in September, two of Bliss's Oakland recruits were nowhere to be found. They had arrived for the spring 1976 semester and simply failed to return to school.

Bliss's emphasis on recruiting transfers and refugees from junior college programs would prove to be a disaster as more of his recruits headed for the door. Some never lasted long enough to suit up for a game. Academic and disciplinary problems were the main reasons for the exodus; two left for personal reasons. Another failed the two-mile run.

The cruelest blow of all came in November on the eve of the opener, when Mike Smith, the leading returning scorer, was declared academically ineligible.

Graceful as a gazelle, athletic, and strong, he had flunked gymnastics. Go figure.

Then another one of the juco recruits flunked out.

The loss of seven talented players severely hampered the Aces. In all the years Mac had been at Evansville, he had never had such problems, which were directly traceable to Bliss and his recruitment of players with less-than-desirable academic performance or unfortunate disciplinary records that he had chosen to ignore. These were costly mistakes and seriously damaged the Aces' chances before they ever played a single game.

Before Bliss arrived in 1975, Mac had signed only two junior college players, both in 1970. Neither had made the team. In all the years Mac had been at Evansville, only two juco transfers had ever seen any game action, and neither had seen much.

In the past, almost all the transfers Mac had welcomed, including Jerry Sloan, had been products of the familiar tristate area, where Mac had mined talent for years. Others had been vetted by former McCutchan players now in the coaching ranks. Few produced any problems and many flourished under Mac.

Now the aggressive Bliss approach had wrought a disaster. The Aces were crippled.

"The loss of Mike Smith before the first game really hurt us. He was the prototypical McCutchan player—a 6-6 guard who could jump, drive, and was fast as lightning," Mike Platt said. "He was our leading scorer coming back and very talented. Somehow he managed to fail gymnastics and was ineligible. It all went downhill from there."[36]

Tony Winburn began to see more playing time. Small, quick, and feisty, he would become a crowd favorite.

"I started a group of students in the stands that all sat together and we'd chant 'Tony, Tony' when he was on the bench. Soon the rest of the crowd in our section picked it up, and invariably Tony would come in and play with high energy and ignite a run," Rory Hennings said.[37]

Mac had to have been more than a little concerned, not just about the impact on the season of losing so many players but about the lower recruiting standards that had brought nothing but problems to his team. All this turmoil was swirling around him as he was closing in on 500 wins and his 31st season at Evansville.

He got his 500th win in the very first game of the 1976–77 season. The Aces turned back an outmanned North Dakota State squad with Mike Platt and Jeff Frey leading the way. Bryan Taylor saw his first action at forward and tallied 10 points as the Aces presented Mac with his milestone victory, 89–82.

Dr. Charles Klamer, a loyal booster, presented Mac with a silver tray. He had joined the ranks of college coaches who had reached an elusive and exclusive level, and he had done it while staying at the same school where he began coaching in 1946.

Arad McCutchan now was in the select company of John Wooden, Phog Allen, Henry Iba, Cam Henderson, Adolph Rupp, Tony Hinkle, and others. Mac had done it the right way and could take great pride in his achievement. He'd never sacrificed academics for athletics. He'd developed scores of coaches from his players, and he had reaped the benefits when they, in turn, sent their players to him.

Yet, here he was, in his thirty-first season, with problems all around him. In fact, he had been thinking about retirement for some time. He had even made his thoughts public a few years earlier when he had told reporters he wanted to have Jerry Sloan replace him. No one ever mentioned an actual retirement date, although back in March 1972 Mac had said he would retire after the 1976–77 season. And with the headaches that he faced this season, he was giving retirement more thought with each passing day. He had turned 63 on July 4.

"We had a pretty good team when we started. We had a lot of basketball talent and four starters returning," Mike Platt said. "But it all changed pretty fast when we started to lose a lot of players that Bliss had brought in."[38]

Mac was still coaching the way he had always coached. "We had drills that we repeated in practice every day on passing and the inbounds plays under our own basket. We practiced the jump ball plays that would produce easy baskets," Platt said.[39] The emphasis on fundamentals and the little things that make a big difference were still part of the McCutchan coaching strategy.

The Aces still wore long multicolored robes, and their jerseys for road trips were still orange.

"He liked us to wear white sneakers because the black ones would draw attention to our feet, and we'd get fewer traveling calls if our feet were less noticeable," Platt said. "Mac could still make in-game adjustments, and his pregame preparation was always meticulous, and he used charts to figure out each opponent's weakness and how to best exploit them."[40]

Mac still applied all the same principles that he had used to accumulate five national titles and more than 500 wins. But the problems he faced this season were a new experience for him and may have hastened his decision to retire.

Adding to those problems and influencing his decision was the fact that since Texas Western's dramatic win over lily-white Kentucky in 1966 the schools in the south had begun accepting black players. That closed a lucrative recruiting door for Evansville which had profited handsomely from the segregation that had foreclosed opportunities for blacks to play at schools in the old south. Mac and Evansville had mined that vein for years and now it had all but played out. Mac had also been the benefactor of an extensive "farm system" of his former players who had entered the high school coaching ranks and would send their best players to him. Through the years Mac had restocked he larder with prize recruits sent his way by his former players. Many of them were now moving on or retiring from coaching and that seemingly endless well of talent was drying up too.

Winning was getting harder and harder at Evansville and there was no sign that it would be any easier at the Division I level where winning is all that really matters.

Following their opening win, the Aces lost successive games to Southwest Missouri State and Ohio State. A win over Western Kentucky on the road saw Frey can 24 points to lead the team.

The lack of big men plagued the Aces. Only two remained on the roster. Then one left school after a four-point game against Xavier that the Aces lost, and he didn't come back. With his departure Mac added Keith Moon to the travel squad as the team boarded a DC-3 operated by Indiana Air for the trip to Georgia. The Aces followed a win in Georgia over Mercer with a two-point loss to the University of Georgia in Athens.

Despite their depleted roster, the Aces remained the top choice of the ICC coaches to win the crown when conference play began. The first ICC game was at Roberts against Valparaiso in January on an evening designated as Arad McCutchan Night. The latest in a series of such celebratory events (others had been held in 1951 and 1965) produced the usual shower of gifts from grateful fans. Mac was joined by his wife, Virginia, his son, Allen, and their daughters, Marilyn and Jean. Some of Mac's former players were also on hand to honor their coach.

The crowd of 4,680 was stunned when Mac sprung this announcement: "I will work at the University of Evansville next year, but I will not work as a basketball coach." Despite his earlier public ruminations about retiring, the news went through Roberts Stadium like a thunderbolt.

Mac had told UE President Graves of his decision a few days earlier. "I believe he made [his decision] because he'd had a brilliant career here and the move up to Division I just set the stage for his retirement," Thornton Patberg said.[41] Jim Byers, the UE football coach at the time, agreed. "Mac would never have been fired. I think it was a combination of things that led to his decision," Byers said. "He'd been there a long time, and his age was a factor. I also think he felt the decision to make the move to Division I gave him an easy way to step down."[42]

After Mike Platt led the Aces with 24 points over Valpo, 67–61, Mac discussed his reasons for stepping down, telling reporters, "Next year we're entering Division I, which is a good time to start a new regime. There's the possibility of somebody being hired, and an early hiring will give him a head start on recruiting."

"He had thought about it for a while," Mac's son Allen said. "It was a combination of things, I think. The move to Division I and his age were the main reasons."[43]

Mac had loudly, clearly, and publicly expressed his preference that Jerry Sloan succeed him as coach. Sloan, still a member of the Chicago Bulls but sidelined with bad knees, had met with Patberg at his request the same day Mac had told Graves of his decision. The exploratory talk had gone well.[44] It seemed like naming Sloan was only a formality, but Jerry had returned to Chicago without making a commitment.

When the Aces lost to Indiana Central, a Division II school, questions about the sanity of the move to Division I began to surface once more. If the Aces couldn't beat a lowly Division II school, how could they hope to compete at the next higher level? The answer, at least for many, was with Jerry Sloan at the helm.

Then the Aces got bad news when Scott Johnson went down with a bad knee and the remaining big man, a reserve forward, left the program.

More bad breaks followed.

"When Jeff Frey broke his ankle, it was pretty much a killer blow for us," Mike Platt said.[45]

Attendance continued to spiral downward. Only 4,114 were on hand to see the Aces go up against long-time rival Kentucky Wesleyan, a game that had drawn overflow crowds in the past. A Panther win did nothing to ameliorate the situation.

During the next game, against DePauw in February 1977, John Ed Washington poured in 31 points for an Aces victory, but only 2,788 were there to witness his best effort as an Ace.

That evening *Evansville Press* sports editor Al Dunning broke the story that Jerry Sloan had decided to become the new Aces coach. An announcement by Graves that accompanied the front-page story informed fans that Sloan had accepted a four-year contract to revive the flagging fortunes of the Aces.

Graves welcomed the decision by Sloan to replace McCutchan and restore the "unique and marvelous basketball program Coach McCutchan has built here, and move it on to a new and higher level. Mac's greatest hope was that Jerry Sloan would come back to replace him."

"I had been on a trip to Chicago earlier that year and while there I looked Sloan up," Graves said. "He was still with the Bulls, and I didn't think he would be interested. I met with him and I . . . told him if he decided to come back he'd be welcomed. When we got Jerry to come down, after Mac's decision, we offered him the job. He accepted and immediately went off to a basketball camp to try to recruit a player that was there. There was elation and disbelief that he'd accepted. The euphoria lasted less than a week."[46]

Jim Byers was in the meeting when Sloan was offered the job. "I think his loyalty to Mac influenced his decision," Byers said. "He accepted it, and we were all pleased. Only Sloan and Wayne Boultinghouse had ever been considered. [Jerry] was a popular player here, and the news that he was coming back was welcomed throughout the community. It was a huge story here." The icing on the cake was that Jerry had talked to Boultinghouse, and he had agreed to become Sloan's assistant.[47]

Jubilation was still warming the hearts of Aces fans when Byers got a call from the newly-hired Sloan. "He said he was coming down to Evansville and needed to talk with me," said Byers. He then called Graves to let him know that something was afoot.[48] Sloan also called Thornton Patberg, saying he wanted to talk to him, too. "I went over to see President Graves in his office," Patberg said. "I told him, 'I think Jerry is going to resign.'"[49]

Patberg's intuition was right. The meeting wasn't very long. "When he got to my office he said, 'I have to renege,'" Graves recalled. "He said that when he'd decided to go to Illinois [out of high school], he'd gotten there and soon had a funny feeling in his stomach that told him he'd made a mistake. He told us he now had gotten that same funny feeling again and was going to resign.

"I asked him not to do anything until I got back from a business trip to New Orleans. While I was in New Orleans, he released the news to the press from his home in McLeansboro. He never gave a reason, publicly, for his decision."[50]

Sloan did make a statement of sorts to Bill Fluty of the *Courier,* who tracked him down at home. "I made a mistake going there in the first place," Sloan said. "Some personal problems developed that I wasn't aware of when I first took the job. I don't want to say anymore about it. People will just have to speculate."

But those closest to the decision cite several factors.

"There was a big difference between what we could pay and what he was making in the Bulls' front office job," Graves said. Sloan's bad knees had ended his career, and he had become a vice president in the Bulls organization. "His wife wasn't crazy about the big cut in pay he'd be taking."[51]

Also, during his one recruiting stop, Sloan had seen immediately that he would have a huge problem competing against the larger, better-known schools for top-level talent, according to Patberg, Byers, Graves, and Boultinghouse.[52]

"He just got cold feet and backed out on us," Graves said.

Jerry Sloan, who had a history of vacillating when it came to important decisions, had waffled once again. His reign as Mac's successor had lasted less than one week.

The man many saw as the savior of the program—the coach who would lead the Aces back to glory in Division I play—decided, instead, to save himself. And his jilting of his alma mater left the University of Evansville with huge shoes to fill. Whoever agreed to take the job would find replacing not one but two Evansville legends to be quite a challenge.[53] But the university was going to have to find someone, and there wasn't a lot of time.

The season still had one month to go as resumes from coaches all over the country began arriving in athletic director Jim Byers's office.

The Aces struggled home but managed to share conference honors with Butler at 7–2. Then they lost a game to Southern Illinois and followed with a win over archrival Kentucky Wesleyan before the season finale against Larry Bird and Indiana State (Terre Haute), now a Division I school and seeking its first NCAA bid.

The appearance of the Sycamores at Roberts with the high-scoring Bird coincided with the final regular season game for Arad McCutchan as coach at Evansville. The farewell for Mac was attended by 11,336 grateful fans clad mostly in red in tribute to their beloved coach.

Although the Aces held Bird, who had been averaging 32 points per game, to just 8-for-23 from the field, it wasn't enough to send Mac off with a win. The Sycamores prevailed, 78–63.

"It was a disappointing season for us. We'd hope to capitalize on our strong finish last season, but the loss of so many players just killed us," Platt said. "Mac never changed, though. He never showed any frustration or anger. We just kept going with what we had."[54]

Arad McCutchan had arrived in Evansville in 1946 and during his thirty-one seasons as head coach had captured five national titles. His coaching success would land him in the Naismith Memorial College Basketball Hall of Fame, where he became the first small college coach to be so honored. He had won 513 games at Evansville and lost 314, a winning percentage of 62.2.

While his accomplishments as a coach were extraordinary, his success on the hardwood year after year brought another, and unique gift to a city that had long been searching for its identity. Evansville had found in its Purple Aces a pride and honor that was its alone. And in basketball-obsessed Indiana, being linked with a successful basketball program was about as much pride and honor as any city could hope for. It was a perfect relationship that had grown into a long-term love affair that had no equal anywhere.

As former Ace Russ Grieger once wrote, "The passion that Evansville had for its Aces was deep and abiding."[55] It had survived a few bad seasons and flourished with the many winning campaigns. Basketball season took precedence over all else. It was a time to be proud, to be loud, to be wearing red, and to be at Roberts Stadium to cheer on the Aces.

But the McCutchan era was over. A move up to Division I was only months away, and the university needed a coach.

It would take a very special person.

(Endnotes)
1   Rick Coffey, telephone interview by author, May 26, 2011.
2   Don Buse, telephone interview by author, May 28, 2011.
3   Al Dunning, "Aces Win One, Lose One," *Evansville Press*, December 16, 1971, UE scrapbook.
4   Pete Swanson, "Utah State Squeaks Past Aces," n.d., UE scrapbook.
5   Pete Swanson, "Aces Chop Down Little Giants," January 9, 1972, UE scrapbook.
6   David Rutter, "St. Louis Strikes Early to Flatten Aces," January 21, 1972, UE scrapbook.

7   Bill Robertson, "Buse Bombards Bears," *Evansville Press,* January 27, 1972.

8   "Sophs Star as Aces Rip St. Joe's for ICC Title," n.d., UE scrapbook.

9   Coffey interview. George Gervin played just two years at Eastern Michigan before leaving for the professional ranks, where he became a perennial All-Star in the NBA. He played in the NBA until 1985, mostly with the San Antonio Spurs, and became one of the league's best performers. He was inducted into the Naismith Memorial Basketball Hall of Fame in 1996.

10   Buse interview.

11   David Rutter, "Eastern Michigan Erases Aces Defending Champs," n.d., UE scrapbook.

12   Coffey interview.

13   "Don Buse," Basketball-reference.com, n.d., www.basketball-reference.com/players/b/busedo01.html.

14   Buse interview.

15   Coffey interview.

16   For this quote from Mac, and others in this chapter that are attributed to no other source, the reader may assume that they come from articles in the *Evansville Courier* and *Evansville Press,* the two local papers at the time. Those articles may be found in the collection of bound scrapbooks kept by Bob Hudson and now housed in the university archives and/or the Bussing manuscript. Bill Bussing graciously made his lengthy manuscript available to me, and I have relied on it for some information, especially attendance figures. The detailed manuscript contains no footnotes, but when I interviewed Bussing in February 2011, he identified his sources as the *Evansville Courier, Evansville Press,* and the combined Sunday edition, the *Courier & Press.* Bussing's manuscript usually makes no distinction between the papers, but the direct quotes are from one daily or the other or the Sunday combined paper and appear in the Bussing manuscript in quotation marks. Bussing also had access to Hudson's scrapbooks. My research assistant and I also used the scrapbooks. Many of the articles do not identify which paper they are from, much less the date and page, but I (and Bussing) assume they are from the *Courier*, *Press,* or Sunday *Courier & Press.*

17   He would later seek political office again and would be successful.

18   Bill Raftery would coach the Pirates until 1981. He led the Pirates to seven consecutive winning seasons and a record of 151–144. His teams made four appearances in the East Coast Athletic Conference Tournament, and he twice

led Seton Hall to the National Invitation Tournament. He retired in 1981 and began a career as a color analyst for ESPN and CBS, where he remains to date. He is consistently regarded as one of the most popular analysts in the game and is one of my best friends. (Full disclosure forces me to admit he paid me to write that.)

19   Olson would go on to win more than seven hundred games at Long Beach State, Iowa. and during his lengthy tenure at Arizona, where he captured the national championship in 1997. He took the Wildcats to the Final Four on four occasions and made twenty-two consecutive NCAA appearances. He was elected to the Naismith Memorial Basketball Hall of Fame in 2002 ("Lute Olson Biography," n.d., www.coachluteolson.com).

20   Larry Humes, telephone interview by author, April 22, 2011.

21   Rory Hennings, telephone interview by author, February 17, 2011.

22   Rick Smith, telephone interview by author, May 2, 2011, and several follow-up conversations.

23   Edna Winburn, telephone interview by author, July 21, 2011.

24   *University of Evansville 1977–78 Media Guide*, courtesy UE Sports Information Office.

25   Hennings interview.

26   Rich Davis, "Three Women Shared Bond That Went Beyond Crash," *Evansville Courier*, December 13, 1997, A-1.

27   Gavitt is best known as the man who conceived the Big East Conference, which evolved into one of the nation's strongest basketball conferences.

28   Mike Platt, telephone interviews by author, June 11 and 25, 2011.

29   Platt interview.

30   Thornton Patberg, telephone interview by author, January 29, 2011.

31   Wallace Graves, telephone interview by author, January 27, 2011.

32   Platt interview.

33   *University of Evansville 1977–78 Media Guide*; Platt interview.

34   Rich Davis, "The Night It Rained Tears," *Evansville Courier & Press*, December 9, 2007, A-1.

35   Mike Platt interview.

36   Mike Platt interview.

37   Hennings interview; "The Players," *Evansville Courier*, December 14, 1977, 1.

38   Platt interview. Bliss would leave after the season and go to Northeastern

Oklahoma as head coach for one season. From there he went to the University of Alaska–Anchorage, where he was head coach from 1978 to 1981 and guided the Seawolves to a record of 44–41 (*University of Alaska–Anchorage Media Guide, 2010*).

39 Mike Platt interview.

40 Platt interview.

41 Thornton Patberg interview.

42 Jim Byers, telephone interview by author, January 27, 2011.

43 Dr. Allen McCutchan, telephone interview by author, February 11, 2011.

44 Patberg interview.

45 Frey, 6-7, was drafted by Seattle but did not make the team. He was also being wooed by the NFL's Dallas Cowboys as an end. The broken ankle ended the interest. He finished his career at Evansville with a career rebounding average of eight per game and having made 547 field goals, both good enough to make the all-time top ten list in each category at Evansville.

46 Graves interview.

47 Byers interview; Wayne Boultinghouse, telephone interview by author, February 11, 2011, and several follow-up calls.

48 Byers interview.

49 Patberg interview.

50 Graves interview.

51 Graves interview.

52 Patberg, Byers, Graves, and Boultinghouse interviews.

53 Sloan accepted an assistant coaching job with Chicago the next season.

54 Platt would finish his career at Evansville with 1,335 points, making him the thirteenth-leading scorer in school history (*University of Evansville 1977–78 Media Guide*).

55 Russ Grieger, "Fans into Redshirts," from the files of Russ Grieger, used with permission.

(l-r) Coach Bobby Watson at home with his family; Bobby Watson kneeling on the sidelines; the 1977-78 Purple Aces and their coaches.

Big Shoes, 1977

"He was destined for greatness."
—Hank Norton, athletic director, Ferrum College

After Jerry Sloan backed out of the Evansville job, about 70 coaches sent their resumes to Jim Byers. When he had the field whittled to a manageable size, **Bobby Watson**, an assistant basketball coach at Oral Roberts University, was among the top 10 candidates.

Robert Lee "Bobby" Watson was 6-7, weighed 230 pounds, and had the feet to match. For someone who was going to have to step into a position previously held by not one but two legends, oversized feet would be helpful.

Size ran in the family. "They called his dad, Carl Watson, 'Big C'—he was as wide as a door," said Hank Norton, retired athletic director at Ferrum College in Virginia who once worked with Bobby Watson.

The family, which included Bobby's younger sister, Lois, lived in a modest frame house at 17 Dorchester Drive in leafy Bethel Park, a suburb of Pittsburgh, Pennsylvania.[1] The handsome Bobby, who was born in 1943, was both a baseball and basketball star in high school. He had earned All-State honors in both sports and was MVP of the basketball team he led all the way to the Pennsylvania state finals.

After graduation he accepted a scholarship to Virginia Military Institute, known as the West Point of the South, a tough place to go to school and compete in athletics at the same time, especially because Bobby was pre-med. The school prided itself on preparing young men for careers in the military, and discipline was strict and rigidly enforced. Cadets wore military uniforms, lived in barracks, and ate in mess halls. Punctuality, order, discipline, courtesy, and respect for authority are the hallmarks of a VMI education.[2] The lessons Watson learned there would shape him and define him.

At VMI he played basketball for coach "Weenie" Miller and was elected captain of the Keydets. The team captured the Southern Conference title in 1964 and went to the NCAA Tournament, where they lost to Princeton (whose starters included Bill Bradley that year). "I coached him and recruited him," Miller said. "He was such a tremendous talent and was a great leader. He was on a club that built something"—the Southern Conference Championship.[3]

Bobby, who graduated from VMI in 1964, was a ninth-round draft choice of the Baltimore Bullets but opted instead to enter the coaching ranks. He served as an assistant at William Fleming High School in Roanoke, Virginia, for one season. Then he joined the staff of George Krajac, head coach at Xavier University who knew Bobby from Pennsylvania, where they had played against each other in high school. But this was the Vietnam era, and Bobby soon was drafted.

His preparation for medical school led the Army to assign him to the medical corps of the 101st Airborne Division in 1965, when U.S. involvement in Vietnam was growing. He played and coached basketball for a time at Fort Bliss, Texas, and was named to the All-Army team. But soon he was in the jungles of Vietnam. "He was over there jumping out of helicopters to rescue and care for wounded soldiers," said Jack Cherry, who was sports information director at Xavier when he met Bobby. "Here he was, 6-7, scrambling around in a combat zone trying to get low enough to dodge bullets and save lives. He did that throughout his tour there." During that year he earned a Bronze Star for gallantry, an Army Commendation Medal, and five Purple Hearts for injuries sustained in battle.

After his tour Bobby rejoined the coaching staff at Xavier. "He'd decided he wanted to be a coach rather than become a doctor," Jack said. "I told him I'd heard of a lot of crazy ideas, but this decision had to be one of the craziest. 'I want to coach,' he told me, and that was what he did."[4]

While at Xavier Bobby completed his master's degree in guidance and counseling. He also met the woman he would eventually marry. Deidra Lang Cavanaugh was a native of Aurora, in southeastern Indiana. Watson fell for the striking brunette with dark flashing eyes, and the attraction was mutual.[5]

Bobby had been assigned to an Army Reserve medical unit in Cincinnati. After two seasons at Xavier he got a letter. The entire reserve unit was being called up. "We started writing letters and calling Washington and the Pentagon to ask them not to send him back there," Jack said. "He'd done his tour, and we felt he shouldn't have to go back.

"We kept at it, and we were eventually told that the Army would station him at Fort Leonard Wood in Missouri rather than send him to Vietnam. Bobby got the letter and said, 'They need medics in Vietnam. They don't need medics at Leonard Wood.' He decided to go back," Jack said.

"I drove him to the airport and gave him a big hug and said, 'I'll see you when you get back.' Bobby looked at me and said, 'You don't come back from a second tour in 'Nam.'

"You will!"

"'No, I won't,' he told me quietly and walked away toward the plane.

"I just stood there crying," Jack said.

"About six months later I was at home when the phone rang. It was Bobby. Apparently, finally, all of our pleas to keep him out of 'Nam had reached a sympathetic ear and he was told, 'You're going home.'"

When Jack picked Bobby up at the airport, he suggested they collect his belongings. Bobby replied that he didn't have any luggage, telling Jack, "They said I could go pack my stuff and catch a plane tomorrow, or I could leave right then on a transport that was ready to go. I wasn't about to spend another day there . . . I said 'Adios,' and hopped that plane."

He rejoined the staff at Xavier, but Krajac was let go after the season and so was Bobby. "I often thought that Xavier made a huge mistake by not moving Bobby up as the head coach," Jack said. "He would have been great at anything he wanted to do."

Jack, like everyone else who knew Bobby Watson, said he never spoke of his tours in Vietnam. But it left some scars that ran deeper than those caused by the wounds he had suffered five times.

Jack related an incident that Paul Ritter, the *Cincinnati Enquirer*'s basketball writer, once told him about.

Ritter and Watson were sharing a room during a road trip after Bobby got back from Vietnam. He had finished shaving and was putting his toiletries in his luggage, when Paul went to the bathroom to shave. When he came out, he walked across the room. Bobby's back was turned to him. Suddenly, Bobby whirled around and grabbed Paul by the throat and threw him up against the wall. He held him there for a few seconds. Then the contorted expression on his face softened, and Bobby released Paul. "I'm so sorry, Paul. It was reflex. I'm sorry," Bobby told the shaken reporter.[6]

After he was fired by Xavier, Watson accepted a job as head basketball coach at Ferrum Junior College in Virginia. Located in the Blue Ridge Mountains, the college is not in a village, town, or city but a "census-designated place." The crossroads of Ferrum was known then, as it is now, as the Moonshine Capital of the United States. It even has a Moonshine Museum.

Ferrum Junior College was established in 1912 so the "mountain kids" could get an education. There the combat veteran from western Pennsylvania would get his chance to coach basketball. "Bobby was a tough, hard-nosed, Bob Knight–type guy," said Hank Norton, who was the college's athletic director at the time. "He favored man-to-man in-your-face–type play. The kids all responded to him."[7]

Bobby Watson's first season at Ferrum was the 1971–72 campaign, and the young mentor soon justified his hiring by recording a 34–4 record, a conference championship, and a trip to the National Junior College Tournament in Hutchinson, Kansas, where the Panthers advanced all the way to the finals before losing.

His second season at Ferrum, the Panthers went 25–4 and were upset in the regional final. "Bobby took the loss hard," Norton said. "They had held the ball on him and beat him that way."[8]

Ferrum had produced successful back-to-back seasons under Watson's tutelage; clearly, he deserved to be coaching at the collegiate level.

A former Ferrum mentor, Carl Tacy, was the coach at Wake Forest University and had been following Watson's success closely. "I had known about Bobby when he played at VMI," Tacy said. "Bobby was a little older, a veteran, and I knew he had done great things at Ferrum, so I offered him an assistant coaching position on my staff. . . . We spent a good deal of time together. He ate with us and lived with us until he could find a place of his own. I liked him like a brother.

"Bobby was strong on fundamentals and techniques, especially on defense. I gave him full responsibility for our defense, and he did a great job. The players all responded well to him. He was a no-nonsense–type guy who earned their respect immediately," Tacy said.

"He was only with me for that one year before he moved on to Oral Roberts. I hated to lose him but I understood at his age he wanted a chance to prove himself and pursue his dream of becoming a head coach. I was pleased for him when I heard he got the job at Evansville and had no doubt he would do well there. He was more than just a good coach. He was a good communicator and could talk to people at any level about things that interested them the most. He was a good recruiter, and I expected he would do very well there."[9]

While at Wake Forest, Bobby and Deidra were married on December 14, 1973, with a small informal reception at a downtown hotel afterward.[10] Deidra had a daughter, Angela Cavanaugh, then about eight, from her previous marriage, so Bobby had an instant family.

Bobby and his family left Wake Forest in the spring for Tulsa, Oklahoma, and Oral Roberts University, where he would become an assistant to coach Jerry Hale. Oral Roberts was a relatively new university founded by its namesake, a charismatic fundamentalist preacher who had built the school after, he said, he received a message directly from God ordering him to do so. It had opened in 1965.

During the three seasons Watson was on staff, ORU won 20 or more games each season.

Glenn Smith has been the athletic trainer at Oral Roberts for more than 40 years and knew Bobby and Deidra when they were there. "He was one of those coaches that you just knew was going to become somebody in the business. He reminded me of a Jim Valvano–type coach. He was enthusiastic, and motivational in his approach to the game, and he communicated that to the players," said Smith, who has worked with eleven head coaches. "We spent a lot of time together; my wife, Mona, and Deidra were best friends. I just knew Bobby was going to do great things when he got a chance to become a head coach somewhere."[11]

Bobby kept his eyes and ears open for head coaching opportunities. When the Evansville job came open, he quickly applied. According to Stafford Stephenson, he had lost out on a head coaching job at Davidson and was determined to land the Evansville job.

Jim Byers recalled that "after Bobby's interview was over, and he had left the office, we all looked at each other, and I said, 'We better get this guy.' Bobby was a vet, good looking, a big guy, and had been an assistant at a major college. There was no question about it, he was our choice."[12]

Thornton Patberg was also a member of the selection committee. "Watson was

'Mr. Personality,'" Patberg recalled. "He was big, good looking, and he just lit up the room when he entered. It was an easy choice."[13]

"He knew what was important to them at Evansville. Given his personality and larger-than life-presence, I am not surprised they were impressed with him," Stephenson said. "He was handsome and a charismatic man. People just gravitated to him. It didn't hurt that he was an excellent basketball coach as well."

Once Watson's hiring was announced, he immediately filled his staff with new people. The first assistant he hired was Stephenson.

After Watson left Winston-Salem for Ferrum, Stephenson had stayed at Wake Forest for another year, then took a head coaching job at Wingate Junior College outside Charlotte. That's where he was when Watson offered him the job at Evansville. The two had stayed in touch—"I'd worked a basketball camp with Bobby at Oral Roberts when I was still at Wingate, and we had renewed our friendship there," he said.

"When he called me and asked me to join him, I jumped at the chance," Stephenson said. "I got there in April [1977], and the first month or so we didn't have our families there with us . . . we spent a lot of time together, and I saw and sensed the excitement in the community wherever we went.

"We knew we had a few holdovers but that we were going to have a very young team. We had no false pretenses about how good we were going to be against a Division I schedule. I was just 30 and Bobby was 34. It was a new and exciting time for us."[14]

Another assistant hired by Watson was Ernon "Ernie" Simpson, who had been highly successful as the coach since 1970 at Union County High School in Morganfield, Kentucky, in Evansville's traditional recruiting area of the tristate region. He had been part of two national championship teams at Kentucky Wesleyan, in 1966 and 1968. His record at Union County was 166–37 over seven years. Simpson's knowledge of the talent in the local area made him a valuable addition to the staff. He and his wife and family arrived in Evansville in August.[15]

Watson also hired Mark Sandy, who had played for him at Ferrum as the point guard on the 1972 national runner-up team. Just 25 when he arrived in Evansville, Mark had gone to Concord College in Athens, Virginia, where he'd earned his bachelor's degree in education. He had played both basketball and baseball there and had earned All-Conference honors in both.

Sandy went directly from Concord into coaching at Herndon High School in West Virginia, where he was the head basketball and baseball coach for two seasons. When Watson called him in March 1977, he was about to enter law school.

"He told me he was interviewing for a head coaching job at several schools and wanted to know if I would come with him if he got hired," Sandy said. "I told him I was planning on law school but I'd think about it. When he got the Evansville job, he called me again. I had just gotten married a few months before, and I decided I'd skip law school and go on to Evansville.

The Sandys arrived in Evansville in June. "As soon as I got there, we held a summer camp, and **Kraig Heckendorn** from Cincinnati made a strong impression on me. He was a scrappy guard, about 6-2, with blond hair and a great mental attitude for the game," Sandy said. "He was coming in as a freshman, and he was just an outstanding young man. I thought if we were getting kids like that, we'd be OK. We also had a kid named Mike Duff who was extremely talented, and you could see he was going to be a very good player from the very beginning.

"I had been hired as a [part-time] coach and had dorm and study hall issues to deal with, in addition to my coaching duties. I took some graduate courses and spent the rest of my time scouting and at practice."[16]

Watson had wasted little time in completing his staff, and all were in place by August. "He wanted people he could trust and who would work with the kids," Stephenson said.[17]

One recruit Bobby failed to land was Glenn Smith, the trainer at Oral Roberts. "I had just bought a new house, and he called me and asked me to come on down with him," Glenn said. "He said that we would be doing great things there together. I turned him down but he kept calling. He called me every month for . . . five months . . . trying to convince me to join him. But the timing wasn't right for me."[18]

Watson's next step was to begin selling himself and his new Division I program to the greater Evansville area.

Tom Collins was the beat reporter covering the Aces for the *Evansville Courier*, and he met Mac's replacement soon after the university had announced his hiring. "After the Sloan hiring, and then leaving, and coming into a place where he would be following a legend, Bobby knew he had to work hard to win over the community," Collins said. "Nobody here really knew who he was. But they soon found out. I went to one of his first speeches in town. While we were walking in, he asked the person with us, 'Anyone here ever heard of me?' The guy said, 'No, I don't think so.' After the speech everyone in the room was won over—he was that good."[19]

Watson and his staff completed the recruiting process that Mac had begun before his retirement. Their returnees were senior John Ed Washington, who had averaged better than 15 points per game to lead the team; Bryan Taylor, who had averaged 13 points per game, shot 53 percent from the floor, and grabbed 152 rebounds in his first season as an Ace; Tony Winburn, a speedy guard; and Steve Miller, who had hauled in 182 boards and averaged just over 8 points per game. All had seen action in almost every game. They were augmented by **Kevin Kingston** from Eldorado, Illinois, who had been a reserve but had earned an athletic scholarship, and **Keith Moon**, a center.

The team would have a plethora of young players who would be facing college competition for the first time. The incoming freshmen, however, were a very talented group; they included many recruited by Mac and some Bobby had been able to sign.

Mark Sandy described Watson's recruiting techniques: "Bobby had strong beliefs about right and wrong which he had developed while at VMI. There was no gray area with him. If you were a parent, and Bobby came to your home to recruit your son, there was no question he was the kind of man you'd want your son to have as a coach. You knew right away he'd care about your son as much as you did."[20]

Stephenson added, "Watson, in his years at Xavier and later at Oral Roberts, had developed a lot of relationships with the high school coaches in the tristate area, and he was well liked. If you met him once, you never forgot him. That helped him a great deal when he got the job there."[21]

Indeed, two incoming players were from outside Evansville's usual recruiting area. Both **Warren Alston** and **Barney Lewis** hailed from Goldsboro, North Carolina. They had played for coach Norvell Lee at Goldsboro High, and he had influenced their decision to attend Evansville. Bobby had approached Lee about becoming one of his assistants in Evansville, but he had backed out of the job at the last minute because his mother was ill. Still, he encouraged his players to enroll there. And they were familiar with Watson because he had frequently visited their school while he was at Wake Forest.[22]

Both had been members of Lee's 24–1 Goldsboro team that won the conference championship in 1977. Alston, 18, had played forward at Goldsboro but would be playing guard for Evansville. He was 6-4 and had a deadly jump shot. He had averaged 24 points per game as a senior. Tall and thin, Warren had a wide and ready smile for everyone. The players called him "Silk" because his moves on the court were silky smooth.

Barney Lewis, also 18, was a 6-7 power forward-center who had won All-Conference honors as a senior at Goldsboro. Lewis was an effective rebounder and had great hustle and desire. His last-second jump shot for Goldsboro had clinched the conference title for his team.

The other freshmen were from the tristate area. **Ray Comandella** had led his Munster, Indiana, high school team to the sectional championship games during his junior and senior years and was ranked second in all of Indiana high school basketball. He averaged 15 points and 8 rebounds per game as a senior. He was 6-9 and weighed just 200 pounds. One of his pet peeves was the food in the university cafeteria—he didn't particularly like it but was constantly encouraged to eat more of it. His coaches felt that with added weight, Ray, who was only 19, would be an important contributor. "He was all elbows and knees but had great potential," Mark Sandy said. "Ray was exceptionally fast for a big man, especially on defense," Stephenson added.

But **Mike Duff** was the prize catch of the 1977 recruiting season. He had led his Eldorado, Illinois, high school team to the Class 1A Elite Eight for three straight seasons. At 6-7 and 205 pounds Mike was an excellent back-to-the-basket player. "He could shoot the ball," Stephenson said. Mike was the only unanimous choice on the UPI Class A All-State team while playing for coach Bob Brown.

Mike was a prep All-America selection by *Basketball Weekly* and *Street and Smith's*. He had tallied 47 points in one game and had averaged 32 points and 16 rebounds per game during his senior year. He was a bona fide blue-chip player, the only Illinois high school player to score more than a thousand points that year.[23]

Mike was widely recruited and had originally signed with Missouri but decided when he got there that it was too big and went home. Evansville reaped the reward when Brown suggested that the "small town kid" might be more comfortable at Evansville. Like Jerry Sloan before him, Mike Duff, just 18, found a comfort level at Evansville, and he was a standout performer in the early practices.

"Mike was a raw-boned, tough, country boy. At practice it was always, 'Yes, sir' or 'No, Sir,' but on the court he was a terror," Stephenson said. "He was going to be a great player. You could see it every time he took the court," Mark Sandy said. Scott Doerner agreed. "Mike had it all. He was an amazing talent. He may have been the best ever to play at Evansville," Scott said of his friend and teammate.[24]

Kraig Heckendorn was the 6-2 guard who had caught Mark Sandy's eye at the summer basketball camp. He was from Oak Hills High School in Cincinnati and had been the play maker on a team that went 45–9 during his career. (Cincinnati is just across the Ohio River from Kentucky and thus is regarded as part of the tristate area.) He was especially proud of his defense, and during his senior year he had set the school record for the most steals. He could also score and proved it in a game his senior year when he accounted for 19 of his team's 21 points in one quarter. He scored 30 points in the game. He was so good that his dad, the assistant principal of a high school, had retired the year before so he could closely follow Kraig's college career.[25]

Several schools were vying for Kraig, but he chose Evansville. Like Mark Sandy said, parents fell in love with Bobby Watson, and the Heckendorns were no exception. "They both felt that he was the ideal person to coach their son," his sister, Kerry Heckendorn Braeuning, said. "They liked him immediately, and that's why Kraig went there. My parents always worried about us when we were growing up. They worried when we started to ride bikes, when we started to drive, but they never worried about anything happening to Kraig when they sent him to Evansville to play basketball."[26] His coaches were counting on the 19-year-old Kraig to spell Winburn, and Kraig welcomed the opportunity to play at the Division I level.

Mike Joyner, 19, loved playing at Roberts Stadium, where he had performed with his Terre Haute South High School team in the state tournament. "He said after being in Evansville that he knew that was where he wanted to go to school," his older brother, Robert, said. "He'd always tell people who asked where he was going to college that Evansville is where he wanted to play. He just loved Roberts Stadium and the people there."

At 6-3 and 180 pounds, Mike was going to have to make the transformation from forward to the back court. He was an All-State honorable mention and had scored the winning free throw in the North-South All-Star game. As a senior Mike had led his team to a 25–3 record and set the school's all-time scoring record. He averaged 18 points and 7 rebounds as a senior at forward. He came from a family that was just nuts about basketball—his dad had played semipro ball and erected a hoop for his sons in the backyard. "My mom would have to come out and get us. Sometimes we'd be out there until one or two in the morning," recalled Robert, who today coaches an AAU team.[27]

Mark Siegel, also 19, had played for his father, Ed, at Pike High School in

Indianapolis, where he had played point guard and earned All-State honorable mention two years in a row. Mark had undergone intestinal surgery shortly after arriving at Evansville and had missed a lot of the early fall conditioning as a result. But he was catching up fast and was showing "quickness and court intelligence," Mark Sandy recalled.[28]

Greg Smith, 18, earned a roster spot as a direct result of Mark Siegel's abdominal surgery. Greg had averaged 18 points per game at Community High School in West Frankfort, Illinois, and would be a reserve for the Aces.

Watson had not been tempted to recruit from the junior college ranks, the route that had proved so disastrous for Evansville in the past. Instead, all but two of the players he sought were from the university's traditional recruiting area. Both those Mac had recruited and the players Bobby signed were local products from strong programs and had good academic preparation.

Rounding out the basketball program were three student assistants, all of whom had grown up in Evansville. **Mark "Tank" Kirkpatrick**, 21, was one of the team's student managers. He was back for his third year with the team. Built like the nickname indicates, Tank was a fun-loving guy who kept everyone on the team loose. He was a graduate of Central High School in Evansville and was planning a career as an elementary school gym teacher.[29]

Mark Kniese, 20, was returning for his fourth year as the team trainer. He was a physical education major and hoped to become a professional athletic trainer.[30]

The other student manager was **Jeff Bohnert**, 21, a product of Evansville's Harrison High. Jeff was majoring in biology and planned to become a doctor—and the athletic scholarship he received as a student manager was a big help toward that goal. He also shot game footage for the football coaches.

All was in place for the 1977–78 season. Now they just had to get down to playing basketball. Bobby could be a strict coach on the practice court; off the court he was someone the players knew they could trust, and they felt increasingly comfortable sharing their personal problems with him. That made the numerous young players, just 18 and 19 years old and away from home for the first time, feel safe and secure.[31]

Watson took the responsibility very seriously. If you were part of Bobby's team, you were part of his family. He and Deidra hosted cookouts and picnics for the team at their home, and Deidra often made cookies and candy for them to take back to school.

The 1977–78 Aces would be young, and they would struggle, but Watson and his staff were pleased with the team they had put together and had reasonable expectations.

"We felt that if we could get through the first part of the season, just weather the storm while everyone got used to playing with each other, we'd be alright," Stephenson said. "It was important to get Taylor, Washington, Winburn, and Miller used to working with the new kids, and they all had to get used to playing at the Division I level together.

"The kids were tough, hard nosed, and competitive, and they took to coaching well. All were new to the experience, and we were new to them, so we all were learning together, and Bobby kept stressing to them that we were all in it together and would all succeed together. Fortunately, they were all really good kids."[32]

When practices started in October, Watson decided to keep all his assistants on campus—no recruiting or scouting—so that they could attend the first four games and evaluate the players, how they worked together, and what the best combinations were. "After that we'd go on and do our recruiting and scouting, but the first four games we planned to all be there together," Stephenson said.[33]

To show his appreciation to Eldorado coach Bob Brown for sending him Duff and Kevin Kingston, a junior, Bobby scheduled a pre-season scrimmage at their alma mater. The event was held in the high school gym where the two had starred, and proceeds from ticket sales went toward a scholarship at the school.

As the beginning of the season approached, the coaches could see that the team was slowly coming together. "In our discussions before the season began . . . we were pretty much in agreement that we had the material to be a .500 team. We felt that by Christmas we'd have a pretty good idea [of] just how good we could be," Stephenson said.

Bobby was very demanding and strict with his players. They knew he expected them to be on time and to be in class when they were supposed to be. "He wasn't an in-your-face-type guy," Stephenson said. "But he would get after kids in a positive way. He wanted them to become better players, and I think they all understood that. They were all good kids who had come from winning programs, and they accepted him and his style."[34]

Evansville was starting to quiver like a tuning fork in anticipation of the season. "Bobby had done a lot of promotion in the area and had spoken everywhere he was asked, so we knew the community was excited about the team and the move to Division I," Stephenson said.[35]

Bob Hudson—whom students had dubbed "Rock" somewhere along the way—was excited, too. He had high hopes for the success of the Aces under Watson, and he was confident from the early season ticket sales that the crowds would be returning to Roberts.[36]

The move to Division I brought new opponents, New Orleans and Loyola of Chicago, to the schedule and created the need to make more travel arrangements than ever before. Hudson had finally gotten some relief from his one-man-band act when Byers hired **Greg Knipping,** 27, as sports information director in July. A 1972 graduate of the University of Missouri School of Journalism, the blond and bespectacled Greg had held that position at Purdue for two and a half years. His new duties included media relations and publications, promotions, and program layout and design, as well as booster group activity.

Greg worked closely with the Tip-Off Club, the booster organization, and he revived the riverboat gambler mascot, Ace Purple, who had been discarded about ten years earlier. The decision to revive the grinning, nattily attired mascot with a pencil-thin mustache and a hand with four aces probably caused lots of indigestion at the NCAA, whose leadership was perpetually paranoid about gambling.

Nonetheless, "Ace Purple" was back, and the fans and student body happily welcomed him. Greg worked closely with Bobby to promote the program.[37] "Whenever we got another recruit, it became front-page news in the paper. Basketball was big in Evansville again," Byers said.[38]

Hudson and Knipping were slam-dunk promoters of the Aces, but they were also getting a huge assist from Bobby Watson. Byers watched in awe as Watson went through a hectic summer and fall schedule of speaking engagements and recruiting trips. "He was tireless in promoting the program, and he impressed everyone who heard him speak. He went to high school banquets, service clubs, church groups, anyone that would have him. He was charismatic and spellbinding behind a lectern and had such a positive image and presence that everyone responded to him immediately," Byers said.[39]

According to Collins, who used to cover the Aces, Watson understood the role of the media and the importance of good public relations. He made about 150 speeches throughout the tristate area.[40]

Early in the fall Thornton Patberg heard Bobby speak at Neu Chapel on campus. "He had everyone in the palm of his hand. He could have become a millionaire as an evangelical revivalist. He was a charmer," Pat said.[41]

Bobby Watson had promoted, recruited, and spoken all he could. He had taught and attempted to mold his returning players and the newcomers into a cohesive winning unit. The Aces had played a scrimmage game in Eldorado, but it was now time to play basketball for real.

The stately sycamores had shed most of their leaves and the fall air was turning crisp.

It was once again basketball season, the only season that counted in Evansville.

(Endnotes)

1   Hank Norton, telephone interview by author, February 4, 2011.

2   "VMI Military Life," n.d., www.vmi.edu.

3   Dave Johnson, "Watson Was Darling of Evansville Fans," *Evansville Press*, December 14, 1977, 1.

4   Jack Cherry, telephone interview by author, September 15, 2011.

5   Rich Davis, "Three Women Shared Bond That Went Beyond Crash," *Evansville Courier*, December 13, 1997, A-1.

6   Cherry interview.

7   Norton interview.

8   Norton interview.

9   Ironically, Tacy was a friend of both Watson and Rick Tolley from their years at Ferrum. Tolley perished in a plane crash with the Marshall University football team in 1971, a tragedy retold in the film, *We Are Marshall* (2006).

10 Marriage license application between Robert Lee Watson and Deidra Lang Cavanaugh, Registrar's Office, Forsyth County, N.C. Information courtesy of Sandra Young, Forsyth County Registrar's Office, August 24, 2011.

11 Glenn Smith, telephone interview by author, September 9, 2011.

12 Jim Byers, telephone interview by author, January 27, 2011.

13 Thornton Patberg, telephone interview by author, January 29, 2011, and several follow-up calls.

14 Stafford Stephenson, telephone interview by author, January 24, 2011; follow-up interview, June 27, 2011.

15 *University of Evansville 1977–78 Media Guide.*

16 Mark Sandy, telephone interview by author, January 31, 2011.

17 Stafford Stephenson interview.

18 Glenn Smith interview.

19 Tom Collins, telephone interview by author, January 24, 2011.

20 Mark Sandy interview.

21 Stafford Stephenson interview.

22 Stafford Stephenson interview; "Funeral Makes Tragedy Real in Goldsboro," *Evansville Press*, December 19, 1977. Lee, who died in 1997, went on to coach at St. Augustine's College in Raleigh, North Carolina.

23 *University of Evansville 1977–78 Media Guide.*

24 Stafford Stephenson and Mark Sandy interviews; Scott Doerner, telephone interview by author, February 22, 2011.

25 AP, "Evansville's Program Was Building to Become a Division I Power," *Lakeland (Fla.) Ledger,* December 16, 1977, http://news.google.com/newspapers?id=4xJNAAAAIBAJ&sjid=o_oDAAAAIBAJ&pg=4833,3557820&dq=keith+moon+1977+basketball&hl=en.

26 Kerry Heckendorn Braeuning, telephone interview by author, July 13, 2011.

27 Robert Joyner, telephone interview by author, September 16, 2011.

28 Sandy interview.

29 *University of Evansville 1977–78 Media Guide*; Sylvia Slaughter, "'Tank': UE 'Manager for All Seasons,'" *Evansville Press,* December 18, 1977, 1-A.

30 *University of Evansville 1977–78 Media Guide.*

31 Stafford Stephenson, Mark Sandy interviews.

32 Stephenson interview.

33 Stephenson interview.

34 Stephenson interview.

35 Stephenson interview.

36 Joan Hudson Roth, telephone interview by author, February 21, 2011.

37 Joan Hudson Roth interview.

38 *University of Evansville 1977–78 Media Guide*; Byers interview.

39 Byers interview.

40 Collins interview.

41 Patberg interviews.

Jerry Sloan, Larry Humes, Sam Watkins, 1965.

Division I Debut, 1977

The move from Division II to Division I is often more difficult than anticipated. The level of play at the top of college basketball is exponentially greater
than that seen at the Division II level. The program may have moved up just one
rung on the ladder, but the distance between the rungs is wide and missteps en
route are commonplace.

In Evansville the move had been preceded by the emotional roller coaster of
Sloan's hiring and resignation— great euphoria followed by a huge letdown.

When Watson was hired in March, he found himself in a basketball-crazy state
at a university with a rabid fan base that had followed the fortunes of a legendary coach and his teams with a passion seldom seen elsewhere. The young coach
and his staff were enthused about the opportunity they had been given to lead
the Aces into the big-time world of college basketball.

After Sloan's messy departure, Watson's arrival was understated. Yet he soon
won over his audience. He'd never be Jerry Sloan and he knew that. But, for
most people, especially those who heard him speak about the Aces' future, just
being Bobby Watson was more than enough.

The first game of the season was scheduled for Roberts on November 30,
1977. Finally, the community was going to get its first look at the new coach and
the 1977–78 edition of the Purple Aces.

Indiana State University–Evansville had "siphoned off a lot of fans, especially
on the west side of town, and had impacted attendance at Roberts, [but] now the

Aces offered the only major college game in town," said Bill Bussing, a local law-yer and major Aces fan. "That was the hope of the administration. They wanted to differentiate and set themselves apart from ISU–Evansville, hoping the move up to Division I would bring the fans back."[1]

A crowd of 8,708 was on hand. The move to Division I and the tireless pro-motional efforts of Watson, Hudson, and Knipping had paid off. The fans were responding to the exciting new era and the charismatic new coach.

There were still some reminders of the McCutchan era at Roberts. Marv Bates was still broadcasting the games, as he had for years. Bob Hudson was still scur-rying around, doing all the jobs no one else knew how to do. Some fans were still wearing red, and, as promised, Ace Purple was back. And, as always at Roberts, the new season was a time for hopes and dreams of a return to the glory days of Aces basketball.

Sportswriters were more realistic about the Aces' prospects. Watson had care-fully cultivated the press and had won their support. "Uppermost in his mind was the hope that fans would be patient," Tom Collins said.

Bobby Watson was both realistic and optimistic. He was confident that, given what he had seen of the team thus far, the Aces could become a competitive team at the Division 1 level. It was a long season, and Christmas was less than two months away. All Bobby was asking for was a little time. "I hope [fans] don't sit in judgment on this team the first game," Watson told Collins. "It will take some time, probably around Christmas, before we get this thing rolling," but after that, "we're going to open some people's eyes."[2]

Western Kentucky University provided the first hurdle for Watson's young team. The Hilltoppers and the Aces scrapped on even terms through most of the game. Neither could manage more than a seven-point lead, and the Aces held a 36–32 lead at the half. Mike Duff's 18 points in the first half kept the Aces in command.

The second half was more of the same. The Aces took a 56–50 lead with about 10 minutes to play as Bryan Taylor started to find his range. Duff had cooled off while Taylor made key buckets, but then the Aces started to falter. Western Kentucky's Greg Burbach and Greg Jackson exploited the Aces' shaky guard play and led the visitors on a 10–2 run.

Bryan Taylor stopped the bleeding with a jumper from the corner to tie it at 60, but the Hilltoppers went on another run, this time 10–0, to seal the Aces' fate. The final score was 82–72.

Duff finished with 26 points and 13 rebounds, while Bryan Taylor had added 21. Overall the Aces had been ice cold from the floor. They had shot only 37 percent from the floor despite Taylor's 10-for-20 performance.

Watson had substituted freely throughout. He had two, and sometimes three, freshmen on the court for most of the game as he searched for the right combination. Warren Alston had come off the bench to steady the guard play and had added nine points.[3]

The inexperience showed, and the Aces' debut was spoiled, but fans were still impressed.

"Fantastic," declared Jerry Scheidler, a former UE student. "They've got good potential. I like the idea of Division I because of the caliber of teams they will be playing against in years to come." Another observer, who had stronger credentials as a critic, was Wayne Boultinghouse. "I'm impressed with their defense," he said. "I was in favor of going to Division I five years ago. Bobby's doing a fine job and I tip my hat to him."

Don Hardesty, an Aces fan since the late 1950s, told a reporter, "I'm glad they went Division I. They had accomplished most of their goals winning five national championships. Now they have a new challenge. I was impressed with Alston, and Duff is a blue chipper."[4] First-game jitters and freshmen mistakes had plagued the Aces, but they had won plaudits for their effort.

Tony Weller, an Evansville fan for 22 seasons, said, "I'm impressed with Bobby Watson. They need a little more muscle, but Duff is going to be a terrific player before he gets out of here. And if anybody is going to lead the Aces out of the wilderness, Bobby Watson will."[5]

Despite his sparkling debut, Mike Duff himself was not impressed with his performance. His self-critique was one word: *rotten*. "I took a lot of bad shots and should have hit some shots I didn't," he said. Bobby had a kinder appraisal of Duff's performance, calling it "better than anticipated." Apparently, Bobby wasn't being overly generous, because Jim Richards, the Western Kentucky coach, was impressed with Mike, too: "Duff showed a lot of poise. He didn't overreact the way a lot of freshmen do. He stuck with it. I think he will be a great one before he's through."

Watson said of his team's overall effort, "We played well at times as a team." Then he noted the 20–4 run that had given the visitors the win and added, "But then we blew it as a team. I was disappointed in our whole guard play. None of them did what we wanted them to do."[6]

Bobby had little time to prepare his squad for the next game, against DePaul in Chicago. The Aces would be facing Dave Corzine, the Blue Demons' 6-11 center and top pro prospect, on Saturday, December 3.

The Aces managed to stay close to their hosts in the early going. They trailed by only a point, 19–18, midway through the first half. Then, with Corzine and William Dise leading the way, the Blue Demons went on a 22–4 blitz that put them in command at the half: 49–28. Evansville never managed to recover.

With 14 minutes remaining, the DePaul lead swelled to 67–34, their widest margin of the game. Once again the Aces had committed crucial turnovers, especially during the Blue Demons' 22–4 run, that had led to Evansville's undoing. It was too much to overcome, and the Aces fell, 94–71.

Steve Miller, the 6-8 junior center, got more playing time and scored 18 points to lead the Aces. Mike Duff added 16, and John Ed Washington and Bryan Taylor tallied 13 apiece.

"We're a young team and we lack size," Watson said. "We're going to have some long nights like this. It's painful while you're learning."[7]

Bobby was pleased with Miller's play. He had held the towering Corzine to just 16 boards while hauling down 12.[8]

DePaul shot 50 percent from the floor, while the Aces could do no better than 40-for-83.[9]

The Aces were now 0–2.

Next up were the Panthers of the University of Pittsburgh, coached by a friend of Watson's, Tim Grgurich. The Panthers had nipped Kent State 55–47 while the Aces were being drubbed by DePaul. No one ever said Division I was going to be easy.

On Tuesday, December 6, the Panthers, 2–1 for the season, faced off against the Aces at Roberts Stadium. Freezing cold temperatures kept the crowd down to just 4,378, but those who braved the chill saw a milestone achievement. In an error-prone game the Aces, led by Steve Miller and Bryan Taylor, managed to get their first win of the season, and their first as a Division I school, turning back Pittsburgh 90–83. Taylor scored 25 points, and Miller continued his stellar post play by adding 23 points.

Bobby had told his charges they needed to get tough, and the youngsters did just that. Miller went to the line 14 times and connected on 13 of them. Bryan had a hot hand from the corners, making 6 of 6 in the second half and 12 of 14 for the game. Overall the Aces shot 57 percent on their home court.

The win was a team effort as Miller's and Taylor's efforts were supplemented by strong performances from Mike Duff, Warren Alston, and Kraig Heckendorn, all freshmen. Duff shot 7-for-10 and had 16 points before fouling out, while Alston, off the bench, added a big offensive lift in the first half by canning four shots and finished with 12 while handling the ball flawlessly after Watson ordered a spread late in the game. Heckendorn, making his first start, canned two critical free throws down the stretch and played effective defense.

Errors still plagued the Aces, but they had hung on and moved their season mark to 1–2.[10] Watson was ebullient.

"Great, great," he said when asked how it felt to get his first win. "There's nothing greater. I've been involved in a lot of wins, but few sweeter than that one. Particularly with an effort like that. I told them all through the game that victory was going to depend on our defense and rebounding. I thought we really took it to them on the boards. I was pleased with our overall aggressiveness and I felt our changing defenses hurt them."

Miller had led the Aces' rebounding effort with nine, and he told reporters about his improved play. "I've been working hard and I know my place," Steve said. "Things are beginning to fall together." Bobby noted, "Miller and Taylor did a great job on the boards. I thought they were our key men."

Mike Duff had made some turnovers, but his long pass down court while the Aces were in a spread broke Pitt's back. He told reporters, "I played a little bit better than the last two games. But, I made a lot of dumb turnovers. It's a lack of concentration, I think. I've got to pay more attention to my passes."

With more than four minutes to go and a two-point edge, the Aces' stall, which Bobby had learned from Oklahoma State's legendary coach Hank Iba, had worked to perfection.[11]

On December 10 the Aces headed to Terre Haute, where a mop-haired kid from French Lick, Indiana, was waiting for them. Larry Bird and the eighth-ranked Indiana State Sycamores wasted little time in bringing the Aces back to earth. It was 10–0 before they even knew it. When it was finally over, the Sycamores had an easy 102–76 win.

As bad as it appeared, Watson wasn't totally dismayed. "Indiana State is as strong as I expected," he said. "All I can say is that two years from now, we'll have the courage to knock some people around."

Bobby was pleased with Mike Duff's performance—he'd scored 23 points and grabbed 8 rebounds. "I was pleased with him offensively, but he's learning some lessons defensively," Bobby said. "But I think in two years Duff will be as good as Bird, and I don't give guys very many accolades. Duff is learning a lot of lessons and he's learning them fast." Placing Mike Duff in the same rarified air as Larry Bird is an indication of just how good Mike Duff was—and he was only a freshman.

To the surprise of no one, Bird had stolen the show, tallying 35 points to lead his team.

The bad start to the game in particular bothered Watson. "One thing we lacked early is what I call courage on the road. By courage I mean poise and patience. But I'm not faulting the kids for that. They never quit. The responsibility for that courage and every loss falls on my shoulders as coach."

"Silk" Alston with 17 and Bryan Taylor with 14 also were in double figures for the Aces. But the Aces had shot a miserable 27-for-80 from the field, a frigid 34 percent, and that wasn't good enough to beat anybody, much less a nationally ranked opponent with a bona fide superstar. John Ed Washington's night had been a nightmare. He managed to hit on only 4 of his 21 attempts.[12]

The Aces had some time to recover from their thrashing before they were to meet Middle Tennessee State in Murfreesboro, Tennessee. They would be flying down a day early, hold a light practice, and then meet the Blue Raiders on Wednesday, December 14.

On Monday, December 12, after the Indiana State game, Bryan Taylor and Art Adye, who coordinated the Aces Brass, the school's pep band, visited several elementary schools in town to talk about the team.

"Bryan was in a pretty good mood. He felt, despite the loss, that the team was improving," Art said. They talked to the school kids about the basketball program and Bryan was especially upbeat.

"I told Bryan, 'I'm sorry I'm not going to be able to see the Middle Tennessee State game.' He said, 'I think there are still a few empty seats on the plane if you'd like to go.' I thought about it for a while, but I had a concert to attend the next night. The faculty string quartet was playing at Wheeler Concert Hall on campus as part of the Fall Concert Series, and I really wanted to see that. I thanked Bryan, wished him luck, and told him I'd see him when he got back."[13]

(Endnotes)

1   Bill Bussing, telephone interview by author, February 14, 2011.

2   Tom Collins, telephone interview by author, January 24, 2011.

3   Tom Collins, "Hilltoppers Spoil Aces Division I Debut, 82–72," *Evansville Courier*, December 1, 1977, 30.

4   Lee Creek, "Aces Fans Say They Like It," *Evansville Courier*, December 1, 1977, 31.

5   Creek, "Aces Fans Say They 'Like It.'"

6   Bill Fluty, "Mike Duff Debts with 26 in 'Rotten' Performance," *Evansville Courier*, December 1, 1977, 30.

7   Chicago, "DePaul Throttles Aces, 94–71," *Evansville Courier*, December 4, 1977, 21B.

8   Corzine would become the first-round draft choice of the Washington Bullets and play thirteen seasons in the NBA ("Dave Corzine," databaseBasketball.com,   www.databasebasketball.com/players/playerpage.htm?ilkid=CORZIDA01%20).

9   "DePaul Throttles Aces, 94–71," *Evansville Courier,* December 4, 1977, B-4.

10   Tom Collins, "Taylor, Miller Crack Pitt," *Evansville Courier*, December 7, 1977, 37.

11   Bill Fluty, "'Few Sweeter' Says Bobby after Notching First Win," *Evansville Courier*, December 7, 1977, 37.

12   "Bird, ISU Fly by Aces, 102–76," *Evansville Courier*, December 11, 1977, C-1. Indiana State would be ranked as high as fourth in the AP poll and finish the season at 23–9. The following season, when Bird was a senior, the Sycamores reached the NCAA Finals, losing to Magic Johnson and Michigan State in a heavily hyped game that drew record television viewers and catapulted the NCAA Tournament into the national consciousness. The NCAA would earn billions in future television revenues.

13   Art Adye, telephone interview by author, January 28, 2011.

Ace Purple Weeps for plane crash victims.

Tears Rain Down: Tuesday, December 13, 1977

This is a song for the one who is doomed,
a blow to the heart that breaks the mind.
—Aeschylus

It had been miserable all day. The temperature hovered in the low to mid-40s, with a cold persistent rain that chilled the bones.

Three days had passed since the loss to Indiana State at Terre Haute, and Monday's practice had not been good. Bobby Watson was not pleased with the effort he was seeing and had dismissed the team early. "The team had been slow in transition and the big guy finally had seen enough. 'Go take a shower. I don't even want to see you. We're just wasting time here. You've got to be tough to play in Division I,'" Tom Collins recalled him telling the Aces.[1]

Despite the verbal outburst and their 1–3 record, "we were getting better," Stafford Stephenson said. "You could feel it."[2]

The team would be flying to Murfreesboro the next day. Bob Hudson had arranged for a charter flight with Air Indiana, a service used by a number of Indiana schools. The company operating the service was National Jet Service of Indianapolis, which had been founded by James Stewart only a year earlier and had since flown 850,000 paid passenger flight miles. Air Indiana had four Learjets as well as a DC-3 in its fleet and had a clean safety record for the short time it had been in operation.

The DC-3 with tail number **N51071** would carry the team, university officials, and some boosters to Nashville near Murfreesboro. The flight, Air Indiana flight 216, would take less than an hour. The players were told to meet at Carson Center with their gear at three for their bus to the Tri-State Aero terminal that served charter flights at Dress Regional Airport. The flight was scheduled to depart at four.[3]

The coaches had scheduled a short practice after arrival in Murfreesboro, then a team meal. Bob Hudson had made all the arrangements.

Bobby Watson had shaved hurriedly that morning in his new home on Newburgh Road. Deidra had been up early with the girls, the two-year-old twins, Leigh and Chandra, and Angela, who was now twelve. He was running a bit late and, after shaving and rinsing his face of excess shaving cream, he put his razor and shaving cream in his toiletries bag and tossed them in his suitcase. Bobby, like most men, forgot to rinse the residue from his shave from the sink. He said goodbye to Deidra and the children and made his way in the rain over to Carson Center.

Around noon Bobby ran into Al Dauble, a booster whom he had invited to make the flight with the team. "With Christmas coming and all, I just didn't have time to go, and Bobby kidded me about it," Al said. "I saw him just after noon and he said, 'So, you're not going to go, huh?' I explained why and then he said to me, 'Well, in that case take care of my wife and send her a dozen red roses for me. Tomorrow's our anniversary.'"[4]

Bobby had also invited Ron Brand and his business partner, **Maurice "Maury" King,** both long-time Aces fans, to make the trip to Murfreesboro with the team. The two men, then in their early 30s, operated Moutoux Furniture and Appliances in the west end of Evansville and sponsored the wrap-up show on radio.

"It was so close to Christmas and our busiest time of year that I thought one of us should stay in the store," Ron Brand recalled. "My daughter Shelly was playing in a high school game that night, so when Maury and I talked about the trip that morning, we decided he should go with the team, and I would stay and close up the store and then go see Shelly play in Poseyville.

"When Maury left for the flight he said, 'You're really not going to go, are you?' I told him no, but he should go on and I would take care of things back here," Ron said. Maury protested that he wouldn't have a car, but Ron promised he'd arrange for a rental, telling his partner, "It will be there waiting for you when you land." King left for the airport shortly thereafter.[5]

Bob Hudson had invited **Charles Goad,** another Aces booster, to make the trip. Like Hudson, Goad was in his early sixties; he operated a local equipment company that bore his name. He had long wanted to travel with the Aces and was looking forward to the trip. Hudson was going too, and so was his best friend, **Charles Shike,** the university's comptroller.[6]

Marvin Bates, the popular radio broadcaster of Aces basketball, was flying down to Murfreesboro to call the game. He had begun doing Aces games for WGBF, where he had remained for 20 years. Now he was doing the play by play for WUEV, the college radio station. In all, he'd been covering Aces games for 30 years. The broadcaster, who was in his mid-50s, was so popular locally, it often took him half an hour to walk a block downtown because people kept stopping him to talk. He had become the familiar voice of the Aces. "It was like listening to an old friend when you tuned in for an Aces game," John Siau, a neighbor, said.[7]

Bates had begun teaching social science at Central High School in Evansville in the fall and was doing public relations work part time for the university. He had little time off and few opportunities to get to away games anymore. But the university radio station sports director, Mark Moulton, had come down with the flu. On Monday he had asked Bates if he could cover the game if he, Moulton, didn't feel well enough to go. Mark was relieved when Marv agreed, and Mark knew that he could count on Marv to do well on his own.[8]

Jennifer Kuster had a lab that afternoon. Bryan Taylor walked his fiancée to the class. "We chatted on the way to my class, and Bryan talked about how he felt the team was beginning to come together. Then he hugged me and gave me a kiss good-bye," she recalled.[9]

Then Bryan headed over to Carson Center.

When the players started to arrive, Mac was getting ready to leave his office, which adjoined Watson's new office at Carson Center. Despite his retirement, Mac was serving as golf coach and still teaching math. He greeted the players and wished Bobby luck.[10]

Scott Doerner was not with his teammates. "I was taking a math class in the evenings at Carson Center, and on Monday I asked Coach McCutchan if I could be excused from his class on Tuesday night to make the trip," said Scott, who had forsaken basketball for baseball but was keeping statistics for the Aces. "He told me I'd miss too much but that I could ride down to Murfreesboro with him the next day to see the game."[11]

Thornton Patberg was also in his office at Carson. Around 2:30 Greg Knipping, whose office was nearby, stuck his head in. "It's about my time to go on one of these trips," Patberg said.

"You can go if you want to," Knipping told him.

"I've got a meeting in a half hour. If I'd known sooner, I would have rescheduled it. Maybe next time," Patberg said.[12]

Knipping left for the airport.

Jim Byers was in his Carson Center office too, waiting for an applicant for the head baseball coaching job. "Under ordinary circumstances I would have gone with them, but the applicant couldn't get there until after four, so I told Bob [Hudson] that afternoon that I wouldn't be joining them," Jim said.[13]

Around 3:30 the team bus pulled up to Tri-State Aero, which ran a fixed-wing service operation and flight school at Dress Regional Airport off Route 41, near the huge Whirlpool factory complex. Tri-State Aero serviced the charter flights that were in and out of Dress.

It was still raining. Low-hanging dark gray clouds and some ground fog made it seem darker than usual for that time of day.

Tri-State's waiting area was small, designed for pilots waiting for planes to be serviced, and it was soon crowded with the players and other passengers for the flight, 25 people in all. The room was at the north end of the Tri-State complex. A few couches lined one wall, along with a few small tables. There were folding chairs but not enough for everyone. Several vending machines stood against the far wall.

"The players were just hanging around in there. They had their duffel bags with them, and a few had radios," said Michael Rasche, a flight instructor who was there that day. "[They] were just sprawled out all over. You had to step over them and their gear all around them to move through the room."[14]

Their plane hadn't arrived yet.

Steve Miller called Vicki, his wife of three months, at around six o'clock to tell her that he'd heard "the plane is having problems and we might charter a bus."[15]

Marv Bates used the pay phone in the waiting room to call his wife, Edie, who was suffering from congestive heart disease. He was worried about leaving her alone overnight and called to see how she was doing. Edie assured him she was going to be alright and told him not to worry.

Edie and Marv had been married for 32 years. She had given up her teaching career shortly after their marriage to be with him and help with stats as he broadcast games. The couple had no children but loads of friends and relatives. Marv, reassured by his wife, ended the call by telling Edie he would be home before she knew it.

Tom Collins, the *Courier*'s basketball reporter, passed the airport on his way to work. "It was foggy, misty, and rainy," he recalled. "When I got to the office a little past three, Bobby Watson called. I asked him, 'Where are you?' He said they were still at the airport. The flight had been delayed."

Collins told Watson he'd be driving down the next day. The coach told the reporter to come by the motel, where they could talk, but Collins demurred, pointing out that Bobby would be busy getting his charges ready. "He said, 'If they're not ready by then, they'll never be ready. Come on over when you get here.'" They talked a few more moments and hung up.[16]

The delay grew longer and longer, caused by the bad weather. Hungry players worked the vending machines. The Aces "were getting fidgety and anxious."[17]

Sophomore Keith Moon feared flying and called home to Cincinnati. He spoke with his father, Donald, an osteopath. "It was about 7 o'clock," his father said. "He said they had canceled the flight three times. He never mentioned why. I never asked because I know how he hated flying. He had never called from the airport before," but he did tell his father he was bored.[18]

Finally, while Keith Moon was talking with his dad, the DC-3 arrived from Indianapolis three hours late, taxiied down the ramp past the passenger terminal, and parked in front of Tri-State Aero to load passengers. The pilot shut down both engines after parking his plane so that the passenger entrance and baggage compartment were facing the Tri-State Aero waiting room area.

The plane, which bore tail number **N51071**, had come off the production line in Santa Monica, California, exactly 36 years and one month earlier. Since that time it had logged almost 20,000 hours of flight time for a plethora of different owners. It had carried without incident corporate executives, freight, business and leisure passengers, and the members of both college and professional basketball teams. It had been maintained in accordance with FAA requirements and had a spotless record of performance.

The players and other passengers moved quickly out of the Tri-State waiting area and made their way, dodging raindrops, the short distance to the plane. Personnel from Tri-State, supervised by the Air Indiana staff, loaded their luggage in the baggage compartment.

When it's just sitting on a runway, the DC-3 looks like the big brother of the Wright brothers' biplane, with its nose up and tail down. The DC-3 was first flown in 1935, only 32 years after Orville and Wilbur made history at Kitty Hawk, and in 1977, about 400 remained in operation—it's known as the most durable airplane ever built.

The plane was designed to fly, if necessary, on only one of its two Wright Cyclone nine-cylinder, air-cooled radial engines. When he was director of TWA, Charles Lindbergh insisted that the plane have that capability. It was a little more than 64 feet long and had a wing span of 95 feet; the sleek fuselage was only slightly wider than 7 feet. Its maximum speed was 216 miles per hour, and it had a range of nearly 1,500 miles.

Indeed, the plane has flown more miles, carried more passengers and cargo, accumulated more flying hours, and performed more impossible feats than any other plane in history. At one point DC-3 aircraft carried fully 90 percent of all the world's air traffic.

The military version of the DC-3 was a favorite of pilots who flew it. It could take off and land safely on very short runways and was virtually indestructible. Their fondness for the plane is demonstrated by their various nicknames for it—from Old Methuselah to Gooney Bird—and it was the workhorse of the skies.

Greeting the players aboard the plane was flight attendant **Pamela Smith** in her crisp blue uniform jacket and skirt. At 24 Pam was only a little older than the players. She was tall and had long dark hair that she parted in the middle. Although she had been born in London, she had lived in Indianapolis for most of her life. She was a 1972 graduate of John Marshall High School in Indianapolis and had then worked for five years at Western Electric. She had joined National Jet Service, Inc. as a flight attendant and had completed her initial training on November 4 and her check flight on December 2. She had only 15 hours of flight time.

The pilot that day was **Ty Van Pham**, 42, who had served as a lieutenant colonel in the South Vietnamese air force, and had fled Vietnam when Saigon fell to the communists. Now he lived in Indianapolis with his wife and four children. During the war he had flown high-level South Vietnamese government and military officials. Ty Van Pham had logged 9,100 flight hours, 4,600 of them in a DC-3. He had been working for National Jet Service for two months. He had completed his last proficiency flight check only two months before, on October 18, a few days after he'd been hired by National Jet Service.

The copilot was **Gaston Ruiz**, 35, who had fled his native Cuba for the United States in 1963 and settled in Miami, where his wife and son were still living. He was a licensed commercial airline instructor who had logged 1,330 hours' flying time and 80 hours in a DC-3. He had been with National Jet Service for three months.

Also on board were **James Stewart**, the 29-year-old son of Paul Stewart, founder and co-owner of National Jet Services, and **William Hartford**, 36, the company's general manager. James Stewart had been president of the company since its formation and had piloted the company's first plane, a Learjet that had carried elected officials and celebrities such Bob Hope. According to his father, James hoped to expand the company to include regular commuter airline service.[19]

Hartford had joined National Jet Service only the year before. But during his tenure the airline had secured business from about 15 midwestern university basketball programs, including those at Valparaiso, Purdue, and Notre Dame, and had transported the Indiana Pacers of the NBA.[20]

Twelve minutes after the plane arrived at Dress, the cockpit contacted the control tower to ask for clearance to use instrument flight rules (IFR) because of the poor visibility. The tower granted the request about 30 seconds later and cleared Air Indiana 216 to taxi to runway 18 via taxiway F.

At 7:16 the tower informed Air Indiana 216 that the "'weather measured 400 [feet], overcast, visibility three quarters [of a mile], light rain and fog.'" The flight crew acknowledged the information.

At 7:16:11 the tower controller called Air Indiana and said the plane was cleared to use IFR to fly to Nashville; the cockpit readback was correct.

In the cabin Pam Smith was giving the preflight safety instructions to the passengers as she stood in the front of the cabin near the bulkhead. The players' eyes were riveted on the pretty young woman as she read them the emergency instructions. As she instructed, they tightened their seat belts securely across their lower waist and hips. Pam then took her position in the jump seat attached to the forward bulkhead, facing the passengers and the rear of the plane.

At 7:16:32 the tower cleared Air Indiana 216 into position on runway 18 and told it to hold until Delta Flight 619, a Douglas DC-9-30, departed from runway 22, which intersects runway 18 at the southeast end of the airport.

At 7:19 the Delta flight lifted off from runway 22.

At 7:19: 54 the tower controller cautioned Air Indiana 216 about possible turbulence from the departing DC-9 and issued takeoff clearance.

It took the plane only 30 to 35 seconds to taxi onto the runway and begin takeoff.

"Air Indiana 216, Evansville tower, cleared on course," the tower transmitted.

At 7:20 the cockpit acknowledged takeoff clearance, "Air Indiana 216," and began its takeoff roll.[21]

With 29 people on board, the aircraft bearing tail number **N51071** rolled down runway 18 at Dress Regional Airport.[22]

Inside the Tri-State Aero building two employees watched through the rain and ground fog as the plane picked up speed as it lumbered down runway 18.

Before the plane reached the main terminal building, its tail lifted up and the plane popped off the ground. By the time it passed Tri-Sate Aero further down the line, it was about 25 feet off the ground. The landing gear was retracted, and the plane banked sharply to the left in an extreme nose-up position, causing the Tri-State observers to believe "the plane wasn't going to make it."

The plane was about 2,500 feet from the runway and headed east-southeast when they lost sight of it in the fog.

"Air Indiana 216, what is your heading?" came the query from the tower.

"Air Indiana 216, what is your heading?"

"Standby" was the response at **7:21**.[23]

That was the last transmission from the cockpit.

The land on which Dress Regional Airport stands is as flat as a pancake in almost every direction around the field. The land had been planted with corn, which had been harvested some months earlier.

The ground rises up in only one place, the site of a housing development known as Melody Hills. The houses were newer structures of one and two stories, and the land surrounding them was heavily wooded. The development is reached from St. George Road, via Twickingham Drive, and rises fairly steeply, about 100 to 200 feet above the road.

A woman who was in her Melody Hills home heard the plane, and it "sounded like it was too low." As she watched, the plane was descending, dipping wildly from side to side. Seconds later she heard the engine noise increase—the noise was tremendous, she said, then ceased entirely. She heard "total silence" followed by a "thud—very dull."[24]

A homeowner in the northeast corner of the development also saw the plane approaching. It appeared to strike or "nearly strike" a stand of trees in his back-yard.[25] The plane's nose was up, and the pilot appeared to be trying to get over and away from the house and trees. The DC-3's landing lights were on, and the man saw the cabin lights. The engines were making a strange noise, "like they were pulling against each other," which continued for about 10 seconds. Then, he said, it was as if the engines were turned off like a radio. Complete silence.[26]

The flight had lasted just 90 seconds of wild, gyrating, ear-shattering terror.

At 7:22 the control tower observed a fireball.

"Oh, he's crashed!" a controller yelled.

The tower sounded the airport crash alarm that alerted emergency crews and vehicles.

It would do little good.

It was so foggy that the tower could not give the emergency crews an exact location for the crash site.

With rescue crews hampered by the lack of visibility and remoteness of the area, people from the Melody Hills subdivision were the first to arrive at the accident site, 10 to 15 minutes after the plane had crashed and the tower had observed a fireball.

They found that the main fire was mostly out or burning itself out. Parts of the fuselage were still burning and glowing in the fog and darkness. Small flames still flickered in the wreckage.

Gene Hollencamp, who had been an army medic in Vietnam, had been at the Patrick Aviation hangar at the south end of the airport with his boss, Pat Alvey, when the plane had taken off. They had seen the flash through the fog-shrouded night and had moved immediately in the direction of the crash. Alvey knew the area was hard to reach. It was east of the main runway, and the road nearest the site dead-ended at the railroad tracks beyond Melody Hills.

As they made their way through the mud and underbrush, they could see the glow of small flames reflecting off the low-hanging fog. "As we got closer, my first impression was it looked like there were a lot of tombstones scattered around," Hollencamp said. "Then I realized they were seats, with many of the passengers still strapped in them. Most of the injuries were from blunt trauma. I think they died quickly."[27]

Upon impact the passengers had been ejected out through the jagged fuselage. Most landed on the muddy plateau, while some tumbled down into the railroad ravine about 15 feet below the crash site. Rain had formed large puddles on the ground, and the mud was knee deep in some places.[28]

Incredibly, some were still alive.

"I put my gray bomber jacket over one," Gene said.[29]

Jess Roberts was fire chief of Scott Township.

"We were working an auto accident on Highway 41 when our dispatcher called, asking if we had a four-wheel-drive vehicle . . . if we could send one over to the airport. I told her we'd send a truck and crew over.

"It was so foggy when we got there, you couldn't see your hand in front of your face," Roberts recalled.[30]

McCutchanville Fire Department had also been summoned. It too sent a four-wheel-drive vehicle to the airport and sought to find a way in to the crash site.

Among those still alive when Melody Hills residents got to the crash site was flight attendant Pam Smith. Strapped in and facing the rear of the plane, she had been in the safest seat in the DC-3. She died before she could be transported to a hospital.

One of the Aces was also still breathing, but he too died before he could be removed.

Finally, fire department and local and state police personnel reached the scene. Thirteen ambulances had been summoned and were waiting at St. George Road, the closest they could get to the site.

They got one player who was still breathing to the emergency room at Deaconess Hospital in Evansville. The ER team transferred the young man to a hospital gurney and wheeled him rapidly to the emergency room. The team had been expecting more injured, but the ambulance driver said no more would be coming.[31]

As the emergency workers had made their way through the wreckage, they had quickly realized that all those ambulance drivers would not be needed. They left the scene, their sirens silent.

What had begun as a rescue operation had become a recovery operation and a very difficult one at that. The only way to get the bodies out, police and fire crews decided, was by train. The tracks lay in the ravine just beyond the site, and a train was summoned from the Whirlpool plant less than a mile away.

Pat Wathen was a reporter for the *Courier* on duty that night. He had grown up in Melody Hills and knew the area.

"I . . . had ridden my bike back there as a kid and knew how to get in to the site through the housing subdivision," he said. "As I made my way, others had already arrived. There were emergency lights casting a white glow that pierced the fog, and a red railroad flare was burning, casting an eerie reddish glow over the area." There was, he said, "a war scene feeling to it."

As he got closer, he could see, "scattered all about, some duffel bags and luggage. As I looked closer, I saw the duffel bags had a logo stenciled on them."

Then Pat realized what the logo on the bags was, and he said, to no one in particular, "My God, it's the Aces." [32]

The city desk at the *Courier* had picked up word of the crash from the police scanner and sent the police reporter and Rich Davis, then a 26-year-old reporter, to the scene.

Rich's sister lived in Melody Hills, so he called her first. "She told me she heard a lot of sirens," he said. "We got out there and parked on Ward Road, which dead-ended at the railroad tracks, and tried to find a way in. I found a house and asked to use the phone to call my editor. He told me, 'We think it's the Aces.'

"It was like a blow to my gut. I thought, 'It can't be.'"

One of the neighborhood kids helped Rich find his way to where the plane had gone down. "Several muddy minutes later I was at the site," he wrote thirty years later. "I stood above duffel bags marked 'Aces.' I saw the tail sticking up above the wreckage and a young man choking back tears as he walked by me. Behind me, a very slow-moving train moaned a sorrowful whistle as it drew near." [33]

He recalled that "there was still smoke hanging in the air, mingling with the fog. In the trees above, clothes were hanging from the bare branches. I stayed there about 15 minutes. No one had any answers for me, so I headed back to my office. I still couldn't believe it had happened. I gave my story to the reporter that was writing the article and tried to give her a picture of the scene. I was stunned and in shock from what I'd seen.

"I wasn't an Aces fan," Rich said, "but I became one that night." [34]

The train was making its way by backing up from the siding at the Whirlpool plant to the Louisville and Nashville Railroad tracks. Its engineer sounded the whistle as it backed up. "It was very eerie. I don't remember any other noise at the scene—just that train whistle that sounded so sad as it approached the site," Pat Wathen said [35]

The engine, a boxcar, and a caboose stopped on the tracks below the wreckage.

The fire and rescue crews had to place the bodies in body recovery bags, put them on stretchers, and wrestle them down the muddy, slippery ravine to the boxcar. The steel-enclosed car bore the logo of the Santa Fe Railroad.[36]

It was a terrible task to perform. "Many of my men who went in there to help with the recovery wouldn't talk about it after," Jess Roberts said. "They still won't talk about it today."[37]

Two of the dead, pilot Ty Van Pham and National Jet Services president James Stewart, were still in the plane's cockpit, which had detached on impact and was badly mangled and burned. The rescue crews lacked the equipment needed to extricate them. The bodies would remain in place until daybreak when they could be removed with the aid of acetylene torches and special tools.

Rev. Calvin Mutti, whose home was nearby, was among those who slogged through the mud and rain to the site.

"It was a terrible place to die," he said.[38]

Eventually, all the bodies were loaded, and the train made its way slowly toward downtown, a distance of about 10 miles.

A temporary morgue had been established at the Community Center, which was located at 100 East Walnut Street, right behind the railroad tracks. The center, where John Ed Washington had liked to play pickup ball, was gaily decorated for the Christmas holiday with wreaths and evergreen boughs and bows.[39] Just inside the main entrance was a large Christmas tree with blinking lights.

Mike Duckworth was the 21-year-old assistant director of the Community Center when he got the call telling him his facility was about to become a temporary morgue. "We immediately went to work setting up the place to receive the bodies, the families, the Red Cross volunteers, and the media that would be arriving," he said.[40]

Ironically, the room they decided to use was a gymnasium, the site of John Ed's pickup games. Community Center personnel shoved aside a volleyball net and set up long tables with white sheets where the bodies would be placed for examination and identification. Then they turned off the heat and waited for the train to arrive.

News travels fast in the electronic age. Bad news seems to travel even faster.

In Evansville WFIE-TV reporter Mike Blake, who was responsible for the six and ten o'clock sports news, was back at the studio after covering a high school game. Blake had been at the station since 1970 and had become sports director a year later. He had covered the Aces since then and had grown to know and like Bobby Watson. "He was a sophisticated Fonzie and was great with the kids," Blake said of Watson.

At the high school game Mike had heard some people talking about a plane crash. "I assumed it was a small plane," he said.

When he got back to the newsroom at about 8:30, the station's general manager was still there, which was unusual.

The manager approached Mike immediately and told him of the plane crash Mike had heard about earlier.

"'It's the Aces,'" he told me.

"After that nothing was the same again," Mike said.[41]

WFIE was the only local television outlet with a mobile unit.

"It was called Live Eye 14," recalled Richard Dietz, a producer at the station. "I rushed out to the scene and got as close as possible. It was very dark, so I turned on all the high-intensity lights on the van to try to help the emergency workers," he wrote years later. "I was waiting for the reporters to arrive when a state policeman walked back from the direction of the crash. I saw his face was ashen white, and he slowly told me, holding in his emotions, that the plane that had crashed was the UE plane and that everyone had perished. I was shocked and couldn't say anything. I never got his name. I was now alone in the cold rain and, except for the lights on the van illuminating in the direction of the crash, the darkness closed in."[42]

Reporters from the Associated Press and UPI were calling the station for updates, and newspapers all across the country called in seeking information. The other two local stations and PBS all took the WFIE feed live. Within 30 minutes of the crash, news of the tragedy—sketchy and often in error—began going out over radio and television.

"David James and I set up in the studio and began coverage that went on for hours," Mike Blake said. "We were on virtually all night and the next day with coverage of the story as it unfolded. We sent the remote unit to the Community Center and did live interviews from there. I was 33 at the time, and I remember thinking to myself, 'God, please help me get through this.'"[43]

Television was how Mike Joyner's family learned his plane had gone down. His father, Robert Joyner Sr., was watching a basketball game on television in his Terre Haute living room when he noticed a news item crawling across the bottom of the screen.

"I heard my father screaming, 'No! No!'" Patricia McGee, one of Mike's younger sisters, recalled. She was in her room listening to music at the time. "We ran in to see what was wrong. My mother was trying to console him."[44]

Robert, Mike's older brother, was married and living four blocks from his parents' home. He was watching a popular sitcom when he saw a news bulletin scroll across the bottom of the television screen. "It said, 'Plane crash in Evansville. Details at 11,'" he recalled.

Shortly thereafter he heard a woman screaming and crying in the street. "It sounded like my sister. I jumped up and went out, and it was her and she was just bawling. She looked up at me and screamed, 'We've lost Michael!'

"I said, 'What are you talking about? What happened?'

"She said, 'He's gone. He died in that plane crash.'

"I just lost it completely. I wandered around in the drizzle in a daze. I couldn't deal with it at all," Robert said.

When he reached his parents' house, he found his father in tears. "It was the first time anyone in my family ever saw my dad cry," Robert said.

The night would be a long one for the tight-knit Joyner family, who had welcomed Mike's teammates Barney Lewis and Warren Alston for Thanksgiving only three weeks earlier. They couldn't get home to North Carolina for the holiday, so Mike had brought them to Terre Haute.

"It usually takes about two and a half hours to get to Evansville," Robert said. "We made it there in an hour and fifteen minutes" on the night of the crash.

At the Community Center he joined his father in identifying Michael's body. "I walked up to the cot where my dad was, and I saw the shoes sticking out from under the blankets," Robert said. "They were Michael's favorite shoes. He wore them so much they had a hole in the bottom. When I saw the shoes, I knew it was him and that he was gone."[45]

A little more than an hour after Steve Miller had called his wife at their apartment, Vicki Miller heard screaming sirens as ambulances raced past. A few minutes later her living room filled with people coming over to check on her and wait with her to learn what had happened.[46]

Bryan Taylor's fiancée, Jennifer Kuster, was in her small apartment near the old armory when the phone rang. "I was . . . sewing a red dress for the Christmas party that the team was having at the Watsons' house in a few days," she recalled. "The phone call was from a childhood friend I hadn't really seen in years. She asked me if she could bring a pizza and come over. I thought it was a little strange, but said sure. The television was on when she arrived. She came in with a friend and, after handing the pizza to her friend, she gave me a big hug. I knew something was very wrong. Pretty soon the news was on the television about a plane crash, and other people were arriving at my tiny apartment. I called my parents and then Bryan's parents in Tell City. They hadn't heard anything, and I told them what little I knew, which wasn't much. The people in my apartment kept urging me to go lie down. It was all very confusing and troubling."[47]

Thornton Patberg, who had passed on the opportunity to make the plane trip because he couldn't miss a meeting, was in his basement den with a fire crackling in the fireplace when the phone rang.

"It was Dee Kalena, director of public relations, calling. She said there had been a plane crash at the airport and that they thought it was the Aces.

"'No, that can't be. They left hours ago,' I told her.

"Then another call came in, and it was then I learned that it was, in fact, our team," he said. "I left to go get President Graves and tell him what I'd learned."[48]

At Wheeler Hall on the University of Evansville campus, the faculty string quartet concert was underway, the one Art Adye had chosen to attend rather than join his friend Bryan Taylor on the plane trip.

"I was sitting one row behind President Graves and his wife. There were about 300 people there to see the faculty string quartet. . . . I saw Thornton Patberg walk down the aisle past me and tap President Graves on the shoulder. Graves got up and looked a little shaken. They walked out together," Ayde recalled.

"When the concert ended at around 8:15–8:30, I left and as soon as I stepped outside, I saw several girls there who were crying. I asked what was wrong, and one of them told me, 'It's the Aces, they were in a plane crash.'

"I left for my house about three blocks away and turned on the television. All the stations were covering the story, and none seemed to know exactly what happened or how many were injured. Switching channels, I saw David James, a young reporter, on the screen. I knew from the look on his face that something terrible was wrong."[49]

Wallace Graves had left the concert immediately. He dropped his wife and her mother at their home on campus and went to Patberg's office.

"Jim Byers and some others were there when I arrived. All anyone knew at first was that there had been a crash and that it 'might have been' our team on the plane," Graves said. "The police called and asked me to come to headquarters downtown near the Community Center. They told me they were trying to get information from the crash site on survivors and asked me not to confirm that it was our team and not to talk to the press until they gave me permission."[50]

Jim Byers, whose interview of a candidate for baseball coach had prevented him from making the trip with the team, had gone home after the interview. He'd had supper, then returned to his office at Carson Center.

"I got a call from someone between 7:30 and 8:00 about a plane crash. The caller was asking if it was our team. The call was very confusing," he said. "After that I got another call almost immediately from Patberg telling me that there had been a crash and that it looked like it was our team.

"I left and went to Pat's office, and we were both pretty much in shock. We soon learned . . . there probably weren't any survivors. Graves, who was also there, left for the police station, and Pat and I went to the Community Center with Coach McCutchan, who had been teaching a class, and Steve Kim, our v.p. for development."

Mac had been teaching a math class at Carson Center that night. Scott Doerner was in the class because Mac had refused his request to skip it and travel with the team. Scott recalled that "Jim Byers walked in our classroom door and called Coach McCutchan outside. They talked for a minute or so, and then the door opened and Coach McCutchan motioned for me to come outside. 'There has been a plane crash near Melody Hills,' Coach told me. My sister lived out there, and my first reaction was that she was involved somehow. When I asked if that were the case, Coach McCutchan said, 'No, it was the team's plane.'

"I knew that they were scheduled to leave at 4:00 so I thought, 'It couldn't be them.' Mr. Byers said he was certain that it was. I couldn't believe it. After that, everything became a whirlwind.

"Byers and Mac were headed down to the Community Center to help identify the bodies, and after a while I decided to go down there, too. I walked back to my frat house to get my car, and when I walked in, my fraternity brothers all looked at me like they were seeing a ghost. They thought I was on the plane," Scott said.[51]

While university officials went downtown to deal with a situation none of them had ever had to face before, news of the crash had spread across the campus. From radio and television reports students learned that the team was involved. On a campus as small and compact as Evansville's, the news made its way rapidly to every dorm, frat, and sorority house.

Soon students began walking through the rain to Neu Chapel.

The chapel has a high, arching ceiling of dark wood from which are suspended fourteen long gold-and-white lights. Five stained-glass windows line each side. A large pipe organ sits in the rear of the chapel, up in a choir loft. The altar sits three steps above the floor and is framed by sturdy stone walls. Behind the altar hangs a cross that is 15 feet high. The chapel has a comforting, strong, and sturdy feel to it.

The arrival of the students had not been arranged; there hadn't been time for that. It was just a place they all were instinctively drawn to. First, just few dozen were there, but soon the chapel was full. It held 500 comfortably, but more than a thousand stood in line in the rain that night, trying to get inside.

As radio and television reported more about what had happened, students relayed the information to the chapel, and what had begun as a prayer vigil became a solemn and sob-filled group memorial service without speakers or counselors. The students had only themselves. They stayed throughout the night, praying, comforting, and consoling each other, facing an awful reality together.

Diana Townsend, a junior, was in her sorority house, practicing with some others for an upcoming music competition.

"It had been a pretty normal day of classes," she recalled. "But it was a gray, drizzly day. Kind of foreboding, when I look back on it."

As she and the other singers stood singing around the piano in the Zeta Tau Alpha sorority house, "someone from one of the evening classes ran in. It was around 8:00 and she said, 'There's been a plane crash. The basketball team's plane crashed.'

"One of the girls, our piano player, got a horrible look on her face and collapsed right on the piano. Her boyfriend was David Furr, and she thought he was on the plane," Diana said.[52]

"After that it was just pandemonium. We were trying to comfort her, and some girls were crying and screaming. Others, the more logical ones, were trying to find out what was really known about the crash. Everyone was just wide eyed and staring at the girl who was crying. Practice broke up, and some stayed to comfort the girl, while the rest of us went back to our rooms to watch TV and try to learn what had happened. At first the reporters said there were some survivors, but as the night went on the reports kept getting worse."

Upset, Diana called her boyfriend and said she wanted to go for a walk. They walked across campus in the rain. "We walked behind Neu Chapel and stopped under a streetlamp. My boyfriend put his arm around me to comfort me, and I had my head nestled against his chest. I was crying."

A photographer from the school newspaper was also there and took a picture. The photo, of an unnamed couple silhouetted in the dark and rainy night, would become a symbol of the shared grief the campus had endured. It appeared in a special section of the *Link*, the university yearbook, later that year.

When she got back to the dorm, Diana found she was "mentally exhausted but couldn't sleep. John Ed Washington was in criminal justice class with me," she said. "I helped him keep up with his assignments while he was playing. He was good hearted—talked tough but really wasn't. He was a funny, funny guy, kind of laidback. I liked him a lot."

Almost every student on campus had a similar experience. The university was small enough so everyone pretty much knew everyone else. "We were all in it together. It brought us all together," Diane said.[53]

In Munster, Indiana, Diane Comandella was in her kitchen baking cookies for her brother Ray. He would be coming home for Christmas soon, and Ray loved her cookies. Ray had called his mother on December 11 to wish her happy birthday.

"I was baking, and *Happy Days* was on the television set in the living room. I could see it from the kitchen, and all of a sudden a news bulletin came over saying something about Evansville. I thought to myself, 'Why would Evansville be on television?'"

Shortly after that she heard a knock at the front door.

"When you open the door and a police officer is standing there looking grim, you know it's not going to be good news," Diane said. That was how she learned about the crash.[54]

Mike Platt was still at the university, working in the admissions office and taking graduate courses. He knew every player on the team.

He was playing intramural basketball when Jim Byers came to the court and called him over. "He asked me when I thought the plane left and then told me that there had been a crash," Mike said. "At first they thought it was a commercial airliner. Later we learned it was our plane that had gone down. It was all very confusing and hard to get information."

Later, Byers asked Mike to go with Scott Doerner to the hospital to try to identify the player that they had taken there. He and Scott went together.

"When we got there, the doctor asked us to just look at some of his clothes to see if we could identify him that way,' Scott remembered. "We couldn't, and so he asked us to come in and look at him."

Scott asked if the player had been dismembered, and the doctor assured him that was not the case.

"When Scott and I walked in, we thought at first it was Mike Duff," Platt said. "He wasn't mangled in any way. But his features were so puffed up it was hard to tell who he was."

Scott too remembered the swelling: "He was all swollen up, and his skin was yellowish. I remember that his fingertips were all split open. I asked the doctor about it, and he said it was from the pressure change caused by the explosion."

Mike had brought a tape measure to the hospital, which was how they were able to positively identify him for the doctor. "We told him the player's name was Greg Smith," Scott said. "Then I asked how he was doing—was he going to make it? The doctor shook his head and said, 'No, there's been too much internal damage done.'"[55]

Scott and Mike left the hospital. Scott went back to campus, and Mike went to the Community Center to help identify the other bodies.

Greg Smith had been a late addition to the travel roster after Mark Siegel's surgery earlier in the year. He had been thrilled at the chance to play Division I basketball, even if he was going to see most of the games from the bench.

His parents, who lived in West Frankfort, Illinois, had learned of the crash through television reports. They tried repeatedly to get information from the school, police, anybody they could think of. Finally, they called Greg's high school coach, Harold Hood, and assistant principal Gail Borton, and all four set out for Evansville, driving as fast as they dared over rain-slickened roads and listening closely to the car radio in the hope of hearing more news. The drive from West Frankfort, about 80 miles, took less time than usual.

They made the trip mostly in silence. "We didn't know what to say. We were hoping he was still alive, but we didn't know," Hood told reporters.[56]

When they arrived in Evansville, they were directed first to the Community Center, and someone there told them to go to Deaconess Hospital.

It was nearly 12:30 a.m.

They were about five minutes too late.

Greg, 18 and the only surviving player, had died at 12:25.

All of the Aces were gone.

As she tried to find out what was going on, John Ed Washington's mother called everybody she could think of and had no luck. She had heard a survivor had been taken to Deaconess Hospital. Hoping against hope, she called there and asked for the emergency room.

The nurse on duty wasn't very helpful. She couldn't say who the patient was.

"Finally she asked her, 'Is he white or is he black?'

"'He's white,' she was told.

"That's when I knew he was gone."

Donna Moon, Keith's mother, was attending a meeting of the Kettering Board of Education when the door to the meeting room swung open. The ashen look on the face of her husband, Don, told her that something was terribly wrong. A neighbor had contacted him with news that the plane carrying the Evansville team, including their son, whom she called "The Gentle Giant," had crashed. As her husband told her what had happened, Donna collapsed in his arms.[57]

The train carrying the bodies arrived at the Community Center around 10:30 p.m.

The place was growing crowded. Staff from the Vandenburgh County Coroner's Office were already there. So were students from the Deaconess Hospital School of Nursing who had volunteered to assist.

"They heard about it before I did. On their own they called the Red Cross and volunteered," said Mary Jo Allgood, nursing instructor at the school and nurse chair of volunteers at the Red Cross. "I've had this role for 18 years, and I've taught disaster nursing to my students for all these years, but this is the first time I've ever had to activate the plans."[58]

The students piled into cars, ten in one car alone.

"This is not like the textbooks. These are people you know," Allgood said. "What they had to do tonight was not an easy thing for them to do. They'd never seen bodies mangled like this."

Because of the police department's instructions to university officials, contacting the families had been delayed. Most learned of the crash from television, radio, or family or friends who had heard a news report or had been told of one by someone else. Most parents, like Edna Washington, tried frantically to get information all night. A lot of them, like the Smiths, simply made their way to the Community Center with little idea of how bad the news was.

From Tell City, Kettering, New Albany, West Hartford, Eldorado, Terre Haute, Munster, Indianapolis, Cincinnati, Jeffersonville, and other towns and cities they came to Evansville.

The Red Cross had quickly assembled another team of volunteers, people who would assist the families that were now beginning to arrive. The Salvation Army, which usually spends Christmas ringing bells to solicit donations from shoppers, was there as well. Ministers, priests, and rabbis from every denomination were there to offer solace and prayers.

As the train pulled to a stop behind the building, Reilly Stansberg, a Louisville and Nashville conductor, stood guard alongside the boxcar, keeping reporters and onlookers away as the bodies were unloaded. "I'd never had a job like this. I've never had to do anything like this, and I hope I never have to again," he said.[59]

More than 300 people had assembled behind the Community Center in the drizzling rain. Some were students from UE and ISU–Evansville, others were local residents. All stood respectfully silent as the bodies were taken inside.

About 90 minutes earlier, Graves and Mike Platt had joined Byers, Patberg, and Mac at the Community Center. "We were all in shock," Byers said. "Scott Doerner was there. When the bodies arrived, we all went from table to table to try to identify each person lying there. It was not an easy or pleasant task."[60]

Reporter Rod Spaw later described a scene that he could never get out of his mind, that haunted his dreams ten years later:

A lobby, lit softly because it was long past the time that anyone is normally there. A wall of glass overlooking a courtyard and a half-dozen people
pressed against it, watching the rain bead against the outside surface and run
down their own reflections. A few whispered words but mostly empty stares
on faces drained of expression.

Across the courtyard, no one had thought to cover the windows in the gymnasium. From the lobby it looks like one row of snowdrifts after another:
white covered tables with white covered bundles and people in white smocks
moving between them. A woman in a dark winter coat enters with a man on
each arm but it is hard to tell who is supporting whom. They stop at a table.
The woman buckles and puts one hand across her face. The men hold her
gently for a moment, then lead her away.[61]

It fell to Deputy Coroner Earl Cox to talk with family members and to try to
get them to identify the bodies. He attempted to secure the identifications with
personal effects—a wallet, a drivers license, an article of clothing. Then he told
the families they didn't have to view the bodies if they didn't want to. But most
wanted to see for themselves.

The nursing students had cleaned up the bodies as well as they could. But bodies that have been propelled at great force through the jagged metal edges of a
fuselage suffer severe damage.

"Some wanted to just see an arm or a hand," said Rev. Kenneth Knapp, director of Catholic Charities.[62]

Among them was Joan Hudson Roth, Bob's daughter. "I'd been at church
working on the Sunday bulletin when my husband called and said I needed to
come home. My mother had seen on the news that the plane had crashed. She'd
worked on the manifest for my dad and was the only person who knew who all
the passengers were," Joan said. "I got the itinerary and manifest from her, and
my husband and our minister went to the Community Center. There were a lot
of support people and medical people there. Nurses were standing by the bodies
that were all covered up.

"They begged me not to look. But I wanted to see him just one last time. I
started to peel the sheet away, and his arm fell out and hit my leg. I felt like it
was a final touch he was giving me. Saying goodbye," she said.[63]

Bob, like most of the victims, had suffered a broken neck, as well as head and chest trauma.

Jennifer Kuster arrived at the Community Center with her father and Bryan Taylor's dad and brother, Grant, who'd arrived together to identify her fiancé.

After a while, Ralph Taylor was called inside.

"When I got there, some of the nurses from Deaconess, who I knew, came over and started hugging me. Then I knew," she said. Moments later Ralph Taylor emerged ashen faced. Jennifer burst into the lobby, crying and clinging to her father's shoulder. "They were supposed to be married," her father said. "That's what they were supposed to do."[64]

A woman was admitted to the gymnasium. A minute later everyone heard her scream, "Oh no, God. Not him. Not him."

The rest of the place went silent.[65]

None of Bobby Watson's assistant coaches were on the plane.

When Mark Sandy heard about the crash, he was at a game in Carbondale scouting a future opponent. He immediately returned to Evansville.

"I helped with the identification. I identified Bobby for them," he said. "There were a lot of the parents there. I talked to some of them but there was nothing I could say to help them get through it."[66]

Ernie Simpson, another assistant coach, had been at a high school game between Apollo High and Owensboro. He was scouting Jeff Jones, a 6-4 guard whom Evansville coveted. When Simpson learned of the crash, his "mind just went blank," he said. He hurried back to Evansville to "do whatever I can. Whatever Jim Byers wants me to do."[67]

The third assistant coach, Stafford Stephenson, was in Florida on a recruiting trip. His wife, Tess, "tried frantically to reach him all evening. Finally, in the morning, I got through, and he got a flight almost immediately after telling the airline who he was and where he was from."

Tess had heard about the crash from Deidra Watson. "She had called my house around 8:00 or so and said she heard there had been a plane crash, and she was concerned that it might be Bobby's plane," Tess recalled. "I told her not to worry about it, I'd make some phone calls and find out what was going on."

Tess knew that if Bobby's plane had gone down, Deidra Watson would find coping especially difficult. Deidra, who was only 31, was an extremely private person, but she had shared with friends that she had a huge fear of death. She said she could spot a funeral director from fifty paces.

"After a few calls I found out her fears [about Bobby's plane] were right," Tess said. "I called back but by then she had already heard the news."[68]

Wayne Boultinghouse was at a local high school game "when the public address announcer said there had been a plane crash involving the Aces. I left immediately.

"When I got home I started to make phone calls to find out what had happened. Rumors were flying everywhere. I called Mac, but he was already at the Community Center. Eventually I found someone who confirmed that it had been the plane the Aces were taking. I left for Deidra's house as soon as I knew." The Watsons lived only a couple of blocks from Wayne's house.

"When I got there, a minister who lived nearby was already there, trying to comfort her. She was all choked up. Very emotional. There was little I could say or do to help," Wayne said.[69]

On a table in a cut glass vase stood a dozen long-stemmed red roses. They were from Bobby to Deidra for their fourth wedding anniversary. Al Dauble had sent them, just as Bobby had requested.

"It was a night of horror," Jim Byers said many years later. "President Graves was really strong throughout."

Graves had fought in World War II with General George Patton. He was a forward artillery observer when his unit was overrun by the Germans and he was captured. He spent months in a prisoner of war camp under severe and horrific conditions before he managed to escape and make his way through enemy territory to freedom.

He'd seen the horrors of war, endured the indignities and deprivation of prison camp, and had lived through it all. None of his experiences had prepared him, or any of the other university officials, for what they had to go through on that terrible night.

All would be haunted by it for months and years to come. "My father didn't get a single night's rest for six months after that," Mac's daughter Marilyn said. "He would wake up every evening. He couldn't sleep."

The images that Mac had seen that night flashed through his subconscious for months. "It was very hard on him. He knew all of them. He'd recruited some of them," Marilyn said.[70]

"Mac was heartbroken," Mike Platt said. "It was a devastating loss for him. The hardest part for him was being there when the parents got there. He felt he'd let the parents down. He was like that. He felt he was a surrogate parent for them and that he'd failed them in his duty. He had to face them and tell them that their sons, whom they had entrusted to him, were gone."[71]

Mac spoke with reporters who had gathered at the Community Center. "There were 24 of our people on that plane. At times like this you must turn around and face things," said Mac, choking back tears. "But I've never had to face anything like this."[72]

Wallace Graves also talked with the reporters. "This is a tragedy that defies description," he told them. "The university will suffer this loss for the rest of its life."

Rod Spaw, then a young *Courier* reporter, was among the many at the Community Center. He'd been at the crash site earlier. That evening he filed his story for the next day's paper and described what he had witnessed that night:

> The sorrow and horror felt by those confronted with the rescue and identification operation was magnified a thousand times over in the faces of the family members as they arrived at the center. . . .
>
> Occasionally, their sounds of grief would shatter the silence and burn the images of tragedy even deeper into the face of the night.[73]

In a later article Spaw summed up the experience of the city on that fateful night: "Evansville is a town that doesn't want to dwell on December 13, 1977, a day of blackness that didn't lift when the night ended. The flight lasted 90 seconds. But the hurt endured far longer. Such is the nature of dreams when waking comes too soon and the wonder of them goes unfulfilled."[74]

The entire city mourned the loss. "A pall set over the city like a cloak of despair," Spaw wrote.[75]

For the next five days there would be only wakes and funerals.

(Endnotes)
1   Tom Collins, telephone interview by author, January 24, 2011.
2   Stafford Stephenson, telephone interview by author, January 24, 2011.

3   National Transportation Safety Board, *Aircraft Accident Report—National Jet Services, Inc., Douglas DC-3, N51071*, NTSB report no. AAR-78-10 (Washington, D.C.: Bureau of Accident Investigation, August 17, 1978), 2.

4   Dave Johnson, "The Irony of It All," *Evansville Press*, December 14, 1977, 4.

5   Ron Brand, telephone interview by author, February 12, 2011. Shelly Brand went on to play at Evansville, where she became the school's all-time leading scorer and a member of the Hall of Fame.

6   "The Dead," *Evansville Press*, December 14, 1977.

7   John Siau, telephone interview by author, January 30, 2011.

8   Herb Marynell, "Illness, Back Pains Were Saviors for Two Who Missed Flight," *Evansville Press*, December 14, 1977, 7.

9   Jennifer Kuster Adkins, interview by author by telephone, October 16, 2011.

10   Don Bernhardt, "After 31 Years Mac Faced His Hardest Job," *Evansville Courier*, December 14, 1977.

11   Scott Doerner, telephone interview by author, February 22, 2011.

12   Thornton Patberg, telephone interview by author, January 29, 2011, and several follow-up calls.

13   Jim Byers, telephone interview by author, January 27, 2011.

14   Michael Rasche, telephone interview by author, February 10, 2011, and follow-up interview, June 29, 2011.

15   Daniel Robinson, "Thirty Years after Evansville Plane Crash, Players' Memories Live On," *New Albany (Ind.) Times*, December 12, 2007.

16   Collins interview.

17   Rasche interview.

18   AP, "Evansville's Program Was Building to Become a Division I Power," *Lakeland (Fla.) Ledger*, December 16, 1977, http://news.google.com/newspapers?id=4xJNAAAAIBAJ&sjid=o_oDAAAAIBAJ&pg=4833,3557820&dq=keith+moon+1977+basketball&hl=en.

19   William J. Booher, "Airline Executives Were Aboard Fatal Flight," *Indianapolis Star*, December 15, 1977, 10.

20   Booher, "Airline Executives Were Aboard."

21   NTSB, *Aircraft Accident Report*, 3.

22   NTSB, *Aircraft Accident Report*, synopsis.

23   NTSB, *Aircraft Accident Report*, sec 1.1, 3.

24 NTSB, *Aircraft Accident Report*, 4.

25 This occurred about one block from Jim Byers's home on Twickingham. His wife was in the kitchen and heard the plane fly low overhead (Byers interview).

26 NTSB, *Aircraft Accident Report*, 5.

27 Rich Davis, "A Night of Tears for UE," *Evansville Courier & Press*, December 13, 2002, http://allnurses-central.com/general-off-topic/25-years-ago-27335.html.

28 NTSB, *Aircraft Accident Report*, 12.

29 Davis, "A Night of Tears."

30 Jess Roberts, telephone interview by author, February 23, 2011, and follow-up, June 30, 2011.

31 Davis, "A Night of Tears."

32 Pat Wathen, interview by author, February 14, 2011, Evansville.

33 Rich Davis, "'We Are Marshall' Stirs Echoes of Another Crash," *Evansville Courier & Press*, December 13, 2006, A-3; Rich Davis, telephone interview by author, January 29, 2011.

34 Davis interview.

35 Wathen interview.

36 Picture with caption, *Evansville Press*, December 14, 1977, 7.

37 Jess Roberts interview.

38 Herb Marynell, "Crash Site Called a Terrible Place to Die," *Evansville Press*, December 14, 1977, 27.

39 Manuel Shiffres, AP, "Entire Evansville Basketball Team Is Killed in Air Crash," *Kentucky New Era*, December 14, 1977, http://news.google.com/newspapers?id=O5AzAAAAIBAJ&sjid=HeEFAAAAIBAJ&pg=984,5231404&dq=basketball+john-ed-washington&hl=en.

40 Robert Heiman, "Oh God, No . . . Not Him . . . Not Him," *Evansville Press*, December 14, 1977, 27.

41 Mike Blake, telephone interview by author, February 2, 2011.

42 Richard Dietz, letter to editor, posted electronically at www.courierpress.com, December 9, 2007, in response to article by Rich Davis, "Crash Hit Illinois Town Extra Hard," courierpress.com, December 9, 2007.

43 Blake interview.

44 David Hughes, "Plane Crash Victim Not Forgotten Thirty Years Later," TribStar.com, December 14, 1977, http://tribstar.com/sports/x1155724503/

Hughes-News-and-Views-Plane-crash-victim-not-forgotten-30-years-later.

45   Robert Joyner, telephone interview by author, September 15, 2011.

46   Robinson, "Thirty Years after Evansville Plane Crash."

47   Jennifer Kuster Adkins, telephone interview by author, October 17, 2011.

48   Patberg interview.

49   Art Adye, telephone interview by author, January 28, 2011.

50   Wallace Graves, telephone interview by author, January 27, 2011.

51   Scott Doerner interview.

52   Furr, a member of the team, had been injured earlier and was not on the travel roster.

53   Dianne Manners Townsend, telephone interview by author, March 25, 2011.

54   "Memories of Evansville Plane Crash Still Haunt Players' Families, Friends," BlueRaiderZone.com,. October 21, 2010, http://mbd.scout.com/mb.aspx?s=349&f=2394&t=6567140.

55   Scott Doerner interview; Mike Platt, telephone interviews by author, June 11 and 25, 2011.

56   Heiman, "Oh God, No."

57   Mary McCarty, "Staying Strong, Donna Moon Recalls Bouts with Tragedy," *Dayton Daily News*, May 22, 1994, 1.

58   Heiman, "Oh God, No."

59   Heiman, "Oh God, No."

60   Jim Byers interview.

61   Rod Spaw, "Ten Years Isn't Enough to Forget Night's Sorrow," *Evansville Courier*, December 13, 1987.

62   Heiman, "Oh God, No."

63   Joan Hudson Roth, telephone interview by author, February 21, 2011.

64   Adkins interview; Heiman, "Oh God, No."

65   Heiman, "Oh God, No."

66   Mark Sandy, telephone interview by author, January 31, 2011.

67   AP, "Tragic Ending," *Page City (Ariz.) Daily News*, December 14, 1977, 7.

68   Tess Stephenson, telephone interview by author, June 29, 2011.

69   Wayne Boultinghouse, telephone interview by author, February 11, 2011, and follow-up calls.

70   Marilyn McCutchan Disman, telephone interview by author, February 22, 2011.

71   Mike Platt interview.

72 AP, "Tragic Ending."

73 Rod Spaw, "Graves Expresses School's Grief," *Evansville Courier*, December 14, 1977,1.

74 Rod Spaw, " A Tragedy Too Painful to Remember . . . A Day Too Tragic to Forget," *Evansville Courier*, December 13, 1978, 10.

75 Spaw, "A Tragedy Too Painful."

Final flight of the DC-3 aircraft with tail number N51071 ended here on a plateau short of the runway. There were no survivors.

Saying Good-bye

Finally, all the bodies had been identified, and hearses lined up to collect them for transport to funeral homes.

University president Wallace Graves, Jim Byers, Thornton Patberg and the surviving assistant coaches would attend the funerals. Over four days Graves attended services for every player on the team.

Evansville funeral homes were hard pressed to cope with the sheer number of services. "When we went to one of the funeral parlors, we would just go from room to room where the bodies were," Jim Byers remembered.[1]

The Aces' opponent for the game that was never played was Middle Tennessee State. They held a memorial service on campus. The Blue Raiders put on their blue-and-white uniforms, pinned on black ribbons, and heard the team chaplain, David Miller, pay homage to the Aces.

"The question we ask is why?" he said. "We realize that all of our questions and guessing fall short of the dimensions of this tragedy." He then asked their coach, Jimmy Earl, to read aloud the scouting report on the Evansville team because, Miller said, "to memorialize someone you must know them."

"All of us thought, 'it could have been us.' Only when we live life to the fullest have we learned how to die. Something like this makes college basketball and winning a very small thing. It puts it all in perspective when you talk about the loss of human lives," Earl said.[2]

The University of Evansville held its memorial service for the players at Neu

Chapel. Bobby had spoken there just a month earlier, on November 13. He had spoken with a religious fervor about the team and the future.

More than a thousand people tried to attend, but the chapel had been built for just half that number. Those who managed to find a seat in the pews found the cross high above the altar bathed in a somber purple light.[3] Graves, Patberg, and Mac were among those who spoke. Many students wept openly as they tried to find solace in the words of the speakers.

Few did.

"We arranged for a community-wide memorial service to be held at Roberts Stadium," Graves said.[4] More than 4,800 attended the service on December 18, 1977, on the court at Roberts Stadium where the Aces had won five national championships.

Seated in the front rows on the court were the immediate families, other relatives, and friends of the players. Governor Otis Bowen, Senator Birch Bayh, Congressman David Cornwall, and Evansville Mayor Russell Lloyd were all present. So were people from every walk of life in the city: laborers, clerks, doctors, lawyers, bankers, sales people, engineers, restaurant staff, auto mechanics, stockbrokers, grocers, hairstylists, carpenters, house cleaners, dentists, judges, landscapers, librarians, painters, teachers, tailors, cobblers, veterinarians, dry cleaners, and snowplow operators.

The stadium was decorated with purple bunting, and the ceremony began with a moment of silence while a spotlight shone on the purple-and-white Aces logo at center court. Then Art Ayde played "The Star-Spangled Banner" on his French horn, in a dark, melancholy tone.

In an arena where once cheers thundered down over the court there was a palpable, dark silence pierced only by muffled sobs. What the nearly 5,000 mourners couldn't hear was the sound of hearts breaking. But they were. What they couldn't see were the hopes and dreams of the inconsolable parents that were torn away and were fluttering towards the rafters. But they were.

"It was," Graves would recall, "as if a black shroud had been draped over the city shutting out all the light and leaving nothing but sorrow and despair."

Graves had composed his remarks alone at his home. Sleep deprived and emotionally drained from all he had had to do over the previous five days, he summoned from within the strength, courage, and wisdom to craft remarks that were both eloquent and moving. It would be his finest hour.

Speaking from a lectern placed on a raised platform in front of a large floral arrangement of purple and white chrysanthemums, Graves assured the assembled crowd:

> "Out of the agony of this hour we shall rise. Out of the ashes of a desiccated team we shall build a new basketball team, stronger, more valiant, than ever before. Out of the brokenness and despair which now grips this institution will burst a new University of Evansville, more sensitive to human needs, more resolute in purpose than ever before. . . . Their dream will be fulfilled."

"My statement was dedicated to the tasks of sharing the university's grief with the bereaved families and with the university's friends everywhere, of wringing hope from the grip of despair, and pulling a devastated university together again and giving it a new meaning, a new purpose," he said years later.[5]

The UE Concert Choir, joined by those assembled, sang a concluding hymn, "O God, Our Help in Ages Past." Many could not finish the song.[6] With Dvorak's New World Symphony playing in the background, the people in the stands began to move down to the court to offer condolences to the families and friends, and Roberts Stadium slowly emptied out.

In the very place where raucous fans dressed in red had cheered the Aces since 1956, silence was all that remained.

Bob Hudson's services were held in Neu Chapel on December 16. Afterward, the pallbearers carried his casket to the waiting hearse. Mac, his head bowed, was one of them. As the hearse made its way slowly to Park Lawn Cemetery, it passed the marquee that promoted UE athletic events. No one had bothered to change the sign touting the Evansville Holiday Tournament that Hudson had worked so hard to market for years. The procession passed Holy Rosary Catholic Church, where services for Jeff Bohnert were underway, and afternoon services for Charles Shike would be held. At the gravesite friends gathered around Hudson's coffin. The director of sports for WFIE television, Mike Blake, looked pale and drawn as he turned around and said to no one in particular, "My God, this is such a nightmare."[7]

The family and friends of Jeff Bohnert remembered the student manager and biology major who wore oversized glasses, had longish dark hair, and wanted to be a doctor. Jeff, 21, had grown up listening to Marv Bates's radio broadcasts of Aces games and was a graduate of Evansville's Harrison High School, where he had been a member of the Thespians Club and the National Honor Society. He had never been comfortable about flying. But serving as a student manager had gotten him an athletic scholarship, so when Bobby Watson had asked him to accompany the Aces and film the game, he had gamely agreed. His younger brother Craig would transfer to UE from Purdue and take Jeff's place as a manager and use his 16 mm camera, recovered from the crash, to film games.[8]

"My dad was never the same. . . . One year later he was in a hospital with congestive heart failure," Craig Bohnert said. The elder Bohnert died at 51, four years after his son's death. "He never got over it,' Craig said.

For many years a single red rose would appear on Jeff's grave on the anniversary of the crash. "It was always a mystery to our family," Craig said. One day he found a posting about Jeff on the university's website, tracked down the poster, and learned that the rose tribute was from Debbie Lankford. She and Jeff had dated in high school and then drifted apart. They had recently reconnected at UE and had made plans to begin seeing each other again and set a date for "'the day [Jeff got] home from the Middle Tennessee State trip,'" Craig said.

When Craig collected his brother's personal effects from the Evansville police, he had found a prom picture in Jeff's wallet. Beaming at his brother's side in her formal gown was Debbie Lankford.[9]

It was sadly fitting that the funeral procession for Bob Hudson passed Holy Rosary, where the funeral mass for his best friend would be celebrated that afternoon. Charles Shike, 36, was a native of Monmouth, Illinois. He had earned his bachelor's degree at Colorado State and a master's at Evansville. The university's comptroller was a member of the Green River Kiwanis Club and a financial adviser to the United Way campaign. He also served on the Youth Services Board. He was survived by his wife, Janet, three sons and a daughter.

Indeed, as hard as it was for small towns and villages throughout the tristate area to bury loved ones cut down in their prime, no place suffered more than Evansville and its immediate environs. The majority of the people who died on the plane were local.

All three student managers were from Evansville: Jeff Bohnert, Mark "Tank" Kirkpatrick, and Mark Kniese.

Kirkpatrick, 21, was a graduate of Central High School, instantly recognizable by his build—hence the nickname—and the blond Beatle mop that framed his round face. He so adored the Aces that he once attended a game in a tuxedo—he was to be an usher in a wedding and wanted to miss as little of the game as possible. He was a referee for basketball games and umpired at volleyball and baseball games in the city youth leagues.[10]

Mark Kniese, 20, was in his senior year and serving his fourth year as student trainer of the Aces. He was a graduate of Harrison High School, where he had been elected president of the student council his senior year. At Evansville he was majoring in physical education and planned to become a professional athletic trainer. The curly-haired Mark had a great smile that he'd flash from beneath a sparse mustache. That grin reflected his personality. "He was very gregarious and fun to be around," recalled John Guild, a fraternity brother in Sigma Phi Epsilon. Mark had spent the summer of 1977 as a counselor at a children's camp.[11]

Greg Knipping's widow, Nancy, and their baby son, Jonathan, took his body back to his hometown of Colorado Springs. The 27-year-old sports information director was a graduate of the University of Missouri's School of Journalism, where he won national awards for his work as a sportswriter for the *Columbia Missourian*. After graduation he had worked as the public relations officer for the Denver Bears' minor league baseball team in the American Association. After a year he became assistant sports information director at Purdue and ascended to the top job there after his boss, Ted Haracz, left to join the Chicago Bears' organization.[12]

In Eldorado, Illinois, the high school gymnasium where Mike Duff and Kevin Kingston had played became the site of their funeral. Thousands gathered, including their high school coach, Bob Brown, who had to be helped to his seat because he was so overwhelmed with emotion that he could barely stand. Duff, 18, had been Watson's most prized recruit. Although only a freshman, he had won the spot as starting forward, and fans loved his aggressive play. In high school he had led his team to the Illinois Class 1-A Elite Eight for three straight years. He was majoring in business. Kingston, 21, had earned his associate's degree at Logan Junior College and planned to become a teacher. He had made the team his junior year by trying out, but his leadership and hustle had earned him a scholarship for his senior year.[13]

In a poignant moment the scoreboard clock was set to 29 seconds and allowed to tick down to zero.[14]

Bryan Taylor's services in Tell City, Indiana, and John Ed Washington's funeral in Indianapolis drew overflow crowds.

Bryan's family and friends remembered the Tom Selleck lookalike who was engaged to Jennifer Kuster, his girlfriend since the seventh grade, who he had followed to Evansville after one year at Louisville.

"I only recently remembered that Bryan's mom had told me once that he had confided in her that he thought he'd die before he got too old. That he just had that feeling," she said.

Other memories are still vivid. Bryan's dad, Ralph, who operated an auto repair shop, had restored and repainted an old jeep for his son. "It was fire engine yellow," Jennifer recalled. "Bryan just loved that jeep. My parents were always a little surprised when he'd pull up in it at 5:30 in the morning with his small bass boat behind. We'd go fishing in nearby Celina Lake. I'd bring a picnic lunch and he'd bring the worms. We spent many quiet peaceful mornings together like that."

The wake and funeral were held at St. Patrick's Catholic Church where Jennifer and Bryan had often attended mass together on Saturday nights before heading to a movie. "The crowds just kept coming and coming," Jennifer recalled. Bryan's parents, older brother, Grant, and Jennifer managed to acknowledge the never-ending line of mourners and got through the services together. "That I was there may have helped them to get through it," Jennifer said. But it wasn't easy for any of them. "I was devastated. I felt my life would not go on," she said.

With the support of Bryan's family, with whom she has remained close through the years, Jennifer did manage to return to school and finish her nursing studies. She graduated in 1979.[15]

John Ed Washington, a 21-year-old senior, had been the Aces' leading scorer during the 1976–77 season. The 6-3 lefthander was a versatile player—he could both shoot and play defense, and was Mac's favorite type of player. He had been recruited by Larry Humes, who had coached him on a junior high team, and John Ed had chosen the University of Evansville over offers from Purdue, Louisiana State, and Oklahoma State.

His high school coach, Ernie Cline, told the *Indianapolis Star* that John Ed was "one of the finest players I have coached in 20 years and was the best 'southpaw' ever to play for [Arsenal] Tech [High School]." The paper noted that John Ed's room at home was "stuffed with trophies he had won" in high school. "I felt he was ambitious and had set goals for himself," Cline continued. "He had achieved most of them. He was level-headed and personable and aspired to play professional basketball."

In high school John Ed had been co-captain of the team, and his teammates had voted him most valuable player. He also won the assist trophy in his senior year, 1974, and played on the city championship team that year.

At Evansville he quickly demonstrated his worth to Mac and was named a starter in his freshman year, seeing action in every game that season, and proved to be a catalyst for the team. He once again was a mainstay of the team in his sophomore season, when the Aces secured an invitation to the NCAA Tournament and a 20–9 record, the best in a long time.

After services at New Hope Baptist Church, John Ed Washington was buried in Crown Hill Cemetery.[16]

The crowd at Kraig Heckendorn's funeral exceeded the capacity of the Westwood First Presbyterian Church in Cincinnati. His family and friends remember "a very caring person," a young man who would drive 90 miles roundtrip to take his grandmother to church on Sundays when he was in high school.

And they remembered how 19-year-old Kraig missed his German shepherd, Igor, when he went away to college. And the Heckendorn family summer vacations when they'd go camping, and how Kraig and his father loved to hunt and fish together. And that he'd planned to marry Karen Zimmer, a cheerleader who was younger than he. "She was the only girl he ever dated," his sister Kerry said. "He said he knew she was the one."[17]

Also from Ohio was Keith Moon, the 20-year-old sophomore who had earned all-conference honors as a senior at Fairmont West High School in Kettering. He had been named to the Dayton All-Star and Midwestern All-Star teams and had gained honorable mention All-America status as a high school senior. As a freshman at the University of Evansville, Keith pledged Sigma Phi Epsilon. "He was a real quiet guy. He didn't attend a lot of our social functions but made it to all the pledge events. He lived in the dorm where most of the other players lived," John Guild, a fraternity brother, said.[18] Keith had planned to become a high school coach.

Keith had a leukemia scare when he was six. It turned out to be no more than measles, but the ordeal created a strong bond between mother and son. A portrait of Keith remained on Donna Moon's desk through the years. Often tears would flow when she gazed at it thinking of his last moments on earth. "I hope he didn't suffer. No one was there for him," she said.

A minister's words helped Donna and her family come to terms with their loss. "God didn't take your son," he said. "Man did."

"I've had despair and heartaches," she told a reporter later, "but have never been angry. But o-o-o-h I've missed him."[19]

Only 20,000 people lived in Goldsboro, North Carolina, and that number included personnel at Seymour Johnson Air Force Base. Nearly 2,000 people attended the joint funeral of Warren Alston and Barney Lewis, both 18. They'd been friends and teammates forever—when they were in the ninth grade, they'd attended a basketball camp at Duke University, where the coach was Bobby Watson. Alston idolized Spencer Haywood and was majoring in business. Lewis excelled at karate as well as basketball: he had earned his brown belt. He sported a medium-length Afro in tribute to his idol, Julius "Dr. J" Erving, and wore glasses when he wasn't on the court. They were popular on and off court, remembered by students as "easy going and smiling." The local sports editor told readers the next day, "I wept unashamedly like some of the rest. Others in the audience sat or stood in dazed, somber, red-eyed silence. They were the mourning parents, relatives, coaches, friends and fans who had come to pay their respects to these exemplary young men."[20]

In Munster, Indiana, they remembered Ray Comandella's sense of humor. How he liked to tell people he wanted to be an engineer but had never driven a train. Ray had been known on campus as "Cool Ray" for his easygoing manner. He was a big fan of the Baltimore Bullets' star center, Elvin Hayes. Ray had led his high school team to the sectional championship games during his junior and senior years and was ranked second in all of Indiana high school basketball. He would have been nineteen on December 27.

Michael Joyner's family delayed his funeral until a week after the crash to give members of the close-knit and far-flung Joyner clan time to get to Terre Haute for the services.

"The church we attended was too small to hold all the people that wanted to come," said his older brother Robert. "We had the services in the Terre Haute Bible Center, a much larger place. Still, the mourners filled the room and spilled over outside." That day they remembered a young man who "loved basketball more than anything and dreamed of someday playing in the NBA—not for the money, just for the love of the game," Robert said. They remembered the big-hearted kid who brought his teammates home for Thanksgiving, who scored the winning free throw when Terre Haute South High School beat archrival Terre Haute North, and who ended his prep career as his high school's all-time leading scorer.[21]

A police escort accompanied the procession to Michael's gravesite at Grand-view Cemetery, where he was laid to rest only four blocks from his childhood home. Robert Joyner's AAU basketball team is called the Purple Aces in his brother's honor.

Friends and family in West Frankfort, Illinois, honored the memory of 18-year-old Greg Smith, who had starred at both basketball and baseball in high school, where he earned ten varsity letters and was elected captain of both teams as a senior. He was a business major who favored leisure suits and was an avid fan of New York Knicks star Walt Frazier.

In Pittsburgh, Bobby Watson was laid to rest next to his father in a rural cemetery as 200 people, half of them basketball coaches, watched the lowering of his casket. The funeral director marveled, "We filled four rooms and still had some people standing." An old friend of Bobby's, the Reverend Lee Roy Hearn of the Bethel Park Christ United Methodist Church, conducted the services for the young coach, telling those assembled, "Bobby was many things to many people. He was a father who knew what it meant to be a son, and he dealt towards all these young people as a loving father would." Charlie Schmaus, a teammate of Bobby's at VMI who went on to become head coach there, said, "He was not like so many other coaches, who think the important thing is to impress, to get ahead. That's not how Bob came across. For him the most important thing was to be honest, sincere."[22]

The *Pittsburgh Post-Gazette* had given extensive coverage to the crash, and on the day Bobby was laid to rest it ran a photo of the graveside services. Deidra Watson, dressed in black, is shown standing between two taller men who are supporting her. She is weeping.

Both Steve Miller, 20, and Mark Siegel, 19, were buried in New Albany, Indiana. Steve was the big man Mac had coveted, captain of the Aces, and the only married man on the team. He and Vicki Lynn Hendrix had been married on August 20, and she had moved to Evansville to be with him. Steve had set a New Albany High School record by blocking 53 shots as a senior while averaging 16 points and 15 rebounds per game. The funeral was held at Our Lady of Perpetual Hope and drew an overflow crowd.

Steve's sister Debbie Reddington said of her brother, "Everything about him was larger than life. He played hard . . . but really he was a teddy bear. He had a big heart." Steve's young widow, now Vicki Peavey, has returned to Evansville only once since 1977—too many unpleasant memories there of things that might have been.[23]

Steve's dad, the New Albany newspaper man, wrote a remembrance for a genealogy website some years later. "At the start, we knew Steve would be a big man. He weighed 9 lbs. 4 oz. at birth and was 25 inches long," Donald Miller wrote. "He achieved a mature height of 6-7. Steve was a gentle, but strong boy and kept these qualities as he grew into life. . . . While time has somewhat dulled the ache of the loss, Stephen still comes into our minds, many times. He was a fine young man and our memories of him make both his mother and father very proud."[24]

Mark Siegel was a member of the National Honor Society, attended Hoosier Boys State, and was active in the Fellowship of Christian Athletes. Mark had played for his father, Ed, at Pike High School in Indianapolis, where he played point guard and earned All-State honorable mention two years in a row. He also lettered in baseball and once pitched a no-hitter in a Little League All-Star contest. In 2001 he was named to the Indiana Basketball Hall of Fame's Silver Anniversary Team. He still holds his high school's record for most assists (180).[25] He was buried in Kraft-Graceland Memorial Park in New Albany.

Marion A. "Tony" Winburn, a crowd favorite at Roberts because he was so quick, had transferred to Evansville from Indiana University–Southeast in New Albany after his freshman year. He had captained both the football and basketball teams at Jeffersonville High School and had led the basketball team to a 58–11 record during his three varsity seasons, including a trip to the state finals in 1972. The 22-year-old was majoring in banking and finance. He could have graduated the previous spring but had decided to stay at Evansville one more season. His best friend, Jeff Frey, a former Aces player, recalled that he and Tony had enjoyed canoe trips down Blue River and that they had attended a Fellowship of Christian Athletes conference in Colorado together. Tony and Jeff "were always together," their high school coach, George Marshall, said. He was buried in Eastlawn Cemetery in Jeffersonville, his hometown.

Within a week the funerals and memorial services were finally over. "I didn't get any sleep for the first three days and don't remember going to bed for a week," Jim Byers said.[26]

Memorial and scholarship funds were established in the names of many of the players, ensuring that they will not be forgotten. Each year at a home basketball game, the University of Evansville announces the recipients of the awards.

Almost immediately after the crash condolences and messages of support had begun to arrive in Jim Byers's office at Carson Center.

"The first call I got was from Bob Knight at Indiana. 'We want to do something for you,'" he told me. "He offered to do anything he could to help. He said he'd ask the NCAA to allow him to play a home game at Evansville that season and donate the money to Evansville."

Another early call came from Wichita State University. "I will never forget it. [The coach there] had gone through a similar situation where they lost their team, and he tried to tell me what we were going to face," Byers said.

Marshall University also contacted Evansville. Marshall had lost its football team in a plane crash seven years earlier, and the athletic director there was calling to tell Patberg and Byers about "what we could expect, including the likelihood of lawsuits," Patberg said.[27]

The last thing the university administrators felt like dealing with was the basketball schedule, but they needed to decide what to do about the remainder of the Aces' season.

"We finally concluded after a lot of back and forth that it didn't make any sense to try to play the rest of the games with walk-ons and get humiliated," Jim Byers said.[28]

It was basketball season in Evansville, but there would be no basketball.

The relationship of the Aces to the city is often described as a deep and passionate one, nurtured through the years by Mac's winning teams. Time after time the visitor is told, "Basketball is big in Evansville."

Thirty-five years later it is hard to fathom just how large an impact the team had on the community. But an editorial published by the *Evansville Press* only a day after the Aces perished provides a strong sense of what the team meant to Evansville:

A PART OF US

They came here to play, some from afar. But, they were Evansville's own.

They were us.

The young team had been a picture window to a city's hopes and dreams.

If memory is the treasury of all things, and we're sure it is, Evansville always will remain the guardian of this young team's hopes and dreams.[29]

Memorial Plaza, honoring the UE's men's basketball team, coaches, and support staff lost in the 1977 plane crash.

Answering Questions

There were still a lot of unanswered questions.

First and foremost was the cause of the crash.

That would be handled by experts from the National Transportation Safety Board (NTSB) who were already on hand, beginning the investigation. It would take more than a year and a half, and the cause came down to human error: the pilot and copilot had failed to make thorough preflight checks, and baggage had been improperly stowed.[30]

The analysis of the NTSB's findings that follow are based on a reading of the report by Robert Stein, a retired colonel in the U.S. Air Force. He is a graduate of West Point who logged more than 700 hours in the hostile night skies over Vietnam in the armed military version of the DC-3, known as "Puff the Magic Dragon." He is intimately familiar with the plane and its preflight checklist, which is identical for civilian and military versions of the aircraft.

The first thing to know, he said, is that "it is a very durable and safe aircraft. It was virtually indestructible and highly reliable. A twin-engine plane, it was designed to fly on a single engine, and pilots loved to fly it."[31]

According to the NTSB report, the external preflight checklist requiring observation of all the external aspects of the aircraft, particularly the leading edge and control surfaces, was not performed in accordance with the protocol.[32]

The preflight checklist is specific to the DC-3. For example, stowed in an open box in the aft baggage compartment are the external control locks. After a plane

lands, they are inserted in each wing and the control surfaces (rudder and elevator) on the tail to keep gusts of wind from moving, and possibly damaging, the
control surfaces. Pilots call them gust locks, and each DC-3 has four.

"The gust locks are . . . V-shaped sheet-metal devices. They are usually bright
red in color with two-inch-wide red streamers attached to make them highly
visible. Additionally, each streamer is embossed with white lettering stating,
'Remove before flight,'" Stein said.[33]

National Jet Service's operating manual called for the copilot to place the
external rudder control locks on the aircraft after landing. Before departure the
copilot was required to remove and stow the rudder locks, during the external
preflight inspection known as the walkaround, then help the flight attendant
close the main door before proceeding to the cockpit. No one observed the copilot performing these functions.[34]

Witnesses on the ground at Tri-State Aero told the NTSB that the walkaround
was abbreviated, halfhearted, and not in accordance with normal operating pro-
cedure.

As the NTSB later determined, two of the four gust locks, which effectively
prevent the control surfaces from being operated, were still in place when the
DC-3 was loaded and were not removed and stored on board.

Two National Jet Service employees who had disembarked from the plane
supervised the loading of the baggage. One was dressed in civilian clothes and
the other in a blue pilot's uniform, cap, and overcoat.[35] The uniformed man was
probably Gaston Ruiz, the 35-year-old copilot. The man in civilian clothes was
either James Stewart, the 29-year-old president of National Jet Services who was
also a pilot, or William Hartford, the 36-year-old general manager of the company. Neither was a member of the flight crew. The pilot, 42-year-old Ty Van
Pham, presumably remained in the cockpit.

Two Tri-State Aero employees watched from the left side of the aircraft as it
was being loaded. They saw the uniformed man go to the left wing, look under
it, and then return to the aircraft. They saw the man in civilian clothes go directly
forward to the left wing and remain there, talking to adults who were accompa-
nying the Aces, while the baggage was being stowed. No witness reported seeing
either man walk to the right side of the plane, where the gust locks remained in
place.

According to Tri-State Aero employees, the man in civilian clothes helped with
the baggage until it was loaded. Proper distribution of baggage is the responsi-

bility of the flight crew. Improper weight distribution or too much weight in the rear of the compartment can alter the plane's center of gravity and cause control problems during takeoff that the pilot might not expect or anticipate.[36]

It was rainy, cold, and Air Indiana 216 had arrived late.

The flight crew was in a hurry.

Twelve minutes after the flight arrived from Indianapolis, it pulled away from the Tri-State Aero building and moved toward the runways. Within minutes the crew gained permission from the tower to use instrument flight rules.

After the pilots were given takeoff clearance by the tower, they began to taxi. The tower controller told the NTSB, "The pilot took some time aligning the aircraft with the runway center line," and the controller saw "the aircraft fish-tail. The tail moved laterally once or twice."[37] According to Stein, a "tail drag-ger" like the DC-3 "tends to fishtail at low speeds. . . . I would expect that, in this instance, the aircraft was being influenced by the wind, and the pilot could not adjust for it because he had no rudder control. That, in itself, should have alarmed him."[38]

Thirty to thirty-five seconds after Air Indiana 216 received clearance from the tower, it had taxied onto the runway and begun takeoff, the controller told the NTSB.[39]

"Part of the preflight [routine] is performed during the taxiing out to takeoff position," Stein said. The protocol calls for the pilot to wiggle the yoke to deter-mine that all surface controls are "free and correct." The pilot "performs this function after the copilot reads the preflight checklist tasks to him and acknowl-edges that he has performed the task," Stein said.

If the gust locks are still in place, "the yoke won't turn and you know that the controls are still locked—assuming, of course, that you perform the tasks on the checklist," Stein said.[40]

The gust locks installed on the right aileron and rudder were still in place as the DC-3 aircraft bearing tail number **N51071** rolled down runway 18 at Dress Regional Airport with twenty-nine people on board.[41]

By the time it passed Tri-State Aero, the DC-3 was about twenty-five feet off the ground. It banked sharply to the left in an extreme nose-up position, causing the Tri-State employees to believe "he wasn't going to make it. He was going to stall." The plane was about 2,500 feet from the runway and headed east-southeast when they lost sight of it in the fog. As the aircraft climbed into the overcast sky, the tower controller lost sight of it too and twice tried to reach the plane. There were no more transmissions.[42]

One person watching the takeoff said the left bank remained fairly constant, and the plane turned toward a housing development southeast of the airport.[43]

With the gust locks still in place, the plane was, according to Stein, "probably unflyable" in any direction except straight ahead.

"You are always taught if there is a problem on takeoff, do not try to get back to the airport unless you have plenty of altitude," Stein said.[44] But Ty Van Pham, unaware that the gust locks had not been removed, made the decision to try to do just that.

With the controls locked, he could not make any turns, so he apparently attempted to maneuver the plane by alternating the engine power, forcing the plane to turn by cutting back power on one engine and increasing it on the other.

Witnesses said they heard a tremendous noise, an "extreme amount of power" being added as the plane climbed.

What they saw next was the plane in a "northbound heading and swooping low into a housing project around Twickingham Drive" (Melody Hill). "The plane then made another correction, and came up above the trees just north of Twickingham."[45]

The plane was at a very low altitude and airspeed.

"At that point you would lose lift and go down in a place not of your choosing," Stein said.[46]

"As it approached the eastern boundary of the airport, the engine rpm and the engine intensity seemed to increase, and about 1 to 2 seconds after the engine increase, the aircraft struck the ground and burst into flames; about a half second later there was a muffled explosive noise," a witness told the NTSB.[47]

The agency determined that the plane had brushed the top of two trees almost due east of the airport. The trees were about fifty feet tall. Pieces of the landing light lens, strobe light lens, and the green right wing navigation light were found beneath those trees.

The nose hit first, followed by the left and then right engines. It traveled about 200 feet from its initial point of impact before coming to rest.

The aircraft broke into three main parts on impact. The cockpit section separated and suffered severe impact force and postimpact fire damage. The fire consumed a major portion of the left side, top, and right side of the fuselage. The rear, including the tail, was torn loose and ended upright, lying on its left side.

The wings had been separated from the fuselage, one to the left and one to the right and forward of the main part of the fuselage. When the wings detached on impact, the fuselage and passenger compartment had been ripped open and the passengers ejected.

The accident, according to the NTSB report, was simply "not survivable."[48]

(Endnotes)
1   Jim Byers, telephone interview by author, January 27, 2011.
2   AP, "Memorial Service," *Evansville Courier*, December 14, 1977.
3   Betsy Morris, "UE Classmates Mourn Loss of Friends and Basketball Squad," *Evansville Press*, December 17, 1977, 27.
4   Wallace Graves, telephone interview by author, January 27, 2011.
5   Wallace Graves, "The Night It Rained Tears," excerpts from manuscript by Wallace Graves, *Evansville Press*, December 8, 1978; Wallace Graves interview by author; remarks used with permission.
6   Robert Heiman, "The Aces: Evansville Pauses to Remember Team," *Evansville Press*, December 19, 1977, 1.
7   Patricia Swanson, "Grieving U of E Buries Bob Hudson," *Evansville Press*, December 17, 1977.
8   "The Dead," *Evansville Press*, December 14, 1977, 7; Rich Davis, "A Night of Tears for UE," *Evansville Courier & Press*, December 13, 2002, http://allnurses-central.com/general-off-topic/25-years-ago-27335.html.
9   Craig Bohnert, telephone interview by author, September 13, 2011.
10 "The Dead"; Sylvia Slaughter, "'Tank': UE 'Manager for All Seasons,'" *Evansville Press*, December 18, 1977, 1-A.
11 "The Dead"; John Guild, telephone interview by author, February 22, 2011; *University of Evansville 1977–78 Media Guide*.
12 "The Dead."
13 "The Dead."
14 Les Wikeler, "Tragedy Remembered," *The Southern.com.*, December 12, 2007.
15 Jennifer Kuster Adkins, telephone interview by author, October 17, 2011.
16 "John Ed Washington Dedicated to Sport," *Indianapolis Star,* December 15, 1977.

17 Kerry Heckendorn Braeuning, telephone interview by author, July 14, 2011.

18 John Guild interview.

19 Mary McCarty, "Staying Strong, Donna Moon Recalls Bouts with Tragedy," *Dayton Daily News,* May 22, 1994,1.

20 Rudy Coggins, telephone interview by author, September 12, 2011; "High School Coach Lost 'Family' in Wreckage," *Washington (D.C.) Afro-American,* December 20, 1977; Jack Lee, "God Love Them and May They Rest in Peace," *Goldsboro (N.C.) News-Argus,* December 19, 1977.

21 Robert Joyner, telephone interview by author, September 16, 2011.

22 AP, "Crash Victim Buried at Forest Lawn," *(Washington, Pa.) Observer-Reporter,* December 17, 1977, D-2; "Watson Was 'A Man on Court and Off,'" *Evansville Press,* December 1977 (date not legible).

23 Daniel Robinson, "Thirty Years After Evansville Plane Crash Players Memories Live On," *New Albany(Ind.) Times,* December 14, 2007.

24 "Spangler-Shriver Clan," www.angelfire.com/ultra2/spanglershriverclan/index_files/Page427.html.

25 Pat McKee, "Silver Team Includes '77 Pike Star Killed in Evansville Crash," *Indianapolis Star,* November 27, 2001; AP, "Silver Anniversary Team Includes Local Name," *Logansport (Ind.) Pharos-Tribune,* November 27, 2001, www.newspaperarchive.com/SiteMap/FreePdfPreview.aspx?img=109269863; "Boys Basketball Records: Most Assists," *2010–2011 Pike High School Winter Sports Magazine,* https://www.pike.k12.in.us/NR/rdonlyres/537510EF-F5DA-430F-B13A-9A86AA44AF9D/20624/20102011PikeWinterProgram_LR.pdf.

26 Byers interview.

27 Byers interview; Thornton Patberg, telephone interview by author, January 29, 2011, and several follow-up conversations. Marshall's experience would become the basis for the movie *We Are Marshall* (2006). Wichita State lost several members of its football team in a 1970 crash.

28 Jim Byers interview.

29 "A Part of Us," editorial, *Evansville Press,* December 14, 1977, 28, used with permission.

30 National Transportation Safety Board, "Probable Cause," *Aircraft Accident Report—National Jet Services, Inc., Douglas DC-3, N51071,* NTSB report no. AAR-78-10 (Washington, D.C.: Bureau of Accident Investigation, August 17, 1978), 31–32.

31 Robert Stein, interview by author, February 15, 2011, Henderson, Nevada.

32 NTSB, "Probable Cause."

33 Robert Stein interview.

34 No. 5 on the pre-takeoff checklist of the *National Jet Service Manual* said, "Controls FREE FULL TRAVEL" (NTSB, *Aircraft Accident Report*, 18). See also p. 16.

35 NTSB, *Aircraft Accident Report*, 18.

36 NTSB, *Aircraft Accident Report*, 25. In fact, the NTSB report found this to be the case. The improper distribution of the baggage, combined with the failure to remove the gust locks, would cause the plane to be virtually uncontrollable.

37 NTSB, *Aircraft Accident Report*, 3.

38 Stein interview.

39 NTSB, *Aircraft Accident Report*, 3.

40 Robert Stein interview.

41 NTSB, *Aircraft Accident Report*, synopsis.

42 NTSB, *Aircraft Accident Report*, 3.

43 NTSB, *Aircraft Accident Report*, 4.

44 Stein interview.

45 NTSB, *Aircraft Accident Report*, 4.

46 Stein interview.

47 NTSB, *Aircraft Accident Report*, 5.

48 NTSB, *Aircraft Accident Report*, 6, 9–12.

Evansville vs. Marquette, 1982.

Rising, 1978–85

In Evansville the grief was everywhere. There was no escaping it. It hung like a veil over the community, smothering the joy of the season with a blanket of inconsolable sadness.

Christmas lights strung on the eaves and shrubbery in front of houses added color to the nights, and Christmas trees were visible through the windows of houses. Carols played as shoppers bought Farrah Fawcett dolls, Play-Doh workbench sets, Tippy Tumbles, and Magic Hair Chrissy. But people in Evansville were just going through the motions.

It was Christmas across the nation, but in Evansville it would be a blue Christmas for everyone old enough to know what had happened.

At the university Wallace Graves, Thornton Patberg, and Jim Byers still faced many decisions and once-unimaginable duties. They had sent students home early for the traditional holiday and semester break. The campus was largely deserted now.

During the memorial service Graves had promised that the university would form a new basketball team. That meant the school had to hire a new coach, the sooner the better. "The Holiday Tournament was coming up," Jim Byers said. "Bob Hudson had always handled that. Now I was doing it."[1]

The university had decided against trying to play out the season. Now the administrators had to figure out what to do with the money season ticket holders had already paid. Eventually, they offered to refund the money.

Two days after Christmas the tragedy of the plane crash was compounded when a university basketball player, 18-year-old David Furr, who had not been on the plane because of an ankle injury, was killed in a car accident.

The 6-2 redhead had been a standout performer at Olney High School and had tried to make the team as a walk-on. He had injured his ankle, ending those hopes, but was keeping stats at home games at Watson's request. He didn't travel to the away games and thus missed being on the flight of Air Indiana 216.

He had attended many of the funerals and had left school early to go home and be with his family for the holidays. "He didn't talk about it much," his mother, Ann Knox, said. "It had a tremendous sobering effect on him."

David and his younger brother, Byron, were both killed when a car David was driving crossed the center line and collided with a utility truck.

Some people suggested it was fate or destiny for God to take the last Aces player. "I don't think that way," Ann Knox said. "I don't think God wanted them to be together. It just happened."[2]

Some of those who lost loved ones in the crash found solace in each other's company.

Edie Bates, Deidra Watson, and Jennifer Kuster, Bryan Taylor's fiancé, formed a small informal support group. They met at Deidra's house most of the time, often at Edie's suggestion. "We were a little like grandmother, mother, and daughter," Edie said. The three, all of whom had lost the most important man in their lives, made spaghetti, played piano, and even shared a few laughs as time went on.[3]

"I only really got to know Deidra and Edie after the crash," Jennifer Kuster said. "We all sort of comforted each other. We'd make ravioli together in Deidra's kitchen, but we had our private moments, too. Edie kept up a very positive persona in public but she grieved as well."[4] Life, for those still living, had been altered irreparably, but they had to find a way to live it.

The Salukis of Southern Illinois filled in as hosts at the Evansville Holiday Tournament.

As they took the floor in place of the Aces, fans greeted the Salukis with a standing ovation at Roberts. They managed to win, defeating Butch Van Breda Kolff's University of New Orleans in overtime.

Students returned to campus after the new year.

The edition of the student newspaper, the *Crescent*, that appeared on January 6, 1978, contained news of the establishment of the University of Evansville Basketball Memorial Fund. The fund drive was headed by Al Dauble, president of the Tip-Off Club; Chris Weaver, president of the student association; and Jerry Linzy, president of the Alumni Association. They promised a united effort to establish a permanent remembrance of the 24 students and staff of the university who had died. Donations could be sent to the president's office.

That issue of the paper also carried a number of letters to the editor about the future plans for basketball and an appropriate tribute to the team.

Diana Townsend had composed a poem in the days following December 13 and had submitted it to the newspaper.

"I did it as a release," she said. "My roommate worked at the *Crescent*, and I knew they were putting out an issue that would be about the students' reactions. I had been writing poetry since junior high, and I said, 'I'd like to write a poem for that.'"

The Night the Stars Went Out
The clouds were gray, the sky was dim,
    misty fog hung low.
The night enfolded tragedy
    which soon we all would know.
As news came in about our loss
    the campus wept with grief.
How could these men so young and strong
    been given life so brief?
Heads were bowed, we all were touched,
    no strangers to us were they.
The chapel became a refuge,
    a silent place to pray.
The shock waves echoed around the world,
    the nation knew our pain,
and encouraged us with thoughts and prayers,
    to learn to live again.
We'll all live life more fully now
    and let more feelings out
because we'll ever remember
    the night the stars went out.

The 19-year-old's poem was later picked up by the *Louisville Courier* and prompted positive letters to the editor.

Diana Townsend never published another poem, but her single published work remains a poignant summation of how the tragedy affected the university's students in the days after the crash.

"For me, personally, the whole experience was horrible but it made me more outgoing. I sought more experiences after that—life is short," she said.[5]

In January the university also announced a new search for a head basketball coach. More than 70 applicants responded. "Both Ernie and I wanted the job," Stafford Stephenson said.[6]

Byers said, "We had considered Stafford Stephenson, and he wanted the position. But after some discussion we decided to conduct a national search. We consulted with Bob Knight and others, and that's the way we went."

Byers headed the committee formed to review the applications. "We hoped to have a new coach in place by March 1," he said.[7]

An Indianapolis lawyer, Earl Townsend, a specialist in aviation law, filed suits on behalf of several families whose sons had perished in the crash. The lawsuits, filed on behalf of the families of Mike Joyner and John Ed Washington, sought to recover damages in excess of $2 million from National Jet Services and the federal government for each family and $5 million in punitive damages for each family from National Jet Services.[8]

Subsequent litigation would be instituted against the university as well. In all, the university was named in several lawsuits, including one on behalf of Greg Knipping's widow, Nancy, seeking $9 million in compensatory and punitive damages.[9]

"We were a small private institution and not a wealthy one. We were very concerned when the litigation began that the lawsuits would bankrupt us," Graves recalled.[10]

Byers said he thinks that the university's efforts to help the grieving families helped to limit the lawsuits. Patberg, Graves, and Byers kept the families informed about everything that was happening. The university paid all funeral costs for the victims and offered free tuition to their immediate relatives who wished to attend Evansville.[11]

The local papers closely followed the investigation into the cause of the accident by the National Transportation Safety Board. Hearings were held in Evansville. Toxicology reports on the remains of the flight crew showed no traces of alcohol or drugs. Eventually, the report, released in August 1978, would determine that the crash was caused by improperly stowed baggage and the failure to remove the gust locks. The flight crew had been hurried that day and failed to adequately perform the preflight protocols; with tragic results[12]

Donations to the memorial fund were arriving in surprisingly large amounts. The Rose Bowl Committee in Pasadena, California, contributed $10,000, as did the Atlantic Coast Conference and the NCAA. The Big 8 Conference sent $8,000.

Schools all across the nation held benefit games and sent the money they raised to Evansville. From tiny Assumption College in Worchester, Massachusetts, to Bakersfield Junior College in California the money poured in.

The popular bandleader Henry Mancini and the impressionist Rich Little appeared at Roberts and donated their fees to the school. In Hawesville, Kentucky, radio station WKCM sponsored an Oak Ridge Boys concert and forwarded the proceeds. In Indianapolis the Wall Street Restaurants held a special benefit dinner for the team. In all, the list of donors was more than 150 pages long and still growing.

Major donations included corporate gifts from Kimball International, the furniture maker, and Smith and Butterfield, the local office supply firm, for $10,000 each. Radio station WIKY sent $6,330 listeners had pledged, and Arkla Industries sent $5,000.[13]

By late spring the memorial fund had received more than $313,000, not including the $50,000 pledged by the Evansville Jaycees.[14] Most of the contributions were small amount—five to twenty dollars—from ordinary people around the country. Kids sold popcorn and baked goods and sent the earnings to Evansville.

The flow of contributions surprised everyone at the university. "Money just began pouring in from all over. I even got one check from Tasmania," Graves recalled. "Some indicated they wanted their money used for rebuilding the program, others for the memorial to the team. We divided the money by the interests they expressed."[15]

Offers of support in terms of fundraising ranged from proceeds from a student play production to an offer from the NFL's Pittsburgh Steelers, who had a basketball team made up of football players—including Franco Harris, L. C. Greenwood, and other members of the Super Bowl championship team—who played exhibition games for worthy charities. Pittsburgh was Bobby Watson's hometown. "The Pittsburgh Steelers' offer was a godsend," said Jim Byers.[16]

"We hadn't had a game at Roberts since the crash, and this was the first opportunity people in the community had to come out and see a game there. It was the first time that they could go to Roberts and have some fun again," Graves said.[17]

The game was played on February 11, and the fans came out in droves to see the gridiron greats take on a team of former Aces coached by Mac. The St. Louis Cardinals of the NFL sent their cheerleaders, and a table tennis exhibition match at halftime featured Dan Seemiller, the U.S. champ. The Hadi Temple Shrine color guard was there, thirty members strong, and the Aces Brass entertained. Tickets were priced at $3 to $5.

The Steelers played the Aces Old Timers for one half and then played the UE football team the second half. There was a lot of applause and a lot of cheering. "After all the university and city had been through, it felt really good to hear those cheers again," Jim Byers said.[18]

"The last time most of those people were there was at the memorial service," Graves said. "To hear them cheer again took the pall off the stadium."[19]

The Steelers' appearance didn't just lift spirits. It also added $25,711 to the memorial fund.

The university made Byers's deadline for hiring a new coach.

The list of applicants had run the gamut. "We'd had coaches who were assistants at major colleges, Division II coaches, junior college coaches all across the country apply," Byers said. The committee ran some of the names past Bobby Knight, who was still acting as a consultant, and got the list down to twelve finalists, then pared it again and interviewed four.

"All of them were high-quality coaches," Byers said.

The man who eventually was hired had been through the process before. He'd been a finalist when the university had picked Bobby Watson a year earlier.

"Dick Walters was coaching at the College of DuPage, a community college just outside Chicago," Byers said. "He had a tremendous record, was a great recruiter, young and energetic. We talked to his athletic director and some others about him and got great references from everyone we talked to. Dick had a lot of confidence in himself, and we felt he could do what was needed."[20]

On March 1 the university called a press conference and announced that Dick Walters would be the new coach of the Purple Aces. He would be paid $40,000 a year by the school, and the boosters would chip in some extra benefits.[21]

"I had wanted to become a major college coach since I was about seven years old," Walters said. "When they offered me the job in Evansville, I felt I had finally reached my goal."

Walters had grown up in a small town, Chatsworth, Illinois, and had gone to Illinois State College, where he studied to become a teacher. He did his student teaching at the high school in Pontiac, Illinois, which was also home to the private Winston Churchill Junior College.

"There were only about 200 to 300 kids in the college, and they hadn't won a single game the year before," Walters recalled. "I applied to become the coach and was accepted. I got paid $1,500, which I thought was great at the time." It was his first job after graduating from college.

"I remember the day of our first home game, the guy setting up the gym had rolled out one set of bleachers that would hold about 40 people and had placed a small card table at center court for the scorekeeper and clock operator," Walters said. "I walked into the gym and asked him what he was doing. 'I thought you were supposed to be setting up the gym,' I said. He looked at me and said, 'I just did. What did you expect it to look like?' He was right—there were just 13 people at our first game."

Walters guided his team to 20 wins the first year and then 24 his second year. "I had 47 kids try out for the team out of a total enrollment of 200 students, half of which were girls," he said.

After his second successful season, with the gymnasium now packed for each game, Dick was summoned to the president's office. "I thought I was going to get a raise. Instead he told me they were closing the school."

Dick applied for the head coaching job at DuPage Junior College in Glen Elleyn, Illinois, a suburb of Chicago. "They had been 7–21 the season before and had never been very good," Dick said.

Walters averaged 29 wins per year in seven seasons at DuPage. He won the state championship in 1974, and his team was ranked first in the nation among junior colleges for his last season.

When he arrived in Evansville, Walters was 31 and had compiled an impressive record as a coach at the junior college level, going 202–56. "My last team there was so good, we would have beaten my first few teams at Evansville easily," he said.[22]

His new job would not be easy. The entire basketball program needed to be rebuilt. It presented an awesome challenge, but Walters thrived on challenges.

He announced he would retain Bobby's staff and begin recruiting and signing players.[23] "We all hit the recruiting trail hard," Stafford Stephenson said. One by-product of the tragedy was that Evansville was now a household name. Name recognition is a vital ingredient in the recruiting process, and it would be impossible to go into a prospect's home and find people who hadn't heard of Evansville.

The other major task that Walters set for himself, as he stepped into the job once held by the sainted Mac and then by the now-martyred Bobby, was courting the boosters and fans, many of whom were eyeing Walters with deep suspicion.

On the one hand, many expected that since Walters had come from the juco coaching ranks, he would begin to bring in a large number of junior college players. The memories of the last time that had occurred, and the disastrous results, were still fresh in the minds of fans.

On the other hand was Walters himself. His persona was something of a liability in Evansville. He was 5-11, blond haired and blue eyed, and given to wearing three-piece suits. He could, reporter Anne Harter of the *Evansville Press* wrote, "pass for a Madison Avenue advertising executive." What Byers and the search committee had seen as confidence, some would see as cockiness. And in a blue-collar town like Evansville, a perpetual tan, three-piece suits, and cockiness could be a problem.

Walters tried hard to win the allegiance of fans in a situation that would have presented a challenge to anyone stepping in. In an interview just before the beginning of his first season, he acknowledged that local exposure for his team was important to him. He had already appeared in television commercials for a lounge chair company, a meat store, and a clothing company.

Sensing perhaps that his image was a bit off-putting, Walters told Harter, "Just because I wear three-piece pin-striped suits, everybody thinks I'm a big city person. And because I coached in suburban Chicago, they associate me with that area. What they don't know is that my high school graduating class had 42 students. I doubt there's anyone in Evansville more country than I am."

Walters acknowledged that he wasn't entirely comfortable with being a local celebrity. "I'm a little bit uneasy when I go out," he said. "A lot of times people will just stare at me. I wish they'd come up and say hello, because I'm a friendly person."

When Harter asked about his being perceived as cocky, Walters had an answer: "When Coach Johnny Orr was in town for a clinic, someone had asked him about that. He told them, 'Don't confuse cocky with confidence. If he's not confident, you're in trouble.'"

Walters also addressed the challenges of the upcoming season, telling Harter, "If we don't win all those first five [games] and people say, 'Well, he can't coach' or 'the team can't play,' we don't need their support. We don't need those kinds of fans."

Walters confessed he'd like to coach until he reached 40 and then retire. "But I came here with one goal in mind—to bring quality Division I basketball to the area. And we're going to get that done," he said.[24]

Walters's recruiting efforts got some help from an unlikely source. The NCAA waived its rule that transfers had to sit out a year before becoming eligible. Any player transferring to Evansville would be able to play immediately. So would the freshmen, because Evansville had no returning players. But Walters had only 15 scholarships to offer. He and his staff still would have to use the scholarships judiciously and then try to form the recruits into a cohesive unit from a group of players who were not familiar with each other on the court.

Stafford Stephenson warned Aces fans about the enormity of the job. "The odds are very great against UE signing any blue-chip prospects," Stephenson said. "Blue chippers have been recruited since their junior year. You have to build rapport, with the recruit and the family, and that takes coaching continuity."[25]

With three coaches in three years there was anything but continuity at Evansville.

But the same day that Stephenson issued his caveat, Walters announced that two former DuPage players were on his radar screen, as were Eddie Layne from Eldorado, Steve Barker and Jeff Jones from Apollo High School in Kentucky (Evansville had been wooing Jones for two years), and Brad Leaf from Indianapolis.[26]

Randy Okrzesik and Steve Long would eventually sign. Both had played for Walters at DuPage. They were joined by three transfers from the University of Iowa, Scott Kelley, Jim Hallstrom, and Larry Olsthoorn. All were big and would give the Aces their biggest front line ever.

Another transfer, Barry Weston, from Southwest Missouri Baptist, was a 6-10 center. Tim Tewksbury from Wheaton, Illinois, and Eric Harris from Washington, North Carolina, committed, as did Darnell McGhee from Memphis who had played at Wabash Junior College in Indiana. Eddie Lane and Theron Bullock from Blue Island, Illinois, also signed with the Aces. By May 8 all the scholarships had been awarded.[27]

A team of freshmen, junior college players, and four-year college transfers would be what Walters had to work with for the 1978–79 season. The job would be difficult at best. He was following in the footsteps of a man whom Evansville had elevated to sainthood and another who had been martyred in a tragedy. Fans also had an inflated notion of how the Aces would do in Division I.

"When I got to Evansville, I soon discovered that a lot of people in town thought that they were going to win national championships at the Division I level the way they had as a small college," he said.[28]

The families of the plane crash victims found to their dismay that Indiana law capped insurance awards at an inordinately small amount when the deceased had no children and no history of earnings. The settlements paid out by National Jet Service and the university's insurance carriers were pitifully small compared with the loss of a son.

The families of team members would receive from $65,000 to $82,000, a fraction of what the parties to the lawsuits had sought to recover. The law in Indiana capped damage awards in a successful lawsuit at $100,000.[29]

After learning of the law limiting liability Mark Siegel's father, Ed, went to the state legislature in January 1978 to testify about the unfairness of the limits. "My son, at only 19 years old with the tremendous potential that was ahead of him—you're trying to tell me his life was only worth $4,500. Is that all his life was worth—$4,500? That's hard for a father to swallow," Siegel told the legislators in a voice choked with emotion and tears.[30]

Some families objected to the way the university had spent the nearly $350,000 in donations to the memorial fund. Some of that money had been set aside to pay for two new vans and other improvements for the athletic department. A local attorney, Richard Adin, representing some of the families of the victims, sued to try to force a public audit of the money the university had received. He said some families "were sickened" by the proposed use of the money.[31]

"We tried our best to allocate the money the way the donors had instructed, but not everyone was happy with it," Graves said.[32]

A full accounting was made in late summer, and the plans for a permanent memorial on campus, costing about $60,000, were revealed. That too stirred up emotions. "Some wanted an eternal flame," Graves said. "We decided on a memorial plaza in a prominent place on campus, with a fountain and two slabs bordering it on either side with the victims' names inscribed."[33] Today, it is known as "the weeping basketball."

Deidra Watson relocated to Louisville with her girls.

"It was months after the crash before she could bring herself to clean the sink where Bobby had shaved at on the morning he left," Tess Stephenson said.[34]

Olga Watson, Bobby's mother, soon moved to Louisville to be closer to the grandchildren.

People began to move on, but they would never forget.

Basketball season would be starting soon, and expectations were high in Evansville. And Walters, with no returning players and a hodge-podge of freshmen and transfers, was expected to meet them.

He started his first season at 0–5.

"I spoke everywhere I could. I recruited as hard as possible. That first year I don't think I spent more than 15 nights sleeping at home," he said. "I put my heart and soul into the job of rebuilding the program."[35]

The team of 15 players who had never played together faced a tough schedule that included top-ranked DePaul and Indiana State, a national finalist. Walters's young Aces managed to win 13 and lose 16 that year. "Thirteen wins with that team was my best coaching job ever," he said.

But at Evansville a losing season is not what fans want to see. They were used to winning national titles and conference championships.

Walters managed to lift the program higher each year in his first four seasons. The second year, 1979–80, his Aces went 18–10, and crowds were returning to Roberts again. Walters followed with a 19–9 mark in his third season. Attendance continued to improve with the winning seasons, and Tip-Off Club membership soared to more than 1,500 members.

In 1981 the Naismith Memorial College Basketball Hall of Fame inducted Arad McCutchan as its newest member. Mac became the first college division coach to be enshrined in the Hall of Fame. At his induction ceremony Mac spoke about his years at Evansville, the five national titles and 514 wins. He also spoke about the worst night of his life, December 13, 1977. "It will always be with me, no matter what I do. There were so many close friends of mine on that plane, and I'd recruited half the team. Those were some of the people who put me here," he said.[36]

In what must be considered one of the most remarkable coaching jobs in major college basketball history, in Walters's fourth season, 1981–82, the Aces produced a 23–6 record, a conference championship, and an NCAA Tournament bid for a team that didn't exist four years earlier. Led by Brad Leaf, they were seeded tenth in the Mid West Regional and lost by five points to the seventh seed, Marquette, in Tulsa, Oklahoma. The loss was disappointing, but just being there with a chance to play for a national championship so soon after all the crash was a major accomplishment.

"I got those kids to believe in themselves. They became a very cohesive unit that was tightly knit," he said. "Our mentality on that team was, 'If you're gonna beat us, you'd better be ready to lace 'em up,'" he said.

Walters was named the Midwestern Collegiate Conference Coach of the Year by his peers. What Dick Walters had done in the span of four seasons was truly a remarkable feat.

"Anywhere else, that season would have been looked upon as a great achievement. In Evansville, though, it was seen as only the beginning of the comeback to national prominence," Walters said.

But the group of freshmen Walters and his staff had recruited upon arriving at Evansville was now graduating, and Walters was faced with restocking the roster.

"The fans and boosters all thought after the 23–6 season we were now ready to take it up a notch," Walters said.[37]

The fans had returned to Roberts. During the 1980–81 season average attendance had soared to more than 10,000 per game, up from the 5,500 in McCutchan's final season.

It wasn't enough.

As a new, young team once more, the Aces would struggle and never could duplicate the 23-win season. After three so-so campaigns of 13–16, 15–14, and 13–16, Walters was dismissed. "President Graves and some of the more prominent boosters felt I had failed to live up to expectations," Walters said. "Maybe we got too good too fast."[38]

Living up to the expectations of a community accustomed to excellence year in and year out was a difficult job. "We were starting over, and they just didn't have the patience," Walters said.

Now, he found, "I couldn't get hired. Everyone thought if Evansville had fired me after what I'd achieved there, then I must have done something wrong." Walters interviewed at the University of Georgia and a few other places, but no one offered him a job, and he had a family to support.

While he was coaching at Evansville, Walters had been treated well by the wealthier boosters. He had been provided with a new Corvette, served on several corporate advisory boards for pay, had the use of three private planes for recruiting, and was a frequent dinner guest. "When I started to make phone calls to some of those same people, looking for work, they wouldn't take my calls," he said. "It was a real valuable lesson for me."

Finally, an old friend helped him get a job with W. E. Follett, a company that operates campus bookstores all over the nation. He is still with Follett and covers a territory in southern California, from Los Angeles to San Diego. He also did some work as a commentator for Prime Ticket, a southern California cable company, but that was a long time ago.

In February 2011, Bob Boxell, UE's sports information director, invited Dick Walters, who is now 62, to attend the last regular season game ever played at Roberts Stadium, along with a host of other former Aces players and coaches. It was his first time back. At halftime he was introduced to the capacity crowd. "I got a standing ovation," he said. It may have come three decades late, but Dick feels "they know what I did now."

More than 30 years after his dismissal Walters said that the bitterness has faded. "I'm proud to have had the opportunity to do what I'd always wanted to do," he said.

Asked to reflect on his arrival at Evansville in the wake of a tragedy, with community expectations high and following in the footsteps of two beloved figures, Walters paused and then said quietly, "I never had a chance."[39]

(Endnotes)

1 Jim Byers, telephone interview by author, January 27, 2011.

2 Rich Davis, "Parent Remembers the Other Aces Player Lost in 1977," *Evansville Courier*, December 27, 2002, B-1.

3 Rich Davis, "Three Women Shared Bond That Went Beyond Crash," *Evansville Courier*, December 13, 1997, A-1.

4 Jennifer Kuster Adkins, telephone interview by author, October 17, 2011. Years later, when Jennifer married Dr. Tom Adkins, Deidra and Bobby's twin daughters, Chandra and Leigh, served as flower girls. Jennifer still considers Deidra a close

friend, and the two have remained in contact through the years.

5   Diana Townsend, "The Night the Stars Went Out," used with permission; Diana Townsend Manners, telephone interview by author, March 4, 2011.

6   Stafford Stephenson, telephone interview by author, January 24, 2011.

7   Jim Byers interview.

8   "Second Suit Is Filed in Crash of Aces Team Plane," *Evansville Press,* December 22, 1977.

9   "Widow Files Suit Asking $8 Million in UE Plane Crash," *Evansville Press,* December 10, 1979.

10 Wallace Graves, telephone interview by author, January 27, 2011.

11 Byers and Graves interviews. Several relatives of victims took advantage of the offer of free tuition. Among them were Leigh and Chandra Watson, the twin daughters of Bobby and Deidra Watson who attended the University of Evansville in the early 1990s. Both earned their degrees from UE and are pursuing careers in the music industry in Los Angeles, where they perform and record as the Watson Twins.

12 Jim Eberle, "Air Crew Autopsies Normal," *Evansville Press,* January 3, 1978; National Transportation Safety Board, "Probable Cause," *Aircraft Accident Report—National Jet Services, Inc., Douglas DC-3, N51071,* NTSB report no. AAR-78-10 (Washington, D.C.: Bureau of Accident Investigation, August 17, 1978), 31–32.

13 "UE Memorial Contributions Come to Over $300,000," *Evansville Press,* August 1978 (exact date illegible).

14 "UE Memorial Contributions."

15 Graves interview.

16 Byers interview.

17 Graves interview.

18 Byers interview.

19 Graves interview.

20 Byers interview.

21 Dick Walters, telephone interview by author, July 8, 2011.

22 Walters interview.

23 Both Mark Sandy and Ernie Simpson would leave for other positions. Stephenson stayed for several more seasons before he too moved on.

24 Anne Harter, "Dick Walters . . . New UE Basketball Coach Is Man on a Mission," *Evansville Press,* November 16, 1978, 26.

25 "Stafford Stephenson," *Evansville Press*, March 3, 1978.

26 "Two Prospective Players to Visit UE," *Evansville Press*, March 8, 1978.

27 Anne Harter, "UE Coaches Could Finish Recruiting by Tomorrow," *Evansville Press*, May 8, 1978.

28 Walters interview.

29 Herb Marynell, "$100,000 Crash Settlements Reached," *Evansville Press*, August 28, 1978.

30 UPI, "Is That All His Life Was Worth—$4,500?" *Evansville Press*, January 20, 1978. The law at the time of the crash limited compensation to funeral expenses, and legal and administrative fees for those who died without any dependents.

31 L. D. Seits, "UE Fund Case Closed, Says Attorney," *Evansville Press*, February 5, 1979.

32 Graves interview.

33 Graves interview; Patberg interview. The Memorial Plaza is situated in a high-foot-traffic area of the campus behind the Olmstead administration building and flanked by Neu Chapel and the university library. Behind it is the dining hall. The area is shaded by two large sycamore trees and features a fountain that has at its center a round object that revolves and emits streams of water.

34 Tess Stephenson, telephone interview by author, June 29, 2011.

35 Walters interview.

36 "Arad A. McCutchan," Naismith Memorial Basketball Hall of Fame, www.hoophall.com/hall-of-famers/tag/arad-a-mccutchan.

37 Walters interview.

38 Walters interview.

39 Walters interview. Walters's record at Evansville was 114–87, a winning percentage of .57.

The Five NCAA Championship Trophies won by the University of Evansville.

Crews Control, 1985–2002

This time, the University of Evansville went about finding a basketball coach somewhat differently. No committee, no solicitation of resumes from coaches nationwide.

This time Jim Byers got a recommendation from Bobby Knight and went to Bloomington to meet the fellow Knight had named, Jim Crews, a graduate of Indiana University, a member of Knight's 1976 undefeated national championship team, and an assistant coach at Indiana for eight seasons under Knight. Crews knew the history and tradition of basketball in Evansville.

Crews recalled that Byers "talked about the great tradition [in Evansville] and he gave me a lot of background on the city and how it had enhanced the program there. I liked Coach Byers immediately. He was very truthful, and everything he told me about Evansville was truthful and honest. He was a great AD [athletic director] and a fabulous person. I couldn't have asked for a better position. Coach Knight was there and sat in on our talks, and I just felt that the time was right, and it just felt like the right fit for me."[1]

Jim, his wife, and their two young children, moved to Evansville. "I knew a lot about the tradition down there from my time at Indiana, and Jerry Sloan had been a speaker at our basketball camps when my dad was coaching at Illinois State. He spoke about Evansville and Coach Mac, so I knew a lot about it even as a kid growing up," Crews said.[2]

Crews didn't arrive at Evansville emptyhanded. Along with him came two transfers who would play key roles in the success of Crews's early teams. Marty Simmons from Indiana University and Scott Haffner from the University of Illinois. They would play prominent roles in returning the Aces to the level of play that the city had enjoyed for so many years.

Scott Haffner, 6-4, grew up in Noblesville, Indiana, a suburb of Indianapolis. He had led his high school team to an undefeated season as a senior before losing to the state's first-ranked team in the state tournament. He had averaged more than 25 points per game as a senior and had been the runner-up in voting for Mr. Basketball in Indiana.

Scott was a bona fide blue-chip prospect. He attended several all-star camps and was widely recruited by the major college coaches. "I wanted to play in the Big 10 Conference," Scott said.

He would get his wish. "I was recruited by six of the ten [Big 10] conference schools and Notre Dame, and I decided on Illinois. As a freshman there I wanted to play more than I was [playing]. The system there wasn't the best fit for me, and I was just not very patient about it," he said. "I wanted to transfer to a program that was using a system better suited to my game."

Before deciding where to continue his career, he considered Norm Stewart's program at Missouri, as well as Miami of Ohio, where a friend was playing.

"My sister had attended Evansville and graduated from there about four years ago. When Marty Simmons transferred there to play for Jim Crews, it was a huge factor in my decision to go to Evansville," Scott said. "They had a great basketball tradition, and I knew it was a great basketball community. Crews was using the motion offense there [that] he had learned at Indiana, and it fit my game better."[3]

Simmons, 6-5 and 225 pounds, was a product of the program at Lawrenceville High School in Illinois, about 65 miles from Evansville. His team posted a state record 68–0 mark in his four seasons there. He enrolled at Indiana University.

"I was recruited by Indiana assistant Jim Crews," Simmons said. "I was there for two seasons but wasn't getting that much playing time. When Coach Crews left for Evansville, I followed him there."[4]

Simmons brought with him the winning attitude that he had acquired in high school, and it quickly became infectious at Evansville.

But that was in the future. As transfers Simmons and Haffner had to sit out a year, and the Crews era began with an inauspicious 8–19 season, one of the worst in Evansville's long history. Happily, that season, 1985–86, proved an anomaly.

"Both Marty and Scott helped develop the culture of winning there," Crews said. "They did so in that very first season when they couldn't even play. Marty was as good a leader as I've ever seen. He told those players, 'Now, this is how we're going to play, how we are going to compete, how we're going to attend every class, and how we are going to behave off the court.' The two of them set the tone for what was to come, and they led by example."[5]

Crews, Simmons, and Haffner ushered in an era of Division I success for the Aces. Crews did it by building on the past. First, he brought back the T-shirt-style jerseys that Walters had eschewed. "Coach Crews did that to show Mac and the fans that they were the reason we were able to play Division I basketball," Simmons said.

Crews also often asked Mac to address the players. "Coach Crews loved having him talk to us," Marty Simmons recalled. "He [Mac] was such a class guy, so positive in every way." One of Mac's talks still resonates with Simmons today. "I will always remember that he told us the best play in basketball is taking a charge because it is the most unselfish thing you can do to help your team," Marty said.[6]

Scott Haffner recalls that "Coach Crews was very demanding but fair. He had the best interests of his players in mind for development as players and as growing from boys to men. He would always challenge you to do more. He believed you could do more than you believed yourself. I learned to appreciate that and respect it.

"One of the things Coach Crews did best was to reestablish tradition there. We were aware of the accident in 1977, and he schooled us on the fact that what we were playing for was a lot bigger than ourselves. The city had high expectations for their basketball team and had endured so much pain and tragedy. We always felt connected to that. We were reminded of it every time we charged out of the tunnel at Roberts onto that court. I'm very proud and fortunate to have been a part of it."

Haffner played at Evansville from 1986 to 1989. Simmons was there one year less. When they got off the bench in the fall of 1986, so did the Aces' fortunes.

Evansville returned to postseason play in the NIT in 1987–88 and managed to defeat Utah in the first round before losing to Boston College by just five points in the second round.

Haffner and Simmons led Crews's teams to winning seasons –three straight for Haffner; two for Simmons who graduated in 1988 -- capped by a 25–6 record in 1988–89, a Midwestern Collegiate Conference title, and an NCAA berth.

The Aces were seeded eleventh. At the West Regionals they faced sixth-seeded Oregon State. The Aces managed their first-ever NCAA Division I Tournament win, defeating the Beavers and Gary Peyton in overtime by 94–90.

The win moved the Aces forward to meet P. J. Carlesimo's Seton Hall Pirates, who eliminated the Aces 87–73 and went on to play Michigan in the national championship game in Seattle. Although they had lost, the Aces had proved they belonged with the elite of college basketball.

The fans were back at Roberts. Attendance soared as the wins mounted. In two seasons, 1987–88 and 1988–89, the Aces' record at Roberts was 30–1, and attendance averaged more than 9,000 per game. In 1989–90 attendance topped 10,000 for the first time since 1981–82. Crews's success led to a growing fan base at Evansville, and attendance at Roberts Stadium stayed at more than 10,000 fans, on average, for six straight seasons.

"We only had about 2,000 students at the time, but that community supported the team. We returned the favor by going out into the community. Our players started a reading program for young kids in the school system, and we became ambassadors to the community," Crews said. "Our teams played like blue-collar guys, tough, hard nosed, and never quit. I think the community saw a lot of themselves in our team, and that's why they responded so well to us. We also had good kids who followed the rules, and they felt comfortable in that city, and I think that was an important component of our success."[7]

Marty Simmons graduated from Evansville with an average for his career there of 24.3 points per game, second only to Larry Humes in the Aces' history. Marty's 750 points scored in 1987–88 are the fourth-highest single-season total, trailing only Humes (in both 1964–65 and 1965–66) and Haffner in that category.

In the three-point era Haffner would score 65 points in a game at Roberts against Dayton on February 18, 1989, setting a new Evansville single-game mark that still stands. Scott shot 11-for-13 from beyond the three-point line and 23-for-29 overall. He was a perfect eight for eight from the free-throw line. His 65 points were the sixth highest in Division I history at the time.

Haffner was drafted by the Miami Heat in the second round in 1989 and played with them for a season before being released. He then signed with Charlotte and played part of a season there before being injured. He had ankle surgery and played briefly in the Continental Basketball Association before going to work for Eli Lilly as a district sales manager in the Indianapolis area.

After Simmons and Haffner graduated, the Aces struggled for two seasons before bouncing back.

In June 1993 Evansville mourned the death of Arad "Mac" McCutchan following complications from a stroke. He had built a retirement home at Christmas Lake Village, about 40 miles northeast of Evansville, where he had spent his time playing golf, doing a little fishing, and enjoying time with his grandchildren. His home was adorned with numerous plaques and trophies from his days as the coach of the Purple Aces.

Mac and his teams had put Evansville on the college basketball map. He had won the plaudits of his fellow coaches and the love and admiration of a city. He was followed into coaching by scores of his former players, and his legacy lives on through them. But his greater legacy is the pride and recognition he brought to the city of Evansville, which realized through Mac's success its long-harbored hopes and dreams and will be forever connected to and known as the home of the Purple Aces.

He was laid to rest near his boyhood home in Daylight, Indiana.[8]

Parrish Casebier picked up where Haffner left off, and the Aces continued to win. The 1992 (24–6) and 1993 (23–7) teams made the NCAA Tournament, although they were eliminated in the first round by Texas–El Paso and Florida State, respectively. Attendance at the Roberts, which had been renovated in 1990, topped 12,000 twice in 1992—against Xavier and Notre Dame.

Casebier left Evansville after his junior year, the 1992–93 season, with 1,535 points, sixth best on the Aces' all-time scoring list, and an average of 20.2 points per game. He tried out for the NBA but failed to make the cut. Trouble, including several felony convictions and prison time, has marked the life of the talented player in the years since. Casebier's story is a glaring and embarrassing exception for former Aces stars. In 1995 he was sentenced to eight years in prison after being convicted of rape. In handing down the sentence, Circuit Court Judge Richard Young told Casebier, "You were very popular. You had a future here. You were the toast of the town. I don't think I've ever seen anyone take such a wrong turn."[9]

The 1993–94 Aces made the NIT field but lost to Tulane in the first round at Roberts and posted a mark of 24–11 in their last season in the Midwestern Collegiate Conference.

On February 11, 1995, the Aces met Tulsa at Roberts with 12,518 fans present, a crowd that set a new Roberts Stadium record since its renovation five years earlier. The 1994–95 season was the Aces' first in the Missouri Valley Conference, and they went 18–9. Three subpar seasons followed before the Aces were back to postseason play.

The fall of 1995 brought Marcus Wilson to campus. He had grown up in South Bend, Indiana, where his father was a high school basketball coach. Marcus tagged along with his dad, going to practice and games from an early age.

"By the time I was twelve, I was shooting 500 shots a day. My dad was a stickler for fundamentals and technique, and I practiced constantly under his supervision," he recalled.

Following a successful high school career and national exposure as a member of the AAU travel team, Wilson, a 6-3 shooting guard, weighed college scholarship offers.

"I had been the leading scorer on every team I'd ever played for at every level. I wanted to go to a school that would permit me to play right away," he said. "A lot of the big name schools wanted me to red shirt a year, and I didn't like that idea at all."

Spurning Purdue, Xavier, and Providence, among others, Wilson finally decided on Evansville. "At the time I was also looking at Valparaiso. It was only an hour away from my home. But South Bend at the time had a lot of crime and gang activity, and I thought if I went there, a lot of local kids would be tempted to follow me and start hanging out there. I didn't like that idea," he said. "Evansville was far enough away to keep the bad influences at home, and they had told me I would play immediately there, so I signed with them."

Wilson had little knowledge of the Aces' storied past but had seen a few of their games on television, including one against Florida State in the NCAA Tournament. "I thought [while] watching that game, 'Who's this team wearing uniforms with sleeves?' he remembered.

He would play a pivotal role in the success of the Aces during his time there. "Our first three years were just mediocre," he said. "But I had been told that everyone that had come to play for Coach Crews and had stayed four years had gotten a [conference championship] ring. I wanted that ring."

He would get it in his senior year, 1998–99.

The season featured an early trip to Hawaii for the Big Island Invitational

Tournament—and a big surprise. "In the first game there, with St. Louis University, Coach Crews pulled me from the game," Wilson recallled. "He was on me about being in the right shooting position when I got the ball. He put a freshman in to replace me. I was the captain and the leading scorer, and he was replacing me with a freshman!

"I was really hot and we got into an argument. I never got back in the game, and we got blown out. In the locker room we started arguing again. It got pretty heated, and Coach told the other players to get on the bus and head back to the hotel. He and I stayed, and we went at it for a while. In the end it all got worked out. We both reached an understanding about my role on the team, and after that everything began to click for us."

The Aces, led by a newly energized Wilson, started conference play at 6–0 and roared through the season. In the last regular season game they played Southwest Missouri State at Roberts. Evansville needed to win to clinch the Aces' first Missouri Valley Conference crown. And with it Wilson would get his ring. He wanted that ring bad.

"We were down by three points in regulation when, with two seconds to play, I put up a three [pointer] that took us to overtime," he recalled. "In overtime, with just two seconds remaining and the game still tied, I put up a baseline jumper that hit the rim, bounced high up to the top of the backboard, came down, and bounced two more times on the rim and went in."

Evansville had won on a shot that fans still talk about a decade later, and Wilson got his ring.

The Aces got an at-large bid to the NCAA Tournament, where Wilson would play a great game against Kansas. The Aces were seeded eleventh, and they faced the Jayhawks of Kansas, the sixth seed, in New Orleans in round one. "I had a hot first half. I had 18 points in the first eight minutes. We were up and down the floor so fast they didn't have time for a TV time-out," he said.

He ended up with 34 points, going 13-for-19 from the floor, but Kansas was "just too big," and with the Jayhawks in control of the boards, the Aces were eliminated.

Wilson finished his career at Evansville with 2,053 points, second only to Larry Humes in Aces history. He wasn't drafted by the NBA but tried out with the Utah Jazz. He didn't make the team and left to play in Europe. For the next eleven seasons he led a vagabond life as a professional basketball player in Israel, Poland, Turkey, and France before he retired in 2010.

"I owe a lot to my experience at Evansville," he said. "It prepared me for life after basketball, and my years there and experiences as an Ace help me every day in business."[10]

And he still wears that ring.

The Crews era at the University of Evansville lasted 503 games over 17 seasons. His record was 294–209 for a winning percentage of .58, slightly better than Dick Walters had produced.

"We had a lot of injuries and adversity while I was there, but each and every time the players just picked up and went on," Crews said. "They never got down, and they always responded positively, even though we had some tough breaks along the way. It was a testament to their character as at team. They faced adversity and saw a challenge and met it head on."

Before the 2001–2002 season he had back surgery, "and I probably shouldn't have coached that season. I did the players a disservice by trying to coach," he said.[11] Crews left Evansville for West Point after that season, when attendance had dwindled badly—an average of 5,822 saw his last Aces team produce a 6–8 mark at home.

Crews' teams at the service academy did not duplicate the success he had enjoyed at Evansville. He remained at West Point through the 2008–2009 season, when he was dismissed. He went on to work as an analyst for the Big 10 television network, and then served as assistant men's basketball coach at St. Louis University, where he is now interim head coach.

His memories of Evansville and the 17 seasons there are fond ones. "We had a big-time basketball atmosphere with individual personalized educational opportunity. We recruited good kids who wanted to earn a degree in four years and win basketball games. It was a very unique and special place, and still is," he said.[12]

(Endnotes)
1   Jim Crews, telephone interview by author, July 21, 2011.
2   Crews interview.
3   Scott Haffner, telephone interview by author, September 13, 2011.
4   Marty Simmons, telephone interview by author, August 23, 2011.
5   Crews interview.

6   Steve Ford, "Arad Will Be Floored," *Courier and Press.com,* November 18, 2008; Simmons interview.

7   Crews interview.

8   "Arad McCutchan, 80, Former College Coach," *New York Times,* June18, 1993; Marilyn McCutchan Disman, telephone interview by author, February 22, 2011.

9   "NCAA Troubles Lie Ahead for New Mexico State," *Sporting News,* November 6, 1995.

10   Marcus Wilson, telephone interview by author, September 7, 2011.

11   Crews interview.

12   Crews interview.

The Ford Center, new home of the Purple Aces, opened in 2011.

Coming Home, 2002–2011

Steve Merfeld, who had been a highly successful coach at Hampton University of the Middle Eastern Athletic Conference, succeeded Jim Crews. Steve had led the Pirates to a 90–57 mark, including back-to-back MEAC titles and NCAA berths in 2001 and 2002.

For the 2002 NCAA Tournament the Pirates were a lowly fifteenth seed, but Merfeld's squad shocked everyone by defeating second seed, Iowa State, in the tournament's opening round.

Merfeld came to Evansville with an impressive resume at a mid-major school, but he failed to duplicate that success at Evansville.[1] In five seasons at the helm Merfeld posted a disappointing 54–91 record. He never produced a winning team at Evansville, and his 7–22 mark in 2003–2004 sealed his fate.

He did manage to post the best Missouri Valley Conference finish since 1999 and the Aces' best nonconference record since 2000. He had signature wins against Purdue, Southern Illinois, and Creighton, but they weren't enough to save his job. Attendance at Roberts hovered around 6,600 during his stay.[2] After five losing seasons the Merfeld era ended with the 2006–2007 season.

The university turned to one of its own to revive the program.

In 2007 the University of Evansville announced the hiring of Marty Simmons as the new head basketball coach. Simmons had played on Jim Crews's successful teams in the late 1980s at Evansville and was part of Crews's winning tradition there.

Simmons's return to the Aces came after he had coached at Wartburg College for a single season in 1996–97 and then at Southern Illinois University, Edwardsville, a Division II school for five seasons. In between he'd served as an assistant to Crews at Evansville.

The boosters were thrilled with Simmons's selection. "He's trying hard to revive the fortunes of the program," said Jay Altmeyer, a long-time Aces fan who serves on the board of the Purple Aces Club, the booster organization that replaced the Tip-Off Club in the late 1980s. "Season ticket holders now number about 5,000, and we have nearly 2,000 members in the Purple Aces Club."

Fans of Aces basketball who recall the program's glory days of the McCutchan era are aging fast. The program is trying hard to develop a new and younger fan base, and Altmeyer believes it will happen. "We're in a tough but exciting conference, and Marty has done a great job of building the program," he said.[3]

Simmons's second season at Evansville produced a 17–14 mark and an invitation to the CollegeInsider.com postseason tournament, a second-tier tournament sanctioned by the NCAA. He duplicated that feat and advanced to the second round of the College Basketball Invitational in 2010–11, the final season at Roberts Stadium, which the city had decided to replace. Attendance at Roberts had continued to drop, averaging fewer than 5,000 in the 2009–10 season and little more in the final season, which was capped by a packed stadium on February 26, 2011.

After wrestling with what to do for several years, the city had made the controversial decision in late 2008 to replace the aging Roberts Stadium. The future of Roberts was a major issue in the 2011 mayoral race. After the election, in the spring of 2012, Evansville's new mayor announced that Roberts Stadium would be torn down, and the site would be converted into a city park.

The new home of the Aces opened in time for the start of the 2011–12 basketball season. Unlike Roberts, it is located in downtown Evansville. And it looks nothing like the Aces' old home.

The new stadium, Ford Center, is an ultramodern design of glass and steel costing $127 million, financed by $95 million in long-term bonds floated by the Evansville Redevelopment Authority and profits from events at Roberts since 2009. The debt service is funded by the city's food and beverage tax, taxes paid by the Aztar Riverboat Casino, and Downtown Development Area Tax Increment Financing, which reinvests a portion of downtown property taxes in development projects. The hope is that the new arena and its 11,000 seats for multiple types of events will spur further growth and development with no increase in real property taxes for residents.[4] If it provides half as comfortable a home-court advantage for Simmons's teams as Roberts did for 55 seasons, everyone in Evansville will be pleased. The inaugural campaign saw Evansville finish at 16-16 and once again advance to the College Basketball Invitational tournament.

On January 22, 2011, the university held a celebration at Roberts of the 40th anniversary of the 1971 championship. "Many of [Mac's] former players returned. They went and knelt down and kissed the floor where his name appears," Thornton Patberg said.[5] In 2008 the court at Roberts was named Arad McCutchan Court in honor of the coach who had led the Aces for 31 seasons. (The court at the new facility is named for him, too.)

"The fact that more than 100 former players came back that night is a testament to just how much playing here at Evansville meant to all of them. The community support for the Aces basketball team is what separates Evansville from other schools," Simmons said.

To validate his point Simmons recounted a recent encounter while on vacation at the World Golf Village Hall of Fame in Orlando.

"I saw a real tall guy there. I said to my father-in-law, 'I know that guy, but I can't think of his name,'" Simmons said.

"'Why not go over and introduce yourself?' my father-in-law said.

"I did so, and when the man saw the Evansville logo on my golf shirt, he broke into a smile. 'Evansville!' exclaimed the man, who turned out to be former Jacksonville University and NBA star Artis Gilmore.

"'I played there,' Artis said," referring to Roberts Stadium.

"That's where those Purple People Eaters played," he added, confusing the Purple Aces with the title character of Sheb Wooley's 1958 novelty song.[6] "Those are the greatest fans in the country," Gilmore said.[7]

The Simmons era at Evansville is just beginning. Marty knows the tradition there; he was a part of it. He played on teams that went to the NCAA Tournament and averaged more than 10,000 fans per game.

But that was then.

Marty Simmons is optimistic about the future of his Aces. "We just have to keep battling. We're headed in the right direction. We had Butler and Indiana come to the new arena for the first two games there and both were sell-outs," he said.[8]

The fans that Artis Gilmore described as the greatest in the country hold the keys to the future.

"Here's the deal," Jim Crews said during that last game at Roberts. "UE is a small university, and it needs three things to succeed. Number one is academics, the highest standards for our players, and we have that. Number two is a leader, a high-character person, and we have that in Marty Simmons. And number three is the fans.

"We are here celebrating the good old days," he said. "But we need the fans to come back tomorrow, next week, and next year to help us create some good new days, too."[9]

Perhaps it's unfair to expect Evansville to resume its dominant role in college basketball. In Division I the Aces come from one of the smallest schools, with an enrollment of about 2,400, and they compete in a very strong mid-major conference.

But the city of Evansville and Aces fans have set a high bar for all who don an Aces uniform.

Not so long ago, the Aces were the best in the land. The University of Evansville's Aces were celebrated as the best small college team in the United States. Their fan support was unrivaled anywhere.

That proud legacy is theirs and theirs alone. And it's why diehard Evansville fans continue to dream of a return to the glory days.

Sometimes, dreams do come true.

(Endnotes)

1   The source of this information was Merfeld's website, www.stevemerfeld. com.

2   *University of Evansville 2010–11 Media Guide.*.

3   Jay Altmeyer, telephone interview by author, January 31, 2011.

4   City of Evansville, "About the Project" and "Financing," Evansville Arena, www.evansvillearenaproject.com; "Mayoral Candidates: More Consideration on Roberts Stadium," New 25–WEHT-TV, June 21, 2011, www. news25.us.com.

5   Thornton Patberg, telephone interview by author, January 29, 2011.

6   Wooley was an actor who appeared in a number of films, including *High*

Noon. He was also a country singer and had significant success in that genre. "The Purple People Eater," which he wrote and recorded, reached the top of the *Billboard* charts in 1958. Wooley died in 2003 at the age of eight-two ("The Unforgettable Sheb Wooley," www.shebwooley.com).

7   Marty Simmons, telephone interview by author, August 22, 2011.

8   Simmons interview.

9   Tom Etheridge, "UE Tries to Turn Past into Future," *Evansville Courier and Press,* February 27, 2011.

BIBLIOGRAPHY

Bigham, Darrel E. *Evansville: The World War II Years*. Charleston, SC: Arcadia Publishing, 2005.

Bird, Larry, with Bob Ryan. *Drive, The Story of My Life*. New York: Bantam, 1990.

Cohen, Stanley. *The Game They Played*. New York: Farrar, Straus and Giroux, 1977.

Denny, Dick. *Glory Days Indiana: Legends of Indiana High School Basketball*. Indianapolis: Sport Publishing, 2006.

Eaton, Ron. *Local Legends: 100 Years of Southwestern Indiana Sports History*. Evansville, Ind.: M. T. Publishing, 2008.

Elliott, Joseph Peter. *A History of Evansville and Vanderburgh County, Indiana*. 1897. Reprint, Whitefish, Mont.: Kessinger, 2008.

Guffey, Greg. *The Golden Age of Indiana High School Basketball*. Bloomington: Quarry Books/Indiana University Press, 2006.

Hayes, Diana. *Crashers*. New York: Minotaur, 2010.

Jones, Marjorie Melvin, and Besse LaBudde. "The Inquiring Visitor's Guide to Angel Mounds State Historic Site." Pamphlet published by Mission Press, Indianapolis, 2000.

Jones, Norman. *Growing Up in Indiana: The Culture and Hoosier Hysteria Revisited*. Bloomington, Ind.: Author House, 2005.

Klinger, George. *We Face the Future Unafraid: A Narrative History of the University of Evansville.* Evansville, Ind.: University of Evansville Press, 2003.

Loewen, James W. *Sundown Towns: A Hidden Dimension of American Racism.* New York, NY. : The New Press, 2005.

Mills, Randy K. and Roxanne. *At The Eye Of The Storm.* Mason, Ind: Cengage Learning, 2007.

McCutchan, Kenneth P., William E. Bartelt, and Thomas R. Lonnberg. *Evansville: At the Bend in the River, An Illustrated History.* Sun Valley, Calif.: American Historical Press, 2004.

Stooksbury, Danny. *National Title: The Unlikely Story of the NAIB Tournament.* Bradenton Beach, Fla.: Higher Level Publishing, 2010.

West, Gary. *King Kelly Coleman, Kentucky's Greatest Basketball Legend.* Morley, Mo.: Steward and Wise, 2005.

White, Samuel W. *Fragile Alliances: Labor and Politics in Evansville, Indiana, 1919–1955.* Westport, Conn.: Praeger, 2005.

White, Theodore H. *The Making of the President 1964.* New York: Atheneum, 1965.

Magazines and Journals

Mills, Randy and Bottoms, Stephen. *"Are You A Communist": The 1948 Evansville, Indiana, Bucyrus Erie Strike:* Journal of the Indiana Academy of the Social Sciences, Volume IX: 2005.

Mills, Randy. *"I Wish To Look Upon Them As My Murderers": A Story of the Cultural Violence on the Ohio Valley Frontier.* Oho Valley History Magazine, Fall, 2001.

Runyon, Carl and Mills, Randy, *"The Most Wonderful Thing I Have Ever Seen": Indiana's Contribution to Petrified Man Hoaxes.* Indiana Magazine of History, 104, December, 2008.

ACKNOWLEDGEMENTS

Many people helped me with the story of Evansville and the Aces. Almost without exception everyone I contacted was more than willing to help. Without their input and recollections I could never have completed the journey. To all who gave of their time I am most grateful.

For the many former university officials and players who were willing to grant me interviews I am especially thankful. Among those were the late Wallace Graves, Thornton Patberg, Jim Byers and Bob Boxell.

Sylvia DeVault in the UE Alumni office and Jen McKee in the Athletic Department helped with my search for many of the former Aces players and were untiring in their efforts.

Many of the former players were willing to allow me access to their scrapbooks and photos including Hugh Ahlering, Wayne Boultinghouse, Harold Cox, Jim Smallins, Rick Smith, Russ Grieger and Ed Zausch.

Jon Siau readily agreed to provide a caricature which he had drawn in the wake of the tragedy. If any picture truly says a thousand words- this is the one.

Those players and coaches who granted interviews are listed in the notes. All were more than willing to share their experiences as members of the Purple Aces. Thanks to Stafford Stephenson, Ernie Enron and Mark Sandy I was able to learn about the members of the 1977 team and their coach, Bobby Watson, from men who knew and worked with them. Coach Stephenson provided a copy of the 1977-78 Media Guide which proved invaluable to me.

I decided at the outset that, despite all the proper rules of journalism, I would not contact any members of the families of those who perished on December 13, 1977. Instead, through Sylvia DeVault, a notice was placed in the Alumni magazine indicating that I was working on a book and asking any who wished to help to contact me. A number did respond and I appreciate their willingness to share with a stranger their thoughts about their loved ones. It was not easy for them to do and I owe them all a debt of gratitude for their cooperation.

I would be remiss if I did not mention the help I received from the families of Gus Doerner, Arad McCutchan and Bob Hudson. All were extremely helpful and willing to scour their attics for material to assist me.

Kathy Bartelt at the UE Library was extremely helpful in providing access to the scrapbooks that are located there and were assembled by Bob Hudson.

Bill Bussing, a prominent Evansville attorney and Aces fan, made available to me his research and draft of a manuscript on the Aces that he assembled. Bill was unstinting in his support of the project and his painstaking research of the attendance records and the early years of the McCutchan era were invaluable to me. Bill is, and will always be, an Aces fan and I am, and will always be, a Bill Bussing fan for his unselfish offer to help me with the book. Thanks Bill.

Once again I want to express my gratitude to the Keiderling support team of Bill Faherty, Bob Casciola and Bill Raftery. Everyone should have friends like them.

My editor for all my books, Polly Kummel, again performed her magic to make the result as good as it could be. She is the best.

For Janet Hulstrand, a special thank you for her copy-editing prowess and sharp eye that shaped the final result.

Lawrence Jordan at the Lawrence Jordan Literary Agency again showed unwavering support from the beginning and throughout the process of assembling the manuscript. To all at Morning Star Books, thanks for all your help. Kelvin Oden at Oh Snap! Design in New York has once again designed the finished product with his usual flair and competence.

My thanks to John Frangelli, Ed McManimon and Henry Kearney for their willingness to read and comment on the book in manuscript form.

Writing about triumph is not hard. Writing about tragedy is. I wish to thank the many who were willing to re-live some painful times with me and to share their innermost thoughts about a horrific event that changed all their lives. I can't thank them enough. I can only hope they will find the result made their efforts worthwhile.

The story of Evansville and the Aces is, in many ways, a history of a town and a team inextricably bound. The bonds were sorely tested at times but have always remained in place. Evansville and the Aces together provide a story that is unique in all of college basketball. There has never been anything quite like it -- and there never will be.

Kyle Keiderling
Henderson, Nevada

ABOUT THE AUTHOR

Kyle Keiderling is the award-winning author of *The Perfect Game: Villanova vs. Georgetown for the National Championship*; *Shooting Star: The Bevo Francis Story*,(www.bevofrancis.com), which has been optioned for a major motion picture, and the critically acclaimed *Heart of a Lion: The Life, Death and Legacy of Hank Gathers*, which was named Best Sports Biography of 2011 by the International Book Awards Committee. He is a member of the United State Basketball Writers Association and has contributed articles to Basketball Times and The Lincoln Library of Sports Champions. You may reach him through the website for his books, at www.kylekeiderlingbooks.com.